50 BEST
TAILWATERS TO FLY FISH

TERRY & WENDY GUNN

STONEFLY
PRESS

PO Box 6146
Bloomington, IN 47407
FAX: 877-609-3814

For information about discounts on bulk purchases, or
to book the author for an engagement or demonstration,
please contact Stonefly Press at info@stoneflypress.com,
or visit us at Stoneflypress.com.

Printed in Korea

17 16 15 14 13 1 2 3 4 5

FSC

Library of Congress Control Number: 2013951656

Stonefly Press

Publisher: Robert D. Clouse

Acquiring Editor: Robert D. Clouse

Managing Production Editor: Bill Bowers

Copy Editor: Bill Bowers

Proofreader: Eileen McNulty

Front Cover Photo: Terry Gunn

Back Cover Photo: Above Judge's Pool on the trophy stretch of the Upper Connecticut
River in Pittsburg, NH. Lopstick Outfitters

Page 1: Middle Provo River. Steve Schmidt

Page 52: Fall *Baetis* fishing on the Madison downstream of Earthquake Lake. John Juracek

Page 142: Rainbow Run on the Cumberland River

Page 200: Fishing a July evening caddis hatch on the Upper Connecticut River
below Murphy Dam. Lopstick Outfitters

We'd like to dedicate this book, with deepest gratitude and appreciation, to the world's fly-fishing guides—the ones who wrote chapters for this book, and all the others who get up early, get home late, row the boats, tie the knots, unsnarl the leaders, and laugh uproariously day after day at the same joke. You guys and gals make fly fishing the pure joy that it is for millions of Americans and countless others around the world.

Whether on the big trout waters of Alaska or at the tip of Patagonia, a British chalk stream or Scottish salmon run, you can count on the guides, each in their own way, to say: "Great cast," "Good job playing him around that log," or if necessary, "Maybe tomorrow . . ."

Contents

Acknowledgments

SOME AUTHORS acknowledge everyone from the local Starbucks guy who served the endless flow of coffee to the computer repair person. We choose not to go that far.

We'd like to acknowledge and thank our chapter authors for all they put into this book while facing the ever-present publishing deadline. These people are the true experts on their respective waters, and you should go out of your way to support them and their businesses.

And thanks to Bennett Mintz for putting all those random and divergent words into something cohesive. Tight lines, Ben.

Cloud of tricos. Jon Kleis

About the Authors

TERRY GUNN has been a full-time fly-fishing guide for more than 30 years, as well as a renowned author, photographer, and public speaker. He and his wife Wendy (a fly-fishing expert in her own right) have owned and operated Lees Ferry Anglers Fly Shop and Guide Service since 1989, and Cliff Dwellers Lodge in Marble Canyon, Arizona, since 2001.

Terry and Wendy co-host *Fly Fish Television Magazine* and have produced two educational videos, *Introduction to Fly Fishing* and *Introduction to Fly Casting*. They have fly fished around the globe in both fresh and salt water, and Terry holds more than ten International Game Fish Association world records for multiple species of fresh- and saltwater fish.

Terry and Wendy and their son Troy live in Marble Canyon, Arizona.

Madison River's famous pockets, pools, and boulders
above McAtee Bridge. John Juracek.

Foreword

Tailwaters are the salvation of fly fishing for trout. These are streams or rivers exiting from dams, with the flow dependent on the amount of water released. They furnish a constant supply of clear, cold water necessary for trout and their food.

Many trout anglers believe all major rivers are located in the West, but some of the finest are in the East, created years ago when the Tennessee Valley Authority dammed many Southern rivers to furnish the region's electric power. Some of these tailwaters are among the best trout rivers anywhere in this country and within easy driving distance of thousands of anglers.

As our country's population grows, many streams and rivers will be depleted to furnish life-giving water. Combined with this will be more development and increased demand for growing more food. All of this will stress our free-flowing rivers, reducing their size, polluting them, and elevating temperatures to levels unhealthy for trout. Because impoundments hold vital drinking water, they will survive, their outlets producing tailwaters benefiting trout. More and more fly fishers will have to depend on tailwater fisheries for their sport.

Tailwaters often produce special hatches and frequently desirable increased aquatic vegetation. Water temperatures within a reasonable distance below a dam's outlet will be constant and cold throughout the season. Nearby waters may be covered with ice and snow, but tailwaters will be flowing and the trout will be feeding on the insects thriving in such an environment. In short, tailwaters furnish 12 months of good fly rodding.

For the above reasons, fly fishers need to know how, when, and what to do when fishing tailwaters, and where to find them.

Terry Gunn has compiled a valuable book, *50 Best Tailwaters to Fly Fish*. Terry and his wife Wendy (one of the top fly-fishing and fly-casting ladies in the country) have for years operated Lees Ferry Anglers and guided the Colorado River in the Grand Canyon. Having fished many tailwaters, I would rate Terry's tailwater flowing below the awesome canyon's cliffs among the most beautiful and most productive places I have ever cast a line.

Terry is a terrific fly-rod guide, but no one can know it all. I started fly fishing more than 60 years ago and learn something new on almost every trip. Terry has asked tailwaters experts around the country to contribute to this book on tailwater fishing.

All rivers are covered by region, from fishing the seasons, how to determine each tailwater's water flow, the necessary tackle and fly patterns, even lists of the hatches on specific tailwaters. There is detailed information on how to find and fish these waters, including information on campgrounds, wireless access, regulations related to specific tailwaters, and more.

Nothing like this volume has ever been published, and serious trout fishers will find this one of the most useful books ever.

—Lefty Kreh

Introduction

ON MAY 18, 1933, the face of North American fly fishing changed forever.

No one knows precisely when the first rod was created, or the first reel, or first fly, but on that date, in the depths of the Great Depression, our sport came of age. The United States Congress passed the Tennessee Valley Authority (TVA) Act. It addressed a wide range of environmental, economic, and technological issues, including the delivery of low-cost electricity and the management of natural resources. TVA's power-service territory includes most of Tennessee, and parts of Alabama, Georgia, Kentucky, Mississippi, North Carolina, and Virginia.

And it began the creation of a virtual nation of tailwaters—the waterways that flow downstream from the power-generating, irrigation, and flood-control dams that stand as tributes to American progress, ingenuity, and creativity.

The success of the TVA subsequently gave birth to flood-control and power-generating dams north and south, east and west—Grand River Dam in Ontario, Canada to Shasta on the Sacramento River in Northern California; Buford Dam, upstream of Atlanta, Georgia all the way to Hugh Keenleyside Dam near Castlegar, British Columbia; the Glen Canyon Dam in northern Arizona and Utah; and Mooselookmeguntic, Maine. (Authors' note: We love that name Mooselookmeguntic!)

No more floods or droughts. No more Dust Bowls. No more farm families with crushed dreams.

We traded in those catastrophes for the chance to catch a trout on a dry fly on Thanksgiving morning or New Year's Day. We can do the previously unthinkable! In a tailwater, we can fly fish literally 365 days a year.

Tailwaters generally start as something between a low rumble and deafening roar, as dams release water from deep in the reservoir above. It churns through power-generating turbines or is directed through bypass tunnels, depending on needs. And then there's a miracle—within a few hundred yards, or a half mile at most, the industrial look of the dam is left behind and suddenly there's a river. The highly oxygenated water is a magnet for trout. There are rapids and glides,

pools and vegetation, birds and insects. By golly, it looks like a river, because it is!

Water comes from the depths of the lake that feeds the tailwater. It is cold, moving, nutritious water, and it provides habitat for trout and other gamefish, for miles and miles.

As an example, on our home stretch of the Colorado River, Lake Powell water is drawn into the Glen Canyon Dam 242 feet below the full-pool level for the electricity generators at the base of the dam. That water is crystal clear and cold, with normal year-round temperatures of 48 to 50 degrees Fahrenheit: perfect trout water. Prior to the dam's completion in 1963, water temperatures fluctuated from 32 to 86 degrees. It is not uncommon for the air temperatures to exceed 110 degrees in the summer. Even so, the water released at the dam warms very slowly—150 miles below Glen Canyon Dam, in the Grand Canyon, the water has warmed an average of only 6 degrees. Here, and in most tailwater fisheries, trout flourish in a river and in an environment where their survival was previously impossible.

Let's be realistic and acknowledge that it isn't all roses. Dams on formerly free-flowing rivers have altered the North American landscape. Stands of tall trees are gone forever; villages, homesteads, and memories were drowned; and some native species extirpated. But in the dark days of World War II, the United States needed aluminum to build bombs and airplanes, and aluminum plants required electricity. To provide power for such critical war industries, TVA engaged in one of the largest hydropower construction programs ever undertaken. That hydroelectric power beat the pants off anything our enemies had. And isn't it great to flip a switch and get instant light, or heat, or a cold one from the fridge?

Tailwaters have changed the way we live our lives, as well as the way we fly fish. Our experiences catching a dozen trout in December would be out of the question if not for the existence of tailwaters.

Tailwaters—like all other waters—are cyclical. Some years they are going to fish better than others. One of the major factors that affect tailwaters is the condition of the reservoirs above. Tailwaters provide an annual uniformity, but don't expect the recreational consistency of Disneyland. There will be wet years when the reservoir fills and even floods the tailwater below. There will be years of drought when the reservoir will drop or in extreme cases actually dry up. Lower water in reservoirs can cause warmer water releases.

The chapters in this book reflect the characters of the authors, together with the character of the waters. Despite the obvious differences, all chapters contain:

Geographic location
Map with turnouts and access points
A general description of the tailwater, along with a
  bit of background
Hatches
Fishing regulations (or where to get them)
Recommended tackle
Closest fly shops
Closest outfitters
Hospital or emergency medical help
Hotels and motels
Campgrounds
Restaurants
Bars
Availability of cell phone service
. . . and so much more!

Be sure to confirm that any business mentioned in this book is still in operation prior to your visit. A phone call or email in advance is a good idea, whether it is a fly shop, guide service, lodge, or restaurant. We did our best to research all the local businesses and unfortunately left some out that probably should have been included. If omissions occurred, we are sorry and take responsibility for that.

There are 56 tailwaters in this book, instead of the advertised 50. When it came to choosing what we felt were the best tailwaters in each region, we ended up with a few extras that warranted inclusion. There are likely others—maybe your personal favorites—that some might argue should be here, too; however, for various reasons these made our cut.

Tailwaters are not ranked one over another; they are listed geographically by region, and south to north. Lees Ferry is not ranked number one; it just happens to be the southernmost tailwater in the West.

When we first considered producing this book, we concluded that we could never write expertly about 56 different tailwaters. So we sought out the people who have worn out a few pairs of wading shoes in the very waters about which they would be writing. We have carefully and thoughtfully chosen the authors of each chapter for their experience, guiding ability, knowledge, and willingness to share that knowledge. Their contact information is in the book. Use it! Call or email them about water conditions and hatches, availability of accommodations, and nearby family activities.

If the author suggests you wear waders even in the heat of summer, take that advice to heart. If they caution that the water isn't safe for an amateur to drift, put your boat away for another day. If they recommend a streamer over a dry—you better believe it.

My deepest thanks and appreciation to each of the chapter authors for their thoughts, words, and photos; to our publisher, Robert Clouse, for his wise counsel and unflagging enthusiasm; to my editor and advisor, Ben Mintz, for being there every step of this incredible journey; to my wife Wendy for taking on another labor of love; and to our son Troy for asking the questions that keep us attempting to unravel the mysteries of being a teenager.

Wishing you good luck, good fly fishing, tight loops, and tight lines!

—*Terry Gunn*

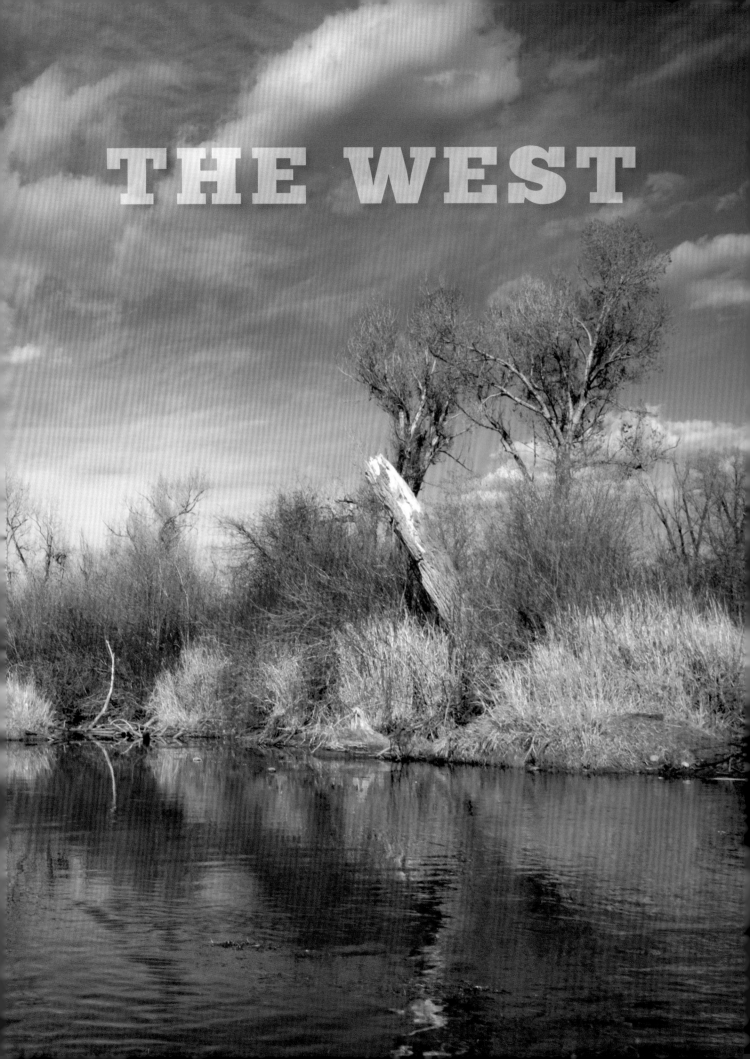

THE WEST

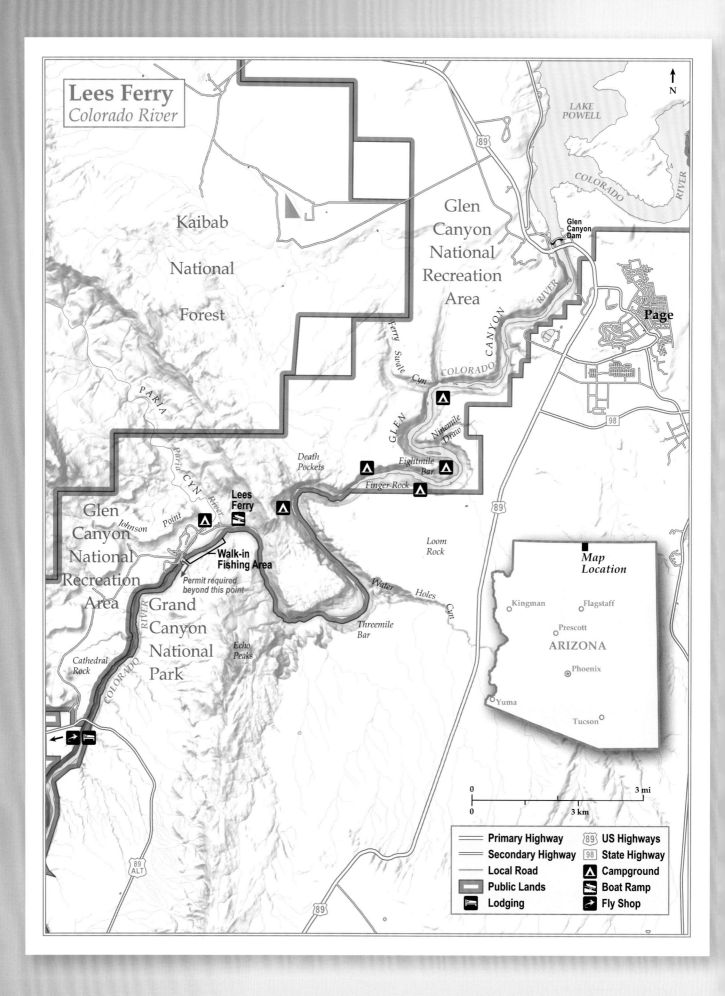

➤ **Location:** Northern Arizona, about a 4-hour drive from Las Vegas, Phoenix, or the San Juan River; about 6 hours from Salt Lake City; and 2 hours from Flagstaff. There is commuter flight service to nearby Page, Arizona.

The 16-mile stretch of the Colorado River that flows from Glen Canyon Dam to Lees Ferry–Grand Canyon National Park is known as Lees Ferry. This tailwater is a year-round rainbow trout fishery that originated in 1963 with the completion of Lake Powell. The river slices through the Paria Plateau, and is bordered by towering vertical sandstone cliffs more than 1,000 feet tall. The river twists and turns through a magnificent landscape, which is the last vestige of Glen Canyon, the rest of which was submerged by Lake Powell. The crystal-clear water is a constant 50 degrees throughout the year and supports what is likely the largest wild trout population (last stocked in the 1990s) of any Western river; trout here are counted by the thousands per mile.

Like many tailwaters, Lees Ferry previously supported warmwater fish that can no longer endure the cold water. In the early 1960s, trout as well as algae, aquatic insects, crayfish, and scuds were stocked below the dam. Few insects survived. However, today the aquatic food base consists of scuds, worms, and myriad species of midges. The lack of a more varied food base is likely related to the water temperature, which remains constant through most of the year, and the large volume of crystal-clear water that warms very slowly (1 degree Fahrenheit for every 25 miles) as it travels downstream.

Indeed, the Colorado River at Lees Ferry is "big water" by any standard. The headwaters of the Colorado are at the highest elevations of the Rocky Mountains. The drainage area of the Colorado River encompasses the entire western slope of the Rockies from Wyoming to New Mexico. Above Lake Powell, the Colorado is joined by the San Juan and Green Rivers, and every tributary that feeds these drainages. These rivers are more dependent on snowpack than on precipitation and, as a result, each year can bring different runoff and flow scenarios.

The water releases from Lake Powell and Glen Canyon Dam fluctuate on an hourly basis. Glen Canyon Dam is used for hydroelectric production, and the water flows are generally low in the evening (low electric demand) and higher during the day and early evening hours (high electric demand). During the day, it is possible to see the water rise or fall by as much as 2 vertical feet. The water releases also change according to the season; higher-release months are usually during the winter (cold weather and higher electrical demand) and the summer months (hot weather and higher electrical demand.) There is also the possibility that the water

Wading the Colorado River at Horseshoe Bend below 1,200-foot sandstone cliffs. Terry Gunn

releases might change from year to year depending on the volume of snowpack runoff—or lack of runoff—and the level of Lake Powell and other reservoirs in the system. The flows are almost always lower during weekends and holidays due to lower electrical demand.

Each new flow level presents its own challenges and opportunities. If you arrive at Lees Ferry planning to nymph

Glen Canyon–Lees Ferry, bordering Grand Canyon National Park, is often considered the most spectacular backdrop in the world to wet a line. Terry Gunn

Below. Troy Gunn, then 11, with a Lees Ferry rainbow. Terry Gunn

fish, you will rarely be disappointed. Lower flows are perfect for wading, and open up several different gravel bars and riffles. The lower flows and warm weather also produce the most prolific midge hatches of the year. The vast majority of midge fishing is subsurface pupa and emerger nymph fishing, using long leaders and fine tippet, with or without a split-shot. A dry fly with a beadhead midge (the Beadhead Zebra Midge was invented here) also works well in the shallower water areas. Expect most of the takes to be on the nymph, though occasionally a fish will eat the dry fly. The

higher flows move the larger food items such as scuds and worms around and the trout are consistently in a feeding mood. Wading areas are limited in these high flows and most of the fishing is done from the boat, either drifting or anchored in riffles. Heavy nymph rigs are the ticket for higher water. This usually means a tapered leader of 9 to 14 feet, with a strike indicator (yarn or Thingamabobber), heavy split-shot, and two larger flies—either a worm and scud, or a worm or scud with a beadhead midge. Dry-fly fishing is sporadic and unpredictable, with the exception of a major cicada hatch that happens in early July and can continue for a month or more.

The only access to this 16-mile stretch of river is by powerboat, motoring upriver from the boat launch at Lees Ferry. Lees Ferry is the launching spot for all the Grand Canyon River trips headed downriver. The upriver section has many good wading areas (depending on water releases), most of which are located above 7.5 miles upriver, as well as plenty

of areas to fish from the boat. The river depth varies from 100 feet to shallow areas that are just a couple feet. Knowing the river and navigating a boat requires local knowledge and experience. Due to the fluctuating flows, navigation hazards can change throughout the day. This is why most of the local guide boats and local rentals run jet boats.

The "Walk-In" is an area of river that can be accessed by vehicle and on foot, and is located just downstream from the Lees Ferry launch. This area is characterized by long, flat stretches of boulders and pocket water. There are times that this stretch of river can fish as well as or better than the upriver section. The best time of year to fish this area is during lower flows, for the best wading access and midge hatches.

➤ **Hatches:** The main food source in the Colorado River is very limited and primarily consists of scuds, midges, and worms. Midges are most prolific in the spring, summer, and fall. Scuds and San Juan Worms are more productive in the summer, when the higher water flows are washing food out from weeds and rocks. Plan on fishing nymphs, since there are no large hatches of aquatic insects that you would normally find on other Western rivers. Lees Ferry has an annual cicada hatch, which typically peaks in July and can last anywhere from 2 weeks to 2 months. Worms work well year-round. Winter is more about sight casting to spawning fish; the spawn lasts from November through May. Egg patterns can be productive during this time.

Water flows are high in July, August, December, and January. During high flows, the best fishing is usually from the boat, either drifting or anchored in riffles. The rest of the year usually presents some great wading in multiple areas. When the conditions are right, there are great sight-casting opportunities here.

➤ **Fishing regulations:** Year-round with flies and artificial lures; barbless hooks. You are allowed to keep four fish less than 14 inches and an eight-fish bag limit. Most of the guides practice catch-and-release.

Most of Lees Ferry is accessible only by power boat. The current runs at 6 to 7 miles per hour in the main channel. You must have a boat that can go against the current. There are also submerged islands, rocks, and logs.

➤ **Tackle:** Use 9-foot or longer, 5-weight rods. Weight-forward floating lines in neutral colors (our water is crystal clear, and bright-colored fly lines spook fish here) are a must. Nine-foot, 4X and 5X leaders with tippet from 5X to 7X are standard. Long-line nymphing is the name of the game here, and long, perfect dead drifts will catch more fish than short drifts. Strike indicators and split-shot are a must.

Headed into Glen Canyon for the 16-mile ride to Glen Canyon Dam, past sheer canyon walls rising 1,400 feet above the river. Terry Gunn

Streamer fishing can be very productive throughout the year. 200-grain or long sink-tip lines for fishing a variety of streamers. Olive Woolly Buggers are the "go-to" streamers for this river.

We often fish a dry with a nymph dropper suspended below. Our "heavy nymph rigs" consist of a 9- to 14-foot leader with a large indicator (yarn or bobber) and split-shot and two nymphs.

Our most productive flies are the Beadhead Zebra Midge (invented at Lees Ferry), Deer Hair Back Scud, and San Juan Worm.

Authors Terry & Wendy Gunn

TERRY GUNN, a full-time guide since 1983, and his wife Wendy started Lees Ferry Anglers Fly Shop and Guide Service in 1989. They acquired Cliff Dwellers Lodge in 2001. They authored the book *50 Best Tailwaters to Fly Fish* and co-hosted the TV program, *Fly Fish Television Magazine*. Learn more at www.leesferry.com.

CLOSEST FLY SHOPS
Lees Ferry Anglers
Milepost 547 N Hwy 89A
Marble Canyon, AZ 86036
800-962-9755
anglers@leesferry.com
www.leesferry.com

CLOSEST OUTFITTERS/GUIDES
Lees Ferry Anglers (above)
Marble Canyon Outfitters
P.O. Box 3646
Page, AZ 86040
928-645-2781
www.leesferryflyfishing.com

CLOSEST LODGES/HOTELS
Cliff Dwellers Lodge
Milepost 547 N Hwy 89A
Marble Canyon, AZ 86036
800-962-9755
info@cliffdwellerslodge.com
www.cliffdwellerslodge.com

Marble Canyon Lodge
Milepost 537 N Hwy 89A
Marble Canyon, AZ 86036
928-355-2225
www.marblecanyoncompany.com

Lees Ferry Lodge
Milepost 541.5 N Hwy 89A
Marble Canyon, AZ 86036
928-355-2231
leesferrylodge@vermilioncliffs com
www.vermilioncliffs.com.

BEST CAMPGROUND
Lees Ferry Campground
(National Park Service) offers dry camping on a first-come, first-served basis.

BEST RESTAURANT
Cliff Dwellers Restaurant
Milepost 547 N Hwy 89A
Marble Canyon, AZ 86036
800-962-9755
info@cliffdwellerslodge.com
www.cliffdwellerslodge.com

BEST PLACE TO GET A COLD, STIFF DRINK
Cliff Dwellers Restaurant
Milepost 547 N Hwy 89A
Marble Canyon, AZ 86036
800-962-9755
info@cliffdwellerslodge.com
www.cliffdwellerslodge.com

CLOSEST EMERGENCY MEDICAL HELP
National Park Service or Kanab, Utah (71 miles)

CELL PHONE SERVICE
Very limited in the canyon.
Good service in the surrounding area.

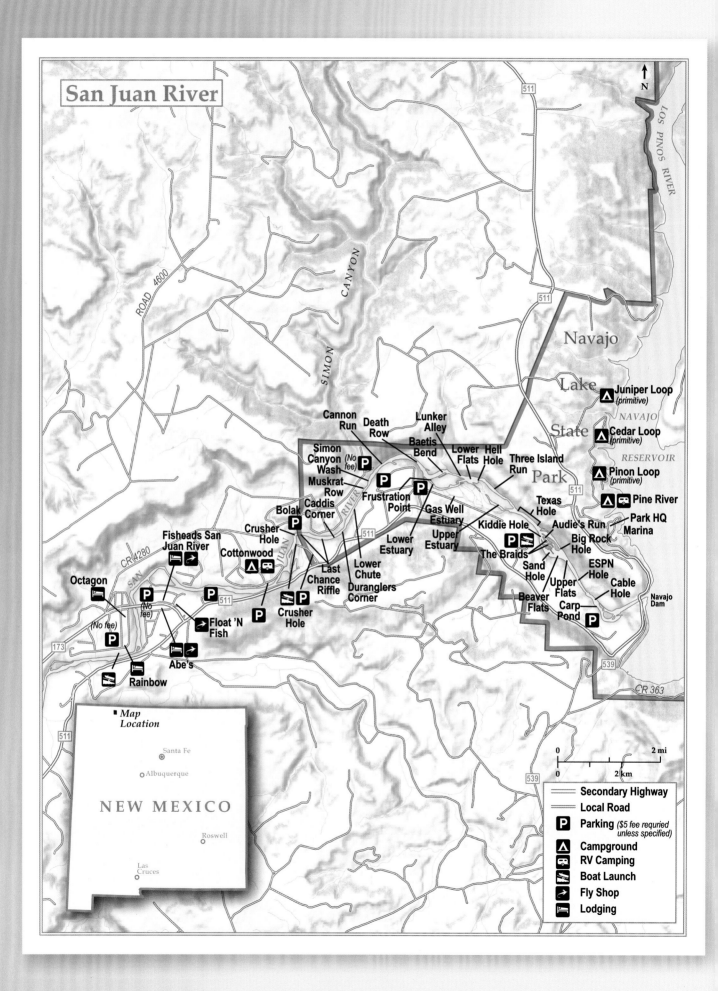

San Juan River

N

Los Pinos River

511

Navajo

Lake

NAVAJO

State

△ Juniper Loop
(primitive)

△ Cedar Loop
(primitive)

RESERVOIR

Park

△ Pinon Loop
(primitive)

△ 🚐 Pine River

Park HQ
Marina

Texas
Hole

Cannon
Run   Death
Row

Lunker
Alley

Baetis
Bend

Lower
Flats   Hell
Hole

Three Island
Run

Simon
Canyon
Wash   P *(No fee)*

Muskrat
Row

P

Frustration
Point

P

Gas Well
Estuary

Kiddie Hole

Audie's Run

Big Rock
Hole

Bolak

Caddis
Corner

Upper
Estuary

P
The Braids

🚤

Crusher
Hole

P

Lower
Estuary

Sand
Hole

ESPN
Hole

SAN   JUAN   RIVER

511

Lower
Chute

Duranglers
Corner

Upper
Flats

Cable
Hole

Navajo Dam

Octagon
🛏

Fisheads San
Juan River
🛏 ➚

Cottonwood
△ 🚐

Last
Chance
Riffle

Beaver
Flats

Carp
Pond

P

CR 4280

SAN

P   P
*(No
fee)*   *(No
fee)*

P

511

🚤   P

Float 'N
Fish   ➚

P

Crusher
Hole

173   *(No fee)*
P

🛏 ➚
Abe's

🚤
Rainbow

**Map
Location**

511

Santa Fe ✸

○ Albuquerque

NEW MEXICO

Roswell ○

Las
Cruces ○

539

CR 363

| 0 | | 2 mi |
| 0 | | 2 km |

═══ Secondary Highway
─── Local Road

P Parking *(\$5 fee required
unless specified)*

△ Campground

🚐 RV Camping

🚤 Boat Launch

➚ Fly Shop

🛏 Lodging

San Juan River *(Northwest New Mexico)*

➤ **Location:** Northwest corner of New Mexico, 1½ hours from Durango and Pagosa Springs, Colorado; 3 hours from Albuquerque; and 8 hours from Phoenix and Denver. Farmington, New Mexico is 30 miles; Aztec and Bloomfield, New Mexico are 18 miles.

The headwaters of the San Juan is in the San Juan Mountains, north of Pagosa Springs, Colorado, and the river flows southwest into the high desert of northwest New Mexico, then northwest through Arizona and into the Colorado River in southeast Utah.

In 1958, construction of the Navajo Dam began. Upon its completion in 1962, the earth-filled dam was the largest of its type in the world, built for flood and sediment control, recreation, and water for irrigation and industry. It also provides irrigation water for the 110,000 acres of the Navajo Indian Irrigation Project (NIIP). With the completion of Navajo Dam, the once high-turbidity, warmwater river became the beginning of one of the finest trophy trout fisheries in the world.

In the early years, New Mexico Game and Fish stocked the river with rainbow, cutthroat, and brown trout. Trout in the San Juan showed phenomenal growth rates, due to the abundance of food. Over the years, rainbows have been consistently stocked in both the Quality Water and the lower river. Browns have reproduced naturally. The result is a unique tailwater river with remarkable consistency offering a year-round high-quality fishery, with approximately 20,000 trout per mile in the Quality Water.

The San Juan presents both challenge and tremendous opportunity to fly fishers. You can catch fish with many methods and without extensive fly-fishing abilities, but your overall skill and willingness to recognize and adapt to the current conditions will determine how many fish you catch. During the day, various parts of the Quality Water will present different angling opportunities, so what is happening on one part of the river may be different than what is happening upstream or downstream. Dry-fly fishing may be great in one location, but fruitless elsewhere.

The most successful trout anglers on the San Juan catch the majority of their fish on nymphs below the surface. The most successful nymph fishers generally use a strike indicator combined with small amounts of weight about 12 to 18 inches above the fly. If you have the right fly, you will still need to adjust the strike indicator and the amount of weight to the water depth and speed you are fishing. Most San Juan anglers fish a two-fly rig. Begin with a 7½- or 9-foot tapered leader attached to the fly line with a loop-to-loop connection or a nail knot. Tie about 18 inches of 4X to 7X tippet to the end of the leader using a surgeon's knot or blood knot. Tie your fly to the end of the tippet and attach weight above the knot at the end of leader. Tie a second tippet to the eye or

Cottonwood Flats (winter), lower part including some new structure from stream improvement projects. Paul Zimmerman courtesy ACS LLC

hook bend of first fly with a clinch knot, then tie on your second fly. Place the strike indicator approximately 1½ to 2 times the water depth from the weight.

Dry-fly fishing is the preference of many anglers. The San Juan presents some of the finest sight fishing for trophy trout using tiny dries, #22 to #30. Most of these large trout are very leader-shy and extremely tough to catch. This is the

7

The bottom of Texas Hole (far left) as it divides into the main channel on the right and the estuaries on the left. Lower Flats is downstream on the right. Paul Zimmerman

challenge fly fishers from across the world accept. Favored patterns are the Parachute BWO, CDC Biot BWO, Parachute Adams, and Hackle Wing Mayfly BWO.

The Quality Water of the San Juan River is located within the Navajo Lake State Park. The park maintains all river access roads, parking lots, boat launches, and trails. All the parking lots are within ¼ mile of the river. Cottonwood Campground is located on the river 4 miles below the dam, providing direct access. Dry camping and electric sites are available, with access to drinking water, restrooms, and telephone.

With the San Juan's relatively flat gradient, most areas can be accessed easily by foot on both sides of the river. Flows remain relatively constant through the year except during high spring flows around the end of May. Duration of the high flows is determined by the winter snowpack in the San Juan Mountains.

➤ **Hatches:** The San Juan River supports a large and diverse insect population that changes as you go downstream and water temperatures increase. The water near the dam is cold year-round—40 to 42 degrees—and supports large populations of midges in various sizes and colors, as well as smaller populations of mayflies, annelids, and scuds. Various midges are available to trout nearly every day of the year in the upper and midsections of the Quality Water. Downstream, the water gradually warms and is influenced more by seasonal conditions, resulting in larger mayflies, caddis, and Golden Stonefly populations. In the Quality Water, midges are con-

sidered the primary food source for rainbow and brown trout most of the year. Typical midge nymph or emerger patterns include the WD-40, Bling Midge, Johnny Flash, Tav's Big Mac, and UV Midge Emerger in #20 to #24. Dry-fly midges are the Brooks Sprout Midge, Fore 'n' Aft, Midge Adult, and Griffith's Gnat.

The San Juan does occasionally have terrestrial action during certain months of the year. During these times, you can fish larger dry flies with success.

➤ **Fishing regulations:** Early on, New Mexico Game and Fish recognized the outstanding characteristics of the river and set aside the upper 3¾ miles as the Quality Water, with catch and method restrictions. Currently the Quality Water is strictly catch-and-release, with up to two flies on single barbless hooks.

There are three access points within the 6-mile stretch of river below the dam for drift boats, rafts, and personal watercraft. No permits are required for private drift boats or personal craft to float the river. No motors or motorized craft are allowed; lifejackets must be worn at all times.

➤ **Tackle:** Use 9-foot, 5-weight rods with disk-drag reels for large trout on fine tippet. Many dry-fly fishers use lighter rods—3- and 4-weights—for softer and more delicate presentations. Leader sizes vary from 7½ to 9 feet, with 4X to 7X tippet and a double-fly rig. Waders are a must, due to the cold water. Dress and layer according to the conditions, and

Authors Wanda and Raymond Johnston. Float 'N Fish

Inset facing. Guide Mike Garrett with very large brown trout. Angler Rick Horning. Dave Horning

Above. Guide Chris Gallegos. Jay Walden

RAY AND WANDA JOHNSTON established their Float 'N Fish Fly Shop and Guide Service in 1997, following Ray's engineering career. He is a life-long fourth-generation resident of San Juan County, New Mexico. Ray learned the fly-tying trade as a teenager, tying commercially exclusively for the San Juan River for Handy Bait & Tackle in Aztec. Ray and Wanda met in the mid-1980s and have been fly-fishing and -tying partners ever since. Ray is a graduate of New Mexico State University and worked as a civil engineer in the soil mechanics and road construction industry for 22 years.

CLOSEST FLY SHOPS, OUTFITTERS, AND GUIDES

Float 'N Fish
PO Box 6460
Navajo Dam, NM 87419
505-632-5385
info@sanjuanfloatnfish.com
www.sanjuanfloatnfish.com

Abe's Motel & Fly Shop
El Pescador Restaurant & Bar
Born 'n' Raised Guide Service
PO Box 6428
Navajo Dam, NM 87419
505-632-2194
abes1958@earthlink.net
www.sanjuanriver.com

Rainbow Lodge
PO Box 6606
Navajo Dam, NM 87419
505-632-5717
info@sanjuanfishing.com
www.sanjuanfishing.com

Soaring Eagle Lodge
PO Box 6340
Navajo Dam, NM 87419
505-632-3721
info@soaringeaglelodge.net
www.soaringeaglelodge.net

Fisheads
Back Cast Café
San Juan River Lodge
P.O. Box 6427
Navajo Dam, NM 87419
505-634-0463
info@fisheadsofthesanjuan.com
www.fisheadsofthesanjuan.com

CLOSEST LODGES

Abe's Motel & Fly Shop (left)
Rainbow Lodge (left)
Soaring Eagle Lodge (left)

BEST CAMPGROUND

Cottonwood Campground
is on the river 4 miles below the dam, providing direct access to the river. Dry camping and electric sites are available; 505-632-2278.

BEST RESTAURANT

Sportsmans Inn Restaurant & Bar,
Intersection of State Hwys. 173 and 511
Navajo Dam, NM 87410
505-632-3271

CLOSEST PLACE TO GET A COLD, STIFF DRINK

Abe's Motel & Fly Shop
El Pescador Restaurant & Bar
PO Box 6428
Navajo Dam, NM 87419
505-632-2194
abes1958@earthlink.net
www.sanjuanriver.com

CLOSEST EMERGENCY MEDICAL HELP

San Juan Regional Medical Center
801 W. Maple
Farmington, NM 87401
505-609-2000

Critical Care Service
604 S. Rio Grande Ave.
Aztec, NM 87410
505-334-5640

CELL PHONE SERVICE

Cell service is limited in this mountainous terrain. Most area businesses have satellite capabilities, but Internet access is slow and limited.

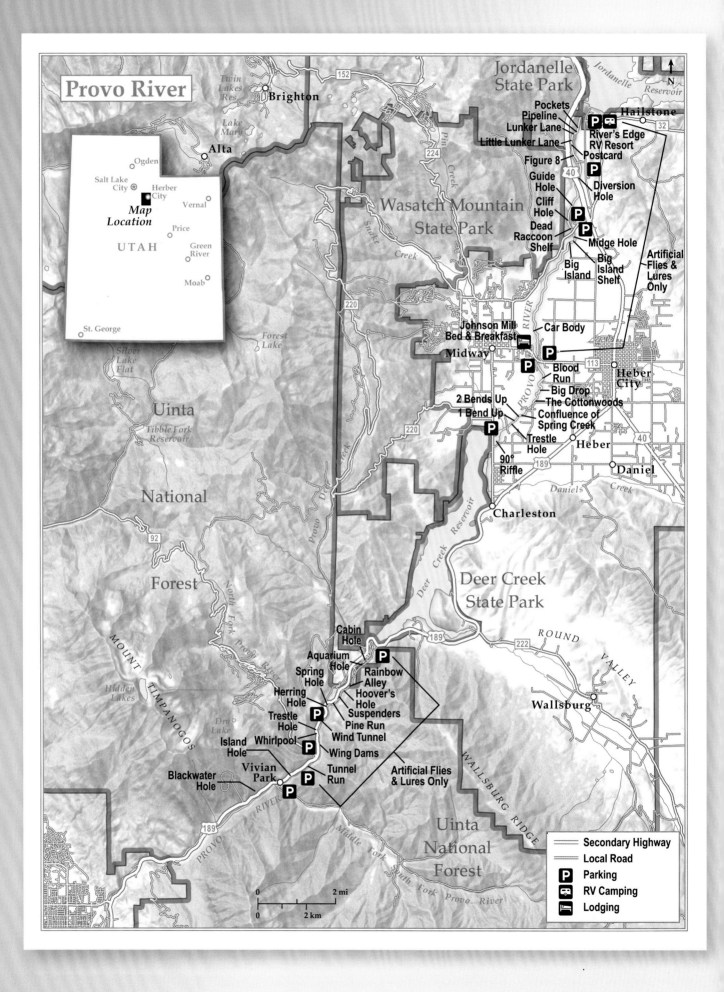

Provo River

Jordanelle State Park

Jordanelle Reservoir

Twin Lakes Res.
Brighton

Lake Mary

Alta

Silver Lake Flat

Map Location
UTAH
Ogden
Salt Lake City
Herber City
Vernal
Price
Green River
Moab
St. George

Pockets
Pipeline
Lunker Lane
Little Lunker Lane
Figure 8
Guide Hole
Cliff Hole
Dead Raccoon Shelf

River's Edge RV Resort
Hailstone
Postcard
Diversion Hole
Midge Hole
Big Island
Big Island Shelf

Artificial Flies & Lures Only

Wasatch Mountain State Park

Pine Creek
Snake Creek

Car Body

Johnson Mill Bed & Breakfast
Midway

Blood Run
Big Drop
The Cottonwoods
Confluence of Spring Creek
Heber City

2 Bends Up
1 Bend Up
Trestle Hole
Heber
90° Riffle
Daniel

Forest Lake

Uinta

Tibble Fork Reservoir

Charleston
Daniels Creek

National

Deer Creek State Park

ROUND VALLEY

Forest

Hidden Lakes

MOUNT TIMPANOGOS

North Fork Provo River

Dry Lake

Cabin Hole
Aquarium Hole
Spring Hole
Herring Hole
Trestle Hole
Island Hole
Whirlpool
Vivian Park
Blackwater Hole
Tunnel Run

Rainbow Alley
Hoover's Hole
Suspenders
Pine Run
Wind Tunnel
Wing Dams

Wallsburg

WALLSBURG RIDGE

Artificial Flies & Lures Only

Uinta National Forest

Middle Fork
South Fork Provo River

Provo River

0   2 mi
0   2 km

Secondary Highway
Local Road
P Parking
RV Camping
Lodging

➤ **Location:** An hour from Salt Lake International Airport and downtown Salt Lake City are two of Utah's more prolific tailwater fisheries: the Middle and Lower Provo Rivers. Each is uniquely beautiful, diverse, offers good access, and provides a myriad of fly-fishing opportunities and experiences.

To the east of Salt Lake City rise the Uinta Mountains, headwaters to Utah's Provo River. Not far downstream from where its tributaries merge, the river enters Jordanelle Reservoir, the first of two major impoundments.

Caddis on the Lower Provo River. Steve Schmidt

Prior to the completion of Jordanelle Dam in 1992, there was little access to the river flowing through the scenic mountain valleys of Kamas and Heber City. Regardless of access, flows were often insufficient, and consequently the trout fishery provided little if any fly fishing. Since Jordanelle Dam became operational, stream flows have been stabilized, water temperatures regulated, and 12 miles of this once dismal trout fishery have been revitalized.

Yet, the dam with its penstocks was only one aspect of this project that led to the river's turnaround. Shortly after its completion, the fishery underwent one of the country's largest mitigation projects. Sections that were once channelized were realigned, minimum stream flowwere implemented, and access was acquired. By its completion, overall trout habitat had been increased fivefold.

The Middle Provo River offers the fly fisher a variety of experiences. This river's prolific and diverse hatches of mayflies, caddisflies, stoneflies, and midges provide consistent fly-fishing opportunities year-round. Although the Green Drake hatch is one of the year's more anticipated event, PMDs, Golden Stoneflies, and late summer's Western Weedy Water Sedge combine with other aquatic insects and terrestrials to create consistent dry-fly, nymph, and soft-hackle fishing during the summer. Spring and fall Blue-winged Olives and winter midges round out the offerings during the cooler months. For those who enjoy throwing the big stuff, some of the largest trout are taken on streamers.

Before emptying into Deer Creek Reservoir, this freestone river descends through rich pasturelands and is easily recognizable by its dense stands of cottonwood, willow, and birch as it meanders through the valley. Its fertile waters are as vital to the surrounding pastures and farmland as they are to the brown and rainbow trout that attract fly fishers from around the world. When the fishing's not up to expectations, the alpine scenery, birds, and wildlife are more than adequate to make a day on the Middle Provo River memorable.

Eventually, the Middle Provo River's 12-mile journey is swallowed up by Deer Creek Reservoir, the older of the river's two reservoirs. Prior to the completion of Deer Creek Dam, the unimpeded river produced some of the country's largest trout. These behemoths often exceeded 20 pounds, with 10-pounders regarded as simply "decent fish." Sadly, the dam put an end to these, but the Lower Provo River still remains a resilient and prolific fishery.

Since the 1940s, the 7½-mile section of the Lower Provo has long been recognized as one of Utah's more notable trout fisheries. Unlike the Middle Provo's open, rural valley, this tailwater follows the close confines of narrow canyons whose glaciated walls dictate its course and define its character. Ancient cottonwoods and dense willows dominate the riparian corridor. Occasionally, clustered stands of pine and

Left. Lower Provo River brown trout. Steve Schmidt

Below. Misty morning on the Lower Provo. Steve Schmidt

scrub oak are also found along the river's edge. On the nearby hillsides, groves of aspen tremble throughout the summer, maturing to shades of yellow in the fall. Several waterfalls fed by Utah's famous snow cascade over the canyon's steep walls, adding to the unique and scenic nature of this fishery.

On the Lower Provo, January's winter midges kick off the year and taper off several months later, replaced by dense hatches of Blue-winged Olives in March and April. Although this tailwater doesn't have the Middle Provo's diverse aquatic hatches, they are equally prolific. Summer hatches of Golden Stoneflies, PMDs, and diverse caddis offer consistent dry-fly, nymph, and soft-hackle opportunities. As summer lingers, terrestrials fill in any voids until fall Blue-winged Olives emerge, with streamers rounding out the Lower Provo's full fly-fishing calendar.

Since Deer Creek Dam was built, the road that borders the Lower Provo has grown from two to four lanes, however in the process of that development, the river corridor was protected and actually enhanced along much of its length. More defined access points were created as part of the changes. Although this corridor suffers from a fair amount of road noise, there are sections where the river provides a quiet and intimate experience.

Another issue that can plague anglers on the Lower Provo is the presence of summer recreational tubers. Once the days warm, there can be a steady stream of them, yet the fish and insects don't seem to mind. There is an advantage to having the tubers around: They deter other anglers from fishing here!

Both tailwaters are impressive year-round fisheries with abundant populations of wild brown trout. You will also find an occasional rainbow trout that has wandered from a reservoir. Given the close proximity to each other and to Salt Lake City, these individually unique tailwaters offer fly fishers an incredibly diverse experience.

Winter and summer flows on both waters are very consistent once spring peak releases have subsided. Generally, spring flushes occur in May. Some years they last into June, just in time for the emergence of Green Drakes, PMDs, and a variety of Golden Stoneflies.

The Provo River tailwaters are of medium size and ideal for wading. Access is readily available along much of their lengths. The Middle in particular—with its streambed of round rock and boulders—can be a slippery wade; studded wading boots are recommended. Generally, 4- and 5-weight rods are ideal during most of the year, but when winter midges are out and the rivers flows are low, many fly fishers enjoy fishing lighter rods.

Nymphing is the most popular technique, as is probably true across most of the West these days, but the Provo offers incredible dry-fly fishing opportunities due to its diverse and consistent year-round hatches. Swinging soft-hackles, a lost art that has recently resurfaced, is another very productive and popular way to fish these tailwaters.

One outstanding aspect is excellent dry-fly fishing during the winter. Midge hatches that begin as early as January will attract a good rise of trout during the most pleasant part of any day. For those who enjoy fishing long leaders, delicate tippets, and small flies, this challenging fishing doesn't get much better. For many, winter fishing opportunities are some of the year's most rewarding.

➤ **Hatches:** Hatch times are generally for peaks; they will often occur in a somewhat lesser degree a few weeks earlier and later. Keep your eyes peeled!

Blue-winged Olives: March through May; October and November.

Pale Morning Duns: June through August, possibly early September.

Stoneflies: June through August.

Mothers Day Caddis: April through June with the heaviest hatches occurring around . . . you guessed it!

Various other caddis: April through October.

Midges: All year.

Scuds: All year.

Sow bugs: All year.

➤ **Fishing regulations:** Lower Provo River: From Deer Creek Dam downstream to Olmstead Diversion Dam, two trout under 15 inches; artificial flies and lures only.

From Olmstead Diversion Dam downstream, Utah general fishing regulations apply. Bait may be used, and four trout of any species may be kept.

Middle Provo River: From Jordanelle Dam downstream to Legacy Bridge, two brown trout under 15 inches. Rain-

bow and cutthroat trout must be released. Artificial flies and lures only.

From Legacy Bridge downstream to Deer Creek Reservoir, Utah general fishing regulations apply. Bait may be used, and four brown trout may be kept. Rainbow and cutthroat must be released.

For more information on Utah fishing regulations, visit: wildlife.utah.gov/guidebooks.

➤ **Tackle:** Use an 8½- or 9-foot rod for a 4- or 5-weight floating line. Use a 9-foot 6-weight with floating and sink-tip lines for streamers. Lighter and shorter rods work for midge fishing during the colder months of the year. Use tapered leaders 9 feet or longer. For dry flies and nymphs, use 4X, 5X, 6X, and 7X tippets, and 4X and 5X for soft-hackles.

Wear waders in winter, spring, and fall. During the heat of summer, wet wading is a nice way to stay comfortable. Cleats or studs on wading boots are highly recommended.

STEVE SCHMIDT owns and operates Western Rivers Flyfisher, a Utah based fly-fishing specialty shop in Salt Lake City. When not fishing, he writes about and photographs the world's waters, and is an avid cyclist and conservationist.

CLOSEST FLY SHOPS

Western Rivers Flyfisher
1071 E. 900 S.
Salt Lake City, UT 84105 (801-521-6424)
info@wrflyfisher.com
www.wrflyfisher.com

Park City Fly Shop
2065 Sidewinder Dr.
Park City, UT 84098 (435-645-8382)
info@parkcityflyshop.com
www.parkcityflyshop.com

Trout Bum 2
4343 Utah 224
Park City, UT 84098 (435-658-1166)
www.troutbum2.com

Four Seasons Fly Fishers
44 West 100 South
Heber City, UT 84032 (800-498-5440)
www.utahflyfish.com

Fish Tech Outfitters
6153 Highland Dr.
Salt Lake City, UT 84121 (801-272-8808)
byron@fishtechoutfitters.com
www.fishtechoutfitters.com

CLOSEST OUTFITTERS/GUIDES
Western Rivers Flyfisher (left)
Park City Outfitters
1295 E. Whileaway Rd.
Park City, UT 84060 (435-647-0677)
bbertagnole@hotmail.com
www.parkcityoutfitters.com

Park City on the Fly
1109 Park Ave.
Park City, UT 84060 (435-649-6707)
parkcityonthefly.com

BEST CAMPGROUND
Lower Provo River Campground
435-783-4338
www.fs.usda.gov/recarea/uwcnf

BEST HOTELS
Convenient to the Provo River are:
Hotel Monoco
15 W. 200 S.
Salt Lake City, UT 84101 (801-595-0000)
www.monaco-saltlakecity.com.

Peery Hotel
110 W. Broadway
Salt Lake City, UT 84101 (801-521-4300)
www.peeryhotel.com

Sundance Resort
8841 N. Alpine Loop Rd.
Sundance, UT 84604 (866-259-7468)
www.sundanceresort.com

Treasure Mountain Inn
255 Main St.
Park City, Utah (800-344-2460)
treasuremountaininn.com

BEST RESTAURANTS
SALT LAKE CITY
Martine Café
22 E. 100 S.
Salt Lake City, UT (801-363-9328)

Frida Bistro
545 W. 700 S.
Salt Lake City, UT (801-983-6692)

SUNDANCE RESORT
The Tree Room
8841 Alpine Scenic Hwy.
Sundance, UT (801-223-4200)

PARK CITY
Zoom
660 Main St.
Park City, UT (435-649-9108)

BEST PLACES TO GET A COLD, STIFF DRINK
SALT LAKE CITY
Redrock Brewing Company
254 S. 200 W.
Salt Lake City, UT (801-521-7446)

SUNDANCE RESORT
The Owl Bar
8841 Alpine Scenic Hwy.
Provo, UT (866-259-7468)

PARK CITY
High West Distillery
703 Park Ave.
Park City, UT (435-649-8300)

CLOSEST EMERGENCY MEDICAL HELP
Utah Valley Regional Medical Center
1034 N. 500 W.
Provo, UT (801-357-7850)

CELL PHONE SERVICE
Yes.

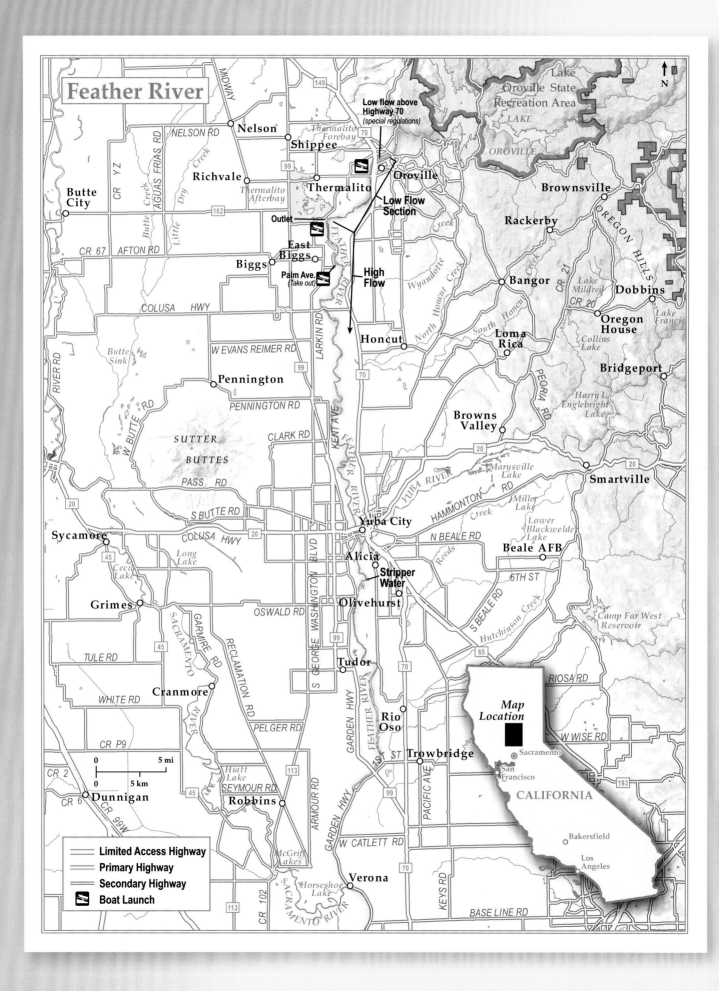

Feather River

Lake Oroville State Recreation Area

LAKE OROVILLE

Nelson

NELSON RD

Shippee

Thermalito Forebay

Low flow above Highway 70 *(special regulations)*

Richvale

Oroville

Thermalito

Brownsville

Low Flow Section

Rackerby

Butte City

Thermalito Afterbay

Outlet

East Biggs

Biggs

Palm Ave. *(Take out)*

High Flow

Bangor

Dobbins

Oregon House

Lake Francis

Honcut

Wyandotte Creek

North Honcut Creek

South Honcut Creek

Loma Rica

Collins Lake

Bridgeport

Pennington

PENNINGTON RD

SUTTER BUTTES

PASS RD

Browns Valley

Harry L. Englebright Lake

CLARK RD

S BUTTE RD

Marysville Lake

Smartville

Sycamore

COLUSA HWY

Long Lake

Yuba City

Alicia

Stripper Water

Olivehurst

Beale AFB

Miller Lake

Lower Blackwelder Lake

6TH ST

Camp Far West Reservoir

Grimes

OSWALD RD

Tudor

Cranmore

WHITE RD

Rio Oso

RIOS A RD

W WISE RD

Map Location

Sacramento

Trowbridge

CALIFORNIA

Dunnigan

Robbins

Verona

Bakersfield

Los Angeles

Legend

— Limited Access Highway
— Primary Highway
— Secondary Highway
— Boat Launch

0   5 mi
0   5 km

➤ **Location:** Northern California, about 3½ hours from San Jose, 3 hours from San Francisco, and 1½ hours from Sacramento.

California's Feather River—a tailwater fishery smack-dab in the heart of 1849 Gold Rush Country—is probably the most unusual in the world by virtue of its assortment of gamefish. Recognized for its prolific run of steelhead, it is also fished for Chinook salmon, shad, striped bass, large-mouth and smallmouth bass, and carp.

From its source in the Sierra Nevada, the Feather River flows from three separate forks into Lake Oroville. Completed in 1968, Oroville Dam is the largest earthen dam in the U.S., at 6,920 feet across and 770 feet high. Over 80 million yards of old mine tailings were used to build it. The Feather River flows from Oroville to the confluence in Verona, where it enters the Sacramento River. Fish entering the system from the Pacific Ocean pass under the Golden Gate Bridge and through San Francisco Bay.

The Feather River hatchery, completed in 1967, was designed to produce salmon and steelhead due to the huge habitat losses above Oroville Dam. It can accommodate 9,000 adult salmon and 3,000 steelhead. Its incubators can hold 20 million eggs, and its 8 concrete raceways can hold 9.6 million fingerlings.

The Feather is known for its fall run of Chinook salmon, and fall- and spring-run steelhead. Fall steelhead follow Chinook salmon in late September. Until temperatures decrease and salmon start to dig redds, steelhead hold in pools where water temperatures remain cool in the hot summer months. Steelhead move onto salmon redds in early October looking for eggs. The first rain is always a good indicator of the fall season starting. Find spawning salmon, and steelhead will be close behind. High-stick nymphing or indicator nymphing with an egg and a green caddis pupa dropper is the proven technique. Get the flies over the salmon to the waiting steelhead below the redds. Sight fishing while walking the river is possible. Look for agitated salmon. The buck salmon will chase the steelhead out of the redd, and then go back to pair up with the hen. Look for buck salmon making a sweeping circle chasing steelhead. The chase is a great indication of steelhead in the area. Sneak up on the salmon and high-stick the egg over the salmon to the waiting steelhead. Stealth and a

good drift are essential to make this work. Salmon are hard to spook, but steelhead are very spooky in the shallow water where salmon are spawning. It's essential to get the flies over the salmon. While salmon are somewhat fresh, they will also take the egg, and then you have a 20- to 40-pound fish on the end of the line that has very little fight left, but just enough to break off your fly.

Not many fly anglers target the spring and fall runs of Chinook salmon. There is a short window for swinging flies in early October when the fall run is bright chrome and moving up from the Pacific. As salmon move through runs in the high-flow section, they are easily agitated. Swing bright chartreuse and hot pink Spey flies on a 7/8 Spey rod to cov-

Mac and Grant with a wild, fall-run steelhead. Jesse Blair

er water. As salmon move upriver, they congregate in deep pools and tailouts to wait for the first rain to pair up and start spawning. As soon as salmon begin pairing up, they start deteriorating.

The most popular rods are 9½-foot 6-weights. The extra length is helpful for turning over an indicator, split-shot, and multiple flies. Switch rods are also ideal; an 11-foot 6-weight with a floating line and indicator is deadly for covering lots of water fast. Drift boats are the most common watercraft for covering both the high-flow and low-flow sections. River Bend Park is the most common put-in. There is a takeout

Hooking up with steelhead in the low-flow section of the Feather River. Mac Noble

at the outlet, or you can continue down through the high-flow section and take out at Palm Avenue, which is an access point off Larkin Road. Gold City Cab Company in Oroville is familiar with all the put-ins and takeouts and will do a shuttle. Both low-flow and high-flow sections are wadable. The low-flow section has riffles between long stretches of slow water. There are nine riffles divided by slow sections within the 6 miles. The low-flow is accessed through the Oroville Wildlife Area, where dirt roads run along the river on the west side. Riffles are easily viewable from the road. Drifting may be done in a drift boat, pontoon boat, kayak, whitewater canoe, or raft. It's common for guides and anglers drifting this section to add an electric motor or kicker motor to a pontoon boat or drift boat to get through the slow sections faster than rowing.

The high-flow section is wadable is some spots, but not crossable in most. The most popular drift in this section is from the outlet to the takeout at Palm Ave. This 4-mile section can be combined with the low-flow drift for a 10-mile drift. The whole drift can be rowed in under 4 hours, but the boat is usually used for access to less accessible spots. The high-flow section is also accessible with a small jet boat or john boat, but can be super-technical, with shallow gravel bars and riffles that are challenging to navigate. Jet boats are more common below Gridley, where the river becomes more channelized.

In addition to steelhead and Chinook salmon, the Feather has a good run of shad in May. Shad fishing is best below the Thermalito outlet, where spring weather warms water to prime spawning temperatures. It's not unheard of to catch

Sydney Williams with a spring hatchery steelhead. Mac Noble

shad as far up as the hatchery, but only when water temperatures are warm enough.

Shad are usually found in soft water on inside bends throughout the high-flow section from the outlet to Verona. A shad dart on a shooting head is enough to entice a grab. Shad darts have a beadhead to give them a jigging action, with a pulse in the swing from the angler. Shad darts are wrapped with bright fluorescent colors to make them visible. Jigging as the fly is on the swing gives the fly action shad cannot resist. Be sure to dangle the fly at the end of the swing with a slight jigging action. The take is ferocious, and there's never any doubt whether or not it is a shad. Because shad form big schools, once one is found, others will be close, often following the hooked shad. Prime time of day is early and late when the sun is low in the sky.

Striped bass follow shad and spring steelhead upriver in the spring. Best fishing is in the high-flow section below Shanghai bend, where deep pools and warm water provide adequate conditions for the striper topwater spawn in late May and June. Stripers are an incredibly adaptive species. Some stripers stay in the high-flow section year-round, spawning in the spring with migrating stripers coming from the San Francisco Delta and the Pacific Ocean. Spring is prime time for stripers because they are in pods and more active pre-spawn than at any other time. Use big flies to imitate shad, spring steelhead, and lampreys, their primary diet in the spring. Best access is by boat. Type 6 or integrated shooting heads are ideal to get down in pools, behind snags, and in riffle tailouts where stripers will hold, ready to pounce on anything within striking distance. Eight- or 10-weight rods are ideal to throw big flies and 300- to 400-grain shooting heads.

Best smallmouth fishing is in the high-flow section throughout the spring and summer. It has good habitat with snags, rock walls, backeddies, and tributaries, where these predators feed on minnows, salmon fry, lampreys, and crayfish. Topwater action can be good in the spring when smallmouth are on their beds along the edges. Warm summer temperatures bring smallies out in the morning and evening eager to crush topwater poppers. Fishing with a sink-tip around structure is the preferred method during the day.

Best section for shad, stripers, and smallmouth is below Shanghai, where incoming water from the Yuba River increases flows, and the water warms, creating plentiful habitat for shad and stripers with deep pools, long runs, and warm inside bends. This is the longest stretch from Boyd's Pump to

Verona. The confluence is a popular shad and striper location during their migration.

➤ **Hatches:** Winter hatches of BWOs and midges are prominent, but the number one food source for steelhead is salmon eggs. Steelhead feed on salmon eggs from October through December. March kicks off the start of March Browns and the beginnings of caddis. Cool mornings and rainy days will still produce hatches of BWOs and midges in the morning. The egg of choice during the spring is the sucker egg. Releasing small yellow or chartreuse eggs, squawfish spawn on flats above riffles where steelhead will pick them up in the riffles below. As temperatures rise, caddis will be the prominent hatch. It's not uncommon to see steelhead slashing caddis on the surface in the afternoon, but the most common fly is a #14 Fox's Caddis Pupa, tan and green.

➤ **Fishing regulations:** www.dfg.ca.gov/regulations.

➤ **Tackle:** The most popular rods for the Feather are 9½-foot 6-weights. Switch rods are also ideal for this area. An 11-foot 6-weight is great for covering lots of water fast. Swinging flies with a light tip and an alevin pattern in riffles is very productive from January to March, when salmon fry are in the river. Another alternative for the switch rod is a RIO Switch line with an indicator on a 7½-foot, 3X leader with eggs, caddis, and/or BWO nymphs in a tandem setup. Be sure to use enough split-shot to get the flies down in riffles and tailouts. Usually one Dinsmore AAA split-shot is enough.

The shad setup is a little different. The switch rod with a Skagit head and a 15-foot sink tip will get a shad dart down on the swing. For single-handed rods, a sink-tip or shooting head with running line behind it will get tandem shad darts down in tailouts and along the flats where shad hold.

Use an egg with an egg dropper during prime-time egg bite, but green caddis pupae are also stirred up when salmon are digging redds. A green caddis pupa on a sturdy 2X-heavy scud hook will get eaten. The egg bite usually goes on until Thanksgiving. As salmon die off, steelhead move to the hatchery and the top section above Highway 70.

After college, MICHAEL M. "MAC" NOBLE moved to Chico, California, where he has managed Fish First! fly shop since 2005. When he's not guiding, Mac divides his time between Chico and Kalispell, Montana, with Pepper, his Lab. Mac's favorite species change with the seasons—striped bass, trout, and steelhead are his primary interests.

CLOSEST FLY SHOPS

Fish First Fly Shop
766 Mangrove Ave.
Chico, CA 95926
530-343-8300
Mac@FishFirst.com
www.FishFirst.com

Sierra Stream Fly Shop
847 W. 5th St.
Chico, CA 95927
530-345-4261
www.sierrastreamflyshop.com

Chico Fly Shop
1154 W. 8th Ave.
Chico, CA 95926
530-345-9983
Info@thechicoflyshop.com
www.thechicoflyshop.com

CLOSEST OUTFITTER
Fish First Fly Shop *(above)*

CLOSEST MOTELS

Motel 6
505 Montgomery St.
Oroville, CA 95969
530-532-9400

Days Inn
1745 Feather River Blvd.
Oroville, CA 95965
800-615-3107

BEST HOTEL
Oxford Suites
2035 Business Lane
Chico, CA 95928
530-899-9090

BEST RESTAURANT
Sierra Nevada Taproom and Restaurant
1075 E. 20th St.
Chico, CA 95928
530-345-2739

Across from Oxford Suites, Sierra Nevada Brewing Company has an excellent restaurant plus brewery tours.

CLOSEST EMERGENCY MEDICAL HELP
Feather River Hospital
5974 Pentz Rd.
Paradise, CA 95969
530-877-9361

SHUTTLE SERVICE
Gold City Cab Co.
530-532-4222

CELL PHONE SERVICE
Excellent all along the Feather River.

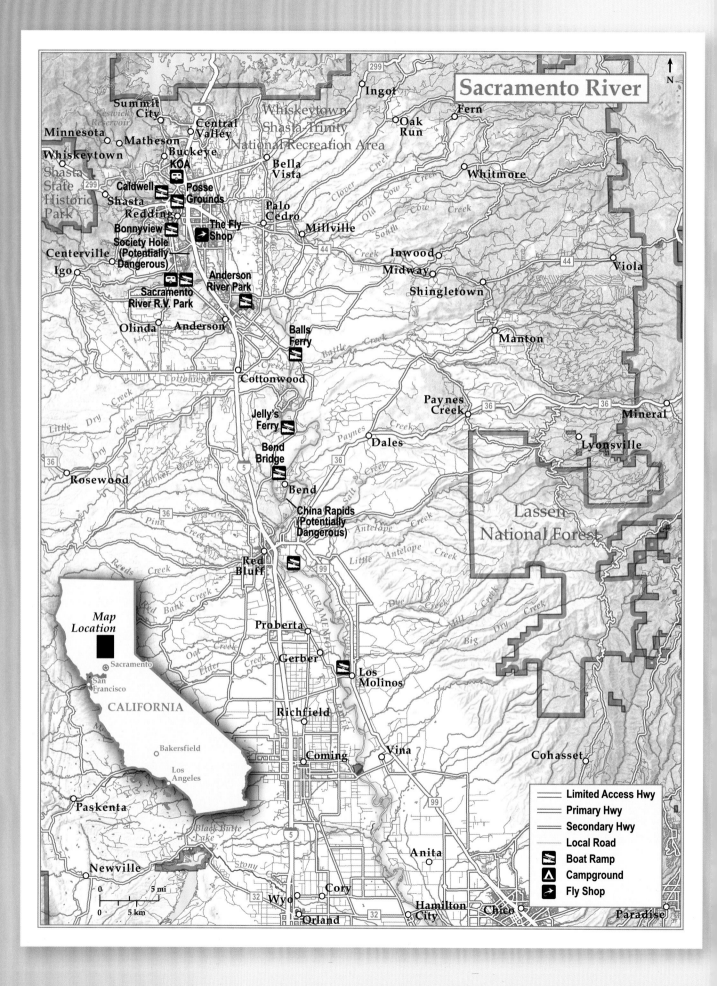

Sacramento River

N

Ingot

Fern

Oak
Run

Summit
City

Whiskeytown
Shasta-Trinity
National Recreation Area

Whitmore

Minnesota

Matheson

Central
Valley

Whiskeytown

Buckeye

KOA

Bella
Vista

Palo
Cedro

Shasta
State
Historic
Park

299

Caldwell

Posse
Grounds

Shasta

Millville

Redding

The Fly
Shop

Inwood

Midway

Viola

Bonnyview
Society Hole
(Potentially
Dangerous)

44

Centerville

Shingletown

Igo

Anderson
River Park

Manton

Sacramento
River R.V. Park

Olinda

Anderson

Balls
Ferry

Cottonwood

Paynes
Creek

36

Mineral

Jelly's
Ferry

Lyonsville

Bend
Bridge

Dales

Rosewood

Bend

36

China Rapids
(Potentially
Dangerous)

Lassen
National Forest

5

Red
Bluff

99

*Map
Location*

Proberta

Sacramento

CALIFORNIA

Gerber

San
Francisco

Los
Molinos

Richfield

Bakersfield

Vina

Cohasset

Los
Angeles

Coming

Paskenta

Anita

Black Butte
Lake

5

Newville

0   5 mi

0   5 km

32

Wyo

Cory

Orland

Hamilton
City

Chico

Paradise

	Limited Access Hwy
	Primary Hwy
	Secondary Hwy
	Local Road
	Boat Ramp
	Campground
	Fly Shop

Lower Sacramento River *(Northern California)*

➤ **Location:** Redding, California, a 4-hour drive (or 1-hour commercial flight) north of San Francisco; a 2¼-hour drive from Sacramento.

The Lower Sacramento tailwater was created by the Shasta Dam in 1945; at the time it was the second tallest dam (behind Hoover) in the United States, and considered one of the greatest engineering feats of all time. It collects the flows of many rivers, creeks, and tributaries, including the McCloud, Upper Sacramento, Pit River, and, indirectly, Fall River and Hat Creek, into Shasta Lake. Below the dam, the Lower Sac is the major aquatic artery of California, supplying a home for many species of both coldwater and warmwater fish, agricultural water for the verdant farmlands to the south, and hydroelectric power to Northern California. It runs high in the summer (10,000–15,000 cfs on average) for agricultural water delivery, and low in the fall, winter, and spring (4,000–6,000 cfs on average), when that demand dwindles.

The river flows clear and cold through the city of Redding, then bisects a vast and largely rural/agricultural watershed for many miles, before becoming a largely channelized water delivery system downstream. The stretch of most interest to trout and steelhead anglers begins in Redding below Keswick Dam, and starts to falter about 75 miles downstream, around Chico, as the water warms. The most impressive reach for numbers and size of fish is the upper 30 or so miles, from Redding to Red Bluff. The Lower Sac is open to fishing all year long, and because of the low-elevation ecosystem it flows through, it actually *does* fish well every month of the year—there is no snow or exceptionally cold weather to negatively impact conditions. Local air temperatures do get quite hot in summer, but because of the coldwater releases, the fishing remains exceptional.

At one time, releases into the Lower Sac came primarily from the surface of Shasta Lake—consequently, downstream the water temps would fluctuate widely, becoming warm enough in the hot Redding summers to significantly restrict the local rainbow trout fishery (as well as the once-legendary Chinook salmon and steelhead escapements). With the construction of a coldwater device on the face of the dam in

1991, water temps are now kept in the mid-50s year-round. Intended to help mitigate the damage done to the historical anadromous runs, as a by-product, this device has helped transform a once-decent wild-trout fishery into one of the finest in the nation. Though the California Department of Fish and Wildlife has not collected data to estimate how many rainbow trout per mile reside in this river, limited angler surveys show the average fish measures just over

The Fly Shop's Mike Mercer nymphing a summertime riffle with guide Bryan Balog. Val Atkinson, courtesy of The Fly Shop

16 inches. These trout are heavy-bodied and thick in the shoulders, and fish over 20 inches are common.

Interestingly, the diversity of aquatic insect species—and their overall populations in the Lower Sac—are improving annually, probably due to the abovementioned coldwater flows, and to the federal cleanup of a copper mine that had been leaking catastrophically poisonous effluent into the Keswick section of the river above Redding for many decades. Where abysmal water quality had once prevented the survival of all but the hardiest insects, the river now boasts strong populations of many species of mayflies, caddis, and stoneflies. And the trout get even fatter.

For an introduction to fishing the Lower Sac, hiring a guide is highly advisable, not so much because the fishing is challenging—it rarely is—but because this is big water. A guide will take the guesswork out of where the fish hold

Fish portrait—a typical wild Sacramento River rainbow.
Val Atkinson courtesy of The Fly Shop

during various flow regimes, and a drift boat is an advantage for accessing the most productive riffles and runs. There are plenty of places for a boat to pull over and allow anglers to get out and wade, but for sheer volume of hookups it's hard to beat driftboat fishing. There are a number of boat ramps—both public and private—scattered along the entire length of the river, making possible any number of different, daylong floats.

For anglers who prefer to fish on their own without a boat, there are plenty of options. First and foremost, the greatest density of great wading water is high in the system—downtown Redding provides the most (and best) wading access

points within close proximity of each other. For those willing to do a bit of research, there are a reasonable number of great walk-and-wade entry points all the way downstream to the small town of Anderson, a stretch of about 10 miles. It would be fair to say that fall, winter, and spring—specifically the months of October through March, most years—are the best wade-fishing seasons on the river, as this is when the flows are traditionally at their lowest. Even during the higher-water summer months, though, there are always a few spots where intrepid wading anglers can catch fish.

Nymph fishing has for many years been the technique of choice among guides and locals on the Lower Sacramento. Fishing a brace of nymphs on a 6-weight outfit, 6 to 10 feet below an indicator, often with a pair of BB or AB split-shot, is devastatingly effective, year-round. Guides line up their boats near the most productive current seams, riffle drops, and sunken clay channels, and have their sports make the relatively short casts to the targets. Anglers then depend largely on the boat to track the indicator's speed—making minor mending adjustments to their floating lines where necessary—allowing for extended dead-drifts. With large numbers of big rainbows per river mile, anglers tend to hook a lot of impressive specimens this way, and they are hot—it's not uncommon to see one's backing when fishing in this manner! Wading anglers fish nymphs in the same way, but depend on feeding slack line into the presentation after the cast—often as much as 60 to 70-feet—to achieve long dead-drifts.

➤ **Hatches:** Though it's not as consistently productive as nymphing, the Lower Sac does experiences some impressive

Fly Shop guide Greg Kennedy with Sarah and Shane Kholbeck downstream from Redding's Sundial Bridge.
Val Atkinson courtesy of The Fly Shop

Inset. Sarah Kholbeck with a Lower Sac rainbow.
Marcel Siegle courtesy of The Fly Shop

seasonal dry-fly action. In a nutshell, there are often heavy PMD emergences (June–September), BWOs (October–March), and various caddis hatches throughout the summer. Other food sources include Salmonflies, Little Yellow Stones, crane flies, and aquatic worms. And in the fall and winter, a strong infusion of spawning king (Chinook) salmon add both eggs and alevins to the menu.

Favorite nymph and dry patterns simply reflect the river's most prolific insect populations (and eggs). With the exception of Salmonfly nymphs, most flies used are in the #14–#18 size range, so heavy hooks are recommended or fish *will* straighten them. 4X tippets are standard for nymphing, and 5X for dries; fluorocarbon is recommended, but not necessary. Despite their size, these rainbows are not usually finicky, requiring only a dead-drift to ensure success.

➤ **Fishing regulations:** From the Redding area (beginning 650 feet below Keswick Dam) down to the Deschutes Road bridge in Anderson, the trout season is year-round, barbless hooks only, with a daily limit of one trout less than 16 inches. Since these are all wild trout, the vast majority of fly fishers and guides release 100 percent of their fish.

➤ **Tackle:** Use a 9-foot, 6-weight rod with a weight-forward floating line and 9-foot tapered leaders ending in 4X and 5X tippet. (If you are wading, be prepared for long, extended dead-drifts.) You need a reel with a smooth drag capable of holding plenty of backing. Wear GORE-TEX or other breathable waders. Leave the studded wading shoes at home if you are going boating with a guide.

Author Mike Mercer

MIKE MERCER has worked at The Fly Shop in Redding, California, for the past 35 years. He currently mans the international travel department, sending people on dream fly-fishing trips all over the world. He is an Umpqua contract fly tier, and wrote the book *Creative Fly Tying*. His articles can be found in all the major fly-fishing magazines.

CLOSEST FLY SHOPS

The Fly Shop
4140 Churn Creek Rd.
Redding, CA 96002-3629
800-669-FISH, ext. 3474
info@theflyshop.com
www.theflyshop.com

CLOSEST OUTFITTERS/GUIDES

The Fly Shop (above)
Confluence Outfitters
20735 Manter Ct.
Red Bluff, CA 96080
888-481-1650
Info@confluenceoutfitters.com
www.confluenceoutfitters.com

BEST HOTEL

Oxford Suites
1967 Hilltop Dr.
Redding, CA 96002
530-221-0100
www.oxfordsuitesredding.com

BEST CAMPGROUND

Sacramento River RV/Campground
6596 Riverland Dr.
Redding, CA 96002
530-365-640
www.sacramentoriverrvresort.com

BEST RESTAURANT

Jack's Grill
1743 California St.
Redding, CA
530-241 9705 (a hole-in-the-wall with the best steaks in town)
www.jacksgrillredding.com

BEST PLACE TO GET A COLD, STIFF DRINK

Shameless O'Leerys
1701 California St. Ste. B
Redding, CA 96001
530-246 4765

CLOSEST EMERGENCY MEDICAL HELP

Mercy Medical Center
2175 Rosaline Ave.
Redding, CA 96001
530-246-3729

CELL PHONE SERVICE
Yes

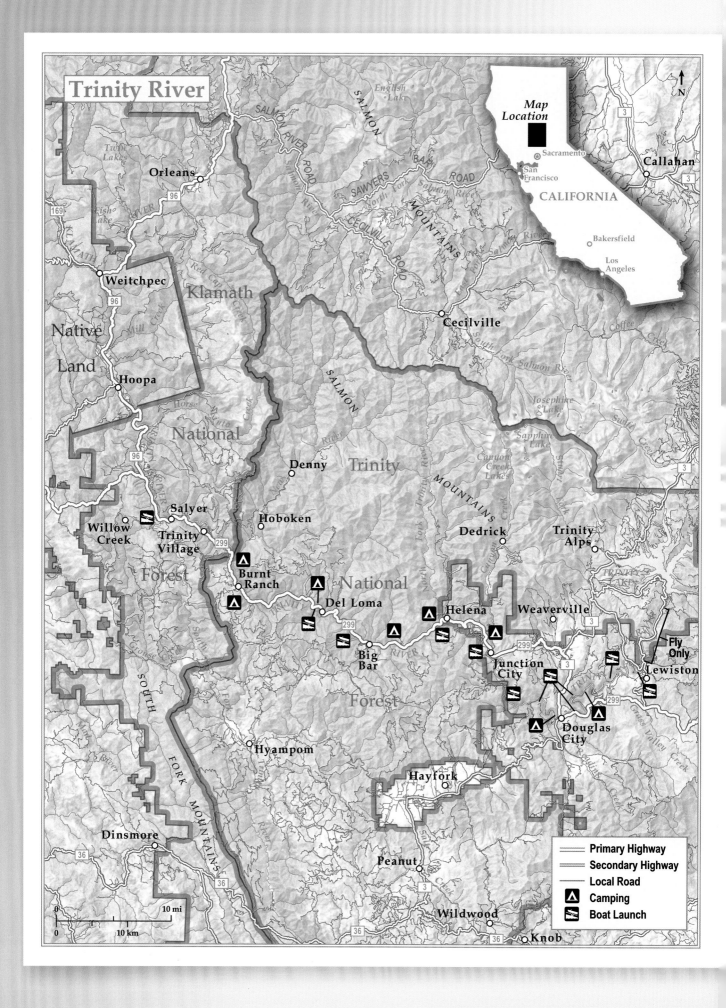

Trinity River *(Northern California)*

➤ **Location:** Northern California, about a 3½-hour drive from Sacramento International Airport; about 1 hour west of Redding, and minutes from historic Weaverville, the place to stay and dine while fishing the Trinity River.

The Trinity River is the longest tributary of the Klamath River, approximately 165 miles from its source to its mouth. The Trinity begins its journey to the sea high in the remote Scott Mountains, flows southwest into Trinity Lake, and immediately into Lewiston Lake. From the Lewiston Dam, the river flows west-northwest past Weaverville to the south of the Trinity Alps, one of the highest points on the entire coastal range. After the Trinity River's confluence with the South Fork, she flows north-northwest and joins the Klamath River about 20 miles from the Pacific Ocean.

The upper stretches are primarily encompassed by Shasta-Trinity National Forest, Bureau of Land Management, and private holdings, while the lower stretches flow through Yurok and Hoopa Native American lands. In 1981, Congress designated the entire Trinity River from the Lewiston dam to her confluence with the Klamath River as The Trinity Wild and Scenic River. The Trinity River's upper reaches (Lewiston dam to Burnt Ranch) would be considered small by most standards; after her confluence with the South Fork, the river almost doubles in volume. The Trinity, being dam-controlled, has more than 20 small tributaries, and five very significant ones, which can turn the main stem into a torrent after a few hours of hard rain. That is the "wild" part of "wild and scenic."

The Trinity River historically was heavily mined, including placer and large-scale hydraulic mining in the days of the California Gold Rush and beyond. Tailing piles are still visible on many sections of the Trinity. Tailings aside, the Trinity is a scenic, semi-coastal river with a Tolkien-like fog that wafts through the evergreen mountainscape every morning. The fog sometimes does not clear until late in the afternoon, and then, like clockwork, rolls right back in. The Trinity supports an abundance of wildlife: waterfowl, coastal black-tailed deer, river otters, and the occasional black bear. In 1828, the Jedediah Smith expedition camped on the banks of the Trinity River in search of the promised land of beaver and otter pelts.

The Trinity River is a unique tailwater, due to its support of healthy runs of several species of anadromous salmonids.

Hook-up on a Trinity steelhead. Jeff English

The Trinity boasts a large run (some years larger than others) of winter steelhead, both hatchery and wild fish. Some people will argue the wild gene, but in California, if the fish's adipose fin is intact it is considered to be wild. The hatchery is located immediately below the Lewiston Dam. The Trinity also has runs of Chinook and coho (silver) salmon. The coho are protected and all-wild fish. The coho run of 2012–2013 was the best witnessed in many years—a good health indicator for the Trinity and her tributaries. The river also has a small resident population of brown trout that can attain 28-plus inches. The steelhead average 25 inches and 4 to 5 pounds, with some reaching 37 inches and 16 pounds, and a very few even larger. Chinook are small by Chinook salmon

Fishin' the goal post. *Jeff Parker*

Inset. An average Trinity steelhead. *Jeff English*

standards and average 18 to 22 pounds, with a few pushing 35 pounds. All coho hooked must be immediately released and never lifted from the water.

The Trinity River has a plethora of boat launch and recovery areas throughout the entire system. Most are unimproved and require a four-wheel-drive vehicle and local knowledge. A few drifts are easy to row, but some sections could get a novice oarsman in trouble, and some sections are not recommended for a drift boat at all, strictly walk-and-wade. Check locally on river conditions and know your put-in and takeout.

Steelhead typically enter the Trinity at her confluence with the Klamath in late August or early September, with steelheading in full swing in the middle to upper reaches by the first week of October. The Trinity is a vast system, with both open and fishable and closed tributaries. Some are permanently closed; others open at certain times of the year. Regulations are strict on the tributaries, but they can offer great opportunities and should be fished as well. Use your imagination, not the crowd. The Trinity can fish very well all the way through February and into March.

➤ **Hatches:** Insect hatches are not really an issue for steelhead. Anglers are not matching a hatch, just triggering a strike.

➤ **Anadromous Fish Runs:**
Steelhead: Mid-August to mid-March.
Chinook (king) salmon: Mid-June into early November.
Coho (silver) salmon: Early July to early November.
Note: Coho salmon may not be taken in any of the waters of the State of California. Incidentally hooked coho salmon must be immediately released unharmed to the waters where they are hooked, and must not be removed from the water.

➤ **Fishing regulations:** Regs are constantly changing, with water conditions and the return of steelhead from the ocean. See www.dfg.ca.gov or shops in the area for up-to-date closures and regulations.

➤ **Tackle:** A 9- to 10-foot, 7-weight rod will cover single-handed casters and be enough rod for the fish. A 10½- or

11-foot, 7-weight switch rod will cover plenty of water for swing fishers. A swung fly can be fished with a dry or various sink-tip lines depending on river flows. You need a matching heavy-duty reel with sufficient drag and at least 100 yards of backing. Use 9- to 12-foot fluorocarbon leaders tapering to 4X or 3X depending upon visibility. (Remember, even though you are fishing for steelhead, you can easily get bit by a 25-pound Chinook salmon on its way to spawn.)

Wear breathable waders with appropriate moisture-wicking underwear and cleated wading boots (obviously not necessary if you'll be in a drift boat) along with a wading staff if you are the least bit edgy about moss-covered rocks. And who isn't?

Small nymphs, Hare's-ear Soft-hackles #8 to #12. Use traditional steelhead patterns—October Hiltons and Green Butt Skunks, for example—their size and sparseness depending on river flow and clarity. Nymphing requires an indicator (many different styles are useful, to each angler their own) split-shot (3/0 or larger), a large nymph up to #4, such as Zack's Thurmanator Stone, Kaufmann Stone, or similar, black or dark brown. Trail this with a much smaller nymph, a #10 to #16 Copper John, Morrish Anatomay, Hotwire Prince, or an egg pattern (vary sizes and colors).

➤ **Historical:** Take an hour or so to visit the Weaverville Joss House State Historic Park in the center of the town. The site is a Taoist temple, which is still in use and is the oldest Chinese temple in California.

The current building, called The Temple among the Trees Beneath the Clouds, was built in 1874 to replace earlier structures that had been destroyed by fires. Much of the material on display inside the temple includes temple equipment, objects of Chinese art, mining tools, and weapons used in the 1854 Tong War.

Salmon spawn in the creek directly in front of the joss (opium) house.

Author Jeff Parker and Riffle. Becky Marston

JEFF PARKER has been a professional fly-fishing guide for more than 20 years. He has guided anglers in Utah, Arizona, Alaska, Chile, Montana—primarily the Missouri River—and California. He currently resides in Northern California and operates J.F. Parker Flyfishing, guiding for trout and steelhead.

CLOSEST FLY SHOP

Trinity Outdoors
1615 Main St.
Weaverville, CA 96093
530-623-4999
theguys@trinityoutdoors-us.com

CLOSEST OUTFITTERS

J.F. Parker Flyfishing
Jeff Parker
435-632-9527
www.jfpflyfishing.com

Fly Fishing NorCal
Gabe Duran
530-526-2044
www.flyfishingnorcal.com

LODGING

Red Hill Cabins
PO Box 234
Weaverville, CA 96093
530-623-4331

Indian Creek Lodge
P.O. Box 100
Douglas City
CA 96024
530-623-6294
indiancreeklodge@wildblue.net

BEST RESTAURANT

La Grange Café
520 Main St.
Weaverville, CA 96093
530-623-5325

BEST PLACE TO GET A COLD, STIFF DRINK

La Grange Café
520 Main St.
Weaverville, CA 96093
530-623-5325

CLOSEST EMERGENCY MEDICAL HELP

Trinity Hospital
60 Easter Ave.
Weaverville, Calif.
530-623-5541

CELL PHONE SERVICE
Sporadic at best on the river.

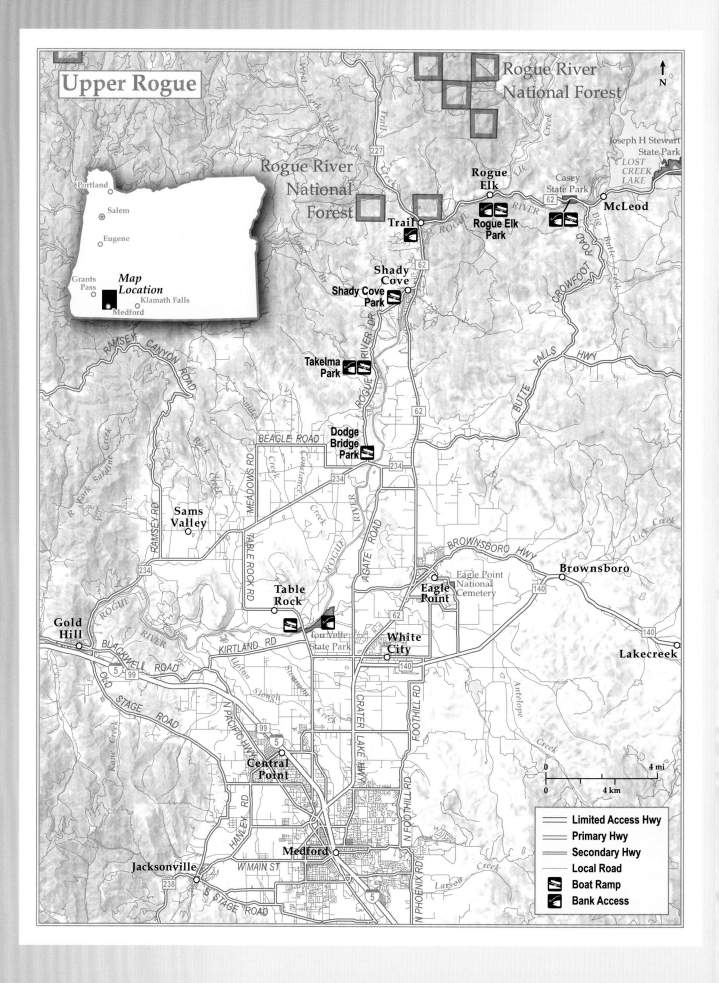

Upper Rogue

Rogue River National Forest

Rogue River National Forest

N

Joseph H Stewart State Park

LOST CREEK LAKE

Portland

Salem

Eugene

Grants Pass

Map Location

Klamath Falls

Medford

Rogue Elk

Casey State Park

McLeod

Trail

Rogue Elk Park

227

62

Shady Cove

Shady Cove Park

CROWFOOT ROAD

Big Butte Creek

BUTTE FALLS HWY

Takelma Park

RAMSEY CANYON ROAD

Sawtel Creek

ROGUE RIVER DR

62

BEAGLE ROAD

Dodge Bridge Park

234

234

MEADOWS RD

Sams Valley

TABLE ROCK RD

ROGUE RIVER

AGATE ROAD

BROWNSBORO HWY

Eagle Point National Cemetery

Brownsboro

234

Table Rock

Eagle Point

140

Lakecreek

Gold Hill

BLACKWELL ROAD

KIRTLAND RD

TouVelle State Park

White City

62

140

5

99

OLD STAGE ROAD

N PACIFIC HWY

99

Strongway Creek

CRATER LAKE HWY

FOOTHILL RD

Antelope Creek

Lick Creek

Kane Creek

HANLEY RD

Central Point

5

Medford

N FOOTHILL RD

N PHOENIX RD

Creek

Jacksonville

W MAIN ST

OLD STAGE ROAD

5

238

Larson Creek

0   4 mi

0   4 km

	Limited Access Hwy
	Primary Hwy
	Secondary Hwy
	Local Road
	Boat Ramp
	Bank Access

➤ **Location:** Southern Oregon, equidistant between Portland and San Francisco. Ten minutes from Medford International Airport (MFR). Historic Crater Lake National Park is 83 miles from the airport.

The world-famous Rogue River is not a tributary, but a combination of its upper forks and a variety of feeders. The 150+ free-flowing miles of tailwater are regulated by William L. Jess Dam. Tributaries of note are the Applegate and the Illinois. The mileage and temperatures below William L. Jess Dam make it among the tops in tailwater length and cool temperatures for the State of Oregon. It is one of the original rivers included in the Wild and Scenic Rivers Act of 1968. This remote section begins about 7 miles below Grants Pass, and ends about 11 miles east of Gold Beach.

The Upper Rogue fishery begins at the dam at the base of the Cascade Mountains. It flows through urban areas and ranchland. Public access is plentiful. Regulations governing steelhead, Chinook salmon, coho salmon, cutthroat, and resident rainbows are extensive, and change with great frequency. Request a copy of the regulations with your license purchase, and read about your targeted species and fishing area.

Even though the fly-caught world-record Chinook salmon was brought to net on the Rogue River, this fishery is wildly hit or miss. A steelhead angler using steelhead gear caught the record fish. Fly anglers actually targeting Chinook on the Upper Rogue are virtually nonexistent. Gear anglers crowd the well-known pools by the thousands, it seems.

Small resident rainbow trout are abundant on the Upper Rogue. These fish are not complicated. Angling pressure for the river's smallest native gamefish approaches zero in 10-mile sections of river. A 2- or 3-weight rod is perfect for these belligerent 6- to 14-inch feeders. A Salmonfly hatch of great duration starts by early June. Surface and subsurface techniques are a must to stay versatile. Cutthroat share real estate with the rainbow trout and can grow to twice their size. Oregon fisheries officials do not understand the cutthroat populations well. Some anglers have decades of observational data but lack the scientific information-gathering methods regulatory commissioners prefer. Cutthroat are a favorite species of many guides, and big smiles and careful handling accompany random encounters with this cherished aquatic all-star.

Cool late fall morning, hidden Spey pockets. Todd Ostenson

Adult steelhead populations *are* well understood in the upper reaches of the Rogue. Both winter and summer steelhead are hooked regularly. The summer fish are significantly more faithful to the fly. And, for summer steelhead, a 61-day, fly-fishing-only season starts September 1. Again, the regulations surrounding the fly-only season change, and reading the yearly handout is necessary to avoiding trouble during this pleasant time of the year.

Sexually mature summer steelhead range from 16 or 17 inches to 30 inches, with occasional larger, spectacular specimens. In the absence of a "low-stretch tape measure," daily chatter of "30-inchers" bounces around public boat ramps like a bad check. Extensive data supports that the Rogue's winter steelhead is *the* fish routinely growing to 30 inches, and beyond. There is no such thing as an "average" Rogue steelhead. They are all special, like the river they swim in.

Dave Culbertson covers the Elks Picnic Grounds. Todd Ostenson

➤ **Hatches:** Not applicable on steelhead water.

➤ **Fishing regulations:** September 1 to October 31, fly fishing only on the Upper Rogue River. Review Oregon's detailed and ever-changing fishing regulations at www.dfw.state.or.us.

➤ **Tackle:** Use 5- to 7-weight, 9- to 10-foot rods for single-handed fishing, and a steelhead-taper WF floating line. A Wet Tip III is a solid subsurface line. Leaders: 9-foot fluorocarbon tapered to 2X or 3X.

Steelhead fly-fishing techniques on the Upper Rogue River vary from traditional wet fly on a single-handed rod, to the more popular Spey, nymph, and center-pin methods. Attentive angling will improve the success of any method. Opportunities for steelhead are usually fewer than those for trout.

Wet-fly patterns of Rogue lore are smaller than on many rivers, some on double hooks. Juicy Bugs, Silver Hiltons, Muddler Minnows, and Rogue River Red Ants are tradition-al on #8 and #10 hooks. Modern Spey anglers also use these historic wet flies.

Nymph anglers put the weight in their flies, not pinched to the leader. Agent Oranges #6, Lingerie Eggs #4, September Soft Hackles #8, Trout Retriever (Chocolate Lab) #6, and Red Copper Swans #8 are consistent producers. The September fishes great on the swing, too! Nymph anglers routinely fish two flies.

For winter steelhead, bump everything up a size or two, including the size of the fish and the number of days it can take to hook one! Catchable numbers of summer steelhead arrive in the Upper Rogue by mid-July, and continue to trickle in through December. The peak of the run is the second or third week of October. The winter steelhead run is a much smaller window on the upper reaches, and lacks a fly-only season. Good numbers of winters show up in March, and drop off by mid-April.

Trout Retrievers for steelhead—Chocolate Lab and Black Lab.
Todd Ostenson

Foot access at Rogue Elk Park, Upper Rogue River. Todd Ostenson

Raised in Corvallis, Oregon, TODD OSTENSON found a
love for fishing as a child after receiving a fly-tying kit
from his father. In 1991, Ostenson became a fly-fishing
guide in Alaska, followed by guiding in central Oregon
on the Deschutes River. In 1998, Ostenson opened
Trophy Waters and has continued guiding in southern
Oregon. He has taught fly-fishing and fly-tying classes
at both Rogue Community College and Klamath Community College, as well as in private lessons. He has
shared fishing tips with viewers and listeners on
NBC, CBS, and ESPN radio.

CLOSEST FLY SHOPS

The Rogue Fly Shop
310 Northwest Morgan Lane
Grants Pass, OR 97526
541-476-0552
customerservice@RogueFlyShop.com
www.RogueFlyShop.com

CLOSEST OUTFITTERS/GUIDES

Spey guide
Scott Howell
541-621-2818
scott@scotthowellfishing.com
www.scotthowellfishing.com

Single-handed guide
Jim Andras
530-772-7992
andrasoutfitters@me.com
www.andrasoutfitters.com

BEST HOTEL

Rogue Regency Inn and Suites
2300 Biddle Rd.
Medford, OR 97504
541-770-1234 or 800-535-5805
regency@rogueregency.com
www.rogueregency.com

BEST CAMPGROUND
Rogue Elk Campground
www.co.jackson.or.us

BEST RESTAURANT

Porters
147 N. Front St.
Medford, OR 97501
541-857-1910

Rogue Regency Inn
2300 Biddle Rd.
Medford, OR 97504
541-770-1234 or 800-535-5805
regency@rogueregency.com
www.rogueregency.com

**BEST PLACE TO GET A COLD,
STIFF DRINK**

Touvelle Lodge
9367 Table Rock Rd.
Central Point, OR 97502
541-826-4855

**CLOSEST EMERGENCY
MEDICAL HELP**

*Providence Medford
Medical Center*
1111 Crater Lake Ave.
Medford, OR 97504
541-732-5000

CELL PHONE SERVICE
Sporadic. Verizon seems to
be the best.

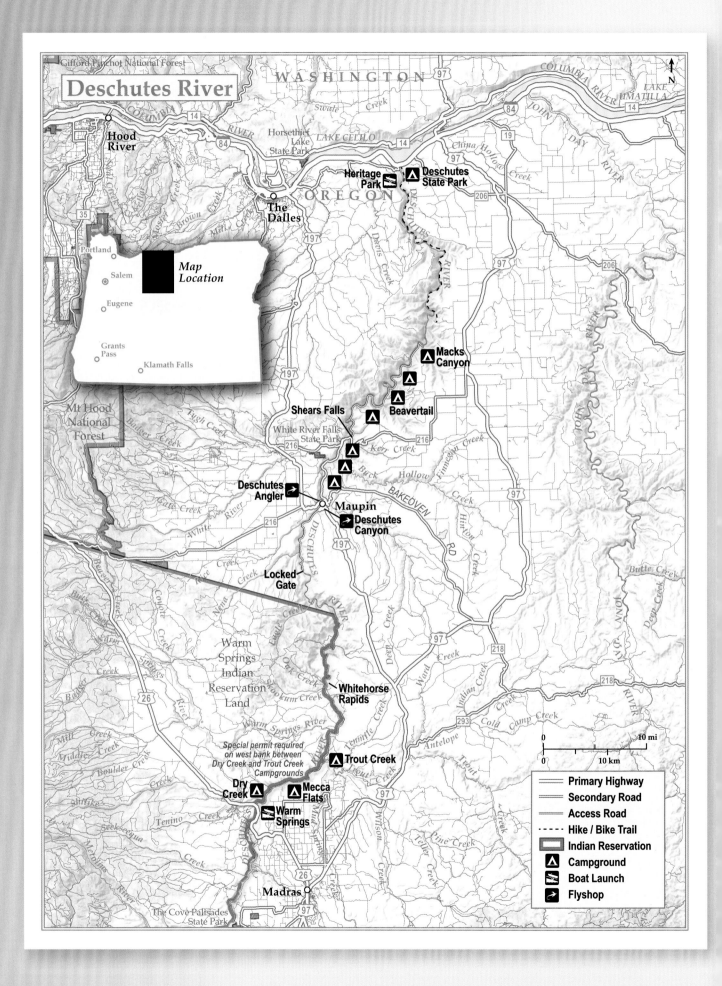

Deschutes River

WASHINGTON

Gifford Pinchot National Forest

COLUMBIA RIVER

LAKE UMATILLA

Hood River

LAKE CELILO

Horsethief Lake State Park

Heritage Park

Deschutes State Park

China Hollow Creek

JOHN DAY RIVER

OREGON

The Dalles

Swale Creek

Davis Creek

Mt Hood National Forest

Map Location

Portland

Salem

Eugene

Grants Pass

Klamath Falls

Macks Canyon

JOHN DAY RIVER

Beavertail

Shears Falls

White River Falls State Park

Kerr Creek

Finnegan Creek

Butte Creek

Deep Creek

Deschutes Angler

Maupin

Deschutes Canyon

Back Hollow

BAKEOVEN RD

Hinton Creek

JOHN DAY RIVER

Locked Gate

Warm Springs Indian Reservation Land

Whitehorse Rapids

Deep Creek

Antelope Creek

Trout Creek

Camp Creek

Special permit required on west bank between Dry Creek and Trout Creek Campgrounds

Dry Creek

Mecca Flats

Warm Springs

Madras

The Cove Palisades State Park

Primary Highway	
Secondary Road	
Access Road	
Hike / Bike Trail	
Indian Reservation	
Campground	
Boat Launch	
Flyshop	

0   10 mi
0   10 km

N

Deschutes River *(Central Oregon)*

➤ **Location:** This fly-fishing mecca in Central Oregon is less than a 2-hour drive from either Portland or Bend. Maupin, the only community on the Lower Deschutes River, is located 90 miles north of Bend and roughly 100 miles southeast of Portland.

The Deschutes snakes its way 250 miles northward through the heart of central Oregon. For the first 150 miles, it is a growing spring creek that flows through the cities of Bend, Redmond, and Madras. Only when it flows out of the Pelton regulating dam is the famous blue-ribbon fishery born. Fed throughout its journey by hundreds of springs that boil from the edges of the desert, it is essentially the largest spring creek in Oregon and one of the most steadily flowing rivers in the world, fluctuating less than 2 feet on average from winter to summer.

For more than 80 years, the law on the lower 100 miles of the Deschutes (from Pelton Dam to the Columbia River) has prohibited fishing from any floating device. This is just one of the unique aspects of the Deschutes that sets it apart from most other tailwaters in the West. This unusual regulation has given thousands of native trout sanctuary water, and has arguably maintained the quality of the fishing experience despite increasing pressure.

The river is spectacular to float, with many roadless miles and riverside camping spots all along the way. No boat? No problem! The lower Deschutes offers 40 miles of road access (mostly gravel) as well as 32 miles of foot and biking trails that parallel the east bank of the river. In terms of access, this is a friendly river to fish and, with few exceptions, including a border with the Warm Springs Indian Reservation and some pockets of private property, you may fish the river nearly anywhere you like.

Trout

While Deschutes River access may be friendly, most first-time anglers are somewhat intimidated by the sheer breadth, depth, and turbulence of this big brawling river. At first glance, there are seemingly few places to wade, and fewer places for a backcast thanks to the alder trees and tall sedge grasses lining both banks. Deep, whirling backeddies and fast, boulder-strewn pocket water make it difficult to control the fly presentation, and simply navigating the steep rocky banks to get to the river's edge can feel like a dance with death. Upon closer inspection, anglers will find navigable paths to the river, will see the gentle and easy foam lines

Amy Hazel guiding big-trout pocket water. John Hazel

that meander adjacent to the turbulent whitewater, and will observe trout noses periodically poking through those foam lines to gulp flies. Once the angler has honed in on this productive trout habitat, it will become quite apparent that the lower Deschutes River is one of the finest dry-fly rivers in America.

The upper 50 miles of the Lower Deschutes River, from Warm Springs to Sherar's Falls (10 miles downstream of Maupin), is considered the premier trout habitat. The river has an estimated population of 2,500 native rainbow trout per mile. Commonly referred to as redsides, these thick-bodied, powerful trout take advantage of the river's fertile bounty, gorging themselves throughout the year on stoneflies, caddisflies, mayflies, midges, and a smattering of terrestrial insects.

The hatches are strongest from April through October, which roughly coincides with the open season for trout on the 40 miles of river that forms the border with the Warm

Amy Hazel casting the Spey in early morning light. John Hazel

Springs Indian Reservation. Only 8 miles of reservation water is open to fishing (with a special tribal fishing permit) so, after drifting below Trout Creek campground, anglers must only fish on the east bank. Once anglers have floated past the northern boundary of the reservation, the river is open to fishing on both banks, and is also open year-round for both trout and steelhead.

The Deschutes has one of the greatest Salmonfly hatches of any river in the West. It begins in Maupin above Sherar's Falls by May 8, and will make its way upstream to Warm Springs roughly through June 20. Both (*Pteronarcys californica*) the large orange adult, size 6, and (*Hesperoperla pacifica*) the smaller golden, size 8 to 10, are on the water together for the major duration of the hatch. The best dry-fly fishing is always during the warmest weather, 85 to 100 degrees. The bugs are in the air, mating and laying eggs, and every fish in the river is looking up.

After the mayhem of the Salmonfly hatch, anglers enjoy months of great dry-fly fishing from June through October. Mayfly hatches include Green Drakes, Pale Morning Duns, Pale Evening Duns, Pink Alberts, and Blue-winged Olives, while evenings with clouds of caddisflies provide a great finale to the day of fishing.

Trout tactics on the Deschutes are simple. Pick your water carefully, and observe the water for a few minutes or longer before you develop your approach plan. Use the river's high and steep banks to observe the shoreline before you make the first cast. Carefully check the upstream side of submerged boulders as large trout surf the cushion of the current to feed above the boulders. So much of the Deschutes River has this type of habitat that it is easy to find big, hungry fish looking for surface flies. Walk a mile of river looking tight to the bank with polarized sunglasses. A good rule of thumb: If it looks like you are going to die climbing down to the river, that is likely a good spot to fish! Choose the banks with the largest rocks and boulders and sudden drop-offs. You will see the big bruisers cruising just below the surface waiting to inhale insects.

A good all-around trout rod is 8½- or 9-foot for a 4- or 5-weight line. The rod should be big enough to handle a 15- to 20-inch trout in fast water, but light enough in the tip section to cushion 5X and 6X tippets. If your rod action is too fast, you will break the tippet when the fish heads out into fast water, which is exactly what a good redside will do the second it is hooked. You will also need 50 to 100 yards of backing. Stay cool and calm when you hook-up. Let them run. The fish will soon come into the bank and you can work it slowly back to you. Anglers lose many a fine trout when the line goes deep into the backing, and they panic.

Steelhead

The lower 50 miles of the Deschutes, from Sherar's Falls to the confluence with the Columbia River, is known worldwide for its summer-run steelhead. With water types so diverse, a steelhead angler could spend a lifetime learning each run, glide, riffle, and pocket. The river is at its maximum capacity in this stretch, so steelhead anglers cover as much water as possible with long casts, and often push their wading abilities to the max to cover each run proficiently.

It is a rare steelhead river that adopts a floating line technique as the most productive methodology, but so it is on the Deschutes River, and it is a delight. The tool of choice for casting a floating line towards center-river is certainly a two-handed rod. Trees line the river's edge and the water gets thigh to waist deep quickly, so there is zero room for backcasting. With an average width of 270 feet, and steelhead holding from bank to bank, the Deschutes is a Spey-caster's river. It's easy to understand why the Deschutes was the epicenter for the rise in the popularity of Spey rods over the past 30 years.

Steelhead begin entering the lower 20 miles of the Deschutes in early July and continue arriving through the end of December. By late September, steelhead occupy good holding water throughout the entire lower 100 miles. The majority of early-run steelhead are wild fish, chrome bright from the sea, and eager to rise toward the surface fly. These fish will average 6 to 10 pounds and larger fish are hooked frequently.

Due to their migratory nature, steelhead are constantly on the move, and finding one with a fly can be a test of an angler's patience and determination. A steelhead angler might cast all day for just one grab, and there are days when he doesn't even get a grab, but others when he hooks six steelhead before lunch. It is impossible to predict what will happen from one day to the next. Making the perfect cast, mending the belly at just the right time in the swing, stepping downstream at the end of each presentation, and repeating those steps hour after hour becomes a very pleasing, satisfying, and relaxing day for a true steelheader. Just one grab on the swinging fly becomes so addictive that steelheaders are willing to put in hour after hour for a chance at another.

Great steelhead holding water is sometimes difficult to identify. Current speed needs to be about the speed of a fast

walk and the water should be three to six feet deep. The run should be boulder-strewn, the larger the better, and wading will be challenging. Many anglers prefer to use a wading staff to keep themselves upright between casts. Summer run steelhead are most aggressive to the fly in low-light conditions, which means that the best times to target them are morning and evening when the sun is not in their eyes. As the Deschutes twists and turns, the sun hits the water at different angles, and knowing where the sun gets on the water later will extend one's productive fishing time. Ultimately, anglers

Early October wild steelhead. John Hazel

who cover the most water the most quickly will hook the greatest number of steelhead. With each cast, anglers tempt fate on the swing, hoping for that violent grab on a near-surface fly and cartwheeling chrome on the end of the line.

A steelhead fly box should be loaded with sparsely dressed wet flies in sizes 6 and 8. Colors should include black, claret, purple, and natural browns and olives. Some of the best patterns are the Lum Plum, Steelhead Coachman, Street Walker, and Engagement. Skating or waking flies are also deadly on the Deschutes. Sizes 6, 8, and 10 are best, quite a bit smaller than those popular in BC waters. Flies resembling natural insects, such as the Spey Skater, Rusty Bomber, Steelhead Caddis, and the Muddler, are proven producers on the Deschutes. It is heart-pounding to watch a fly skate the glassy surface of a tailout, knowing that a steelhead could erupt in an immense explosion of water at any moment.

Boating can be tricky and in many places downright dangerous. Most rapids are class I and II, with class III and IV scattered throughout the lower 100 miles. The river is large

Fly fishing off a rock bar on the lower Deschutes River near Maupin, Oregon. Mark Lisk

Deschutes Angler guide Evan Unti taking inventory. Evan Unti

and extremely powerful and it claims both boats and lives every year. Refer to the BLM's Deschutes River Boaters Guide and talk to a local fly shop before attempting to float the Deschutes.

Maupin (population 450) is the only town on the Lower Deschutes, and from this riverside hub, anglers can drive upstream 10 miles or downstream 30 miles to access the river at any point. There are plenty of public campsites along this stretch, with primitive but well-maintained facilities; boat launches and takeouts are sprinkled along the access road. Maupin has four hotels, a handful of restaurants, a city park with fee camping and full hookups, and two fly shops.

➤ **Fishing regulations:** Regulations are complex, and change from year to year, and section to section. Refer to www.dfw .state.or.us for up-to-date info.

The lower 100 miles, from Pelton Dam to the Columbia River, is divided into two parts. From Pelton Dam to the northern boundary of the Warm Springs Indian Reservation, the river is open for trout fishing from the fourth Saturday in April through October 31 and for steelhead fishing from the fourth Saturday in April through December 31. From the northern boundary of the Warm Springs Indian Reservation

to the confluence with the Columbia River, the river is open for trout and steelhead fishing year-round. Coho and Chinook salmon regulations change annually.

Fishing is restricted to artificial flies and lures only. Bait and soft rubber is illegal on all parts of the lower Deschutes except for a small section from Sherar's Falls to the first railroad trestle. The limit is two rainbow trout per day between 10 and 13 inches. Anglers may keep two hatchery steelhead per day (adipose fin is clipped). All wild, nonclipped steelhead must be released unharmed.

No angling from any floating device.

Motorized boats are allowed from Mack's Canyon north to the Columbia River from June 15 to September 31, except during motorized boat bans every other Thursday through Sunday during this time. From October 1 through June 15, motorized boats may go upstream of Mack's Canyon up to Buck Hollow, during which time there are no bans on motorized boating.

Every floating device must have a valid Deschutes River Boater Pass, available at www.boaterpass.com.

➤ **Tackle**

Trout:

Rods: 4- and 5-weight, 8½ to 9 feet, medium action. Reels: Good drag and capacity to hold at least 100 yards of backing. Leaders: 9-foot 5 or 6X. Waders should be breathable and chest high. Felt soles with or without studs are best.

Steelhead:

Rods: 6- and 7-weight, 12- to 13½-foot Spey rods. Reels: 3¾ to 4 inches with a strong drag and capacity to hold Spey lines and a minimum of 100 yards of backing. Floating lines and floating poly leaders are best. Waders should be chest-high and breathable. Felt soles with or without studs are best. Flies: Green Butt Lum Plum, Engagement, Recon, Spey Skater, Steelhead Coachman, Steelhead Muddler, Rusty Bomber.

JOHN AND AMY HAZEL live and work on the Deschutes River in Maupin, Oregon. They own and operate Deschutes Angler Fly Shop and their guide service, John Hazel & Company. John, Amy, and the select group of guides they employ guide the entire 100 miles of the lower Deschutes. John has been guiding the Deschutes since 1978, and Amy joined him in 1999. Together they have been featured on several Spey-casting instructional DVDs as well as the acclaimed fly-fishing film, *Drift*. When not hunting or fishing, they relax on their ranch with good friends and family.

Authors John and Amy Hazel

CLOSEST FLY SHOPS

Deschutes Angler Fly Shop & Guide Service
504 Deschutes Ave.
Maupin, OR 97037 (541-395-0995)
www.deschutesangler.com

Deschutes Canyon Fly Shop
599 S. Hwy 197
Maupin, OR 97037 (541-395-2565)
www.flyfishingdeschutes.com

Fly & Field Outfitters
35 SW Century Dr.
Bend, OR 97702 (866-800-2812)
www.flyandfield.com

The Fly Fishing Shop
67296 E. Hwy 26
Welches, OR 97067 (800-266-3971)
www.flyfishusa.com

OUTFITTERS
(other than fly shops above)

John Hazel & Company, Inc.
541-395-0995
www.deschutesangler.com

Brian Silvey
541-328-6369
www.silveysflyfishing.com

River Runner Outfitters
541-978-0152
www.riverrunneroutfitters.com

CLOSEST LODGES

Imperial River Company
304 Bakeoven Rd.
Maupin, OR 97037 (800-395-3903)
www.deschutesriver.com

River Run Lodge
210 Hartman Ave.
Maupin, OR 97037 (541-980-7113)
www.riverrunlodge.net

BEST MOTELS

Sonny's Motel
1539 U.S. Hwy 97
Madras, OR (541-475-7217)

Imperial River Company
Maupin (800-395-3903)
www.deschutesriver.com (Lodge)

Deschutes Motel
606 Mill St.
Maupin, OR 97037 (541-395-2626)
www.deschutesmotel.com

Oasis Resort
609 U.S. Hwy 197 S.
Maupin, OR 97037 (541-395-2611)
www.deschutesriveroasis.com

BEST CAMPGROUNDS & RV PARKS
Maupin City Park (541-395-2252)
www.cityofmaupin.com
(Restrooms, showers, full RV hook- ups, tent camping, free WiFi; reservations recommended.) BLM Drive-In campgrounds are all along the river—dry camping, outhouses
www.blm.gov/or/districts/prineville

BEST RESTAURANTS

Imperial River Company
304 Bakeoven Rd.
Maupin, OR 97037
800-395-3903
www.deschutesriver.com

Rainbow Tavern
411 Deschutes Ave.
Maupin, OR 9737
541-395-2497

BEST PLACES TO GET A COLD, STIFF DRINK
Same as best restaurants

CLOSEST EMERGENCY MEDICAL HELP

Mid-Columbia Medical Center
1700 E 19th
The Dalles, OR 97058
541-296-1111

Mountain View Hospital
470 NE A St.
Madras, OR 97741
541-475-3882

CELL PHONE SERVICE
Limited at best.

WIRELESS ACCESS
Available at Imperial River Company, Maupin Market, across from Deschutes Angler Fly Shop.

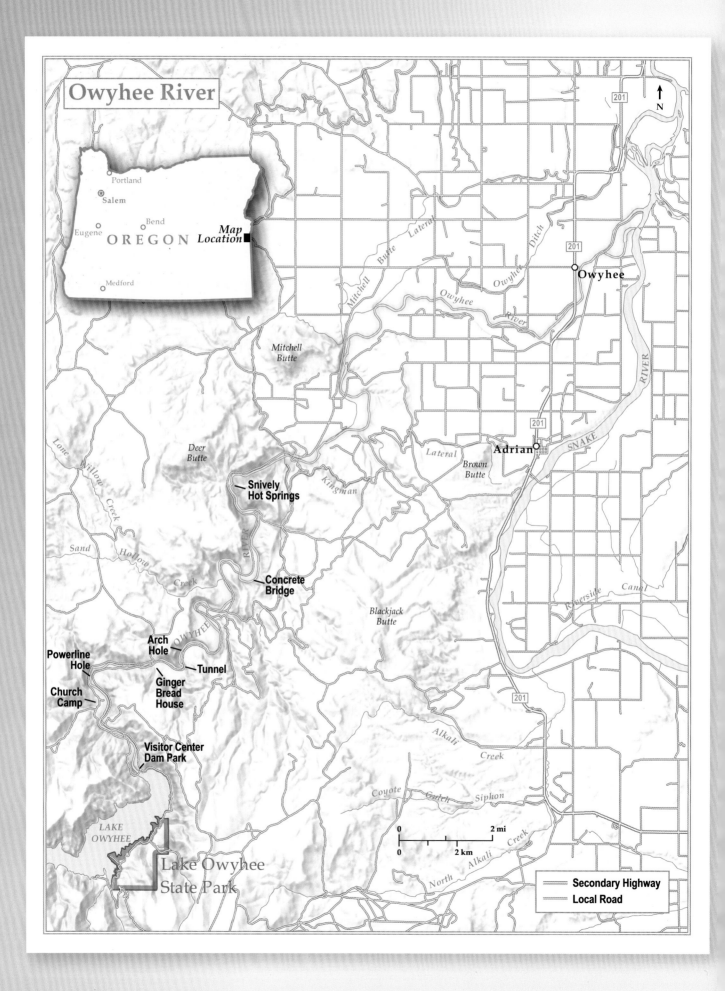

Owyhee River

N
[201]

OREGON
Portland
Salem
Bend
Eugene
Map
Location
Medford

Owyhee

[201]

Mitchell Butte Lateral

Owyhee Ditch

Owyhee River

Mitchell Butte

Adrian
[201]

Deer Butte

Lateral

Brown Butte

SNAKE RIVER

Snively Hot Springs

Kingsman

Lone Willow Creek

Sand Hollow Creek

RIVER

Blackjack Butte

Concrete Bridge

Riverside Canal

Arch Hole
OWYHEE
Tunnel

Powerline Hole

Ginger Bread House

Church Camp

Visitor Center Dam Park

Alkali Creek

Coyote Gulch Siphon

LAKE OWYHEE

North Alkali Creek

Lake Owyhee State Park

0   2 mi
0   2 km

Secondary Highway
Local Road

➤ **Location:** The Owyhee River is 1 ½ hours west of Boise, Idaho; 45 minutes south of Ontario, Oregon; 5 ½ hours east of Bend, Oregon; and 4 hours from Sun Valley, Idaho. Flight service into Boise.

In 1932, the Owyhee Dam was completed near Adrian, in eastern Oregon, creating the 53-mile-long Owyhee Reservoir. This fishery is fairly new, compared to many other tailwaters. In 1990, the Oregon Department of Fish and Wildlife started stocking brown trout, and protected them with catch-and-release angling to provide a trophy fishery. Traditionally, the river has been managed as a put-and-take fishery for rainbows, and different rules for the different trout species continue. Over the last 20 years, the browns have thrived, making the Owyhee one of the finest tailwaters in the nation for trophy brown trout. Browns here average 16 to 18 inches, with many fish in excess of 20 inches.

The high desert canyon is comprised of towering cliffs and unusual rock formations. Sagebrush and wildlife abound. The willow-lined river encompasses a series of pools connected with shallow runs, but few traditional riffles. The pools are slow-moving, almost stagnant, and usually deep. The runs are mild, with large rocks creating countless holding areas for fish. The river is a walk-and-wade fishery due to its narrow riverbed and several shallow runs. There is little need to float the river, as the road parallels it and access is extremely easy.

It's common to find brown trout sipping insects from the surface, another aspect that makes the Owyhee a unique fishery. Most of the food base is insects, and the Owyhee's brown trout are not shy about feeding on the surface, even within a rod's length of an angler. Fishing is open year-round, and quality fly fishing begins early. During mild winters, February can be excellent, as abundant midge hatches keep fish feeding actively during this usually dormant time. March often ushers in the *Skwala* hatch. *Skwalas* are dark, olive-brown stoneflies commonly found in the Bitterroot River in Montana.

Late spring and early summer are among the best and most pleasant times to fish the Owyhee. The weather is typ-

ically warm and sunny, and the canyon comes alive with wildflowers and wildlife. Fishing is most productive when Pale Morning Duns, finally ready to end their underwater lives and emerge, bring with them eagerly awaiting trout. At times, the water boils with rising fish eagerly feeding on naturals. The PMDs last throughout the summer, but as each day passes, fewer and fewer fish rise with such reckless abandon. Many begin sipping, barely breaking the surface, and plucking emergers from the film. Anglers turn to long leaders, small tippets, and accurate casts, and often have to stalk individual fish.

Summer day. Roger Phillips

Summer brings forth terrestrials, and often triple-digit heat. Ants, beetles, and hoppers cling to the shore grass and willows and frequently lose their holds during frequent afternoon winds. Many become easy meals for strategically placed bank feeders, who will also eagerly take an imitation.

As summer fades into fall, the river changes. Crane flies appear, buzzing lightly above the water in search of suitable place to deposit their eggs. Mahogany Duns, *Baetis*, and midges replace PMDs and caddis, and the brown trout start staging for the spawning season. By mid-October, the irrigation flows from the dam drop to winter levels, and the river erupts in spawning activity.

Many local anglers refuse to fish the river at this time, and those who do are cautious to avoid spawning fish. They leave

Above. Erick Moncada with a heavy Owyhee brown during the caddis hatch. John Wolter

Left. Casting to rising Owyhee fish. Roger Phillips

Inset. Maja Wolter releasing an Owyhee brown. John Wolter

stretches of the river with redds alone and concentrate on the slower pools where fish are not spawning. Despite the year-round fishing season, many frown upon fishing for spawning browns. By mid- to late November, most fish are through spawning and return to feeding, usually on the abundant afternoon midge hatches.

Similar to other tailwaters, the Owyhee's flows are managed for agriculture and flood control. Typical summer flows are between 200–300 cfs, and are then reduced to about 30 cfs from October until mid-April. Although the winter flows seem low, the fish experience little stress, thanks to the large holding pools dotted throughout the 11 miles of prime habitat. It's also worth noting that winter flows were increased several years ago from about 10 cfs or less to the current winter flows after an agreement between dam managers and Oregon Fish and Wildlife.

River flows below Owyhee Dam are generally predictable because the 53-mile reservoir absorbs most or all of the snowpack from the vast desert and mountains that feed it. On rare occasions, there's a big spring runoff and flooding.

During the spring of 2006, the river that normally flows a 300 cfs reached 12,000 cfs and flooded a small portion of the town of Owyhee near the Snake River, along with several nearby farms. While flooding is rare, over the span of a decade, there are usually several years the Owyhee flows at more than 2,000 cfs for several weeks in the spring, when snowmelt exceeds reservoir capacity.

The Owyhee anglers generally prefer standard trout outfits: 4-, 5-, or 6-weight rods, at least 8½ feet, with floating lines. Waders are recommended even in the heat of the summer, as is a wading staff. If you travel there for the day, or plan on camping overnight, keep an eye on the local advisories, particularly during the drought season. The amount of care and conservation poured into the Owyhee is amazing; it takes all of us to keep the Owyhee River an enjoyable and memorable river to fish.

► Hatches:

Blue-winged Olives: Nymphs from February into May; dries beginning in March and continuing to mid-May.

Midges: All year.

Caddis: June through October. The various caddis species are generally determined not to be major hatches at any time, but they still can be prolific.

Skwalas: March and April; peak from mid-March to mid-April.

Pale Morning Duns: Late April through July, with peak season June to mid-July.

Scuds: All year.

Sculpin: All year.

➤ **Fishing regulations:** Open year-round. All brown trout must be released unharmed.

Indicators are helpful from late fall to early spring when the river is low; they are optional the rest of the year. Leader lengths will vary with technique. However, keep in mind the flies work best when they are presented near the bottom.

Streamer anglers usually settle on powerful 6-weights, 9 or 9½ feet. Leaders should be short and heavy to turn over flies in excess of 4 inches in length.

JOHN WOLTER has owned and operated Anglers Fly Shop in Boise since 1997. His passion for fly fishing has taken him further in conservation efforts, reaching out to local organizations along with personally helping with the restoration and protection of local tailwaters, free-flowing streams, and reservoirs.

CLOSEST FLY SHOPS

Anglers Fly Shop
7097 Overland Rd.
Boise, ID 83709
208-323-6768
www.boiseanglers.com

Idaho Angler
1682 S. Vista Ave.
Boise, ID 83705
208-389-9957
www.idahoangler.com

Faded Fly
1401 1st St. North
Nampa, ID 83687
208-615-8228

Anglers Habitat
716 Blaine St.
Caldwell, ID 83605
208-454-8118

CLOSEST OUTFITTERS

Dreams on the Fly
(by appointment only)
203 N. Roswell Blvd.
Parma, ID 83660
208-861-2853
dreamsonthefly@gmail.com
www.dreamsonthefly.com

Owyhee Fly Fisher
Dan Bofenkamp
208-642-7898
dan@owyheeflyfisher.com
www.owyheeflyfisher.com

BEST HOTEL

Holiday Inn Express
212 SE 10th St.
Ontario, OR 97914
888-465 4329

BEST CAMPGROUND
No formal campsites on the river

BEST RESTAURANT

The Mirage, 605 1st St.
Adrian, OR 97901
541-372-2338
(best prime rib Friday and Saturday)

CLOSEST EMERGENCY MEDICAL HELP

West Valley Medical Center
1717 Arlington Ave.
Caldwell, ID 83605
208-459-4641

CELL PHONE SERVICE
No cell service in the canyon.

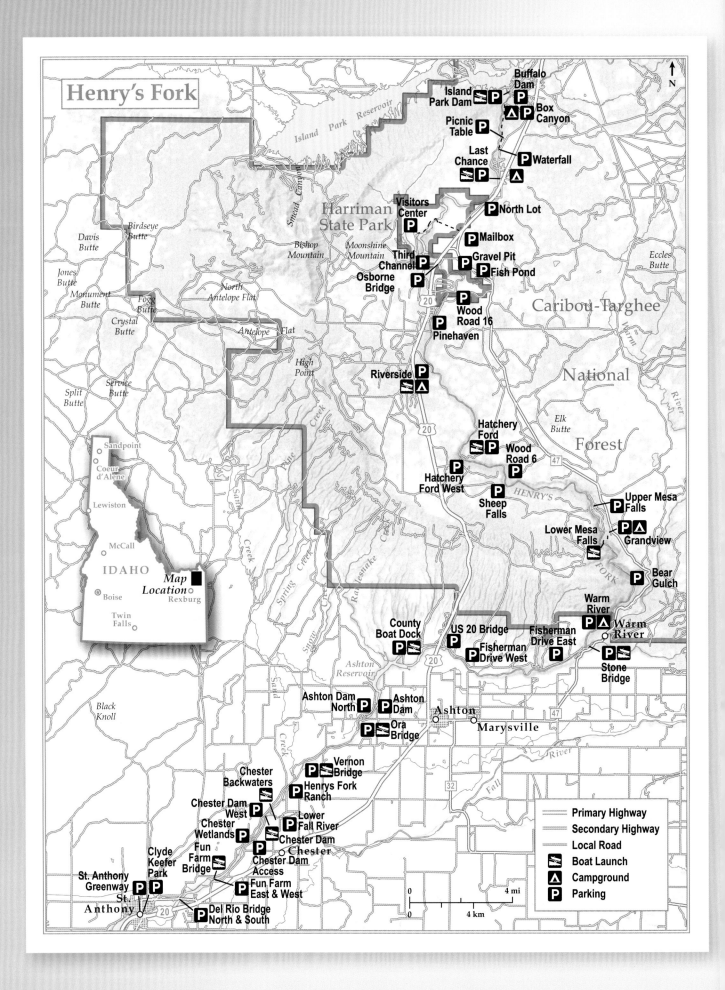

Henry's Fork

Island Park Dam

Buffalo Dam

Box Canyon

Picnic Table

Last Chance

Waterfall

North Lot

Visitors Center

Harriman State Park

Mailbox

Moonshine Mountain

Gravel Pit

Third Channel

Fish Pond

Osborne Bridge

Caribou-Targhee

Wood Road 16

Eccles Butte

Pinehaven

Bishop Mountain

Davis Butte

Birdseye Butte

Jones Butte

Monument Butte

Fogg Butte

Crystal Butte

North Antelope Flat

Antelope Flat

Service Butte

Split Butte

High Point

Riverside

National

Hatchery Ford

Elk Butte

Wood Road 6

Forest

Hatchery Ford West

Upper Mesa Falls

Sheep Falls

Lower Mesa Falls

Grandview

Bear Gulch

Warm River

Warm River

Fisherman Drive East

Sandpoint

Coeur d'Alene

Lewiston

McCall

IDAHO

Map Location

Boise

Rexburg

Twin Falls

Black Knoll

Stone Bridge

County Boat Dock

US 20 Bridge

Fisherman Drive West

Ashton Reservoir

Ashton Dam North

Ashton Dam

Ora Bridge

Ashton

Marysville

Vernon Bridge

Chester Backwaters

Henrys Fork Ranch

Chester Dam West

Lower Fall River

Chester Wetlands

Chester Dam

Fun Farm Bridge

Chester

Clyde Keefer Park

Chester Dam Access

St. Anthony Greenway

Fun Farm East & West

St. Anthony

Del Rio Bridge North & South

Snow Creek

Sand Creek

Pine Creek

Spring Creek

Rattlesnake Creek

Fall River

Island Park Reservoir

Smead Canyon

HENRY'S FORK

Warm River

Legend

— Primary Highway
— Secondary Highway
— Local Road
Boat Launch
Campground
P Parking

0   4 mi

0   4 km

The Henry's Fork of the Snake *(Southeast Idaho)*

➤ **Location:** Southeast Idaho, less than an hour north of Idaho Falls; less than an hour south of West Yellowstone, Montana, and about 1½ hours from Jackson Hole, Wyoming.

The Henry's Fork of the Snake is not a true tailwater. Rather, it is a large spring creek with two dams. The Island Park Dam, located at the top of the Box Canyon section, creates the Island Park Reservoir. There is also a small hydroelectric facility at Island Park. The Ashton Dam, about 45 miles downriver, is strictly for hydropower.

Above Island Park Reservoir, the Henry's Fork is a true spring creek. The river changes dramatically below the dam. While many dams create trout fisheries where previously trout could not survive, the Island Park Reservoir creates more diversity in temperature and water chemistry than the cold spring creek waters above the reservoir. Water temperature is one of the most limiting factors in diversity of aquatic life. The river hosts a great population of midges, caddisflies, mayflies, stoneflies, and many other invertebrates. It is unlikely there's another trout stream in the world with more variety in the aquatic community than the Henry's Fork.

Below the 3½-mile section known as the Box Canyon, the river opens up and meanders quietly through the Harriman State Park, formerly known as the Railroad Ranch. This is where anglers come from all over the world to test their skills on some of the most selective rainbow trout on the planet. It's a place where you can find out what you're made of, like a rookie stepping into the batter's box in Yankee Stadium to find out if he can really hit a Major League fastball.

Below the Harriman Park, the river cascades through a deep canyon, flowing through the sidewall of the Island Park Caldera and dropping almost 1,000 feet in elevation in fewer than 20 miles. There are several serious waterfalls in this section, including Upper Mesa Falls, with a 113-foot drop. Below the canyon, the river joins up with Warm River, another spring creek. From there it flows another 8 miles into the Ashton Reservoir.

The Henry's Fork is a true tailwater below the Ashton Dam. Like many tailwaters, the reservoir enriches the water

and stabilizes the temperature. This section supports some of the fastest-growing trout in the entire system. This tailwater stretch is diluted with the waters of Fall River, a major freestone tributary, about 6 miles below the Ashton Dam. From there, the Henry's Fork resembles many typical Western trout rivers, with a great diversity of water types including runs, riffles, pools, and glides. Below the City of St. Anthony, the river swings through thick woodlands as it channels its way to its mother river, the South Fork of the Snake.

A beautiful drift through Box Canyon.

The Henry's Fork is like six different rivers in one. Above Island Park Reservoir the river is managed with very liberal fishing regulations, with the objective of maintaining a large population of small trout. This makes the upper stretch a great place to take a family or help a novice angler get into some fish. Before and after the summer tourist season, there is an opportunity to catch some large, quality trout. These trout move up from Island Park Reservoir in the late autumn and hold in the river through the winter.

Box Canyon has a good population of trout that range from 10 to over 20 inches. This section is so full of aquatic larvae, nymphs, leeches, crayfish, sculpin, and other forage fish that the trout show little interest in feeding on the surface, except when the big stoneflies are emerging from mid-June through early July. Sometimes you need to use some

Top. Think of a word to describe this little corner of the world . . . magnificent!

Inset. Mike Lawson with a nice Henry's Fork rainbow.

very small nymphs to score with the largest trout. My favorites are red, olive, or brown Zebra Nymphs in #14 to #18. Old standbys like Pheasant-tail and Prince Nymphs also work well. The most important thing is to get them down deep in the fast water.

Volumes have been written about the storied Railroad Ranch, now known as the Harriman Park. You'll likely find at least one species of aquatic insect emerging no matter what day of the year you decide to fish. It is important to note that most of the largest aquatic insects, such as the famous Green Drake, emerge soon after the season opens on June 15. Later on in August and September the bugs get small, and you will

likely need to use a #18 fly or smaller with 6X tippet. This fact, along with sophisticated trout and dense aquatic vegetation, really thins out the crowds. However, my personal favorite time to fish this water is August. I'd rather deal with tough fish than crowds!

The canyon water from Harriman State Park downstream to the Ashton Dam flows mostly through public land. Yet this water doesn't get much pressure because you need to wear your climbing shoes to get down to the river. From Hatchery Ford downstream below Lower Mesa Falls, the river is not navigable. There is good boating access below Warm River. You can also drag a raft down into the deep canyon below Lower Mesa Falls. Most of the fishing techniques here are very much the same as you would use in the Box Canyon.

The Ashton tailwater section provides great dry-fly fishing from February through early July and again from September until the weather gets nasty in December. The flies and techniques are similar to those used in the Harriman State Park. Some of the bugs are different. For example, the Harriman section gets Brown Drakes while the Ashton stretch gets Gray Drakes.

Below St. Anthony, the river turns into mostly a brown trout fishery. Browns are abundant upstream to Lower Mesa Falls, but they really take charge in the lower river. They are born with an attitude that intensifies the older they get. Most that reach trophy proportions are caught with streamers and nymphs, but it is possible to score on a 6-pound brown trout with a stonefly pattern in June or a hopper in August.

➤ **Hatches:** The hatches of the Henry's Fork are extensive. This is a massive and complex fishery, and the information below is just the tip of a very large iceberg. For a much better view of things, visit www.henrysforkanglers.com.

Midges: All year, with a greater concentration May through September.

Blue-winged Olives: March through October, generally peaking in April.

Grannoms: April and May peak seasons, lesser hatches in August and September.

Stoneflies: Lesser hatch in May and July, greater activity in June—sometimes it must be seen to be believed!

Golden Stoneflies: May well into September, with peak months June and July.

Various caddisflies: April through October, with the best months traditionally May through July. In reality, you can find caddis hatches anytime except maybe the depth of winter.

Speckled Spinners (Callibaetis): March through September, with peak months May through July.

► **Fishing regulations:** Fishing regulations on the Henry's Fork are somewhat complex. For the most part, the river is open to fishing year-round, but some stretches are open only to catch-and-release during the off-season; some sections are under a "two-over-16-inch" slot limit; others are pretty much anything goes with a six-trout limit. The Harriman Park is fly-fishing-only, catch-and-release, with a June 15–November 30 season. Visit the Upper Snake Region on the Idaho Fish and Game website: fishandgame.idaho.gov.

► **Tackle:** Use an 8½- or 9-foot, 3-, 4-, or 5-weight rod for dry flies, and a 6- or 7-weight for big streamers and nymphs. You need fluorocarbon tippet, 2X to 6X. Use a 12-foot tapered leader for the Harriman Park, and a 9-foot tapered leader for other sections. Waders are required, with good studded boots. Hip boots are not an option. Some anglers opt to wet wade during the heat of the summer.

MIKE LAWSON started guiding in 1973. He and his wife, Sheralee, started Henry's Fork Anglers in 1976. Mike currently serves as general manager and outfitter. He has authored several books, including *Spring Creeks* and *Fly Fishing Guide to the Henry's Fork*. Signed copies are available at www.henrysforkanglers.com.

CLOSEST FLY SHOPS

Henry's Fork Anglers
3340 Hwy. 20
Island Park, ID 83429
208-558-7525
info@henrysforkanglers.com
www.henrysforkanglers.com

Trouthunter
3327 Hwy. 20
Island Park, ID 83429
208-558-9900
info@trouthunt.com
www.trouthunt.com

CLOSEST OUTFITTERS/GUIDES

Henry's Fork Anglers (above)

Trouthunter (above)

Three Rivers Ranch
PO Box 856, Warm River
Ashton, ID 83420
208-652-3750
info@threeriversranch.com
www.threeriversranch.com

CLOSEST LODGES

Henry's Fork Lodge
2794 So. Pinehaven Dr.
Island Park, ID 83429
208-558-7953
info@henrysforklodge.com
www.henrysforklodge.com

Elk Creek Ranch
PO Box 2
Island Park, ID 83429
208-558-7404
information@elkcreekid.com
www.elkcreekid.com

The Pines at Island Park
3907 Phillips Loop Rd.
Island Park, ID 83429
208-558-0192
cabins@pinesislandpark.com
pinesislandpark.com

BEST HOTEL

Ponds Lodge
PO Box 260
Island Park, ID 83429
208-558-7221
res@pondslodge.com
www.pondslodge.com

BEST CAMPGROUND

Buffalo Run Campground
3402 Hwy 20
Island Park, ID 83429
208-558-7112
www.buffaloruncampground.com

BEST RESTAURANT

Ponds Lodge
PO Box 260
Island Park, ID 83429
208-558-7221
res@pondslodge.com
www.pondslodge.com

BEST PLACE TO GET A COLD,
STIFF DRINK

Trouthunter
3327 Hwy. 20
Island Park, ID 83429
208-558-9900
info@trouthunt.com
www.trouthunt.com

CLOSEST EMERGENCY
MEDICAL HELP

Madison Memorial Hospital
450 E. Main St.
Rexburg, ID 83440
208-359-6900
www.madisonhospital.org

CELL PHONE SERVICE
Good with Verizon.
AT&T has some dead spots.

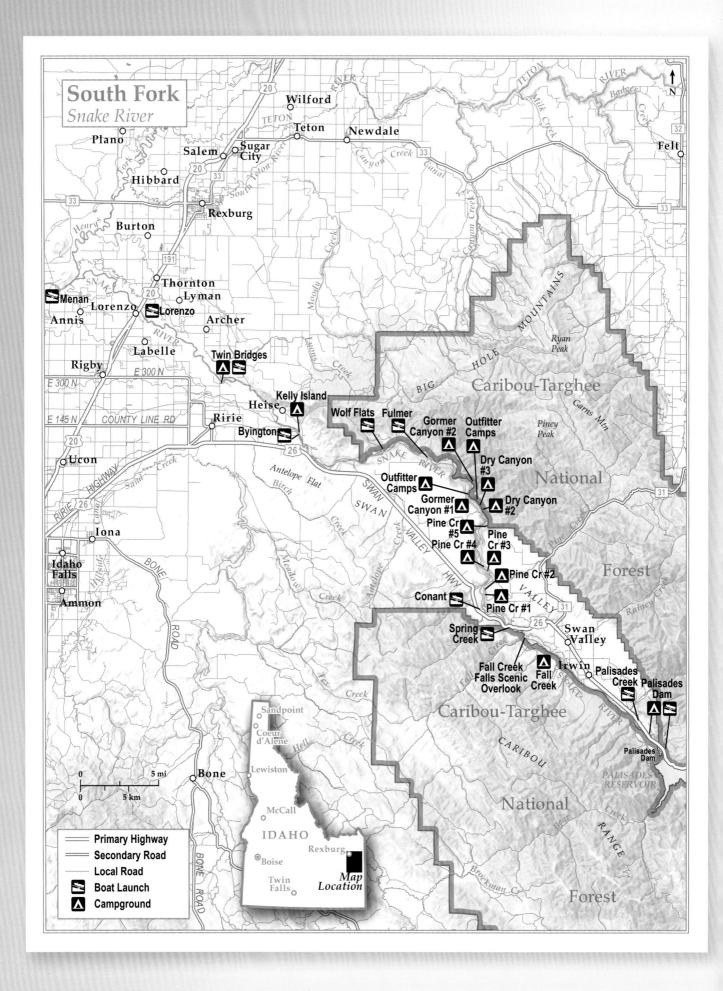

South Fork
Snake River

Plano

Wilford

Salem · Sugar City · Teton · Newdale

Hibbard

Felt

Rexburg

Burton

Thornton · Lyman

Menan · Lorenzo · Lorenzo · Archer

Annis

Labelle

Rigby

Ririe

Heise · Kelly Island

Byington

Twin Bridges

Wolf Flats · Fulmer

Gormer Canyon #2 · Outfitter Camps

Ryan Peak

Caribou-Targhee

Piney Peak

Dry Canyon #3

National

Outfitter Camps

Gormer Canyon #1

Dry Canyon #2

Pine Cr #5

Pine Cr #4 · Pine Cr #3

Forest

Pine Cr #2

Ucon

Iona

Idaho Falls

Ammon

Conant

Pine Cr #1

Spring Creek

Swan Valley

Fall Creek Falls Scenic Overlook

Irwin · Palisades Creek

Fall Creek

Palisades Dam

Caribou-Targhee

Palisades Dam

PALISADES RESERVOIR

CARIBOU

Sandpoint

Coeur d'Alene

Lewiston

Bone

National

RANGE

McCall

IDAHO

Rexburg

Boise

Map Location

Twin Falls

Forest

0   5 mi
0   5 km

Legend
— Primary Highway
— Secondary Road
— Local Road
🚤 Boat Launch
⛺ Campground

South Fork Snake River *(Southeast Idaho)*

➤ **Location:** Southeast Idaho, 45 miles east of Idaho Falls and 55 miles west of Jackson Hole, Wyoming. Most major airlines serve Idaho Falls Regional Airport and Jackson Hole Airport.

If the question: "Pick one river to fish for the rest of your life" were posed, the South Fork of the Snake would be a common answer among those who have spent time fishing it. And for good reason: The South Fork has it all: more than 4,000 fish per mile; exceptional dry-fly fishing from a drift boat; sight fishing in riffles while wading; productive streamer and nymph fishing; abundant wildlife; incredible hatches; well-organized campsites; ten well-maintained public boat launches; and more.

There is some confusion regarding the South Fork of the Snake, due solely to its name. While technically it is the Snake River, locals refer to the 60-mile stretch from Palisades Dam to the confluence with the Henry's Fork as the "South Fork." The Snake River originates in Yellowstone National Park, flows south in Wyoming through Grand Teton National Park into the Snake River Canyon, and empties into Palisades Reservoir. The Wyoming–Idaho line divides the reservoir, a 1,600-acre impoundment with healthy populations of brown and cutthroat trout, and Kokanee salmon. Completed in 1957, the Palisades Dam is an earth-filled structure with a discharge capacity of 48,000 cfs! It is below the dam that the "South Fork" begins.

From high mountain valleys, rugged canyons, and towering cliffs to broad floodplains, the South Fork changes dramatically and often annually along its 65-mile course. Due to its size, the river is best fished from a boat. Even for wade fishing, a boat is advantageous to access the many gravel bars, riffles, and islands. There are multiple wade-fishing opportunities on the upper river, although it is harder work than accessing the river from a boat during optimal fishing season.

The South Fork is large and at times unruly. While there are no significant rapids, the volume of the river can be deceptive, and is something boaters and rafters must beware of. From June to September in normal years, the river flows consistently at 14,000 cfs. In September, the flows start to de-

crease as irrigation demands are met, and usually by October the river is at 4,000 cfs and tapering down.

The South Fork boasts the largest riparian cottonwood forest in the West, and is considered one of Idaho's most varied ecosystems. It is home to 126 bird species, including 21 raptors. Other wildlife includes moose, deer, elk, mountain goats, black bears, coyotes, river otters, beavers, foxes, and mink.

The South Fork is primarily a cutthroat fishery, but also holds healthy populations of brown, rainbow, and cuttbow trout. Idaho Fish and Game is campaigning to remove the rainbows through a no-limit harvest on rainbows and cuttbows, which endanger the native cutthroat. While the

Drift cutty. Doug Barnes

average size of the fish remains 12 to 18 inches, fish over 20 inches are common, and the trout of a lifetime is always within reach. The South Fork held the Idaho state record brown trout—a 26-pounder—for 26 years until the record fell in 2007.

Locals call the 15-mile stretch from Palisades Dam to Conant Valley "Section 1," and it flows through Swan Valley. With four developed boat launches here, there are plenty of options. From Palisades Dam 4½ miles downstream, the river is one channel; then it changes dramatically into vari-

A spectacular backdrop on the South Fork. Doug Barnes

ous braids, with multiple channels and islands. While Section 1 is the most heavily fished, it holds some of the largest fish in the river.

From Conant Valley the river veers away from the highway for 26 miles and enters the Canyon. From Conant Valley to the Cottonwood takeout (north side of the river) is Section 2, approximately 15 miles long. Arguably the prettiest stretch, Section 2 flows into a rugged canyon with no road access and again boasts several braids and side channels that offer incredible dry-fly fishing, and multiple campsites for overnight trips.

From the Cottonwood boat ramp to the Byington boat ramp, roughly 11 miles, the river begins to flow out of the Canyon and ends up in the plains, while still offering up some dramatic cliffs and braids as it descends out of the canyon. This is Section 3.

From the Byington Boat Ramp to the Lorenzo Boat Ramp, a 15-mile stretch that flows through broad floodplains, the river changes dramatically. This is Section 4, and boaters must beware, as the river changes constantly, and debris-blocked side channels can be dangerous.

From the Lorenzo boat ramp to the confluence with the Henry's Fork River, a 6-mile stretch referred to as Section 5, the river can change appearance annually. At the confluence with the Henry's Fork the "South Fork" turns back into the main stem of the Snake, and the next takeout is 3 miles below the confluence on the Snake River at Menan Buttes, 9 miles downstream of the Lorenzo boat ramp.

The South Fork is known for its incredible hatches from the end of June until October. From the legendary Salmonfly hatch to Golden Stoneflies, Yellow Sallies, caddis, Pale Morning Duns, Pink Alberts, Mahogany Duns, grasshoppers, beetles, ants, *Baetis*, and midges, the South Fork is not short on bugs!

➤ **Hatches:** *Blue-winged Olives:* March to early May; September and October.
Western Green Drakes: Late June through July and occasionally early August.
Mahogany Duns: Late July or early August into early October.
Grannoms: Late April through May, can be prolific!
Spotted Sedges: Late June through August.
October Caddis: Mid- to late September and October.
Salmonflies: Mid-June to early August. July is peak.
Yellow Sallies: June and July.

➤ **Fishing regulations:** Open year-round. No harvest of cutthroat trout. Brown trout limit is two, none under 16 inches. No limit on rainbow trout or trout hybrids.

Wade fishing can be very productive during the low-water months of winter, early spring, and late fall. High flows of spring and summer remove wade fishing as an option, and the use of a drift boat or raft is more effective. Most boat ramps are operated by the BLM or Forest Service and require a self-service parking pass and fee. Idaho boating regulations apply to the South Fork of the Snake for those using drift boats (non-motorized watercraft) or motorized watercraft.

State law requires an Invasive Species Sticker for all watercraft except inflatable non-motorized vessels less than 10 feet. These stickers are available through the Idaho Parks & Recreation website at idpr.idaho.gov.

➤ **Tackle:** Use 5- and 6-weight rods with midsize or large-arbor reels, occasionally a 4-weight rod for dry flies, and a 7-weight for streamer fishing. Use weight-forward floating lines, and sink-tips and/or full-sinking lines while streamer fishing. Use 7½- to 9-foot leaders and tippets from 0X to 5X to accommodate flies from #2 to #22. We recommend 4X and 5X fluorocarbon for dry-dropper setups in the summer and early fall.

➤ **Rigging:** Be ready for everything. Double nymph rigs with indicators can very effective all season, especially in the winter and spring when water temps are cold. Dry-dropper rigs work well during the Salmonfly, Golden Stone, and Mutant Stone hatches, as well as on summer days with hoppers and terrestrials. Small dry flies that require long leaders and light tippets are used on riffle complexes, slack-water seams, and flats during the summer PMD, Caddis, and Yellow Sally hatches. Streamers can be fished all year, but are most deadly on overcast days and in the fall. Sink-tip lines with short leaders work very well.

Waders and wading boots are needed when the water temps are cool. This coincides with winter, spring (sometimes early summer), and late fall. Summer months are fine for wet wading, with quick-dry pants or shorts, and wading boots, shoes, or sandals.

South Fork Salmonfly. Aaron Otto

MIKE DAWES joined the WorldCast Anglers management team in November 2001 and now serves as president of the company. Mike has been immersed in the sport since the age of five, when he caught his first trout on the fly. A 1996 graduate of St. Lawrence University, Mike moved to Denver, where he received a MBA in marketing from the University of Denver Daniels College of Business in 2000. Mike has been featured on ESPN, ESPN2, ABC, OLN, and in *Fish & Fly* magazine, *The Angling Report*, Orvis catalogs, and others. Mike has won the prestigious March Merkin Permit Tournament, as well as the Jackson Hole One Fly.

CLOSEST FLY SHOPS

WorldCast Anglers
38 West Center St.
Victor, ID 83455 (800-654-0676)
gofish@worldcastanglers.com
www.worldcastanglers.com

Victor Emporium
45 S. Main St.
Victor, ID 83455 (208-787-2221)
www.victoremporium.com

Lodge at Palisades Creek
3720 Hwy. 26
Irwin, ID 83428 (208-483-2222)
www.palisadeslodge.com
palisades@tlapc.com

Three Rivers Ranch
30 E. Little Ave.
Driggs, ID 83422 (208-354-1200)
www.threeriversranch.com
driggsflyshop@gmail.com

Natural Retreats
40 Conant Valley Loop Rd.
Swan Valley, ID 83449 (208-483-3112)
www.naturalretreats.com
concierge@naturalretreats.com

Teton Valley Lodge
3733 Adams Rd.
Driggs, ID 83422 (208-354-2386)
www.tetonvalleylodge.com

CLOSEST OUTFITTERS/GUIDES

WorldCast Anglers (above)
Lodge at Palisades Creek (above)

Three Rivers Ranch (left)
Natural Retreats (left)

CLOSEST LODGES

Lodge at Palisades Creek and Natural Retreats (left)
Teton Springs Lodge and Spa
10 Warm Creek Lane
Victor, ID 83455
(208-787-7888) (877-787-8757)
www.tetonspringslodge.com

BEST HOTELS

Cowboy Roadhouse
381 N Agate Ave.
Victor, ID 83455 (208-787-2755)
www.cowboyroadhouselodge.com.

Moose Creek Ranch (cabin rentals)
W. 960 S. Rd.
Victor, ID 83455 (208-787-6078)
www.moosecreekranch.com
info@moosecreekranch.com

BEST CAMPGROUND

Full service with hook-ups:
Teton Valley RV Park and Campground,
1208 Hwy. 31
Victor, Idaho 83455 (877-787-3036)
www.tetonvalleycampground.com

Primitive:
Falls Campground is next to the Snake River near Swan Valley, 45 miles east of Idaho Falls. Spring Creek and Conant boat ramps

are nearby. Palisades Reservoir is less than 20 miles away. The Falls Creek area has trails for hiking, mountain biking, horseback riding, and ATVs. Roads and parking spurs are gravel. Campground provides restrooms and drinking water; wheelchair-accessible.

BEST RESTAURANTS

Big Hole BBQ
22 W. Center St.
Victor, ID 83455 (208-270-9919)

Knotty Pine Supper Club
58 S Main St.
Victor, ID 83455 (208-787-2866)
www.knottypinesupperclub.com

BEST PLACE FOR A COLD, STIFF DRINK

Knotty Pine Supper Club (above)

CLOSEST EMERGENCY MEDICAL HELP

Eastern Idaho Regional Medical Center,
3100 Channing Way
Idaho Falls, ID 83404 (208-529-6111)

Madison Memorial Hospital
450 E Main St.
Rexburg, ID 83440 (208-356-3691)

Teton Valley Hospital
120 Howard Ave.
Driggs, ID 83422 (208-354-2383)

CELL PHONE SERVICE

Best on the upper and lower portions of the river; spotty in the canyon.

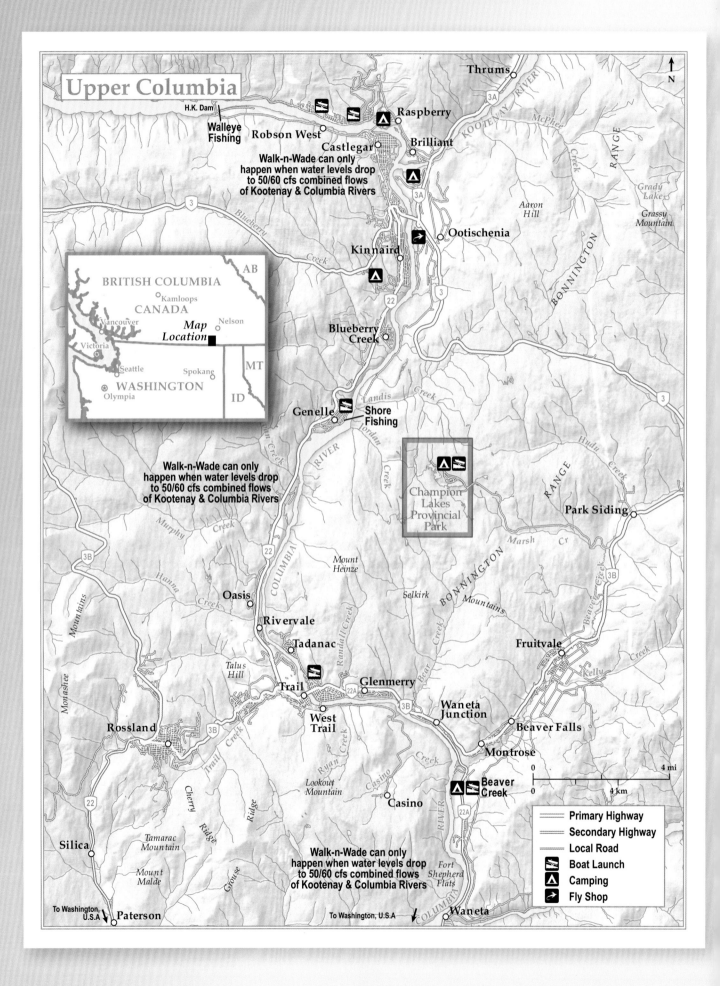

Upper Columbia

Thrums

H.K. Dam
Walleye
Fishing

Robson West

Raspberry

Castlegar
Brilliant

**Walk-n-Wade can only
happen when water levels drop
to 50/60 cfs combined flows
of Kootenay & Columbia Rivers**

Ootischenia

Kinnaird

KOOTENAY RIVER
3A
McPhee Creek
Grady Lakes
Aaron Hill
Grassy Mountain
BONNINGTON RANGE

Blueberry
Creek

Landis Creek

Genelle
Shore
Fishing

**Walk-n-Wade can only
happen when water levels drop
to 50/60 cfs combined flows
of Kootenay & Columbia Rivers**

Champion
Lakes
Provincial
Park

Park Siding

Hudu Creek
RANGE
Marsh Cr

COLUMBIA RIVER

Mount
Heinze

Selkirk

BONNINGTON Mountains

Murphy Creek

Oasis

Rivervale

Tadanac

Talus
Hill

Trail

West
Trail

Glenmerry

Waneta
Junction

Fruitvale

Kelly Creek

Beaver Falls

Montrose

Rossland

Monashee Mountains

Hanna Creek

Randall Creek

Bear Creek

Beaver Creek

Casino Creek

Cherry Ridge

Trail Creek

Ryan Creek

Lookout
Mountain

Casino

Beaver
Creek

4 mi
0
0
4 km

Silica

Tamarac
Mountain

Mount
Malde

Grouse Ridge

Fort
Shepherd
Flats

**Walk-n-Wade can only
happen when water levels drop
to 50/60 cfs combined flows
of Kootenay & Columbia Rivers**

To Washington,
U.S.A

Paterson

To Washington, U.S.A

COLUMBIA RIVER

Waneta

N

Map Location inset

BRITISH COLUMBIA
AB
CANADA
Kamloops
Vancouver
Nelson
**Map
Location**
Victoria
Seattle
Spokane
MT
WASHINGTON
Olympia
ID

Legend

Primary Highway
Secondary Highway
Local Road
Boat Launch
Camping
Fly Shop

Upper Columbia River *(British Columbia, Canada)*

➤ **Location:** British Columbia, Canada, a 3-hour drive north of Spokane, Washington; 7 hours east of Vancouver, BC; or 7 hours west of Calgary, Alberta. Both Castlegar and Trail have airports with service from larger cities such as Vancouver. There are 42 miles (68 kilometers) of free-flowing water draining from Hugh Keenleyside Dam (on Arrow Lake) starting the Columbia River, with the added bonus of a mile (2 kilometers) of the Kootenay River from Kootenay Lake, below Brilliant Dam off Highway 3A or Highway 25 from Spokane to Highway 22 at Trail, BC.

Both rivers join in the small city of Castlegar. The flows in summer vary between 30,000–150,000 cfs. In 2012, high-water flows reached 230,000 cfs; fishing was fantastic for those willing to brave the currents. There are four places to launch boats in the Castlegar area: one at Genelle and three in the Trail-to-border area. Currents are quite swift in places and not for the amateur boater. The river has a wide variety of shallow runs, small pocket eddies, and big backeddies, some over 100 feet deep. Yes, this is big water.

The most impressive change over the past 30 years has been the cleanup of the water and shorelines by the big industries. The hatches have responded, as well as the size and quality of fish. The other draw to this fishery is the lack of fishing pressure. You can pick your spot any day or evening and seldom be challenged for the water you want to fish. It's a fishery you will want to fish and cherish all your life.

The big draw to the Columbia is its big, hot, wild fish taken on dries in the summer. The caddis fly hatch starts in May and June, with the cloudlike hatches coming in July and August. Fish averaging 4 to 6 pounds gorge on the caddis hatch that occurs every evening into dark. Long, accurate casts of 60 to 80 feet are often necessary to take these shy but powerful rainbows. Many people hook fish weighing much more than 6 pounds—but landing them is another story. The river is open and fishes 12 months a year. The fall, winter, and spring months are best fished with sinking-line methods. Streamers, weighted Buggers, or nymphs drifted through a run will almost certainly be rewarded. There are the terrestrial hatches of cicadas in April and May, and flying carpenter ants in May and June. This usually turns the fish on to dry-fly action for the upcoming season.

The normal mayfly hatches occur throughout the seasons. Early season sees Blue-winged Olives and *Baetis* mixed with

Five-year-old Jacob with his 22-incher caught on a Beadhead Pheasant-tail.

midges and chironomids. In early summer, you'll see Pale Morning Duns, *Baetis*, and Pale Evening Duns. In midsummer (July and August) you will often witness Brown Drakes, Green Drakes, and the large *Hexagenia*. September and October bring the big October Caddis, with all sorts of other hatches, including mayflies, smaller caddis, midges, and chironomids. Along with the different bug hatches, the minnow population should never be excluded from the fly fisher's arsenal. Sculpin and minnow patterns will get a fish's attention. Access to the river can be difficult in the winter.

➤ **Hatches:** The spring spawn happens in April and May in the mainstream and in June in the side streams. Good, clean fish are taken all year, with dark, pre-spawn fish coloring up in November and December and on until the spawn is completed.

January to March: Chironomids, BWOs, bloodworms, caddis larvae.

April to May: First terrestrials with flying black ants, cicadas, chironomids, mayflies, and early caddis; some feeder streams have stoneflies washing down into the Columbia.

June and July: Good mayfly hatches, BWOs, *Baetis* gray, Brown Drakes, PMDs, Pale Evening Duns, *Hexagenia*, and the big caddis hatches start. The net-spinning caddis comes off in a cloud almost every night for a month to two months.

August: Caddis hatches are still present, but slowing; mayflies.

September: Still caddis and mayflies, but now the terrestrials come back into play. Hoppers, bees, ants, larger caddis, and October Caddis.

October and November: Hatches slow; BWOs, chironomids, and October Caddis.

December: Brrrrrr. Merry Christmas to you all.

➤ **Fishing regulations:** All streams in BC require single barbless hooks. This section fishes 12 months a year. There is a two-fish limit per day on rainbows: one over 50 cm, the second under 50 cm. Walleye limit is 8 per day. Northern pike are unlimited. Whitefish: 15 per day. Bull trout: one per day counted on the two-trout quota. There is no angling for sturgeon.

➤ **Tackle:** Rods: 9- to 10-foot, 4- to 6-weight if dry-fly fishing; 6- to 8-weight for wet lines or nymphing. Leaders: 9- to 15-foot, 4X or 5X for dry flies; 7- to 9-foot, 3X to 1X for wet lines. A minimum of 100 yards of backing on reels is necessary.

Drift boats should be 16 feet or longer. Motorboats 14 to 18 feet with 25-horsepower minimum, and larger for bigger boats. Props can be used if you have knowledge of the river. Rafts or pontoon boats can be used on limited-distance trips.

➤ **Flies:** Nymphs: Pheasant-tail from #16 short shank up to #8, 3X-long; Prince, flashback style #16 to #6 in a 2X-long, gold beadhead. Black and Golden Stonefly Nymphs, #8 to #4; a size #2 is acceptable. Orange and gold Beadhead Woolly Bugger variations with rubber legs and lots of flash in a variety of colors. Don't forget San Juan Worms with extra weight and indicators.

Dries: BWOs, midges, chironomids, Gray *Baetis* from #22 to #14. From May through summer, Black Ants #10 to #6 on 3X-long hooks; Flying Black Ants in deer hair or foam body. Cicadas, same as Black Ants in #8 and #6. Elk-hair Caddis variations, #12 and #14.

The Upper Columbia River. Derek Kaye

Fishing the early evening caddis hatch. Derek Kaye

A chunky Columbia rainbow.

Author Rod Zavaduk. Derek Kaye

ROD ZAVADUK has been an owner/operator of Castlegar Sports Centre and Fly Shop for 29 years and likes to spend most of his free time fishing the Columbia River. He writes, "You will find me at the fly-tying bench every day. I like to create patterns that will work on the fussy big trout of the Columbia. I also enjoy fishing on lakes in the area when time allows. I enjoy teaching the sport of fly fishing, as well as fly casting and instructing in fly tying. I have built rods for over 40 years. I am a passionate fly fisherperson, very lucky to be living on one of the greatest trout streams in the world."

CLOSEST FLY SHOPS
Castlegar Sports & Fly Shop
1951A Columbia Ave.
Castlegar, BC V1N 2W8 (250-365-8288)
rodz@tellus.net

GUIDES
Rod Zavaduk
Castlegar Sports & Fly Shop (above)

Dwayne D'Andrea
Mountain Valley Fly Fishing
2612 4th Ave.
Castlegar, BC V1N 2W8 (250-365-5771)

Kirk Daley
Action Angling
4092 Bonnington
South Slocan, BC (250-359-2943)

CLOSEST LODGING
Sandman Inn
1944 Columbia Ave.
Castlegar BC V1N 2W8 (250-365-8444)

Quality Inn
1935 Columbia Ave.
Castlegar, BC V1N 2W8
(250-365-2177) (restaurant)

Super 8 Motel Castlegar
651 18th St.
Castlegar, BC V1N 2W8
250-365-2700 (restaurant)

CLOSEST CAMPGROUNDS
Castlegar RV Park & Camping
(go online for booking)
1725 Hwy 3
Castlegar, BC
(250-365-2337 or 866-687-7275)
www.castlegarrvpark.com.

Kootenay River Kampground
651 Rosedale Rd.
Castlegar, BC (250-365-5604)

BEST RESTAURANTS
Sunshine Café (new, with great breakfasts)
Quality Inn
1935 Columbia Ave.
Castlegar, BC (250-365-2177)

The Greek Oven
400 Columbia Ave.
Castlegar, BC (250-365-2311)

Chopsticks
789 Columbia Ave.
Castlegar, BC (250-365-5330)

Pub food:
Lionshead Pub
(great food, small brewery ales), Robson
Black Rooster Bar & Grill, next to Super 8
(250-365-7779)

B&Bs:
(Call for directions and availability.)
Genelle House B&B (250-693-2189)
Windbourne B&B (250-365-6697)
Robson Homestead B&B (250-365-2374)

CLOSEST EMERGENCY MEDICAL HELP
Castlegar and District Community Health Centre
709 10th St.
Castlegar, BC V1N 2H7 (250-365-7711)

Kootenay Boundary Regional Hospital
1200 Hospital Bench
Trail, BC V1R 4M1 (250-368-3311)
Call 911 for any emergencies.

CELL PHONE SERVICE
Limited. Some service near motels and restaurants.

THE ROCKIES

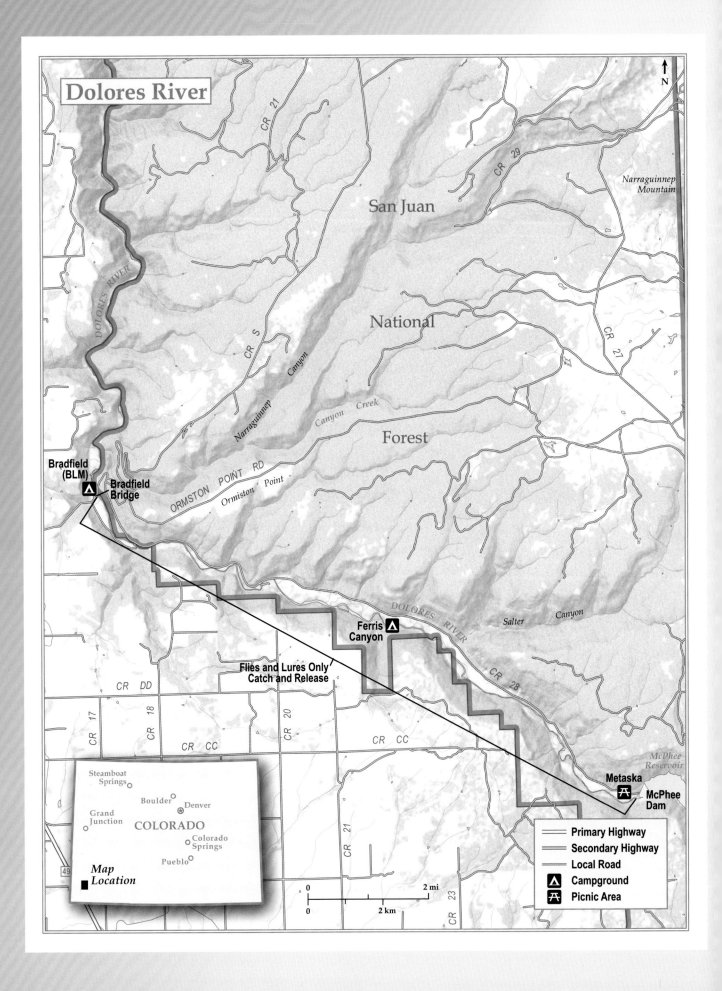

Dolores River

N

San Juan

National

Forest

Narraguinnep Mountain

CR 21

CR 29

CR 27

CR 28

CR S

CR CC

CR DD

CR 17

CR 18

CR 20

CR CC

CR 21

CR 23

Narraguinnep Canyon

Canyon Creek

Salter Canyon

DOLORES RIVER

ORMSTON POINT RD

Ormiston Point

Bradfield (BLM)

Bradfield Bridge

Ferris Canyon

Flies and Lures Only Catch and Release

McPhee Reservoir

Metaska

McPhee Dam

Steamboat Springs

Boulder Denver

Grand Junction

COLORADO

Colorado Springs

Pueblo

Map Location

49

	Primary Highway
	Secondary Highway
	Local Road
⛺	Campground
⛲	Picnic Area

0   2 mi

0   2 km

➤ **Location:** Southwest Colorado, about 1½ hours west and a little north of Durango; 7 hours from Phoenix or Denver; about 5 hours from Albuquerque, New Mexico; and 2½ hours from the San Juan River tailwater. Flight service is available to Durango, Farmington, and Albuquerque.

The Dolores River tailwater was born when cold water was first released from McPhee Dam in 1983 and the Colorado Division of Wildlife stocked 10,000 fingerlings each of rainbow, brown, and Snake River cutthroat trout. The first 12 miles from the dam down to Bradfield Bridge are restricted to catch-and-release, flies and lures only.

There is easy access to the 12 miles of special-regulations water, with Forest Service Road 504 paralleling the river from Bradfield Bridge upstream to the dam. The river flows through a beautiful, wide valley with steep, Jurassic-age Entrata sandstone walls, which have entombed the ancient sand dunes from a massive desert. The elevation is moderate at 6,500 feet, and the sides of the canyon are covered with juniper and piñon woodlands, but also support Ponderosa pine and Douglas fir. The river valley is lined with large cottonwoods.

The lands adjacent to the Dolores from McPhee Dam down to Bradfield Bridge are managed by both the San Juan National Forest and Colorado Parks and Wildlife, giving public access. There is one small piece of private property about 5 miles up from the bridge, but if you follow the signs you can still access the river. There is overnight camping at the Bradfield Recreation Site just downstream from the Bradfield Bridge, and at Ferris Canyon Campground on San Juan National Forest about 8 miles up from the bridge.

This is not big water, with summer flows generally running between 70 and 100 cfs, and the typical low winter flows between 25 to 40 cfs. Unlike many tailwaters, the Dolores is not a year-round fishery, and much of the river freezes over.

Along with easy access, the Dolores is user-friendly, with easy wading, low gradient, and plenty of room to work into position for a cast. There is not much pocket water, but mostly a series of riffle, pools, and slow bends. Holding water is

scattered, and anglers should expect to cover a significant distance through the day.

Being relatively small water, the Dolores does not support huge populations of trout, but has a modest population of predominantly browns mixed with rainbows. Most fish are in the 10- to 15-inch range, and it does grow quality fish over 20 inches.

Low gradient, clear water, and low flows make the Dolores temperamental, and it is not always easy to catch fish. Fishing the Dolores is rarely a game of numbers. But those who seek out beautiful places and thrive on challenging fishing will most likely love it.

A nice, high-country rainbow. Rob Coddington

The 12 miles of special-regulation water below McPhee Dam is a tale of two rivers. Closer to the dam the tailwater effect—constant coldwater conditions—is more pronounced. This provides consistent hatches of small aquatic insects, such as midges, Blue-winged Olives, and Pale Morning Duns. These bugs typically range from #18 to #24, and you can expect daily hatches of these small insects from early June into November, creating selective feeding behavior. Matching the hatch, small flies, accurate presentations, and

Great riffles and deep runs about a mile below the dam. Glenn Tinnin Photography

Scenery abounds on the Dolores. Spencer Schreiber

light tippets are mandatory for these challenging conditions. Patterns to carry include Parachute Adams, #18 to #26; Black Biot Midges, #24 and #26; CDC Compara-dun BWOs, #18 to #22; and CDC Compara-dun PMDs, #16 to #20. There are more browns here, but mixed in with a good number of rainbows, and you will see larger average-size fish than farther downstream.

Farther from the dam we lose the tailwater effect, and there is a greater fluctuation in temperatures more typical of free-flowing waters. There is more diversity in aquatic insects, but less total biomass. Sometimes the fish feed selectively on caddis and mayflies, but mostly they are opportunistic feeders, and fly selection is less important than closer to the dam. Terrestrials like hoppers and ants are important throughout the 12 miles, but increasingly more important farther from the dam. Throughout the summer and fall, hoppers and hopper-dropper rigs are very productive. There's also an increase in crayfish, sculpin, and other baitfish such as speckled dace, hence stripping Zonkers or your streamer of choice can be very

effective. Expect smaller average-size fish, mostly browns but in greater numbers than closer to the dam.

This is a handsome valley with bald eagles, mule deer, elk, black bears, mountain lions, and the occasional rattlesnake. The persistent angler might even catch a glimpse of the few otters. With the right attitude and mindset, a fishing trip to the Lower Dolores can be a very satisfying experience.

➤ **Hatches:** Dry flies are the most popular way to fish the Dolores. It is best to try to match the hatch and fish to rising trout. Hatches are more intense near the dam and become sporadic lower down. Pale Morning Dun hatches occur in midsummer in the late morning. Caddisflies are also important on the Dolores, but hatches are not predictable or consistent. The Blue-winged Olive is the most consistent hatch on the river. Hatches are most numerous in spring and fall, but summer hatches are not uncommon, particularly on overcast days.

In season, terrestrials are particularly effective on the Dolores. Ants and beetles are frequently found on the water, making foam beetles and ant patterns good choices at any time of year. Carry patterns ranging from #10 to #16. Grasshopper season runs from June to mid-fall. Large hopper patterns—#6 to #10—are particularly good fished along the banks.

By late September, the insects on the river are small. A #24 Blue-winged Olive is the main hatch through November, and thin to heavy midday hatches make the trout active feeders. In the absence of a hatch, attractors are good choices after midday. Below the surface, large populations of dace and sculpin make streamers an effective method.

➤ **Fishing regulations:** Open year-round. From McPhee Dam to Bradfield Bridge, flies and lures only, catch-and-release.

➤ **Tackle: A** 5-weight, 8½- or 9-foot rod with a floating line is a great choice for throwing dries, hopper-droppers, streamers, and indicator rigs. For dry-fly enthusiasts, a 3- or 4-weight rod can work, but there are situations where distance is needed to reach spooky fish in flat water. For most situations, go with 9-foot, 5X or 6X leaders, and carry tippet down to 7X. During spring and fall, waders are necessary; in the summer, many find wet wading comfortable.

Coauthors John Flick, above and Tom Knopick, below

In 1983, longtime fly-fishing buddies JOHN FLICK and TOM KNOPICK moved to Durango, Colorado and opened Duranglers Flies and Supplies. John and Tom still guide, manage the shop, and fish the waters of southwest Colorado. Their home waters are the Animas, Dolores, Piedra, Los Pinos, Florida, and San Juan below Navajo Dam.

CLOSEST FLY SHOPS

Duranglers Flies & Supplies
923 Mail Avenue
Durango, CO 81301
970-385-4081
888-347-4346
www.duranglers.com
duranglers@duranglers.com

Telluride Outside
121 W. Colorado Ave.
Telluride, CO 81435
970-728-3895
800-381-6230
info@tellurideoutside.com

CLOSEST GUIDES/OUTFITTERS

Duranglers Flies & Supplies (above)
Telluride Outside (above)

CLOSEST HOTELS

Strater Hotel
699 Main Ave.
Durango, CO 81301
800-247-4431
www.strater.com

O-Bar-O Cabins
11998 CR240
Durango, CO
970-259-3649
www.obaro.com

Blue Lake Ranch B & B
16919 Hwy 140
Hesperus, CO
888-258-3525
www.bluelakeranch.com

BEST CAMPGROUND

Ferris Canyon Campground
3 miles from Cabin Canyon
Campground along Forest Rd. 504
www.fs.usda.gov/recarea/sanjuan

BEST RESTAURANTS

Ore House
147 E. College Dr.
Durango, CO 81301
970-247-5707

Olde Tymer's Café
1000 Main Ave.
Durango, CO 81301
970-259-2990

Dolores River Brewery
100 S. 4th St.
Dolores, CO
970-882-4677

BEST PLACE TO GET A COLD, STIFF DRINK

Dolores River Brewery
100 S. 4th St.
Dolores, CO
970-882-4677

CLOSEST EMERGENCY MEDICAL HELP

Mercy Regional Medical Center
1010 Three Springs Blvd.
Durango, CO 81301
970-247-4311

CELL PHONE SERVICE
No cell service in the canyon.

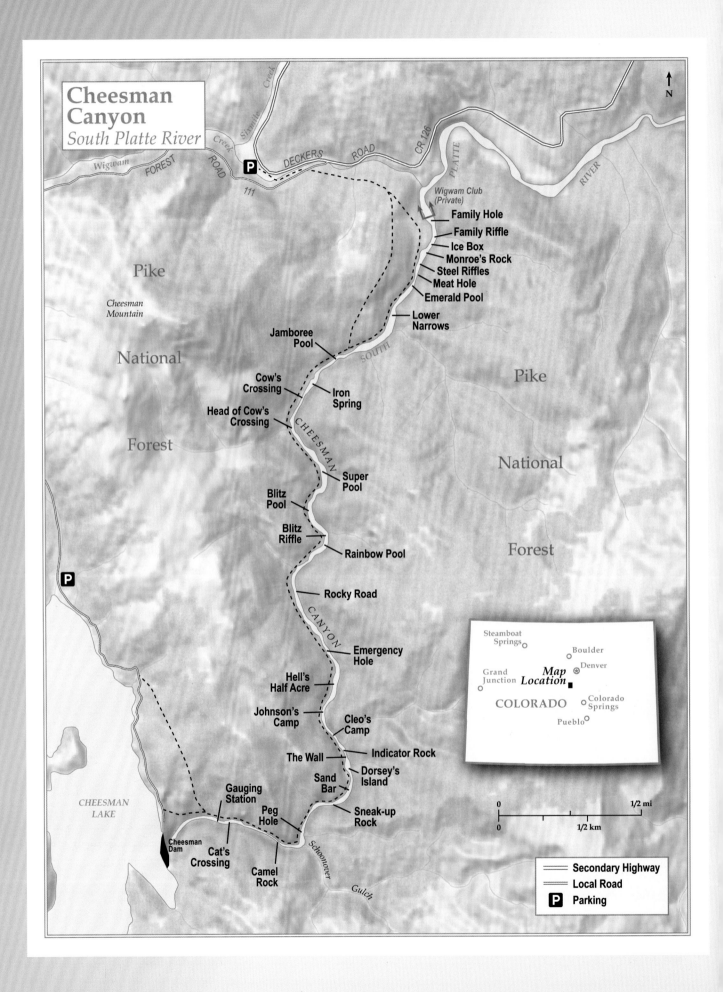

Cheesman Canyon
South Platte River

Pike

Cheesman Mountain

National

Forest

CHEESMAN LAKE

Wigwam Creek

Sixmile Creek

FOREST ROAD 111

DECKERS ROAD

CR 126

PLATTE

RIVER

Wigwam Club (Private)

Family Hole
Family Riffle
Ice Box
Monroe's Rock
Steel Riffles
Meat Hole
Emerald Pool
Lower Narrows

SOUTH

Jamboree Pool

Cow's Crossing
Iron Spring

Head of Cow's Crossing

CHEESMAN

Super Pool

Blitz Pool

Blitz Riffle

Rainbow Pool

Rocky Road

CANYON

Emergency Hole

Hell's Half Acre

Johnson's Camp
Cleo's Camp

The Wall
Indicator Rock
Dorsey's Island
Sand Bar
Sneak-up Rock

Gauging Station
Peg Hole

Cheesman Dam
Cat's Crossing

Camel Rock

Schoonover Gulch

Pike

National

Forest

Steamboat Springs

Boulder

Grand Junction

Map Location

Denver

COLORADO

Colorado Springs

Pueblo

N

0   1/2 mi
0   1/2 km

Secondary Highway
Local Road
P   Parking

Cheesman Canyon *(South Platte River, Colorado)*

➤ **Location:** Cheesman Canyon is 60 miles southwest of Denver and 50 miles northwest of Colorado Springs. There are major airports in both cities.

Many consider the Cheesman Canyon section of the South Platte one of the best tailwaters in the United States. Constructed in 1905, Cheesman Reservoir was named after Walter Scott Cheesman, president of the Denver Union Water Company. From the base of the 221-foot dam, the South Platte River carves it way through a majestic, boulder-filled canyon lined with dense stands of ponderosa pine, Douglas fir, blue spruce, and willow. Bald eagles, black bears, mountain lions, mule deer, raccoons, turkeys, and beautiful butterflies all add to the experience.

Fly-fishing aficionados affectionately call it "the canyon." There's a common belief among South Platte regulars that if you can catch fish in Cheesman Canyon you can catch fish anywhere in the world. I wholeheartedly agree—Cheesman Canyon is a world-class, technical fishery, loaded with some of the most finicky trout anywhere.

There is approximately 3½ miles of public water between the dam and the upper boundary of the private Wigwam Club. Access is via the Gill Trail, named after Henry C. Gill, one of the first settlers in the area. The well-defined trail parallels the river throughout the canyon, affording anglers easy and convenient access. Anglers can park their vehicles in two parking facilities, one off Highway 126 (2 miles west of Deckers) and the other adjacent to Cheesman Reservoir.

Most anglers park in the lower lot (off Highway 126) and hike into the canyon. It takes about 30 minutes to get into the lower river and about an hour to get into the middle reaches. The hike from the upper canyon (Cheesman Reservoir) is not for the faint of heart. Steep grades and rigorous terrain make this hike considerably more difficult than the lower access.

Anglers should consider putting their fly-fishing paraphernalia into a backpack before hiking into Cheesman Canyon. The walk can be strenuous, so hiking in waders and wading shoes can become cumbersome. Hiking shoes are recommended because the decomposed granite along the trail can be slippery. Make sure you take plenty of water, sunscreen, lunch, camera, and a first-aid kit. It's a good idea to take a spare rod in the event you break a tip. This will save a lot of frustration, as it is entirely possible that you will be several miles from your vehicle.

The South Platte in Cheesman Canyon is a classic, bottom-release tailwater supporting rich and diversified aquatic life and providing anglers with a consistent, four-season

Pat Dorsey nymphs the Wall in the upper section of Cheesman Canyon. Mark Adams

fishery. Cooler releases during the summer and warmer outflows during the winter keep the trout active all year. Flows fluctuate regularly to meet downstream urban electricity demands supporting more than three million people, plus the agricultural needs of livestock, irrigating pastureland, and watering other crops and grains. Flows can range between 50–1,000 cfs depending on the snowpack. A typical winter flow is 50–200 cfs; summer releases often range between 400–800 cfs, and autumn flows average 200–400 cfs.

The anatomy of Cheesman Canyon is simply stunning. Anglers can sample classic riffles and runs, deep plunge pools, glassy flats, and superb pocket water. Huge boulders are sprinkled throughout the canyon, making this one of the prettiest landscapes you'll ever encounter.

Above. Jim Cannon fishes to rising fish during a Blue-winged Olive hatch in the Jamboree Pool. Pat Dorsey

Inset. Mark Adams fooled this rainbow near Cleo's Camp. Rainbows between 16 and
20 inches are not uncommon in the fabled Cheesman Canyon stretch. Pat Dorsey

Anglers will have the opportunity to catch a mixed bag of both rainbows and browns. The rainbows average 12 to 18 inches, with a few exceeding the 20-inch mark. Brown trout range from 10 to 14 inches, with the occasional fish surpassing 16 inches. Colorado Parks and Wildlife has designated Cheesman Canyon as Wild Trout Water. Furthermore, the canyon has been catch-and-release since 1972. All fish must be returned to the water immediately after being caught.

Anglers will experience good to excellent hatches. Midges hatch year-round, providing consistent nymph fishing. Matching the hatch requires anglers to be familiar with all stages of a midge's life cycle: larva, pupa, and adult. Dry-fly enthusiasts will find their fair share of rising fish feeding on midge adults.

Late March and early April brings reliable Blue-winged Olive hatches between 1 and 3 P.M. Inclement weather produces the best hatches because rainy or snowy conditions stall the development of the mayfly duns, keeping them on the water longer. If the flow is 100 cfs or less, anglers will experience moderate to heavy hatches. During nonhatch periods, in the absence of mayfly duns, nymphing with *Baetis* imitations is always a good option.

Late May and early June brings forth excellent caddis hatches. Anglers will fool fish on caddis larvae, pupae, and adults. Skated caddis can produce explosive dry-fly fishing.

Dry-dropper rigs are especially effective, particularly in the shallow riffles where selective trout often become suspicious of conventional nymphing rigs. Caddis pupae, *Baetis* nymphs, and Pale Morning Dun nymphs are all excellent droppers. Yellow Sallies also hatch this time of year, providing anglers with exciting dry-fly fishing in 18 to 24 inches of riffled water.

Dry-fly anglers come out of the woodwork to fish the Pale Morning Dun hatch in late July and early August. This hatch typically comes off between 1 and 3 P.M. Flows can make or break this hatch, as high water will produce poor dry-fly fishing. Flows are dependent on snowpack, rainfall, and downstream demand. If the flows are above 500 cfs, nymphing with Pale Morning Dun nymphs might be a better option, as the Cheesman Canyon fish are always willing to eat dead-drifted imposters.

➤ **Hatches:** August and September bring stellar Trico hatches. The duns begin hatching about 7 A.M., and the spinner fall takes place between 9 and 11 A.M. This can be one of the most reliable hatches in Cheesman Canyon. Appropriately named the "white wing curse," this hatch will bring out the best in any serious dry-fly angler.

September and October bring more Blue-winged Olives and dense midge hatches. The *Pseudocloeons* (tiny Blue-winged Olives) also appear during the autumn months. They are one to two hooks sizes smaller than the spring BWO hatches, so pick your flies accordingly.

Midges: Year-round.
Blue-winged Olives: Mid-March to May; September and October.
Caddis: Late May and June.
Golden Stoneflies: July.
Pale Morning Duns: July and August.
Tricos: August and September.

➤ **Fishing regulations:** Strictly catch-and-release, flies and lures only.

➤ **Tackle:** Bring a 9-foot, 5-weight rod with a WF floating line. A two-fly, dry-dropper nymph rig is usually a good bet.

Author Pat Dorsey. Kim Dorsey

PAT DORSEY is a Colorado native who has been guiding for more than 22 years and runs The Blue Quill Angler. He spends 200 days a year on the water, enjoying a unique quality of life both personally and professionally. Pat writes the central Rocky Mountain stream report that monitors stream flows and conditions on the Blue, Colorado, South Platte (Cheesman, Deckers, Spinney Mountain Ranch, and Elevenmile Canyon), North Fork of the South Platte, and Williams Fork Rivers. He is also Southwest Field Editor for *Fly Fisherman* magazine.

Mark Adams fights a powerful rainbow in the upper narrows. Cheesman Canyon is a pocket water paradise. Pat Dorsey

CLOSEST FLY SHOPS
Flies and Lies
8570 South Hwy. 67
Deckers, CO 80135
303-647-2237
danny2@southplatteoutfitters.com
www.Fliesnlies.com

CLOSEST OUTFITTERS/GUIDES
Blue Quill Angler
1532 Bergen Pkwy.
Evergreen, CO 80439
303-674-4700
flyfish@bluequillangler.com
www.bluequillangler.com

Anglers Covey
295 South 21st St.
Colorado Springs, CO 80904
719-471-2984
www.anglerscovey.com

CLOSEST LODGE
Flies and Lies offers cabin rentals (left)

BEST HOTEL
Country Lodge
723 U.S. Hwy 24 W.
Woodland Park, CO 80863
719-687-6277
www.woodlandcountrylodge.com

BEST CAMPGROUND
Lone Rock Campground, about 0.6 mile west of Deckers on Hwy. 126 next to the South Platte River.
877-444-6777
campincolorado.com/federal, search for Lone Rock Campground.

CLOSEST RESTAURANT
Woodland Park, 25 miles from river.

BEST RESTAURANT
Small café at *Deckers* that serves the basics: coffee, sandwiches, and beer.

CLOSEST PLACE TO GET A COLD, STIFF DRINK
Liquor store and general store at *Deckers.*

CLOSEST EMERGENCY MEDICAL HELP
Pikes Peak Regional Hospital and Surgery Center
16420 W. Hwy. 24
Woodland Park, CO
719-687-9999
www.pikespeakregionalhospital.com

CELL PHONE SERVICE
Not on the river.

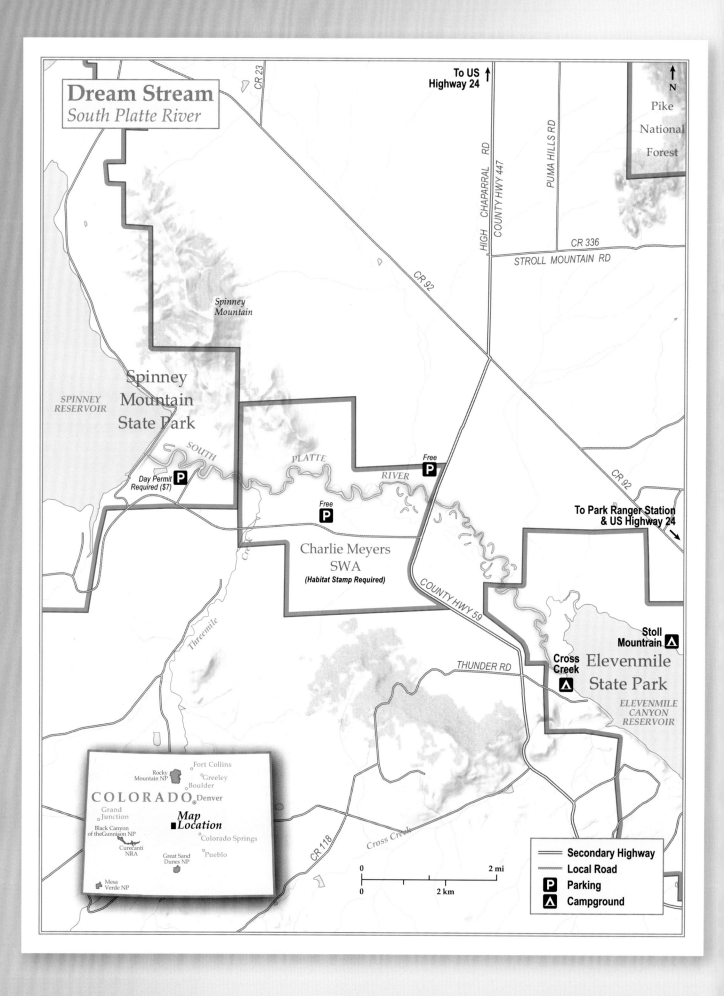

Dream Stream
South Platte River

To US
Highway 24

N

Pike
National
Forest

CR 23

HIGH CHAPARRAL RD

COUNTY HWY 447

PUMA HILLS RD

CR 336

STROLL MOUNTAIN RD

CR 92

*Spinney
Mountain*

Spinney
Mountain
State Park

SPINNEY
RESERVOIR

SOUTH

PLATTE

RIVER

Free
P

CR 92

Day Permit
Required ($7) **P**

Free
P

To Park Ranger Station
& US Highway 24

Charlie Meyers
SWA
(Habitat Stamp Required)

Creek

COUNTY HWY 59

Stoll
Mountrain **▲**

Cross
Creek
▲

Elevenmile
State Park

Threemile

THUNDER RD

*ELEVENMILE
CANYON
RESERVOIR*

Fort Collins

Rocky
Mountain NP

Greeley
Boulder

COLORADO ® Denver

Grand
Junction

Black Canyon
of theGunnison NP

Curecanti
NRA

Great Sand
Dunes NP

**Map
Location**

Colorado Springs

Pueblo

Mesa
Verde NP

CR 118

Cross Creek

	Secondary Highway
	Local Road
P	Parking
▲	Campground

0   2 mi

0   2 km

Dream Stream *(South Platte River, Colorado)*

➤ **Location:** Southwest Colorado, 1 hour west of Colorado Springs and 1 ½ hours southwest of Denver. Both have major airports with direct flights.

For ages, anglers around the world have known the South Platte River below Spinney Reservoir as the Dream Stream— the land of giants, where anglers wade softly and carry big sticks. For anyone wanting to test their merit as a tailwater fly fisher, this is the proving grounds. Fishing pressure, changing water conditions, and the legendary South Park County wind all combine to make this one of the most technical tailwater fisheries in the country.

In 2010, famous *Denver Post* columnist and book author Charlie Meyers passed away, and the Dream Stream from Highway 59 up to the last free parking area below Spinney Dam was renamed Charlie Meyers State Wildlife Area.

The Dream Stream flows from Spinney Dam roughly 3½ miles through scenic high-country meadow before it dumps into Elevenmile Reservoir. The valley the river travels through is surrounded by beautiful mountains, including the iconic Spinney Mountain. The completely open valley makes the Dream Stream a corridor for wind gusts from 15 to 35 mph. Anglers should come armed with a fast-action 5- or 6-weight fly rod.

At its widest, the Dream Stream is slightly more than 20 feet across. The deeper pools are 4 to 6 feet (depending on water level) and because the river is too skinny to float, all fishing is done by walk-and-wade. Proximity to nutrient-rich Spinney and Elevenmile Reservoirs makes the Dream Stream an ideal place to hunt for trophy fish, and trout over 10 pounds are landed here yearly.

There's a surprising amount of variation between the types of structure and water conditions found closer to Spinney Dam compared to the Elevenmile inlet. From the dam to the bridge, water moves faster as a result of boulders and trees installed to create holding water. Lines of strategically placed boulders cross the river to create plunge pools, and dead trees along the sides provide cover and stabilize the banks. All this extra cover has made the upper half of the Dream Stream the best place to look year-round for what locals affectionately refer to as "resident hogs." The upper half is also where fishing is most technical because of high fishing pressure.

From the Highway 59 bridge down to Elevenmile Reservoir, the water moves more slowly, and the river resembles a typical spring creek. Without as much structure, fish rely on deeper pools and undercut banks for protection from anglers and birds of prey. Fishing on the lower half benefits greatly from higher flow rates, as well as the spring and fall spawning runs. During low flows, and in the dog days of summer, this stretch of river can have considerably fewer fish in it.

Fish enter and leave the river system based on water temperature and the amount of water coming through Spinney

Spinney Mountain bliss. Jon Kleis

Dam; water levels fluctuate according to Denver's and Aurora's needs. As this is a city water supply and demands for water are constantly changing, so does the water level. Time of year, weather conditions, and water level all affect water temperature. Like every other fish species, trout have a certain temperature range where they are comfortable spawning. The months where conditions are most favorable for fish to migrate up from Elevenmile Reservoir are March through May, and August through October.

Species that call the Dream Stream home are rainbow trout, Snake River cutthroat trout, a hybrid of the two known as a cuttbow, brown trout, and (for a brief period in the autumn) Kokanee salmon. Rainbows, cutthroat, and cuttbows take over the river in the spring to spawn, and the browns and Kokanee take over in the fall. Often there is a resurgence of cutthroat a few weeks before the browns and Kokanee move

Kokanee salmon landed during the fall migration.

A view of the Dream Stream and Elevenmile Reservoir from Spinney Dam. Jon Kleis

in. The sudden appearance of voracious cutthroat looking to feed on the protein-rich eggs of brown trout and Kokanee is a sign that the fall spawn is about to happen.

Eggs aside, there is no shortage of insects or crustaceans in the Dream Stream. Scuds are a common food source in both surrounding reservoirs, and scuds as well as sow bugs are found in abundance for the first mile and a half below Spinney Dam. The same way that scuds are prevalent the closer you get to the dam, crayfish are found in abundance near the Elevenmile inlet. Both crustaceans make great meals for hungry trout.

Insects include midges, *Baetis*, Pale Morning Duns, Tricos, caddis, annelids (worms), leeches, and small stoneflies. One of the challenges anglers face is discovering which bugs are hatching, and which stages of the hatch the trout are feeding on. For instance, in the fall, fish could see Tricos, midges, Blue-winged Olives, and caddis—all in the same day. Experienced anglers know that it's important to carry imitations of all these insects in their different stages to master the dreaded multiple hatch.

Fishing with a tandem nymph rig under an indicator is the most common method to fool fish. Popular nymphs are Copper Johns, Graphic Caddis, Barr's Emergers, Black Beauties, and Rojo Midges. The hopper-dropper setup is used during late summer and early fall. Schroeder's Parachute Hopper with a heavily weighted nymph such as a Copper John can be deadly when thrown tight against an undercut bank. Heavily weighted black-and-olive streamers are also deadly during late summer and fall. In fact, when fishing gets tough it can be very productive to tie on your favorite streamer and start covering a lot of water.

Of course, the adversity that anglers face chasing large trout in ever-changing conditions is what makes the Dream Stream so special. The challenge is sight fishing to spooky, trophy-class fish in gin-clear water with insanely small flies. These things embody tailwater fly fishing, and are what make it an incurable disease for many anglers. Anyone afflicted by the tailwater virus who doesn't mind a challenge needs to add this destination to the bucket list. The Dream Stream is one of the most rewarding fly-fishing experiences in the country.

➤ **Fishing regulations:** All year. From Spinney Dam to the Elevenmile inlet, fishing is catch-and-release, flies and lures only. All fish must be returned to the water immediately.

➤ **Hatches:** The Dream Stream is one of the most insect-prolific North American waters, with some 45 identifiable caddisflies, mayflies, midges, stoneflies, and terrestrials—far too many to name here. For a complete list including identifying pictures, visit coloradoflyfishingreports.com.
Grannoms: March through mid-May.
Gray Spotted Sedges (caddis): June through mid-July.
Little Sister Sedges (caddis): mid-May through August.
Dark Sedges (caddis): June through mid-August.
Blue-winged Olives: early March through mid-November
Brown Drakes: mid-June to mid-July.
Mahogany Duns: September through October.
Tricos: mid-July through mid-September.
Salmonflies: mid-May to mid-July.
Yellow Sallies: mid-June through August.

Dream Stream Snake River cutthroat. Jon Kleis

Tailwater #26 midge pupa. Jon Kleis

Author Jon Kleis. Kristen Kleis

➤ **Tackle:** Bring a 5-weight rod with a WF floating line. The size of your leader and tippet depends on the type of fishing you're doing—streamers, nymphs, hoppers, and so on—but for most situations and most of the year, 5X fluorocarbon is the most common. Come armed with 6X fluorocarbon during the colder months, when the water is low and clear. There is the potential to do a lot of walking while looking for fish, so bring breathable waders and dress in layers. A jacket with an outer shell for wind protection is also highly recommended.

JON KLEIS is a Colorado native and a fly-fishing convert who grew up fishing on the South Platte tailwaters with his father using in-line spinners and spoons. Around age 15, he decided to take the plunge and started fly fishing and tying, has spent the last 16 years mastering his craft on some of the country's most technical trout streams. He runs Anglers Covey.

CLOSEST FLY SHOPS

Anglers Covey (45 minutes away)
295 21st St.
Colorado Springs, CO 80904
719-471-2984
www.anglerscovey.com

The Peak Fly Shop
301 E. Highway 24
Woodland Park, CO 80918
719-687-9122
www.thepeakflyshop.com

CLOSEST OUTFITTERS

Anglers Covey (above)
The Peak Fly Shop (see above)

BEST HOTEL

The Broadmoor Hotel
1 Lake Ave.
Colorado Springs, CO 80906
719-634-7711
www.broadmoor.com
The Broadmoor is a five-star hotel.

CLOSEST AND BEST CAMPGROUND

Elevenmile State Park
4229 Co. Rd. 92
Lake George, CO 80827
719-748-3401
eleven.mile.park@state.co.us

BEST PLACE TO GET A COLD, STIFF DRINK

Colorado Mountain Brewing Company
600 S. 21st St., Ste. 180
Colorado Springs, CO 80904
719-466-8240
www.cmbrew.com

CLOSEST AND BEST RESTAURANT

Paravicini's Italian Bistro
2802 W. Colorado Ave.
Colorado Springs, CO 80904
719-471-8200
www.paravicinis.com

CLOSEST EMERGENCY MEDICAL HELP

Pikes Peak Regional Hospital and Surgery Center 16420 W. Highway 24
Woodland Park, CO
719-687-9999
www.pikespeakregionalhospital.com

CELL PHONE SERVICE

Depending on your carrier, there is usually some signal for making calls out. The town of Lake George, roughly 10 or 15 minutes from the Dream Stream, always has a strong signal for both Verizon and AT&T.

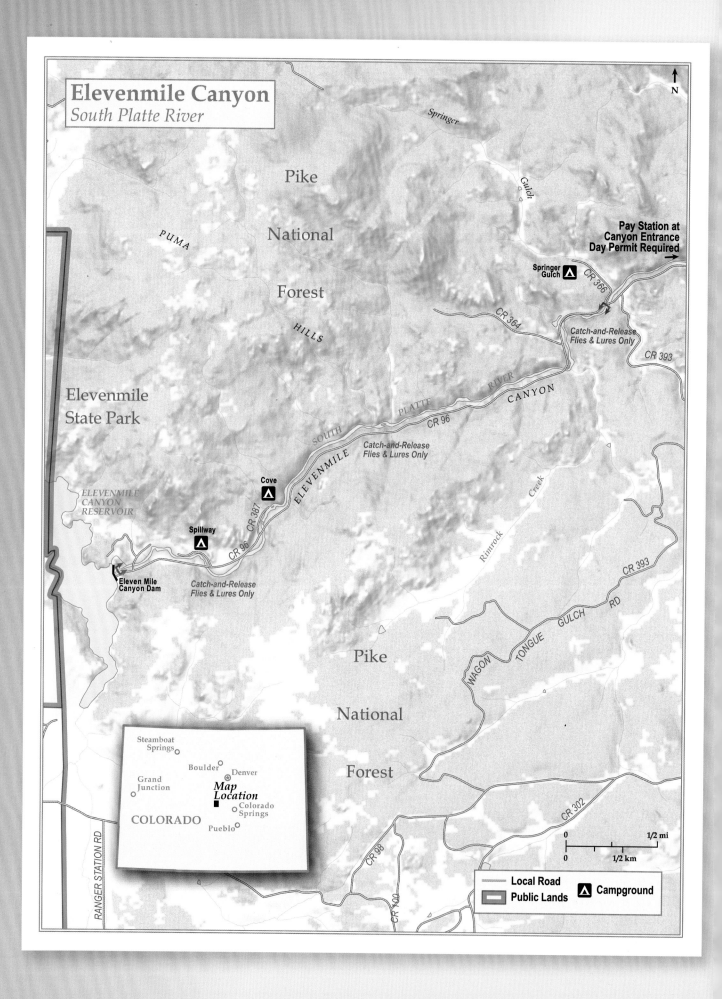

Elevenmile Canyon
South Platte River

N

Pike

National

Forest

PUMA

HILLS

Pay Station at Canyon Entrance Day Permit Required

Springer

Gulch

Springer Gulch

CR 366

CR 364

Catch-and-Release Flies & Lures Only

CR 393

Elevenmile
State Park

SOUTH   PLATTE   RIVER   CANYON

CR 96

Catch-and-Release Flies & Lures Only

ELEVENMILE
CANYON
RESERVOIR

Cove

ELEVENMILE

CR 387

Spillway

Rimrock   Creek

CR 96

Eleven Mile
Canyon Dam

Catch-and-Release Flies & Lures Only

Pike

WAGON   TONGUE   GULCH   RD

CR 393

National

Forest

CR 302

CR 98

RANGER STATION RD

CR 100

Steamboat
Springs

Boulder

Denver

Grand
Junction

**Map
Location**

Colorado
Springs

COLORADO

Pueblo

0   1/2 mi
0   1/2 km

Local Road   Campground
Public Lands

Elevenmile Canyon *(South Platte River, Colorado)*

➤ **Location:** Southwest Colorado, 1 hour west of Colorado Springs and 1 ½ hours southwest of Denver. Both have major airports with direct flights.

The South Platte River as it runs through Elevenmile Canyon is home to more fish per mile through the catch-and-release section than just about any other tailwater in Colorado. When anglers aren't busy catching Snake River cutthroat, rainbows, or brown trout, they can look up and admire the unmatched beauty of their surroundings. In fact, the Canyon is considered so gorgeous that it attracts more than just anglers looking to harass fish. On a warm summer day you could see rock climbers, joggers, and hikers on the many trails; campers; artists painting images of steep canyon walls; and, depending on the flow, kayakers and others playing in the cool, clean water.

In 2002, Colorado was dealing with the Hayman Fire, which was its largest fire to date and threatened a large portion of the South Platte River. Hayman brought with it a lot of attention directed at the health of the South Platte, and a new project called Trees For Trout was born. The goal was to take burned trees from the Hayman fire and use them to stabilize the banks of the South Platte, and to also provide winter homes and structure for fish. This was the first program of its kind, and a great way for the USDA Forest Service, Trout Unlimited, and local fly shops such as Anglers Covey to take a huge negative and try to turn it into a positive. Evidence of Trees For Trout's benefits can be found throughout the Elevenmile Canyon corridor.

The South Platte River as it runs through the Canyon is similar in size to the Dream Stream. It's roughly 30 feet across at its widest, and has every form of structure and water type. There are slow-moving runs with an average depth of 2 to 6 feet, fast pocket water, and deep plunge pools beneath falls. Ideal flows for the best fishing are 120–240 cfs.

Fishing access is found by pulloffs along County Road 96, a dirt road that goes the length of the Canyon. County Road 96 originated as a railroad track which served to transport ore from mining operations in Park County to Colora-

do Springs beginning in 1887. Keep an eye out for the three train-shaped tunnels with ceilings still stained black from the smoke of steam-powered locomotives. The road itself is maintained fairly well, except for occasional washboarding, and can be driven by smaller vehicles.

The bottom two-thirds of the Canyon is open to bait fishing, and receives a ton of pressure during the summer

Sunrise in Elevenmile Canyon. Kristen Kleis

months, but sees relatively little in the spring and fall. Anyone wanting to harvest fish in the bait section should be mindful of the limits. As of this writing you can keep 4 trout with no size limit. The catch-and-release flies- and lures-only water begins at Springer Gulch campground and covers the entire stretch of river between there and Elevenmile Dam.

The catch-and-release section is by far the most popular destination for fly fishers from the Colorado Springs area. Almost all trout found in this stretch are wild, naturally reproducing fish. With an average around 14 inches, rainbow trout comprise the bulk of the population. Trout in the Canyon grow fast, feeding on a steady diet of midges (which hatch year-round); Blue-winged Olives and caddis during the spring and fall; Pale Morning Dun mayflies in the summer; and starting around July, Tricos, which last into late fall.

Angler from high in the canyon. Daniel Zimmerman

The Trico hatch is the stuff of legend, and even though you can catch fish while throwing dry flies during all the major hatches, it's hard for passionate dry-fly purists not to get chills just thinking about the wall of Tricos that line the river during the peak of the hatch. A wind gust strong enough to knock copious numbers of Tricos into the water will cause an eruption on the surface unlike anything most anglers have witnessed.

During winter, anglers are relegated to imitating super-small midges while fishing in freezing cold, gin-clear water. Two flies hanging under an indicator with a little bit of weight strategically placed on your 6X fluorocarbon leader usually does the trick. Whereas ridiculously tiny midges are on the menu during winter, the opposite holds true during summer. The most productive rig used for fooling trout during higher flows and summer heat is the hopper-dropper. Weighted nymphs hung under a hopper imitation such as a #10 or #12 olive Amy's Ant absolutely hammer fish.

Unlike the Dream Stream, where reward is found in fooling extremely large and spooky spawners, in Elevenmile Canyon anglers are rewarded with catching large numbers of healthy, pan-size trout. Because conditions are ever-changing, there is always something new to learn. Even though it can be challenging at times, the sheer numbers of fish that call this tailwater home make it a place where experienced anglers can count on bending a 9-foot, 5-weight rod on any given day. It's all of these things that make this place so special. Anybody who doesn't mind a mellow day of catching fish while surrounded in all directions by postcard-worthy views needs to add Elevenmile Canyon to their list.

► **Hatches:**

Midges: year-round.
Baetis/Blue-winged Olive mayflies: late February to June.
Caddis: early April to June, then again September through late October.
PMDs: early June through August.
Yellow Sally Stoneflies: June through August.
Hoppers: July to September.
Tricos: late July through October.
Annelids: all year.
Scuds and sow bugs: all year right below the dam.

► **Fishing regulations:** From Springer Gulch Campground upriver to Elevenmile Dam, catch-and-release only, flies and lures only. From Springer Gulch downriver to the Elevenmile Canyon entrance is standard Colorado bait-fishing regs. Anglers can keep four trout with no size limit.

► **Tackle: A** 5-weight rod with a WF floating fly line. The size of leader and tippet depends on the type of fishing—

Cutthroat in the canyon. Jon Kleis

Elevenmile Dam. Jon Kleis

Author Jon Kleis. Kristen Kleis

streamers, nymphs, hoppers, and so on—but for most situations and most of the year 5X fluorocarbon is the best. Come armed with 6X fluoro during the colder months when the water is low and clear. There is the potential to do a lot of walking while looking for fish, so bring your breathable waders and dress in layers. A jacket with an outer shell for wind protection also comes highly recommended.

JON KLEIS is a Colorado native and a fly-fishing convert who grew up fishing on the South Platte tailwaters with his father using in-line spinners and spoons. Around age 15, he decided to take the plunge and started fly fishing and tying, has spent the last 16 years mastering his craft on some of the country's most technical trout streams. He runs Anglers Covey.

CLOSEST FLY SHOPS
Anglers Covey (45 minutes from the stream)
295 21st St.
Colorado Springs, CO 80904
719-471-2984
www.anglerscovey.com
The Peak Fly Shop
(in the mountain town of Woodland Park)
301 E. Hwy 24
Woodland Park, CO 80918
719-687-9122
www.thepeakflyshop.com

CLOSEST OUTFITTERS
Anglers Covey (above)
The Peak Fly Shop (above)

CLOSEST LODGES
Eagle Fire Lodge
777 E. Hwy 24
Woodland Park, CO 80863
719-687-5700
www.eaglefirelodge.com

11 Mile Lodge
38122 U.S. Hwy 24
Lake George, CO 80827
719-748-3220
www.11milelodge.com

CLOSEST AND BEST HOTEL
Broadmoor Hotel
1 Lake Ave.
Colorado Springs, CO 80906
719-634-7711
www.broadmoor.com
The Broadmoor is a historic, 5-star hotel located 5 minutes from Anglers Covey Fly Shop on the west side of Colorado Springs. Nearly every president, actor, and professional athlete has stayed there. There are several stores located at the hotel, and no shortage of things to do, including spending a day at the Broadmoor spa, checking out the Cheyenne Mountain Zoo, or playing a round of golf on the 18-hole golf course.

BEST CAMPGROUND
Elevenmile Canyon has four campgrounds located along the river with 61 sites available.

CLOSEST AND BEST PLACE TO GET A COLD, STIFF DRINK
Colorado Mountain Brewing Company
600 S. 21st St., Ste. 180
Colorado Springs, CO 80904
719-466-8240 www.cmbrew.com
Located in the historic Roundhouse Building, corner of Hwy. 24 and 21st St.

CLOSEST AND BEST RESTAURANT
The Sunbird Restaurant
230 Point of the Pines Dr.
Colorado Springs, CO 80904
719-598-8990

CLOSEST EMERGENCY MEDICAL HELP
Pikes Peak Regional Hospital
16420 West Hwy 24
Woodland Park, CO 80863
719-687-9999
(Roughly 25 minutes from fishing location.)

CELL PHONE SERVICE
Most of the Canyon has no signal. Drive down the length of the canyon to the town of Lake George.

FLY-FISHING CLUBS
Cheyenne Mountain Chapter of Trout Unlimited
Pikes Peak Flyfishers

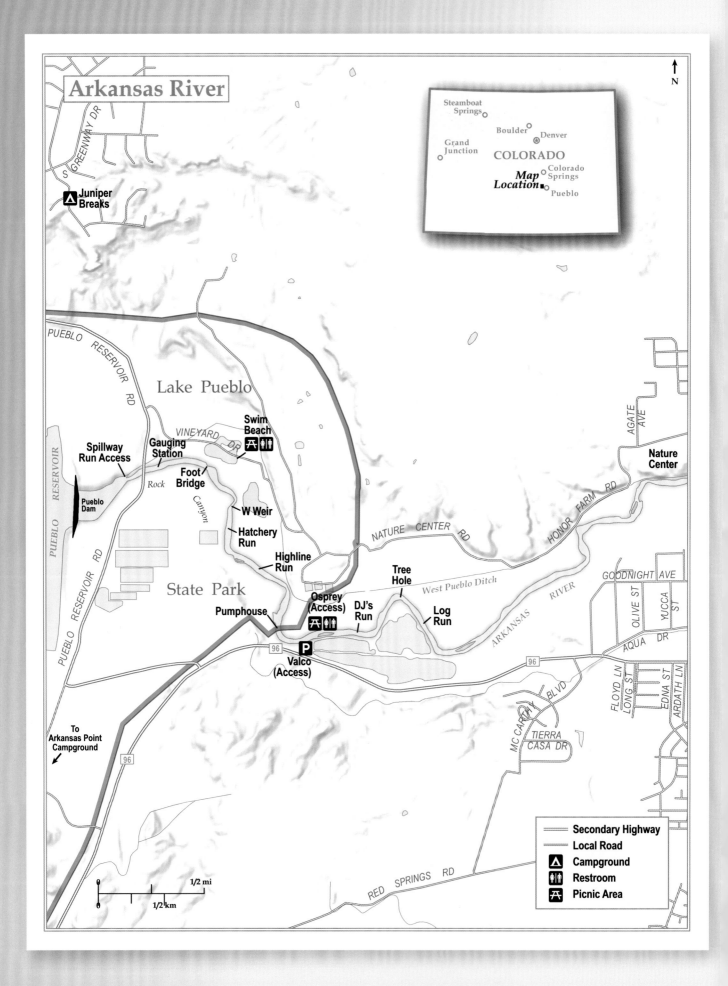

Arkansas River

Juniper Breaks ⛺

Map Location Inset
Steamboat Springs
Boulder ○ Denver
Grand Junction
COLORADO
Colorado Springs
Map Location ■
Pueblo

N ↑

PUEBLO RESERVOIR RD

Lake Pueblo

VINEYARD DR

Swim Beach 🏕 🚻

Spillway Run Access

Gauging Station

Nature Center

Rock

Foot Bridge

Canyon

PUEBLO RESERVOIR

Pueblo Dam

W Weir

Hatchery Run

NATURE CENTER RD

HONOR FARM RD

Highline Run

GOODNIGHT AVE

Tree Hole

West Pueblo Ditch

State Park

Arkansas River

OLIVE ST
YUCCA ST

Osprey (Access) 🏕 🚻

DJ's Run

Log Run

AGATE AVE

Pumphouse

PUEBLO RESERVOIR RD

96

Valco (Access) 🅿

96

AQUA DR

FLOYD LN
LONG ST
EDNA ST
ARDATH LN

MC CARTHY BLVD

To Arkansas Point Campground
↙

96

TIERRA CASA DR

RED SPRINGS RD

Scale
1/2 mi
1/2 km

Legend
—— **Secondary Highway**
—— **Local Road**
⛺ **Campground**
🚻 **Restroom**
🏕 **Picnic Area**

Arkansas River *(South -Central Colorado)*

➤ **Location:** The Arkansas River below Pueblo Reservoir is approximately 100 miles south of Denver. About an hour's drive from Colorado Springs, it is easily accessible via Interstate 25, which runs from Fort Collins to Trinidad. The closest airport is the Pueblo Memorial Airport, about 20 minutes from the water. From I-25 in Pueblo, take the W. 4th St. Exit, which turns into Thatcher Ave. Thatcher Ave. headed West turns into CO-96, which follows the river to Pueblo Reservoir.

When most anglers envision the Arkansas River, they think of a large and high-gradient freestone river that runs through a gauntlet of rugged canyons and Colorado's High Desert. Truth be told, the Upper Arkansas drainage, which starts high in the Collegiate Range near Leadville, overshadowed the Arkansas Tailwater fishery until recently. In 2005–2006, a major structural renovation of the first 8 miles of river below the dam was completed, as part of a long-term effort to increase trout survival habitat. A multimillion-dollar development, The Arkansas River Legacy Project will continue its work with additional renovation. Because throughout its history the Arkansas River has been a major artery for agricultural use, not only in southern Colorado but also throughout the Great Plains, release demands have often displaced fish during the summer months. With the addition of the new structure, fish survival rates during high flows have dramatically increased, along with aquatic insect growth and subsequent size growth in the trout population. Since 2008, studies show per-mile trout population and average size to be higher than ever. Additionally, the structural work offers anglers a much easier fishery when it comes to reading water. The Arkansas Tailwater offers a much different look than its freestone counterpart upstream, with meandering bends, deep holes, and large cottonwood groves. However, do not be fooled by the difference at first sight, as this section offers the angler just as many fish as the upper river, and shots at trophies.

This tailwater stretch fishes best between September and March, when flows are maintained in the 75- to 300-cubic-feet-per-second (cfs) range. During an average water year, summer flows will vary erratically between 500 and 2,000 cfs, following water demands downstream. This section can be very tough to wade when flows exceed 600 cfs. With the bottom-release dam at Pueblo Reservoir, this fishery maintains a constant water temperature of between 42 and 46 degrees regardless of flow or season, allowing for excellent aquatic insect growth and year-round reliable hatches. Additionally, due to the temperate nature of the weather in southern Colorado, this section is one of the Rocky Mountains' most productive and popular fisheries during the fall and winter months.

Between spring and fall, anglers can expect unbelievable variety in aquatic insect activity. March will see heavy hatches of larger Blue-winged Olives, followed by excellent Tan Caddis, Pale Morning Dun, Yellow Sally, and Trico hatches during the summer months. The winter months contribute excellent micro BWO and midge hatches and can be some of the best dry-fly months of the season. Anglers see productive emerger and dry-fly activity 365 days a year.

Winter angler's paradise. Taylor Edrington

The highest trout numbers are in the 2-mile stretch immediately below the dam at Pueblo Reservoir. This stretch offers fish an extraordinary amount of holding structure, including large J-hooks, rock outcroppings, and some good, long riffles. The average fish in this section is between 11 and 14 inches, and anglers can expect to see many rainbows and cuttbows in the 16- to 18-inch range. This section offers up a few trophy-size browns every year as well, but these are older and more seasoned fish and can be difficult to hook.

Clint Werthman with a great
rainbow at Osprey. Joe Bower

Right. Summer season sunset
at Valco. Taylor Edrington

The lower sections between Tortilla Flats and Valco Bridge offer the best experience and shots at much larger fish. This section has fewer fish, and the water is more technical, but the rewards can be worth it. Most fish in this lower section average between 13 and 16 inches, but many are over 17 inches. There are many brown trout in this lower section, and several 30-inch fish are landed each year. This lower section also offers anglers more solitude. The Arkansas Tailwater is not stocked from Valco Bridge downstream, however many fish migrate into the lower stretch. A bike path/hiking trail runs the entire length of the river, with seven parking areas for anglers, including a free lot just below the dam.

Several rigging procedures work well here. Throughout the season, anglers can be productive running a two- or three-fly static nymph rig, focusing on the active aquatic insects of the given time period. Guides usually run a fairly heavy lead fly or attractor nymph, such as crane fly imitations, worm cluster imitations (during high water), and egg patterns during the spring and fall. Dropper flies depend on the depth where fish are stationed. If fish are active on deeper emergers and feeding in the riffles and tailout runs, some standby droppers may include, but aren't limited to, Barr's Emergers, RS2s, and WD-40s in a variety of colors. Of course, a variety of midge pupae and drowned Tricos can also be very productive during those specific hatch periods. Much of the time, however, fish will hold tight to structure or deep in current seams below J-hooks. In this case, heavy dropper nymphs may be required. Some favorites include:

Craven's Poison Tung, Gunkel's Shotglass, Garcia's Rainbow Warrior, Garcia's Rojo Midge, Dorsey's Medallion Midge, and Barr's Pure Midge. When rigging these two- or three-fly rigs, successful anglers run a 9- to 12-foot leader with 5X to the lead fly, ending in 6X to the droppers. Fluorocarbon can be helpful here, as fish can be very selective.

During hatches, trout will congregate in the larger tailouts and riffles to feed on emerging pupae and adults. The best tactic for approaching fish during hatch periods is with a dry-dropper rig and a long greased leader. Focus on both the adult and emerger with this rig, as the majority of your fish will take the emerger during heavy hatches. Ten- to 12-foot leaders to the dry with a 5X or 6X, 14- or 16-inch fluorocarbon drop to the emerger will work best. In the fall and spring, during both spawning phases, fish are very territorial and aggressive, and streamers can work very well. Best rigging for streamers is with a short, fast-sinking poly-leader and a short section of heavy fluorocarbon, as flows are usually 100–300 cfs. A variety of streamers work well, but we tend to focus on small baitfish imitations: blacknose dace and sculpin.

➤ **Hatches:** With an enormous and varied aquatic insect population, this is just a basic sample. For a complete hatch chart, visit the Royal Gorge Anglers website: royalgorge anglers.com.

Blue-winged Olives: March and April; September through October.

Pale Morning Duns: August through September.

Western Green Drakes: July and August.

Giant Salmonflies: June and July.

Golden Stoneflies: June and July.

Little Yellow Stoneflies: June to late August.

Midges: All year; heavy in winter.

Caddis: Various caddis with color and size differences from April through October.

➤ **Fishing regulations:** Open year-round. A state parks day pass is required for parking areas within Lake Pueblo State Park. State regulations are four fish any size. Flies and lures only from the Valco Ponds to Pueblo Blvd.; all fish 16 inches and longer must be released in this section. The Nature Center is exempt and runs on normal state regulations. No motorized vessels.

➤ **Tackle:** Bring a 9-foot, 5-weight, fast-action fly rod with matching reel. Indicator-tip nymphing lines are recommended for nymphing, while standard WF trout taper fly lines are perfect for dry-fly and emerger fishing. Use 9- to 12-foot fluorocarbon leaders for nymphing; 10- to 12-foot trout taper leaders for dries and emergers; and 9-foot, fast-sink poly-leaders with 3X terminal ends for streamers. Breathable waders and boots year-round. Studded Vibram rubber soles on boots are recommended.

Owned and operated by TAYLOR EDRINGTON, Royal Gorge Anglers is in its 25th year. Taylor is the son of founder Bill Edrington, who has since retired to days on the river and part-time retail management. Taylor has been guiding the watersheds of Colorado for over a decade, and spent almost 10 years guiding at and managing several flagship fly-out lodges in Alaska. Taylor is a global angler, hosting fly-fishing travel adventures to destinations on five continents.

CLOSEST FLY SHOPS

Royal Gorge Anglers
49311 U.S. 50 West
Canon City, CO 81212
888-994-6743
www.royalgorgeanglers.com

The Anglers Covey
295 S. 21st St.
Colorado Springs, CO 80904
719-471-2984
www.anglerscovey.com

CLOSEST OUTFITTERS

Royal Gorge Anglers (above)

The Anglers Covey (above)

CLOSEST LODGE

Royal Gorge Anglers' Skyline Lodge at the Royal Gorge
49311 U.S. 50 West
Canon City, CO 81212
1-888-994-6743
www.royalgorgeanglers.com

BEST HOTEL

Pueblo Marriott
110 W. 1st. St.
Pueblo, CO 81003
1-866-460-7440

BEST CAMPGROUND

Arkansas Point Campground
Lake Pueblo State Park
640 Pueblo Reservoir Rd.
Pueblo, CO 81005
719-561-9320
www.parks.state.co.us/parks/lakepueblo

BEST RESTAURANTS

Do Drop Inn
1201 S. Santa Fe Ave.
Pueblo, CO 81006-1040
719-542-0818

Mi Ranchito Mexican Restaurant
2450 U.S. 50 Business
Pueblo, CO 81006
719-583-1098

BEST PLACE TO GET A COLD, STIFF DRINK

Gray's Coors Tavern
515 W. 4th St.
Pueblo, CO, 81003
719-544-0455

CLOSEST EMERGENCY MEDICAL HELP

Parkview Medical Center
400 W 16th St.
Pueblo, CO 81003
719-583-4006

CELL PHONE SERVICE

Yes, along the entire river.

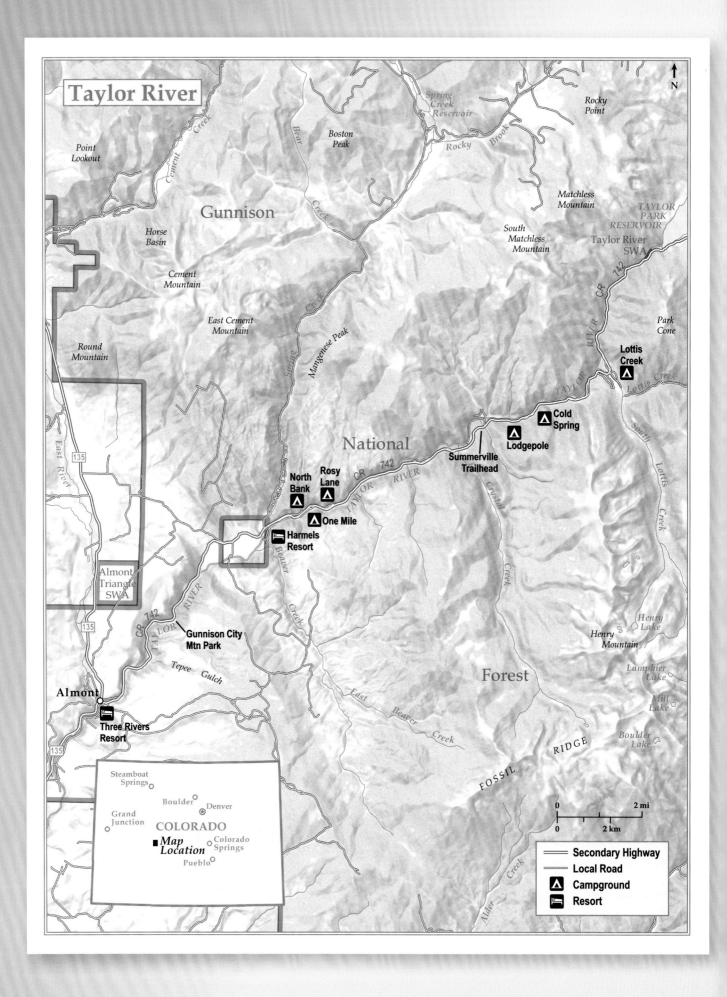

Taylor River

Point Lookout

Cement Creek

Bear Creek

Boston Peak

Spring Creek Reservoir

Rocky Brook

Rocky Point

Gunnison

Horse Basin

Matchless Mountain

TAYLOR PARK RESERVOIR

Cement Mountain

South Matchless Mountain

Taylor River SWA

East Cement Mountain

Spring Creek

CR 742

Park Cone

Round Mountain

Mangenese Peak

Lottis Creek ▲

Lottis Creek

135

East River

National

▲ **Cold Spring**

Rosy Lane ▲

CR 742

TAYLOR RIVER

▲ **Lodgepole**

Summerville Trailhead

North Bank ▲

▲ **One Mile**

Crystal Creek

🛏 **Harmels Resort**

South Lottis Creek

Almont Triangle SWA

CR 742

TAYLOR RIVER

Beaver Creek

Henry Lake

135

Gunnison City Mtn Park

Henry Mountain

Lamphier Lake

Tepee Gulch

Forest

Mill Lake

Almont

East Beaver Creek

🛏 **Three Rivers Resort**

Boulder Lake

RIDGE

FOSSIL

| | 0 | | 2 mi |

| | 0 | | 2 km |

Steamboat Springs

Boulder *Denver*

Grand Junction

COLORADO

■ *Map Location*

Colorado Springs

Pueblo

135

Alder Creek

	Secondary Highway
	Local Road
▲	Campground
🛏	Resort

N ↑

Taylor River *(Southwest Colorado)*

➤ **Location:** Southwestern Colorado, a 4-hour drive from Denver; 3 hours from Colorado Springs; 3 hours from Grand Junction; 45 minutes from Gunnison County Airport.

The Taylor River tailwater begins at its release from Taylor Reservoir and flows 25 miles to the small town of Almont, where it meets the East River to form the Gunnison River. The Taylor Reservoir, at 9,300 feet, was created by the building of the Taylor Dam in 1937. Water is released from the bottom of the reservoir. This release will have varying temperatures throughout the year; winter months 39 to 42 degrees. Due to this variation, the elevation and very cold winter temperatures, the tailwater will be a year-round fishery from the point of release to 5 or 6 miles downstream. Steep canyon walls shade a lot of the river during the winter months, causing snowfields and ice to completely encompass the sections further from the dam, deeming them un-fishable. Mid-March to early November will see the entire 25-mile section become very fishable and productive.

Water releases from Taylor Reservoir fluctuate seasonally and stay consistent throughout. The snowpack runoff dictates release, with a normal year seeing flows coming up by late April to 500–800 cfs, usually stabilizing by late June between 225–375 cfs. September will see a ramping down of flows, with reductions of 50–75 cfs staggered reaching a winter flow of 79–100 cfs for the winter months.

The 25-mile section of the tailwater parallels County Road 742 winding through varying terrain of open ranch meadows to rugged rocky canyon walls. November 2012 saw the completion of major road improvements, making road travel in the narrow canyon much easier and safer, with access to the river painless. The makeup of the tailwater consists of both public and private sections. Traveling upstream from Almont, every few miles you will see a change in status from public to private and back to public. Local maps are a good investment for the fishermen new to the Taylor, as Colorado law prohibits wading into private water.

The tailwater of the Taylor River can be divided into two different sections, with one section fishing differently than the other. Section 1, the public section directly below the out-

put of the reservoir, is a little over ½ mile of water strictly managed for trophy trout. It is a catch-and-release-only area restricted to artificial flies and lures. Access to this area is easy, and angling pressure can be high. This section can be fished year-round and the fish in this section become highly educated, creating challenging angling. The management of this section, combined with the emission of *Mysis* shrimp from the Taylor Reservoir, creates perfect conditions for

The Taylor River is one of the highest-elevation tailwaters and is surrounded by spectacular mountain scenery. Wendy Gunn with fish on. Terry Gunn

browns and rainbows to grow exceptionally large. The section features slow, deep water, where wading is not necessary. Numerous fish will average 4 to 6 pounds, with many opportunities for trout 8 to 10+ pounds.

Water levels and time of year will dictate fishing methods. Generally, nymph fishing with long leaders and light tippets will give you the best chance to hook a monster. Use 10- to 12-foot leaders tapered to 5X or 6X. Many anglers will use a two-fly rig with weight to be adjusted according to the depth of the water. The water is crystal-clear and sight-fishing to the larger fish is an exciting experience. The most productive times seem to be when water levels come up and stay high to relieve the reservoir filling in April-June. Normally high, brown, and valley wide, this section stays clear throughout that period. Fly choices are ever-changing, and creativity is highly suggested. Have numerous flies, and watch the

Above. The gin-clear water on the Taylor lets you pick your target—and this is a target-rich environment. Terry Gunn
Inset. Angler Gary Mitchell prepares to release a Taylor brown trout. Terry Gunn

reaction of the fish to indicate when it's time to change. Flows will come down when the reservoir has maintained its level. Summer crowds will educate fish and productivity can become a little tougher.

Late July and August can be as exciting as fishing gets on this section, with the arrival of the Green Drakes. It is wise to have many different Drake imitations in #10, #12, and #14, and to watch the river for fish that are looking to the surface. Stay with 10- to 12-foot leaders with fluorocarbon tippet to 5X. This is one of the best opportunities to witness enormous fish feed on the surface. Other mayflies will be prevalent, and Parachute Adams as well as Parachute Red Quills in #12, #14, and #16 can be productive. The fall months on this section will see the levels drop and the fish become a bit spookier. Tippets may go to 6X, and Blue-winged Olive hatches can bring medium-size fish to the surface. This is also a great time to strip midges across the current just below the surface, for fish suspended at that depth. You will see many brown trout 12 to 19 inches, as well as the larger fish. Winter flows will normally drop below 100 cfs, and fishing becomes more difficult combined with winter conditions. Fish will congregate in the deepest holes and nymphing will be the best method.

Expect icy winds daily and dress well for winter. Also, expect the guides on the rod to freeze regularly.

The trophy section of the Taylor is bordered on the downstream boundary by a private ranch with a little over 3 miles of private water, accessible only to the ranch owner. Below the ranch is the continuation of 20 miles of the tailwater. This section flows through many different public and private pieces. It also has a steeper gradient, large boulders, and numerous opportunities for great pocket water fishing. The public access areas offer excellent dry-fly and dry-dropper fishing throughout the late spring to late fall. Use 8- to 9-foot leaders for pocket water fishing. High-stick tight-line techniques work well. Caddis hatches in May and June; Green Drakes and Golden Stoneflies during the summer; and Blue-winged Olive hatches in the fall are the insects to target.

Caution: When summer flows are between 200–300 cfs, wading is extremely difficult. Fall water levels will drop and wading access increases dramatically, providing anglers the ability to work every pocket in the river. As you get farther downstream from the release of Taylor Reservoir, expect the fish to consist of browns and rainbows 10 to 14 inches, with many opportunities for fish 15 to 20 inches.

➤ **Hatches:** *Mysis* shrimp patterns #16 to #20; small midges #18 to #22, including RS2s, WD-40s, Black Beauties, Brassies, Pheasant-tails, and the various variations are your go-to choices.

With the arrival of the Green Drakes, late July and August can be as exciting as fishing gets on this section. Other mayflies will be prevalent, and Parachute Adams as well as Parachute Red Quills in #12, #14, and #16 can be productive.

➤ **Fishing regulations:** Section 1: The public section directly below the output of the reservoir is a little over ½ mile of water strictly managed for trophy trout. It is catch-and-release restricted to artificial flies and lures.

Section 2: The remaining public access is not restricted; statewide bag and possession limits apply. In general, these include a daily bag limit of four trout and a maximum of eight trout in possession. In addition, an angler may keep up to 10 brook trout, 8 inches long or less, per day.

➤ **Tackle:** 9-foot, 5-, or 6-weight rod; floating fly lines in neutral colors; 10- to 12-foot leaders tapered to 5X or 6X. Tippet 4X, 5X, and 6X (fluorocarbon preferred).

ROD CESARIO owns and operates Dragonfly Anglers Fly Shop and Guide Service in Crested Butte, Colorado. Rod has been guiding in the Gunnison/Crested Butte region for 25 years.

CLOSEST FLY SHOPS
Dragonfly Anglers
307 Elk Ave.
Crested Butte, CO 81224
(970-349-1228) (800-491-3079)
www.dragonflyanglers.com
rod@dragonflyanglers.com

Willowfly Anglers
130 County Rd. 742
Almont, CO 81210 (970-641-1303)
fish@willowflyanglers.com
www.willowflyanglers.com

Almont Anglers
10209 Hwy 135
Almont, CO 81210 (970-641-7404)
fish@almontanglers.com
www.almontanglers.com

Gunnison River Fly Shop
300 N. Main St.
Gunnison, CO 81230 (970-641-2930)
info@gunnisonriverflyshop.com
www.gunnisonriverflyshop.com

Gene Taylors/High Mountain Drifters
201 W. Tomichi
Gunnison, CO 81230 (970-641-1845)
www.genetaylors.com

CLOSEST OUTFITTERS/GUIDES
Dragonfly Anglers (left)
Willowfly Anglers (left)

CLOSEST LODGES
Harmel's Guest Ranch
6748 County Rd. 742
Almont, CO 81210 (970-641.1740)
stay@harmels.com
www.harmels.com

Three Rivers Resort
130 County Rd. 742
Almont, CO 81210 (970-641-1303)
email@3riversresort.com
www.3riversresort.com

Old Town Inn
708 6th St.
Crested Butte, CO 81224 (970-349-6184)
www.oldtowninn.net

BEST HOTEL
Old Town Inn
708 6th St.
Crested Butte, CO 81224 (970-349-6184)
www.oldtowninn.net

BEST CAMPGROUND
Three Rivers Resort
130 County Rd. 742
Almont, CO 81210 (970-641-1303)
email@3riversresort.com
www.3riversresort.com

BEST RESTAURANT
Soupcon
127 A Elk Ave.
Crested Butte, CO 81224 (970-349-5448)

BEST PLACE TO GET A COLD, STIFF DRINK
Harmel's Guest Ranch
6748 County Rd. 742
Almont, CO 81210 (970-641.1740)
stay@harmels.com
www.harmels.com

CLOSEST EMERGENCY MEDICAL HELP
Gunnison Valley Hospital
711 N. Taylor St.
Gunnison, CO 81230 (970-641-1456)

CELL PHONE SERVICE
Spotty.

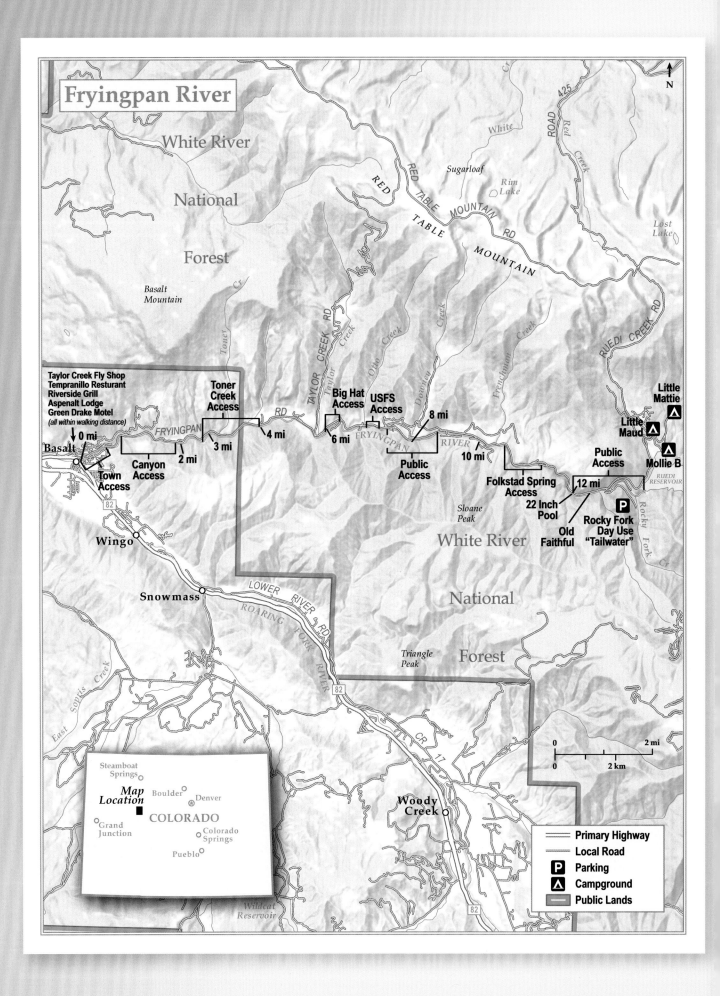

Fryingpan River

White River

National

Forest

Basalt Mountain

White River

National

Forest

Sugarloaf

Rim Lake

Lost Lake

RED TABLE MOUNTAIN

RED TABLE MOUNTAIN RD

ROAD 425

Red Creek

White Cr

RUEDI CREEK RD

Toner Cr

Taylor Creek RD

Taylor Creek

Otto Creek

Dowdy Creek

Frenchman Creek

Little Mattie

Little Maud

Mollie B

RUEDI RESERVOIR

Rocky Fork Cr

Taylor Creek Fly Shop
Tempranillo Resturant
Riverside Grill
Aspenalt Lodge
Green Drake Motel
(all within walking distance)

Toner Creek Access

Big Hat Access

USFS Access

8 mi

Public Access

4 mi

FRYINGPAN RD

3 mi

2 mi

FRYINGPAN   RIVER

10 mi

Folkstad Spring Access

Public Access

12 mi

0 mi

Basalt

Town Access

Canyon Access

Sloane Peak

22 Inch Pool

Old Faithful

Rocky Fork Day Use "Tailwater"

82

Wingo

Snowmass

LOWER RIVER RD

ROARING FORK RIVER

Triangle Peak

White River

National

Forest

East Sopris Creek

82

CR 17

Woody Creek

Map Location

Steamboat Springs

Boulder

Denver

Grand Junction

COLORADO

Colorado Springs

Pueblo

Wildcat Reservoir

82

Scale
0 — 2 mi
0 — 2 km

	Primary Highway
	Local Road
P	Parking
▲	Campground
	Public Lands

Fryingpan River *(West-Central Colorado)*

➤ **Location:** Western Colorado's Roaring Fork Valley, Basalt. Twenty minutes from Aspen, 1½ hours from Vail or Grand Junction, and 3 hours from Denver. Full-service airports are available at all four locations.

The Fryingpan (aka "the Pan") is rich with angling lore. Home to the H&L Variant, popularized by the writings of John Gierach and A.K. Best, this river is certainly Colorado's most noted year-round tailwater. Since the completion of Ruedi Dam in 1968, the introduction of *Mysis* shrimp, fabled mayfly hatches, and trout often measured in pounds rather than inches, the Pan has certainly garnered a reputation among anglers for being a must on the bucket list.

The Fryingpan flows 14 miles from Ruedi Dam downstream to the town of Basalt where it merges into the Roaring Fork River. The Pan is an intimate, medium-sized Western tailwater, offering a variety of angling opportunities 365 days a year. Too small to float, the Pan is known for its ease of wading and readily available public access. The entire 14 miles is designated "Gold Medal" water. Gold Medal is Colorado's defining measure of quality coldwater fisheries and states that, at a minimum, an acre of water must support no less than 60 pounds of trout with at least 12 of these fish being 14 inches or greater. A unique note is that the 14-mile stretch from Ruedi Dam downstream initiates the beginnings of the single-longest continuous stretch of Gold Medal water in the state. This encompasses 14 miles of the Pan and about 28 miles of the Roaring Fork, collectively providing 40-plus miles of unrivaled Colorado angling opportunities.

What's all the fuss about this tailwater? Green Drakes, *Mysis* shrimp, and double-digit fish, to mention a few. Introduced into Ruedi Reservoir, *Mysis* shrimp were originally poised as the primary food source in anticipation of supporting a Kokanee salmon sport fishery, which unfortunately never materialized. However, an unintended benefit was soon realized as these shrimp were being flushed into the river below the dam. The Fryingpan is not a large river—average flows range from 100 cfs to 250 cfs—and all of a sudden fish were growing to grotesquely unimaginable proportions for such a medium-size river. Typical of many Western tail-

waters, the challenges of sight-fishing to large fish with light tippet is certainly exhilarating, even more so when casting to fish weighing 5 pounds, 10 pounds, or larger!

Hatches abound year-round, arguably distinguishing this river as Colorado's finest dry-fly fishery. The Fryingpan is a mayfly-dominant fishery and its legendary Green Drake hatch is known throughout angling circles. Beginning in late July and extending into October, some years this midday hatch is heaviest throughout August and September. Pale Morning Duns of two species (*Ephemerella inermis* and *E. infre-*

Solitude and good company. Angus Drummond

quens) also overlap the drakes during the same months and hours of the day. Anglers can set their timepiece to daily hatches, thus evening hatches are often overlooked on this "banker's hours fishery." Daily PMD hatches produce epic evening Rusty Spinners falls, often beginning an hour or so before last light and continuing into the depths of darkness. Anglers can blindly drift imitations in complete blackness, prying the powers of their inner Zen, to sense the subtle take and a tight line. On opposite ends of drakes and PMDs, the shoulder seasons provide solitude coupled with a bountiful and varied mix of smaller mayflies belonging to spring and fall species of Blue-winged Olives.

Spring hatches of Blue-winged Olives, referred to by many self-appointed entomologists as *Baetis*, begin sporadically in March, but hatches are most prolific in April and May. It is not uncommon to witness a varied mix of Blue-winged

Olive species emerging at the same time. Anglers should be prepared with a varied mix of patterns ranging from #18 to #22 in a spectrum of olive, olive dun, and gray to match the subtle complexities of this hatch. The fall hatches share many of the same nuances as spring BWOs. Fall hatches typically start during late summer, thus it is not uncommon in August, September, and even October to witness BWOs, PMDs, and drakes hatching all at once. Anglers will be forced to distinguish what fish are keyed into during the complexities of the overlapping hatches; however, one could certainly encounter worse angling scenarios. For instance, an angler could turn a corner and witness hordes of fish eagerly rising to *Serratella ignita*.

Serratella or Sara tells us what? The *Serratella* is an intrinsically unique Fryingpan hatch rumored to also occur on the Henry's and South Fork, and possibly only on these three tailwaters! The Fryingpan *Serratella*—a morphed hermaphroditic, flightless Blue-winged Olive—brings lots of trout to the surface, driving even the most arduous and devout dry-fly angler frantic.

In discussion of Fryingpan hatches, it should be noted that due to the elevation and the constant 40-degree water being released 365 days a year from the depths of Ruedi, hatches are often several weeks to a month later on the Pan than on many other fisheries. For example, Drakes, which are expected in July on many Western waters, are almost nonexistent until August on the Pan. The same is true for our spring BWOs. While many anglers would expect heavy BWOs in March, these little critters begin to peak in April and are often heaviest in May; a blessing for many anglers who discover this because much of the West is in peak runoff during May.

Beyond the beautiful red sandstone walls of the Fryingpan Canyon, a plethora of other angling opportunities are close at hand. From small cutthroat-filled creeks, brookie-laden ponds, to the classic Western float fishing on the Fork and Colorado rivers, there's a vast anglers' menu complementing the main course. In addition to all the great fishing, the surrounding communities extending between Aspen, Basalt, Carbondale, and Glenwood Springs host a multitude of year-round activities to accommodate families, romantic escapes, and groups looking to mix or balance their fishing habits with other life responsibilities. There are hot springs, hiking, horseback riding, 10th Mountain Division huts, hunting, skiing, and mountain biking, to mention a few for starters—and yes, of course, one can come and do nothing but fish and possibly sleep and eat between hatches!

➤ **Hatches:** Although the Pan is a mayfly-dominant river; caddis, stoneflies, crane flies, and midges are important depending on time of year. Streamer fishing is very productive through the fall and winter months, and any overcast day can also produce good chases. Bring your fly boxes into local shops to see what you have and what you might be missing.
Stoneflies: April through June.
Blue-winged Olives: mid-March through May; late-September through November.
Pale Morning Duns: mid-June through August.
Green Drakes: July until mid-September.
Caddis: mid-June through mid-October.
Midges: mid-November through mid-April.
Mysis *shrimp:* All year.
Others: Terrestrials July through September.

Fryingpan rainbow colors are so vibrant they appear electric. Kirk Webb

Winter yields stunning scenery, dramatically less fishing pressure, and bigger fish. Kirk Webb

➤ **Fishing regulations:** Fishing 365 days a year; there is no closed season on the Pan. Anglers may keep two brown trout less than 14 inches; all other fish must be released immediately. Rainbows and brown trout are the predominant species, but cutthroat and brook trout are present too.

➤ **Tackle:** Use a 9-foot, 4-weight; a 9-foot, 3-weight for fishing dries is serious fun. Soft- or slow-action 5-weights are suitable as well, however, given the necessity of fishing 6X and 7X throughout much of the year, coupled with large fish, lighter, softer rods protect delicate tippet much better. Many anglers break off large fish when using fast, stiff, 5- or 6-weights with light, delicate tippets. Floating fly lines are standard and are fine for streamer fishing. Fluorocarbon tippets are highly recommended for both nymph and dry-fly fishing.

Drifting to the West to work as a USFS backcountry ranger, WILL SANDS discovered the bountiful waters of the Roaring Fork Valley, and his career path was altered. Since 1999, he has worked at Taylor Creek Fly Shop and plied the waters throughout the valley. Saltwater fishing and wingshooting excursions fill his free time.

CLOSEST FLY SHOPS

Taylor Creek, Basalt
183 Basalt Center Circle
Basalt, CO 81621
970-927-4374
www.taylorcreek.com

Taylor Creek, Aspen
408 E. Cooper St.
Aspen, CO 81611
970-927-4374
www.taylorcreek.com

Alpine Angling
995 Cowen Dr., Suite 102
Carbondale, CO 81623
970-963-9245
www.alpineangling.com

Roaring Fork Anglers
2022 Grand Ave.
Glenwood Springs, CO 81601
970-945-5800
www.froutfitters.com

CLOSEST OUTFITTERS

Aspen Trout Guides
520 E Durant Ave.
Aspen, CO 81611
970-379-7963
www.aspentroutguides.com

Taylor Creek, Basalt (left)
Taylor Creek, Aspen (left)

BEST HOTEL

Aspenalt Lodge
157 Basalt Center Circle
Basalt, CO 81621
877-379-6476
www.aspenalt.com

Green Drake Motel
23286 Two Rivers Rd.
Basalt, CO 81621
970-927-4747

Snowmass Cottages
26801 Highway 82
Snowmass, CO 81654
907-927-5313
www.snowmasscottages.com

BEST CAMPGROUND

Little Maude, Little Maddie
Molly B., Sopris Ranger District
Carbondale, CO 81623
970-927-0107
recreation.gov, search Carbondale

BEST RESTAURANTS

Val's Gourmet
227 Midland Suite 17A
Basalt, CO 81621
970-927-3007
www.valsgourmet.com

Riverside Grill
181 Basalt Center Circle
Basalt, CO 81621
970-927-9301
www.riversidegrillbasalt.com

Brick Pony
202 Midland Ave.
Basalt, CO 81621
970-279-5021

CLOSEST EMERGENCY MEDICAL HELP

Aspen Valley Hospital
0401 Castle Creek Rd.
Aspen, CO 81611
970-925-1120

CELL PHONE SERVICE

Cell phone service is available from Basalt (mile zero) to Mile Marker 4. From Mile Marker 4 upstream, there is no cell service available.

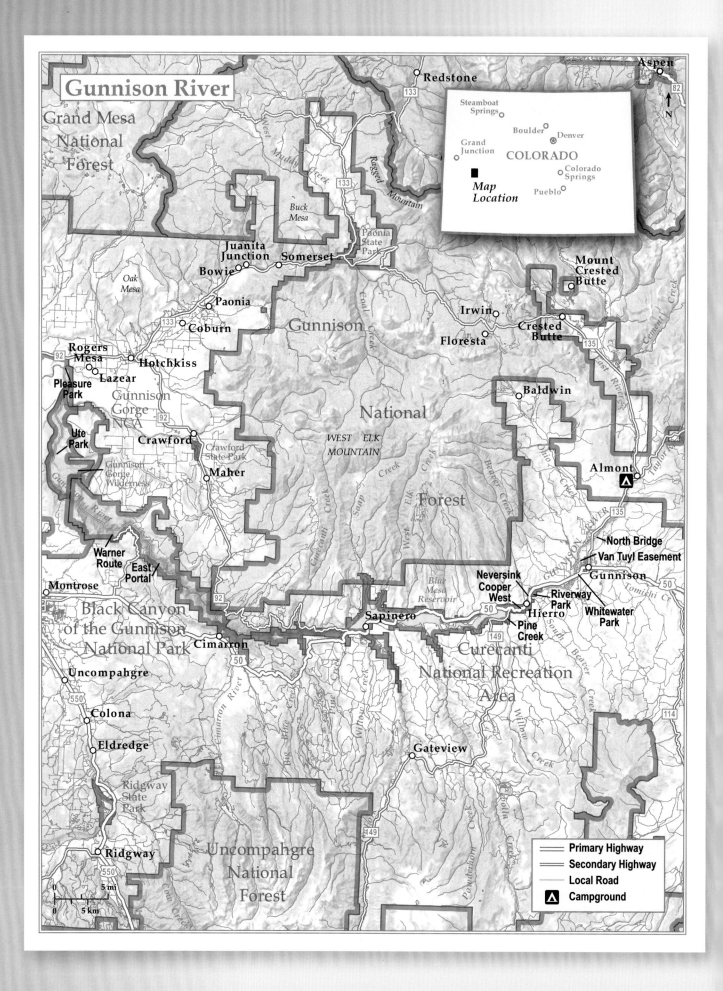

Gunnison River *(South-Central Colorado)*

➤ **Location:** Western Slope, south-central Colorado about a 4-hour drive from Denver, 3 hours from Colorado Springs, and 2 hours from Grand Junction. Gunnison has an airport with service from Dallas and Denver.

The Gunnison River system is one of the more complex in the Western U.S. With three dams and numerous tributaries, it has many types of water and topography to fish. The Gunnison River from Almont to Austin is one of the best trout fisheries in the state. The river has rainbow, brown, and cutthroat trout. It flows through high desert, deep canyons, and a beautiful gorge. The trails and routes that allow access to the more remote sections of the river are difficult at best. Warner Route in the Black Canyon National Park is just over 3 miles long and has a 2,700-foot vertical drop. The river through the national park and gorge is a Gold Medal fishery with special regulations to help the river rebuild the rainbow trout population, decimated by whirling disease in the 1990s.

The Taylor and East Rivers meet in Almont, Colorado, to form the Gunnison. The river then flows south and west past the town of Gunnison to Blue Mesa Reservoir. Below Blue Mesa Dam is Morrow Point Reservoir. There is great fishing below the dam, where the water flows for a short distance before becoming the reservoir. Morrow Point Dam is the second of the three main dams, and there is no access to fishing below it. The third dam on the Gunnison is Crystal Dam. This is the dam with the best access and the best fishing below it. The waters from Crystal Dam first flow into a long, slow pool with a small, low-head "dam" that backs up enough water for some to flow into the Gunnison Tunnel. Water from the Gunnison Tunnel flows into the Uncompahgre Valley. What remains passes over the aforementioned low-head dam and flows through Black Canyon National Park and Gunnison Gorge National Recreation Area before meeting up with the North Fork of the Gunnison, which flows into the arid lands of western Colorado and meets the Colorado River at Grand Junction.

The river once flowed undammed through a great canyon, and boasted some of the best fishing in the world. The famed "willow fly" hatch brought presidents and movie stars to fish its fabled waters. Now, the river lies below three reservoirs, one of which is the largest lake in Colorado. The fishing, while not as famous as is days past, is nonetheless spectacular. Every year, trout over 10 pounds are landed on public water.

Since the entire length of the Gunnison River is influenced by dams, let's begin at the very upstream end and work down to where the water warms and trout fishing diminishes. Fishing in the upper stretch (above Blue Mesa Reservoir) gets going in the early spring. While the air is still cold enough to freeze water in your guides, the fish are looking to feed.

Gunnison River, downstream of Almont. A float trip is the best way to fish the Upper Gunnison above "North Bridge." Oscar Marks

Techniques for early spring let you get your flies deep and detect strikes from sometimes sluggish fish. Deep indicator nymphing or Czech nymphing works best. Flies include big, heavy stonefly nymphs, caddis larvae, and Copper Johns. Egg patterns work on the Gunnison from September through May. A pattern such as a Zebra Midge trailed behind the egg in a three-fly rig can catch the more selective trout.

Runoff may seem, a strange consideration on a tailwater, but the Gunnison is formed by two rivers, only one of which is dam-controlled. During runoff, the river becomes more difficult to fish. Flows are up, and sometimes the color is off. This affects the fish, but not as much as it affects anglers. If you are floating, use extreme caution, as there are several low bridges that cross this stretch of the river. Drift boats and rafts become pinned against structures. I recommend hiring a guide if this is new water to you.

As the weather warms, the fishing only gets better. The hatches on this stretch include Blue-winged Olives, Pale Morning Duns, Green and Gray Drakes, caddisflies, stoneflies, and midges. With the amazing diversity of insect life, the variety of flies that catch fish is nearly endless. A dry-dropper rig is most commonly used. A big stonefly with a caddis pupa dropper is a sure bet most of the spring and summer and into fall.

During the fall, Kokanee salmon run up the Gunnison to Roaring Judy Fish Hatchery on the East River. A 5-weight rod with a beefy nymph drifted through pods of salmon provides great sport during a time when the river has few anglers. Many big trout are on egg patterns caught in and behind pods of salmon.

The stretches below Blue Mesa Dam and Crystal Dam are the more classic tailwaters, at least for a couple of hundred yards below each dam. Pine Creek is the access below Blue Mesa Dam. A short but steep hike down a bunch of steps gets you to the river (really dependent on flows released from Blue Mesa dam) above Morrow Point Reservoir. This is an interesting fishery; when flows are up, the fishing can be incredible, with deep nymphing the most effective way to fish.

Below Crystal Dam, the Gunnison flows through Black Canyon National Park and then through the Gunnison Gorge National Recreation Area. The river just below Crystal Dam is accessed through Black Canyon National Park via East Portal Road. East Portal Road is steep and winding, with a campground and river access at the bottom. This is National Park land and requires entrance and camping fees. The river runs into the depths of the Black Canyon, and access downstream is tricky—in some cases, treacherous. Obtain information regarding access, flows, and fishing techniques at Gunnison River Fly Shop in Gunnison. This is classic tailwater, so bring small flies and skinny tippets.

Below the East Portal Road, canyon access is limited to trails and routes from either the North or South Rim of the park. Backcountry permits are required and are available at all park visitors centers. Do not go in without a permit (they're free) because there are fines for doing so. Trails such as SOB and the Warner Route provide good river access and great fishing, but are extremely difficult at best.

The Gorge stretch of the Gunnison is home to a Salmonfly hatch in early June. The river here really looks like a freestone stream, but the regularity of the flows and temperatures are great for the bugs and abundant fish here. Fall fishing in the Gorge is about as good as fishing can get. Hoppers are everywhere, and big fish key in on them or streamers stripped through holding areas. Late fall brings about the brown trout spawn and the last of the really great fishing of the year.

The top end of Ute Park. Gunnison Gorge National Recreation Area. Oscar Marks

The Gunnison River below "The Painted Wall," Black Canyon of the Gunnison National Park. Oscar Marks

Kokanee salmon are great game during their fall run up the Gunnison River. *Oscar Marks*

Upper Gunnison. Terry Gunn

➤ **Hatches:** Spring: Stonefly nymphs, subsurface caddis, BWOs, midge patterns, and streamers.

Summer: Early mayflies, incredible stonefly hatches throughout summer (Salmonflies in early June), and PMDs. July has a great Green Drake hatch. Caddisflies are on almost every evening in the summer.

Fall: Late stones, BWOs, eggs (both Kokanee salmon and browns spawn in the fall), and streamers.

➤ **Fishing regulations:** Visit wildlife.state.co.us/fishing.

➤ **Tackle:** Use a 9-foot 5-weight for all but the heaviest streamers. Another option is a 10-foot 5-weight—the extra length helps in mending and hook setting. Use heavier tippet than you might think necessary, since some trout are large. Early in the season, waders are a necessity; in the heat of summer, wet wading becomes a good way to access the rivers.

OSCAR MARKS is owner and head guide at Gunnison River Fly Shop on Main St. in Gunnison. He has been an avid fly fisherman for more than 45 years. Oscar can be found on the river most days. When he's not, he can be found at the shop: www.gunnisonriverflyshop.com.

CLOSEST FLY SHOPS

Gunnison River Fly Shop
300 N. Main St.
Gunnison, CO 81230
970-641-2930
www.gunnisonriverflyshop.com

Almont Anglers
10209 Hwy. 135 N.
Almont, CO 81210
970-641-7404

CLOSEST OUTFITTERS/GUIDES

Gunnison River Fly Shop (above)
Almont Anglers (above)

CLOSEST LODGE

Rocky River Resort (cabins on the river)
4359 County Rd. 10
Gunnison, CO 81230
970-641-0174
www.gunnisoncabins.com

BEST HOTEL

Holiday Inn Express
901 E. Tomichi Ave.
Gunnison, CO 81230
970-641-1288
www.hiexpress.com

BEST CAMPGROUND

Mesa RV Resort
36128 U.S. Hwy. 50
Gunnison, CO 81230
970-641-3186
www.mesarvresort.us

BEST RESTAURANT

The Trough
37550 U.S. Hwy. 50
Gunnison, CO 81230
970-641-3724
www.troughrestaurant.com

BEST PLACE TO GET A COLD, STIFF DRINK

The Ol' Miner Steakhouse
139 N. Main St.
Gunnison, CO 81230
970-641-5153
www.olminersteakouse.com

CLOSEST EMERGENCY MEDICAL HELP

Gunnison Valley Hospital
711 N. Taylor St.
Gunnison, CO 81230
970-641-1456

CELL PHONE SERVICE

Verizon and AT&T

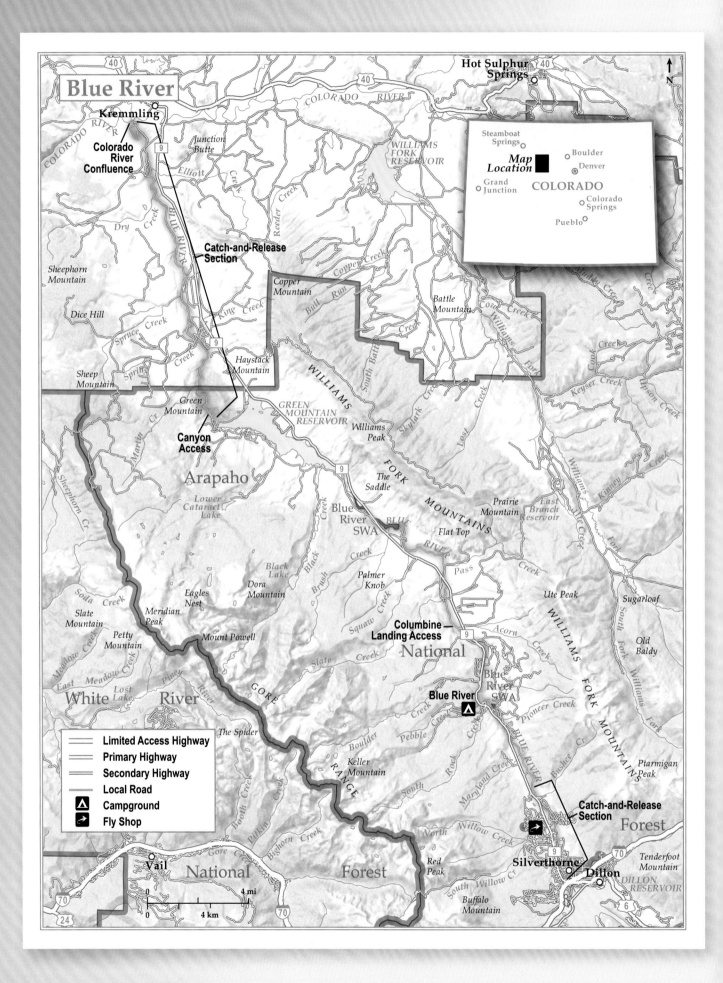

Blue River

Hot Sulphur Springs

Kremmling

Colorado River Confluence

Catch-and-Release Section

Map Location

Steamboat Springs
Boulder
Denver
Grand Junction
COLORADO
Colorado Springs
Pueblo

Junction Butte

Elliott Creek

Reeder Creek

Copper Creek

Dry Creek

Sheephorn Mountain

Copper Mountain

Bull Run

Battle Mountain

Williams Fork

Dice Hill

King Creek

South Battle Creek

Spruce Creek

Spring Creek

Haystack Mountain

Canyon Access

Sheep Mountain

Green Mountain

Williams Peak

GREEN MOUNTAIN RESERVOIR

The Saddle

Prairie Mountain

East Branch Reservoir

Cook Creek

Keyser Creek

Upson Creek

Arapaho

Lower Cataract Lake

Martin Cr.

Flat Top

Pass

Ute Peak

Sugarloaf

Sheephorn Cr.

Soda Creek

Black Lake

Dora Mountain

Black Creek

Brush Creek

Palmer Knob

Blue River SWA

Acorn Creek

Old Baldy

Slate Mountain

Meridian Peak

Eagles Nest

Squaw Creek

Columbine Landing Access

Pioneer Creek

WILLIAMS FORK MOUNTAINS

Petty Mountain

Mount Powell

Slate Creek

National

Ptarmigan Peak

White

East Meadow Creek

Lost Lake

Piney River

River

The Spider

GORE

Boulder Creek

Pebble Creek

Rock Creek

Blue River SWA

Blue River ▲

Bushee Cr.

Legend
- Limited Access Highway
- Primary Highway
- Secondary Highway
- Local Road
- ▲ Campground
- Fly Shop

Keller Mountain

RANGE

Booth Creek

Pitkin Creek

Bighorn Creek

South Willow Creek

North Willow Creek

Catch-and-Release Section

Forest

Vail

National

Forest

Red Peak

South Willow Creek

Buffalo Mountain

Silverthorne

Dillon

Tenderfoot Mountain

DILLON RESERVOIR

0   4 mi

0   4 km

Maryland Creek

➤ **Location:** The mountains of north-central Colorado, in Summit and Grand Counties. It's 75 minutes west of Denver on I-70 to Silverthorne, then south on Colorado Highway 9. Nearest airport is Denver International, about 90 minutes.

This river enjoys two distinct tailwater sections. From below Lake Dillon in Silverthorne to the Green Mountain Reservoir, the river rolls north, starting at about 9,000 feet. The Blue winds its way for about 15 miles before emptying into the lake. The section below Green Mountain Reservoir joins the Colorado River 15 miles downriver, near the town of Kremmling. Both sections hold very large fish, for two distinctly different reasons: On the upriver section, through a 2-mile stretch in the town of Silverthorne, the food source

Blue River near Silverthorne. Charlie Lockwood

from Lake Dillon is the answer. *Mysis* shrimp are continually swept through the dam's outlet, providing a steady high-protein diet for the trout below. (This phenomenon also prevails on the Fryingpan and Taylor Rivers.) Rainbows grow to well over 10 pounds here. On the section below Green Mountain, the story is stocking. The largest landowner has stocked a long segment for a number of years. As you may expect, this has created mixed feelings. Fish to 15 pounds are not uncommon! The river is open year-round to the public for a few miles below both dams. Lower sections begin to freeze over by December. Water temperatures from both dams average in the mid-40s, and warm downstream.

The Blue River flows through a variety of landscapes, all beautiful. As you travel north down the Blue River Valley,

the Gore Range Wilderness Area and its massive peaks tower overhead. Views of mountain formations such as the Sleeping Indian will haunt you for years. The Blue passes through numerous cattle ranches dating from the mid-1800s. In each section, the river winds through a canyon. On the upper reach, the canyon section is the confluence of Boulder Creek, about 7 miles from the dam. On the lower river, the canyon area is directly below the Green Mountain Dam and winds its way for about 3 miles before opening into mostly private ranchland. Both these canyon sections are open to the public, with great angling opportunities. Great riffles, runs, pockets, and every type of water fly anglers crave is available. The Blue has runs of wild browns, but also boasts a large rainbow population. There is a fly-catchable fall run of Kokanee salmon from Green Mountain Reservoir that travel all the way to the dam in Silverthorne to spawn. The Blue is designated a one of Colorado's Gold Medal trout rivers, and rightfully so.

Flows are the key on the Blue River. The minimum stream flow is 50 cfs. During the winter months, as you might expect, flows are quite low on both sections. During an average runoff, flows go up to 1,500 cfs on both sections. However, flows on the lower section can reach 3,000 cfs. Best flows for wading anglers are from 100 to 300 cfs. Of the approximately 30 miles of water, about 15 are publicly accessible for wading. The section from Silverthorne to Green Mountain Reservoir has numerous state wildlife areas and U.S. Forest Service accesses that parallel Colorado Highway 9. These areas are all well signed and most have parking lots. On the lower river, most of the public access is directly below Green Mountain Reservoir.

Some small sections of the upper river are floatable at flows between 400 and 1,200 cfs. Below Green Mountain Reservoir, best flows are 500 cfs and above. Note that in Colorado, the landowners own the river bottom. Therefore, it is illegal to wade, anchor, or even touch the rocks or bottom of the river. Generally, the upper river is not considered a floating river during July and August. Flows on the lower section are usually best from July through September. Most of the floats are up to Class II rapids.

Techniques and flies vary. The most difficult angling is in the Silverthorne area, where there is more pressure. Here, 9-foot, 5-weight rods, 10-foot leaders, 6X fluorocarbon tippets, small midge patterns, and *Mysis* shrimp patterns are standard. Two-nymph rigs with camo split-shot are most effective. During the summer and fall, there are decent hatches of *Baetis*, PMDs, and caddis. In the winter, midge hatches are common between 11 A.M. and 2 P.M. Hopper-dropper and dry-dropper rigs work quite well during prime flows of 100 to 300 cfs. Downriver on the upper stretch, the best fishing is from April through September. The area just above Green Mountain Reservoir fishes very well in April and May. Flies on this section tend to be larger, with similar hatches as the on upper river, as well as Green Drakes, Sallies, and Golden Stones in June. Runoff can affect this section. It remains somewhat clear in average runoff years.

Below Green Mountain Reservoir in the wading section, similar hatches prevail as on the upper river. Deep nymphing with shot and both larger and smaller patterns will produce. Copper Johns, Barr's Emergers, Pheasant-tails, and midge patterns work best. As on most rivers, when the water is high or muddy, worm patterns work well. If you are floating this section—the float is about 14 miles—streamers can work very well. Because of large fish, a 7- or 8-weight rod works best. As for tippet, 0X may not be enough! No outfitters are permitted to float guide any section of the Blue River at this time.

➤ **Hatches:** *Midges:* April through November and into December.

Mysis shrimp: All year, heaviest April through November.
Caddis: A cornucopia of caddis ranging from #10 to #20; June through September.
Blue-winged Olives: April through May; September to early November.
Pale Morning Duns: July and August.
Golden Stoneflies: May and June.
Green Drakes: July and August.
Terrestrials: July into September.

➤ **Fishing regulations:** The 2-mile stretch through the town of Silverthorne and the 15-mile stretch below Green Mountain Reservoir to the confluence of the Colorado River are catch-and-release only, artificial flies and lures only. All other sections of the upper river: two fish, 16 inches or longer.

➤ **Tackle:** Bring 4- to 6-weight, 8½- or 9-foot rods. Use 7- or 8-weight rods for floating below Green Mountain reservoir. Use 8- to 10-foot, 0X to 6X leaders, depending on location and flies. Methods include dry-fly, dry-dropper, indicator nymphing, and streamer fishing. Wet wading is not recommended due to the cold water. Cleats work best—the Blue River can be very slippery.

Inset. Blue River above Green Mountain Reservoir. Scott Gongaware
Below. Scenic backdrop on the Blue

Blue River below Green Mountain Reservoir. Jackson Streit

JACKSON STREIT moved to Colorado from New York in 1973. He has owned and operated Mountain Angler in Breckenridge since 1985. Jackson started the first guide business in the area in 1977. He is the author of *Fly Fishing Colorado: A No Nonsense Guide to Top Waters*. Besides fishing and guiding his local Colorado rivers, Jackson travels to the great waters of New Zealand, Argentina, Christmas Island, and the flats of Mexico.

CLOSEST FLY SHOPS

Mountain Angler
311 S. Main St.
Breckenridge, CO 80424
970-453-4665
www.mountainangler.com

Breckenridge Outfitters
101 N. Main St.
Breckenridge, CO 80424
970-453-4135
www.breckenridgeoutfitters.com

Cutthroat Anglers
400 Blue River Pkwy.
Silverthorne, CO 80498
970-262-2878
www.fishcolorado.com

CLOSEST AND BEST HOTELS
Numerous in Silverthorne,
including *Day's Inn* and *La Quinta*.

CLOSEST AND BEST CAMPGROUND
Blue River Campground, about 5 miles north of Silverthorne on the Blue.

CLOSEST AND BEST RESTAURANTS

Chipotle
247 Rainbow Ave.
Silverthorne, CO 80498
970-468-0671

Red Mountain Grill
703 E. Anemone Trail
Dillon, CO 80435
970-468-1010

BEST PLACE TO GET A COLD, STIFF DRINK

Murphy's Irish Pub
501 Blue River Pkwy.
Silverthorne, CO 80498
970-468-2457

Red Mountain Grill (above)

CLOSEST EMERGENCY MEDICAL HELP
St. Anthony Summit Medical Center – Summit County Hospital
340 Peak One Dr.
Frisco, CO 80443
970-668-3300

WIRELESS SERVICE
None on most sections below Silverthorne.

CELL PHONE SERVICE
There is cell coverage; some carriers work better than others.

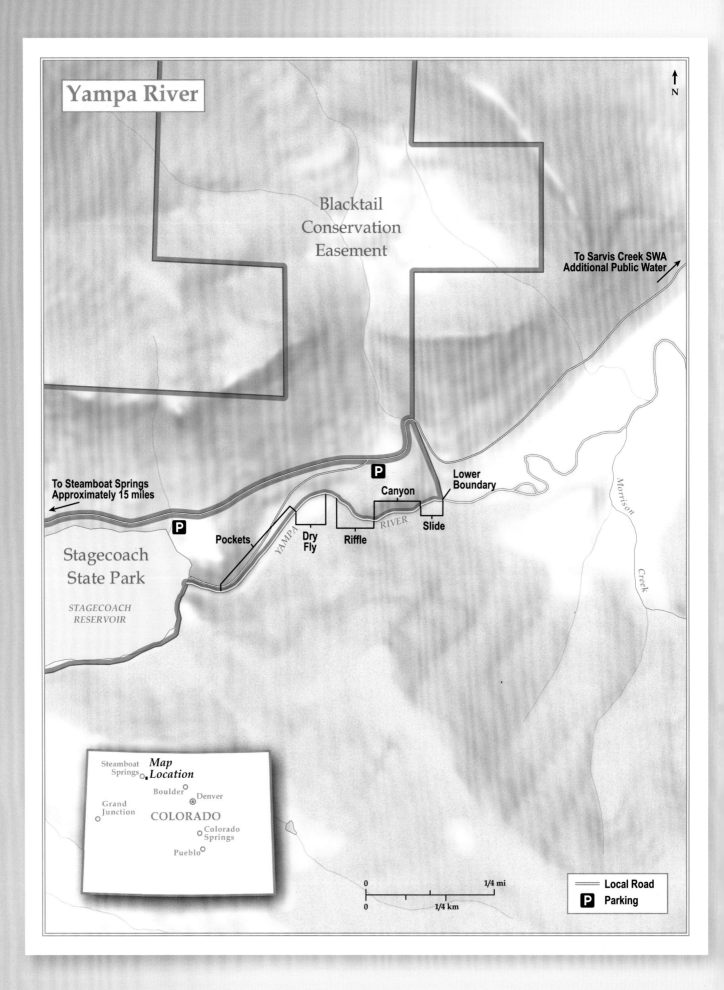

Yampa River

Blacktail
Conservation
Easement

To Sarvis Creek SWA
Additional Public Water

P

Canyon

Lower
Boundary

To Steamboat Springs
Approximately 15 miles

P

Pockets

Dry
Fly

Riffle

RIVER

Slide

Morrison

Creek

YAMPA

Stagecoach
State Park

STAGECOACH
RESERVOIR

Steamboat
Springs

Map
Location

Boulder

Denver

Grand
Junction

COLORADO

Colorado
Springs

Pueblo

0   1/4 mi

0   1/4 km

Local Road

P   Parking

➤ **Location:** About 180 miles northwest of Denver International Airport.

The Yampa River below Stagecoach Reservoir is an intimate tailwater, full of character and intrigue. Despite offering less than ¾ mile of public access, this tailwater will challenge and frustrate even veteran anglers.

The Yampa River starts in the Flattops Wilderness Area near the town of Yampa, Colorado, about 40 miles south of Steamboat Springs. At its headwaters, the river is called the Bear River; as it flows from south to north and meets up with Chimney Creek, the river changes names to the Yampa River, and continues its northward journey. The river empties into Stagecoach Reservoir, 15 miles South of Steamboat Springs, near the town of Oak Creek. The reservoir itself offers anglers good opportunities to catch trout and northern pike, which are a kick in the pants for fly anglers to pursue with a 7- or 8-weight rod. However, the true gem of the state park for anglers is found below the dam, in the tailwater section.

Gin-clear water; Volkswagen Beetle–size boulders; deep, narrow runs pouring into long, mellow riffles—these are some of the ingredients that create fun, fishy rivers. Anglers will find all these features and more when exploring the tailwater below Stagecoach Reservoir. The river ranges in width from 15 to 50 feet, and in depth from inches to several yards. It feels designed for wading anglers. What make this tailwater so special are the variety of techniques anglers can incorporate to catch these big Rocky Mountain trout. For anglers who love streamer fishing, the lower reaches of the public section offer ideal features to swing streamers. Those anglers who have embraced European-style nymphing will find plenty of spots where those extra 12 to 18 inches of rod length are necessary. But anglers who find joy in punishing themselves with #26 and #28 midges, tied on 7X and even 8X tippet, often produce the best days for numbers of fish. These folks are easily identifiable; you'll see them with magnifiers on their hat brims, or bifocal sunglasses draped around their necks. You'll find an appropriate spot at the Stagecoach tailwater for whatever angling technique turns you on.

This tailwater remains open and fishable year-round, and the winter months are often the most productive. The main access road, County Road 18 on the north side of the reservoir, is closed to motorized traffic from January 1 through March 31, as it lies in an elk migratory range. However, the access road must remain plowed through the winter months for the dam service trucks to have access to the dam. So,

Paul Russell approaching the Yampa River below Stagecoach Reservoir. Jim Henderson

while access is slightly trickier, the winter months are often the most exciting, because the fishing pressure is limited. Anglers can walk, bike, or ski into the tailwater and often have the whole public section to themselves. For groups of anglers and non-anglers looking for a great trip in the wintertime, this is a great opportunity to combine a few activities to keep everyone happy during a trip to Steamboat Springs.

From a fly selection point of view, midges are the most consistent year-round patterns. Anglers should ensure they have a good selection of tungsten Zebra Midges, WD-40s, RS2s, Buckskins, and Mercury Midges, in various colors and sizes. This is a part of the Yampa River where tippet size is critical; 6X and smaller tippets are vital for catching good numbers of fish. A 5-weight rod is the right rod, although many folks do well with a favorite 3- or 4-weight rod. Because of the stacked pour-over features, being able to quickly steer and land a big fish becomes vital, as many fish are lost

Some happy anglers on the Yampa River below Stagecoach Reservoir. Jim Henderson

by anglers unable to keep them in the pool in which they were caught. For that reason alone, I recommend having a heavy enough rod to land these big fish quickly and safely.

In addition to midges, the *Baetis* hatch picks up as the temperatures begin to increase in early spring. Blue-winged Olive dries and emergers become very effective, and this is often some of the best dry-fly fishing of the year. Stonefly nymphs and dries are particularly dangerous in the spring and fall; Golden Micro Stones, Girdle Bugs, and Yellow Sallies are some of my favorites. The caddis show themselves in mid- to late summer, and Elk-hair Caddis and slickwater caddis imitations are staples in the fly box. Fall brings on good terrestrial activity, with ants, crickets, and hoppers working well along the banks. Folks who enjoy fly tying will adore spending time at the tailwater below Stagecoach, as it is a great place to study the insect life. In many respects, it is a perfect example of a "student's river." The more time an angler puts into learning how the fish feed, on what they feed, and how they react to food in the feeding lanes, the more fish that angler will catch.

Any fishing trip to Steamboat Springs or northwest Colorado would not be complete without spending a few days at the tailwater below Stagecoach Reservoir. The combination of natural beauty, challenging water, and world-class quarry makes this section of the Yampa River a must for the wading angler. While I haven't fished all the other tailwaters mentioned in this book, I feel very confident that the Yampa more than deserves its place here.

➤ **Hatches:** *Midges and scuds:* throughout the year. *Blue-winged Olives:* throughout the spring. *Stoneflies:* in the spring and continuing through the fall. *Caddis:* mid- to late summer. *Terrestrials:* late summer through the fall.

➤ **Fishing regulations:** Open year-round, however the main access road is closed to motorized traffic from January 1–

Beautiful rainbow on the Yampa River below Stagecoach Reservoir. Jim Henderson

March 31, when access is by foot, ski, or bike. This section is designated as catch-and-release, flies and lures only. Anglers must have a valid Colorado fishing license and a state parks pass for that day, or an annual pass.

➤ **Tackle:** Bring a 4- or 5-weight rod, floating fly line, 6X or smaller tippet (fluorocarbon if you use it), small split-shot if needed, small indicator, or high-stick tackle. Studded rubber wading boots are a must.

Author Tim Kirkpatrick with a bonefish in Los Roques, Venezuela.

Paul Russell with a nice Stagecoach Tailwater fish! Steamboat Flyfisher

TIM KIRKPATRICK grew up in Denver, but spent most of his summers at his family's ranch in Yampa, Colorado. Tim has owned Steamboat Flyfisher since April, 2005. When not in Steamboat, Tim prefers to be on the flats, chasing bonefish.

CLOSEST FLY SHOPS
Steamboat Flyfisher
35 5th St.
Steamboat Springs, CO 80487
970-879-6552
info@steamboatflyfisher.com
www.steamboatflyfisher.com

Bucking Rainbow Outfitters
730 Lincoln Ave.
Steamboat Springs, CO 80487
970-879-8747
john@buckingrainbow.com
www.buckingrainbow.com

Straightline Sports
744 Lincoln Ave.
Steamboat Springs, CO 80487
970-879-7568
FlyFishing@straightlinesports.com
www.straightlinesports.com

CLOSEST OUTFITTERS/GUIDES
Steamboat Flyfisher (above)

Bucking Rainbow Outfitters (above)

Straightline Sports (above)

BEST HOTEL
Rabbit Ears Motel
201 Lincoln Ave.
Steamboat Springs, CO, 80487
970-879-1150
info@rabbitearsmotel.com
www.rabbitearsmotel.com

BEST CAMPGROUND
Stagecoach State Park
Oak Creek, CO 80467
970-736-2436
www.parks.state.co.us
search for Stagecoach

BEST RESTAURANT
Mahogany Ridge Bar and Grill
435 Lincoln Ave.
Steamboat Springs, CO 80487
970-879-3773
www.mahoganyridgesteamboat.com

BEST PLACE TO GET A COLD, STIFF DRINK
Mahogany Ridge Bar and Grill (below left)

CLOSEST EMERGENCY MEDICAL HELP
Yampa Valley Medical Center
1024 Central Park Dr.
Steamboat Springs, CO 80487
970-879-1322

CELL PHONE SERVICE
Cell phones work on CO 131 and U.S. 40, but not at the tailwater because of the sheer canyon walls.

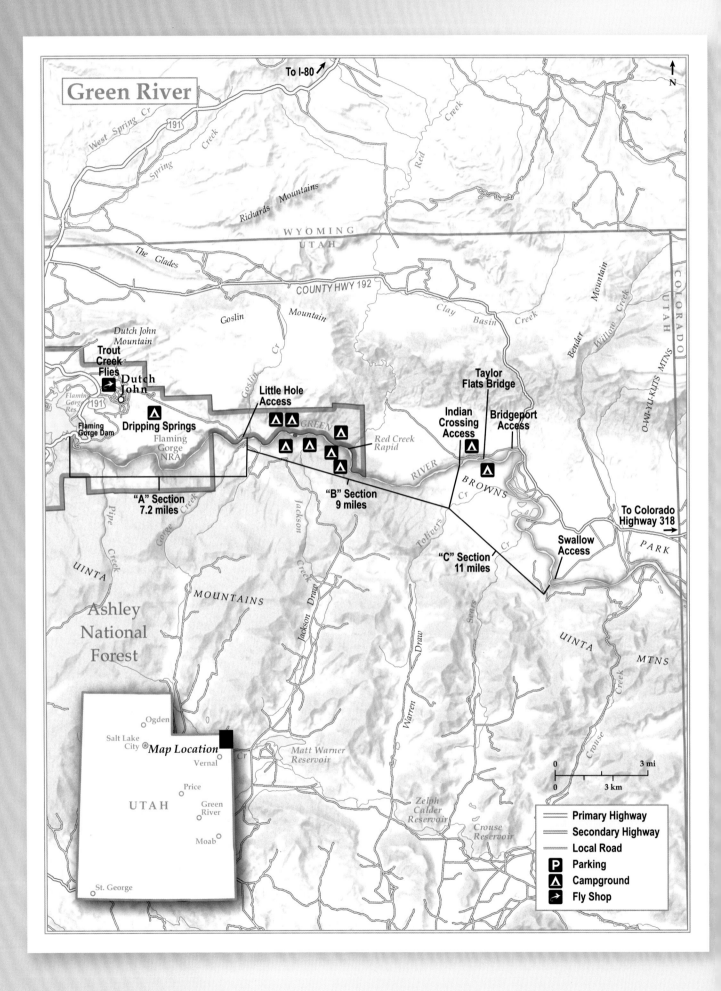

Green River

To I-80 ↗

N

West Spring Cr

191

Spring Creek

Red Creek

Richards Mountains

WYOMING
UTAH

The Glades

COUNTY HWY 192

Clay Basin Creek

Bender Mountain

Willow Creek

COLORADO
UTAH

Goslin Mountain

Goslin Cr

UINTA MTNS

Dutch John Mountain

Trout Creek Flies

Dutch John

Flaming Gorge Res

191

Taylor Flats Bridge

Little Hole Access

Indian Crossing Access

Bridgeport Access

Dripping Springs

GREEN

Red Creek Rapid

Flaming Gorge Dam

Flaming Gorge NRA

RIVER

BROWNS

Cr

"A" Section
7.2 miles

"B" Section
9 miles

To Colorado
Highway 318 →

Pipe Creek

Gorge Creek

Jackson Creek

Tolivers Cr

Swallow Access

PARK

UINTA

"C" Section
11 miles

Ashley
National
Forest

MOUNTAINS

Jackson Draw

Warren Draw

Seans Draw

UINTA MTNS

Crouse Creek

Ogden

Salt Lake City ◉

Map Location

Cr

Matt Warner Reservoir

Vernal

Price

Green River

UTAH

Zelph Calder Reservoir

Crouse Reservoir

Moab

St. George

0   3 mi

0   3 km

Primary Highway
Secondary Highway
Local Road
🅿 **Parking**
⛺ **Campground**
➤ **Fly Shop**

➤ **Location:** Northeast corner of Utah near Wyoming and Colorado borders, about a 3½-hour drive from Salt Lake City. Take U.S. 191 south off I-80 just west of Rock Springs, Wyoming. You can also take 191 north out of Vernal, Utah. Commuter flight service and car rentals are available at both towns.

The Green River tailwater below Flaming Gorge Dam is 27 miles of trout-fishing paradise. The impressive Red Canyon is formed by the river carving its way through the north side of the Uinta Mountain range, where it meets with the high Red Desert. This is Flaming Gorge country. The Green has it all: gin-clear water, aquatic vegetation, huge boulders in the river, and steep canyon walls. One of the things that helps make the Green River such a unique trout fishery is controlled water temperature. The dam was retrofitted with a set of penstocks to blend warmer water closer to the surface with water from the bottom to supply an optimal 55- to 60-degree water release temperature for the trout fishery. This has helped maintain a diversified aquatic plant and insect population not seen on many tailwaters. The river supports an incredible number of trout per mile, with estimates upwards of 16,000 to 20,000 fish. This is for the upper canyon, with an average size being 14 to 17 inches, with many fish over 20. The number estimate of trout is somewhat smaller downriver, but in the 2012 season, sizes grew the farther downstream you went. Included in all of this is the variety and color of the trout. Different strains of browns, rainbows, and cuttbows inhabit the river. There are not the numbers of cutthroat left, but mixing with the rainbows has supplied the river with an abundance of beautiful, varied-color cutthroat/rainbow hybrids.

The Green is a somewhat large and intimidating river at higher flows. During low flows, however, the river can be very wader-friendly. The lowest flows are around 800 cfs. At this rate, parts of the river can be crossed—with care! Almost everyone tries to avoid the high flows, which generally occur in mid-May through mid-June. One real problem is that most anglers fish close to the access points. During the high-use times of the year, this means either a long hike or floating to get a little solitude.

In order to understand the river better, let's talk about the three sections into which it is divided:

The A section starts below the dam and runs 7.2 miles through what is considered the Red Canyon, and ends at Little Hole. On the north side of the canyon is a trail that runs the entire length of this section. This trail is accessible from parking lots at either end. The river at the bottom end of this section at Little Hole has the most wader-friendly water. The

Dead Man's Rapid in the A Section.

river canyon is more open here and has much shallower riffle/pocket-type water, while the top end of the canyon closer to the dam has deeper pools and large backeddies. Accessing fish in some of these hard-to-reach, deep pools is next to impossible. This is why most anglers prefer to float. The Green may not always run clear. Most years the runoff coming in above the dam at Cart Creek and 1 mile down in the canyon from Pipe Creek can muddy the water a little, although don't panic as the river is still fishable. There is no camping allowed on the A section of the river; day use only!

B section begins at Little Hole and ends 9 miles downriver at the top of Brown's Park at Indian Crossing. It is more open than the upper canyon, hence it is shallower for better wading. There is a rough trail on the north side of the river here also, extending about 3 miles downriver and ending at Trails End campsite. The B section can muddy up from runoff, as numerous creeks join the river around Little Hole. Red Creek enters the river 5 miles downstream of Little Hole, and this can present problems with the river muddying up (or blowing out!) from runoff or severe rains. This can occur often, so plan accordingly if you want a B- or C-section camp or float. Below Red Creek in 2012, many floaters noticed the opportunity to catch very large fish. I personally had numerous clients boat fish in the 20- to 25-inch range. B section has campsites located along the river, accessible only by hiking or floating. There is no vehicle access. Camping is allowed only in designated sites.

C section starts at Indian Crossing and ends 11 miles downriver at Swallow Canyon takeout. There are many different put-in/takeout spots in this section, and access is much easier since Brown's Park Road parallels it. If Red Creek blows out, C section can be unfishable. Also, one of the problems with C section is the warming of the water during low-flow years. This can make it difficult to move larger trout in late summer. There are two large campsites at the top of C section—Taylor Flats Bridge and Indian Crossing.

For nymphing, scuds, San Juan Worms, and egg patterns are all effective. On cloudy days, streamers also produce well. But the real fun is casting dry flies to imitate the many types of terrestrials that inhabit the river corridor. The Green has such a variety of trees and vegetation along its banks that it hosts an amazing list of land-based insects: cicadas, crickets, ants, beetles, and grasshoppers. Most guides recommend a terrestrial dry fly like a Chernobyl Ant (invented on the Green) with a Tungsten Zebra Midge dropper when the weather starts to warm. Midge and Blue-winged Olive mayfly hatches starting as early as January are two of the best aquatic hatches in late winter/early spring. Little Winter Stoneflies and large Golden Stones round out the spring hatches. Some of the best aquatic bug hatches are Yellow Sally stoneflies and Pale Morning Dun mayflies, usually starting at the end of June or beginning of July. Fishing Boomer's

Tungsten PMD/Sally Nymph can be productive during this time. August presents Tricos along with the appearance of a new bug—a bright, fluorescent green midge. Caddis can also be important, with hatches starting in June. Large October Caddis in the fall end a fun season of hatches. However, we are not finished fishing, as the fall spawning season can be amazing some years.

➤ Hatches: *Midges:* All year, with peak months January through May and then October through December.
Baetis: mid-February through mid-June and September and October; prime time mid-April to mid-May.
Yellow Sallies: Mid-June to mid-August, with prime time the month of July.
Caddis: May through October; prime time beginning mid-June.
Scuds: All year, with prime months mid-April through August.
Small cicadas: mid-April through mid-July; prime time beginning mid-June.
Mega cicadas: mid-May to mid-August; prime time beginning mid-June.
Ants, field crickets, hoppers, and beetles: mid-May through September, depending on the usual variables of temperatures.

➤ Fishing regulations: Open to fishing all year. Creel limit: two fish under 15 inches, one fish over 22 inches. Artificial flies and lures only. No bait. No scents. No motors of any kind, including electric. No single-chamber float tubes allowed. Pontoon boats allowed. All boats must carry a spare oar and a bailing device. Boats over 16 feet must carry a throw bag.

A Section: Life jackets must be worn at all times while floating.

B Section: Life jackets must be worn from Little Hole to Red Creek camp. Below Red Creek Camp to Indian Crossing, life jackets are not required except for children under 12.

C Section: Life jackets must be worn from Indian Crossing to 100 yards past Taylor Flats Bridge. After that they may be removed.

➤ Tackle: Bring a 9-foot, 5- or 6-weight rod. Anglers preferring smaller dry flies should use a 9-foot 4-weight for midges, Blue-winged Olives, or ants. A 7-weight rod with a sink tip is recommended for streamers—very large streamers can be very productive on cloudy days or in muddy water. Leaders: Use 9-foot 4X or 5X for spring, going to 9-foot 2X or 3X for large summer terrestrials. Waders are useful, but in midsummer can be a little too hot for comfort. Don't wear boots with cleats when floating in a guide's boat.

Dramatic cliffs in the Red Canyon, A Section, Green River. Carl "Boomer" Stout

Gee . . . why do they call this the Green River? Emmett Heath

Below. Beautiful hybrid caught in November.

CARL "BOOMER" STOUT, head guide for Trout Creek Flies since 1998, started guiding in Colorado in 1986. Boomer also guided in Alaska for four years. Boomer has become a master fly tier, designing many patterns for Alaska and more for the Green River. He is currently a royalty tier/designer for Umpqua Feather Merchants.

CLOSEST FLY SHOPS
Trout Creek Flies/Green River Outfitters
Corner U.S. Highway 191 and
Little Hole Road
Dutch John, UT 84023
435-885-3355 or 800-835-4551
www.fishutahsgreenriver.com

Western Rivers Flyfisher
1071 East 900 South
Salt Lake City, UT 84105
801-521-6424
www.wrflyfisher.com

Fish Tec Outfitters
6153 Highland Dr.
Salt Lake City, UT 84121
801-272-8808
www.fishtecoutfitters.com

Trout Bum 2
4343 Utah 224
Park City, UT 84098
435-658-1166
www.troutbum2.com

Four Seasons Fly Fishers
44 West 100 South
Heber City, UT 84032
800-498-5440
www.utahflyfish.com

Flaming Gorge Resort
1100 Flaming Gorge Meadows
Dutch John, UT 84023
435-889-3773
www.flaminggorgeresort.com

CLOSEST OUTFITTERS/GUIDES
Trout Creek Flies/Green River Outfitters (left)
Western Rivers Flyfisher (left)
Flaming Gorge Resort (above)

CLOSEST LODGES
Red Canyon Lodge
2450 W. Red Canyon Lodge
Dutch John, UT 84023
435-889-3759
www.redcanyonlodge.com

Flaming Gorge Resort (above)
Trout Creek Flies (above)

BEST HOTEL
Flaming Gorge Café & Motel
18 E. Hwy 43
Manila, UT 84046
435-784-3088
www.fgmotel.com

BEST CAMPGROUND
Mustang Ridge Campground
Ashley National Forest
www.fs.usda.gov/ashley

BEST RESTAURANT
Red Canyon Lodge (left)

BEST PLACE TO GET A COLD, STIFF DRINK
The Snag at Cedar Springs Marina
Flaming Gorge, UT
435-889-3795
cedarspringsmarina.com

CLOSEST EMERGENCY MEDICAL HELP
Ashley Valley Medical Center
151 West 200 North
Vernal, UT
435-789-3342

CELL PHONE SERVICE
Very intermittent.

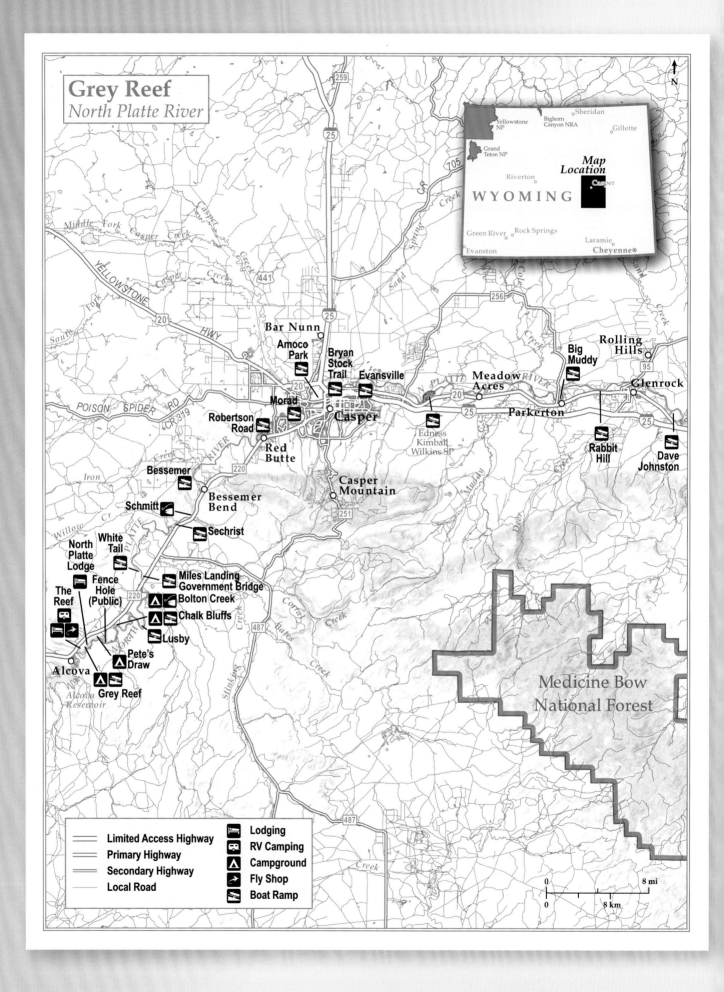

Grey Reef
North Platte River

WYOMING
Map Location

Yellowstone NP
Bighorn Canyon NRA
Sheridan
Gillette
Grand Teton NP
Riverton
Casper
Green River
Rock Springs
Evanston
Laramie
Cheyenne

N

Bar Nunn
Amoco Park
Bryan Stock Trail
Evansville
Morad
Casper
Meadow Acres
Big Muddy
Rolling Hills
Glenrock
Robertson Road
Red Butte
Parkerton
Rabbit Hill
Dave Johnston
Edness Kimball Wilkins SP
Bessemer
Casper Mountain
Bessemer Bend
Schmitt
Sechrist
White Tail
North Platte Lodge
Miles Landing
Government Bridge
Bolton Creek
Fence Hole (Public)
The Reef
Chalk Bluffs
Lusby
Pete's Draw
Alcova
Grey Reef
Alcova Reservoir

Medicine Bow National Forest

YELLOWSTONE HWY
POISON SPIDER RD
CR 319
CR 441
CR 259
CR 705
CR 256
CR 95

Middle Fork Casper Creek
South Fork
Casper Creek
Sand Creek
Spring Creek
N PLATTE RIVER
MUDDY
Willow Cr
Iron Cr
Corral Creek
Bates Creek
Stinking Creek

Legend

Limited Access Highway	Lodging
Primary Highway	RV Camping
Secondary Highway	Campground
Local Road	Fly Shop
	Boat Ramp

0   8 mi
0   8 km

➤ **Location:** The Grey Reef section of the North Platte River originates in central Wyoming near Alcova, about 25 miles southwest of Casper. Grey Reef is a 4-hour drive from Denver and 5½ hours from Salt Lake City. Casper is served by flights from major airlines in Denver and Salt Lake City.

Although the most popular sections of Grey Reef are in the upper 13 miles, there are actually 83 miles of highly productive trout water in the Grey Reef system. The upper 13 miles maintain good water quality through the brief spring runoff; the entire stretch fishes well during the rest of the year. Grey Reef produces year-round, as it's ultra-insulated from runoff by five reservoirs tightly spaced upstream. Grey Reef Dam was completed in 1961 and has performed its duty as an afterbay to Alcova Reservoir ever since. Prior to the Grey Reef Dam, the North Platte River below Alcova Dam was subject to wild changes in daily flow due to electricity demands. Now, the flows are consistent and increase or decrease only with seasonal demand. The river intersects classic Western sagebrush prairie and is flanked by a variety of landscapes, including rolling hills, mountains, and cottonwood bottoms.

The North Platte originates in northern Colorado just across the Continental Divide from major tributaries of the Colorado River system. It relies on snowpack from the mountains of the Routt National Forest in northern Colorado and the Snowy and Sierra Madre Ranges in the Medicine Bow National Forest of southern Wyoming. The river flows north out of Colorado to Casper, where it turns east and joins the Missouri River in Nebraska. Grey Reef was historically a warmwater environment, but the construction of several dams—most importantly Grey Reef Dam—gave rise to a spectacular coldwater fishery. The lower North Platte was stocked with trout in the 1980s, and Grey Reef was first stocked the spring following the dam's completion. The lower sections are still stocked today. The upper 8 miles from Grey Reef Dam to the Lusby Access are a "trophy fishery," where natural reproduction is the only source of trout recruitment. The Wyoming Game & Fish Department and the U.S. Bureau of Reclamation have instituted a flushing flow program for Grey Reef. For 5 days each spring (and sometimes in the fall) the flows from the dam are dramatically in-creased and systematically decreased to purge the spawning gravel of silt that might otherwise inhibit survival of trout eggs. Since 1996, the flushing flow program has helped create a venue for excellent natural reproduction on the entirety of Grey Reef.

Wyoming shares the same stream access laws as Colorado. The river bottom belongs to the landowner, thus there is no public access between the ordinary high-water marks on private property. Much of the Grey Reef System flows over private land, limiting fishing access to remain in the boat without anchoring, beaching, or wading. However, there are

Grey Cliffs. Trent Tatum

many public fishing accesses along the entire reach, allowing for miles of excellent wade fishing and solitude. Many public access sites have boat ramps that give the Grey Reef angler many combinations of floats of varying lengths. The lower North Platte River is easy to navigate, with the exception of the winds, which can create difficulties for inexperienced rowers. Rental drift boats and river shuttle services are available at The Reef Fly Shop.

Trout populations average 3,000 fish per mile, with 90 percent rainbows and 10 percent browns and Snake River cutthroat. Grey Reef is renowned for the large average size of its trout and the massive size of its trophy-class trout. The average rainbow is 16 to 17 inches, while a trophy is generally regarded as starting at 25 inches and up. Trophy fish can weigh from 6 to 15 pounds and more. Nymphing is the

A beautiful evening on upper Grey Reef. Trent Tatum

A closeup view of a Grey Reef 'bow. Trent Tatum

primary mode of fishing during all seasons and water levels. A long leader of 9 to 12 feet, and heavy weight can be used with great success, but a short, 3- to 6-foot leader with light weight will target trout actively feeding on emergers. Tippets of 3X to 5X are appropriate, depending on the hatch, flies, and water conditions. Streamers can be tethered to a sink-tip line with a 4-foot leader, or a floating line with 7 to 9 feet of leader. Dry flies are best presented with 4X or 6X tippet and a leader of at least 8 feet.

The trout at Grey Reef are generally oriented toward the deeper troughs in the middle of the river, as Grey Reef has little edge structure, especially at lower flows. You'll typically find greater success by placing your boat close to the bank and fishing out toward the runs, troughs, and tailouts rather than fishing along the banks. The same is true for wading. The exception would be in high-water conditions, when the depth becomes conducive for trout to forage and seek refuge along the banks. Aquatic life in Grey Reef is abundant, and scuds, midges, leeches, worms, and crayfish are always available. Spring is generally regarded as prime time, but Grey Reef fishes well all year. Spring features a healthy *Baetis* hatch, which presents great emerger-style nymphing, some dry-fly opportunities, and even some effective streamer options. As the *Baetis* hatch wanes in mid- to late May, the Pale Morning Duns, caddis, and Little Yellow Sallies make their appearance. Nymphing remains king during these hatches, but dry-fly fishing, while isolated, can be excellent. Tricos are present in mid- to late July, and offer by far Grey Reef's most productive and predictable dry-fly opportunities.

Tricos will be a force nearly every morning until mid- to late September. Caddis are an important source of food throughout the summer and fall, with nymphing primarily in the afternoon and switching to dry flies near dusk. Streamer fishing also gains steam during the summer as fry and crayfish become more available for trout forage. Hopper fishing can be excellent from late July to mid-September, but this is not a predictable phenomenon. September welcomes temperate weather conditions and the forgotten *Pseudo* hatch. The *Pseudos* normally hatch in early afternoon, and the trout will snug themselves into shallow, tight riffles to snack on the emergers. However, they will soon orient themselves to take the duns off of the surface until early evening. Late September to early October will usher in the fall *Baetis* hatch, where light nymph rigs and dry flies are effective. Fall is streamer time on Grey Reef. Targeting a trophy trout with a sink-tip and a short leader or a floating line and a longer leader can be heart-pounding. After the fall *Baetis* have disappeared, prolific midge hatches will offer nymphing and dry-fly fishing throughout the winter, while solid streamer fishing remains. Nymphing leeches, scuds, worms, and midges will be staples until the next year's spring *Baetis* arrive.

Visit Grey Reef with the expectation of nymph fishing for the highest productivity, and be pleasantly surprised when dry-fly and streamer opportunities present themselves. Fishing pressure is comparatively low, and often you may not see another boat during your day. There are several campgrounds and lodging facilities in the vicinity, although dining options are limited. It is close to Casper, Wyoming's second-largest city, which has all the services you may need. Grey Reef is easily accessible, is easy to navigate, and is a consistent and reliable fishery, with a strong potential to produce the trophy trout of a lifetime.

➤ **Hatches:** November–April: Midges combined with a staple of scuds, leeches, crawdads, and worms.
   April–May: *Baetis*, midges.
   May–July: PMDs, Yellow Sallies, caddis, and midges.
   Late August–mid-September: Tricos, caddis, and *Pseudos*.
   Mid-September–October: *Baetis*, caddis, and midges.

➤ **Fishing regulations:** Open year-round, with the exception of a small stretch closed in April.

Limits on the upper 8 miles are one trout over 20 inches in possession. Below that, the limit increases to one trout over 20 inches and one trout under 20 inches in possession.

No bait allowed on the upper 8 miles. Barbed hooks are legal, but we strongly suggest fishing barbless.

All watercraft must display an Aquatic Invasive Species decal, available at most Wyoming Game & Fish license agencies. All watercraft must have suitable personal floatation devices for each individual in the boat. PFDs do not have to be worn, but must be readily available. Floaters may not anchor, beach, or wade on private property without permission.

➤ **Tackle:** Rods: Use a 9-foot 6-weight for nymphing; 8½- or 9-foot 5-weight for dries; and a 9-foot 7-weight for streamers.

Reels: Large-arbor with reliable and smooth starting drags.

Lines: WF floating with tapers appropriate for bulky flies and wind for nymphs. Six- to 20-foot sink-tips or floating lines are appropriate for turning over heavy streamer flies; traditional tapered floating lines for dries.

Wading gear: Mid-September through mid-June, wear breathable chest waders with appropriate and layered insulation. Rarely will there be a need for a waterproof jacket, but you'll wish you had one when the situation arises.

Mid-June through mid-September, you can wear quick-dry wading pants and long-sleeve shirts and sandals. Wet wading is very comfortable, but bring waders and rainwear, as summer downpours can be very cold.

ERIK AUNE has been a professional fly-fishing guide since 1996 and is co-owner, with Trent Tatum, of The Reef Fly Shop and North Platte Lodge.

CLOSEST FLY SHOPS

The Reef Fly Shop
22222 Grey Reef Rd.
Alcova, WY 82620
307-232-9128
info@thereefflyshop.com
www.northplatteflyfishing.com

Ugly Bug Fly Shop
240 S. Center St.
Casper, WY 82604
307-234-6905
www.crazyrainbow.net

Platte River Fly Shop
7400 Hwy. 220
Casper, WY 82604
307-237-5997
info@wyomingflyfishing.com
www.wyomingflyfishing.com

CLOSEST OUTFITTERS/GUIDES

North Platte Lodge
20400 Grey Reef Rd.
Alcova, WY 82620
307-237-1182

info@northplattelodge.com
www.northplattelodge.com

Crazy Rainbow Fly Fishing
13800 W. Hwy. 220
Casper, WY 82604
307-234-6905
www.crazyrainbow.net

The Reef Fly Shop (left)

CLOSEST LODGES

North Platte Lodge (left)
Crazy Rainbow Fly Fishing (above)

BEST CAMPGROUND

The Reef Fly Shop (above)

CLOSEST RESTAURANT

Sunset Grill
22250 Hwy 220
Alcova, WY 82620
307-472-3200

BEST RESTAURANT

J's Pub & Grill
3201 Wyoming Blvd.
Casper, WY 82604
307-472-3100

BEST PLACE TO GET A COLD, STIFF DRINK

Sunset Grill
22250 Hwy 220
Alcova, WY 82620
307-472-3200

CLOSEST EMERGENCY MEDICAL HELP

Wyoming Medical Center
1233 E. 2nd St.
Casper, WY 82601
307-577-7201 or 800-822-7201

CELL PHONE SERVICE

Available in most places, but it may require hiking to the highest point in hilly areas.

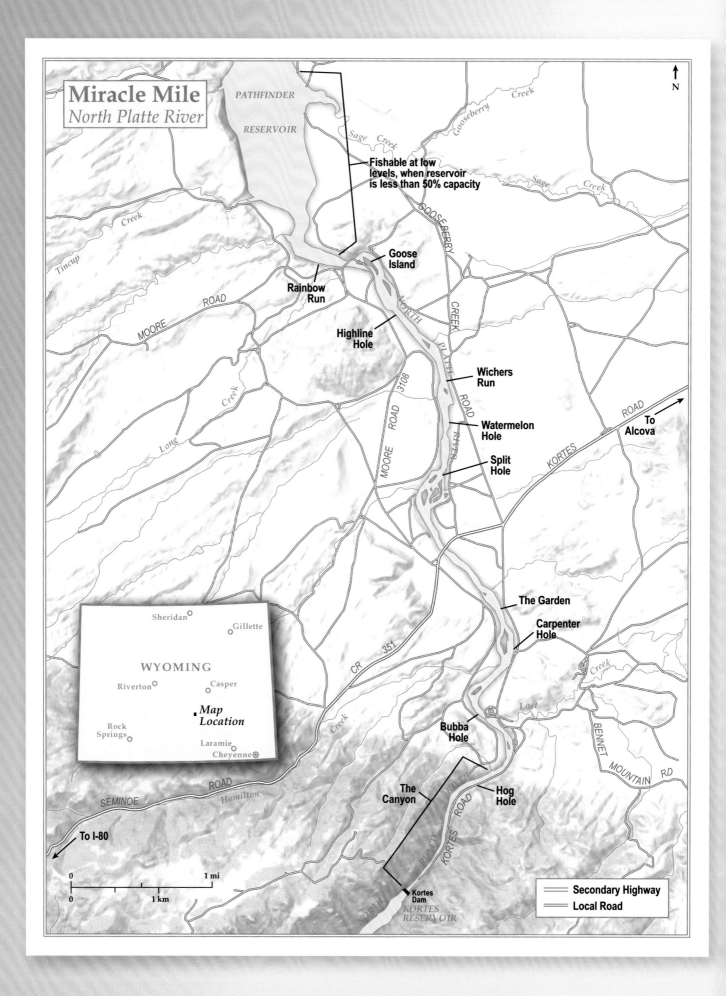

Miracle Mile
North Platte River

PATHFINDER

RESERVOIR

Fishable at low
levels, when reservoir
is less than 50% capacity

Goose
Island

Rainbow
Run

Highline
Hole

Wichers
Run

Watermelon
Hole

Split
Hole

The Garden

Carpenter
Hole

To
Alcova

Bubba
Hole

The
Canyon

Hog
Hole

Kortes
Dam

KORTES
RESERVOIR

WYOMING

Sheridan

Gillette

Riverton

Casper

Map
Location

Rock
Springs

Laramie
Cheyenne

To I-80

0   1 mi
0   1 km

——— Secondary Highway
——— Local Road

MOORE ROAD

Creek

Tincup

Creek

Sage Creek

Gooseberry Creek

Sage Creek

GOOSEBERRY CREEK

NORTH PLATTE RIVER

MOORE ROAD 3708

KORTES ROAD

Long Creek

CR 351

Creek

SEMINOE ROAD

Hamilton

Lost Creek

BENNET MOUNTAIN RD

PLATTE RIVER

KORTES ROAD

NORTH PLATTE

Miracle Mile *(North Platte River, Central Wyoming)*

➤ **Location:** Central Wyoming, 59 miles from Casper, and 50 miles from Rawlins. The closest airport is in Casper (Natrona County International Airport). There are no paved roads directly accessing the Mile. Travel is dependent upon the weather and season. It is essential to use good judgment when traveling to this part of Wyoming.

The Miracle Mile section of the North Platte River is located below Kortes Reservoir and flows into Pathfinder Reservoir. The largest impoundment upstream of the Mile, Seminoe Reservoir and Dam, was completed in 1939—Kortes was added in 1951 to serve as an afterbay dam for power production. An inherent part of the Reclamation Act of 1902, these water projects were essential in providing sustainability to the arid lands of the American West. Due to its location and design, the Mile is one of the largest stretches of public water on the North Platte. The river is completely accessible through Bureau of Reclamation land.

Despite its name, the Miracle Mile is substantially longer. This section of the North Platte fluctuates in length from about 5 to 8 miles, depending on the level of Pathfinder. Nestled between the Seminoe and Pedros Mountains, the Miracle Mile boasts a dynamic range of water—steep canyon walls, large boulders, and pocket water to classic riffle runs. Flows can range from 500–3,000 cfs during an average year, but can exceed 10,000 cfs in years with abundant snowpack. This section of the Platte is extremely important to hydroelectric production, therefore it can fluctuate on a daily and even hourly basis. Regardless of fluctuating flows, this fishery would not exist without the dams. The consistent water temperatures provided by the upstream reservoirs and the close proximity to Pathfinder make it an ideal tailwater.

Multiple subspecies of rainbows, browns, and Snake River cutthroat, along with suckers, carp, and walleye call the Miracle Mile home. The Mile's trout population is roughly 50 percent rainbows and 50 percent brown trout. Good numbers of resident trout are in the river year-round, but there are also large numbers of migratory rainbows and browns

from Pathfinder Reservoir. These fish will move into the Mile during certain times of year, with larger numbers of migrants seen in the spring and fall. This interchange between river and reservoir environment is one of the most interesting and important aspects of the Miracle Mile. Pathfinder Reservoir has a very high growth rate when it comes to trout—a 20-inch fish is approximately 3 years of age. The health of the Pathfinder trout fishery is dependent upon the level of the reservoir. The increased productivity and additional habitat of a full reservoir yields increased growth and overall health in the trout population.

The Miracle Mile is great swinging water. Trent Tatum

Along with various species of baitfish, the Mile has a multitude of invertebrates, and is a virtual food factory for the fish that call it home. Some of the signature food sources include crayfish, Golden Stoneflies, caddis, scuds, leeches, midges, and many different mayflies. Make no mistake, the Mile is second to none when it comes to productivity. With this large food base, it is easy to understand why the fish can grow to such large sizes. Fish in the 25- to 30-inch class are caught annually.

The Mile, without question, is a world-class fishery and offers anglers the possibility of catching fish on nymphs, streamers, and dries. All things considered (weather, water

Above. When Pathfinder Reservoir is low, new water opens up. Trent Tatum
Inset. Miracle Mile brown. Trent Tatum

conditions, and season) it is, day in and day out, a nymph fishery. The nymph rig is king on the Mile! But nymphing on the Mile is far more than packing on length and weight. It's about understanding the hatches, water, and preferences of the fish. Any hatch on the Mile can bring fish to all levels of the water column, and understanding this can make the difference between a slow and a good day on the water.

Streamer fishing and swinging would be the second most productive methods on the Mile. These fish are not afraid of a big meal. Stripping flies with a single-handed rod or swinging with a two-hander can yield some of the best big fish days of the year. Matuka- and Bugger-style patterns are the most productive—sufficiently imitating the leeches, crayfish, and baitfish. Good selections of articulated flies are also important to have in your box. When it comes to streamer fishing, it is critical to utilize both floating and various types of sinking lines to hit the right depth.

Last, and surely not least is the potential for dry-fly activity on the Mile. It's there and it does exist, just not with the consistency of the other two methods. There are, without question, hatches that will get the fish to the top. Year in and year out, the Golden Stones and caddis are the go-to hatches for those looking to fish dries. Any of the other hatches can bring them to the top, when conditions are prime—it's just being there on the right day, under the right conditions. As with many other fisheries, overcast days and some degree of calm weather is the recipe for success.

The Miracle Mile is a truly amazing fishery. Big fish and public access are the most attractive features of this great Western tailwater. But let's be honest, it is not for everyone. The location can make getting there a challenge, and the weather and river can test your angling skills. However, for those willing to put in the time and effort on this section of river, the rewards are spectacular.

➤ **Hatches:** Year-round: Nymphing with a variety of midge, scud, leech, crawdad, aquatic worm, and Golden Stone patterns.

April and May: *Baetis.*

June–August: PMDs, Golden Stones, caddis, and terrestrials.

August–September: Tricos, caddis, and terrestrials.

➤ **Fishing regulations:** Open year-round. Three trout per day or in possession. No more than one trout can exceed 16 inches. There are no designated boat ramps on the Miracle Mile.

➤ **Tackle:** Rods: Nymphing: 9-foot 6-weight; Dry Fly: 8½- or 9-foot 5-weight; Streamers: 9-foot 7-weight; Switch: 11- to 13-foot, 6- to 8-weight.

Reels: A large-arbor reel with reliable and smooth starting drag will be the most effective. Use the reel rather than handlining.

Lines: Nymphing: floating with a taper appropriate for bulky flies and wind; Streamers: full- sinking lines, sink-tips, and floating lines for larger flies; Dry fly: weight-forward floating; Switch/swinging: Skagit compact lines with a wide variety of interchangeable tips.

Wading gear: Mid-September through mid-June: Breathable chest waders with appropriate layered insulation. Rarely will there be a need for a waterproof jacket, but you'll wish you had it when the situation arises.

Mid-June through mid-September: Quick-drying wading pants and a long-sleeve shirt with sandals. Wet wading is very comfortable, but have waders and a raincoat, as a summer downpour can be very cold.

TRENT TATUM grew up fly fishing East Texas lakes and the coasts of Texas and Louisiana. In 1999, he moved to Wyoming to pursue a degree in fisheries biology and management. During his tenure as a student, he guided on the North Platte. After receiving his bachelor's degree, he continued guiding full time. Several years later, he and Erik Aune purchased the North Platte Lodge and The Reef Fly Shop. Trent continues to guide and work with the North Platte's most prestigious outfitter.

Miracle Mile Golden Stone. Trent Tatum

CLOSEST FLY SHOPS

The Reef Fly Shop
22222 Grey Reef Rd.
Alcova, WY 82620
307-232-9128
info@thereeflyshop.com
www.northplatteflyfishing.com

Ugly Bug Fly Shop
240 S. Center St.
Casper, WY 82604
307-234-6905
www.crazyrainbow.net

Platte River Fly Shop
7400 Hwy. 220
Casper, WY 82604
307-237-5997
info@wyomingflyfishing.com
www.wyomingflyfishing.com

CLOSEST OUTFITTERS/GUIDES

The Reef Fly Shop (above)

North Platte Lodge
20400 Grey Reef Rd.
Alcova, WY 82620
307-237-1182
info@northplattelodge.com
www.northplattelodge.com

Crazy Rainbow Fly Fishing
13800 W. Hwy. 220
Casper, WY 82604
307-234-6905
www.crazyrainbow.net

CLOSEST LODGES

North Platte Lodge
20400 Grey Reef Rd.
Alcova, WY 82620
307-237-1182
info@northplattelodge.com
www.northplattelodge.com

Crazy Rainbow Fly Fishing
13800 W. Hwy 220
Casper, WY 82604
307-234-6905
www.crazyrainbow.net

BEST CAMPGROUND

The Reef Fly Shop (left)

CLOSEST RESTAURANT

Sunset Grill
22250 Hwy 220
Alcova, WY 82620
307-472-3200

BEST RESTAURANT

J's Pub & Grill
3201 Wyoming Blvd.
Casper, WY 82604
307-472-3100

BEST PLACE TO GET A COLD, STIFF DRINK

Sunset Grill
22250 Hwy 220
Alcova, WY 82620
307-472-3200

CLOSEST EMERGENCY MEDICAL HELP

Wyoming Medical Center
1233 E. 2nd St.
Casper, WY 82601
307-577-7201

CELL PHONE SERVICE

None on the river.

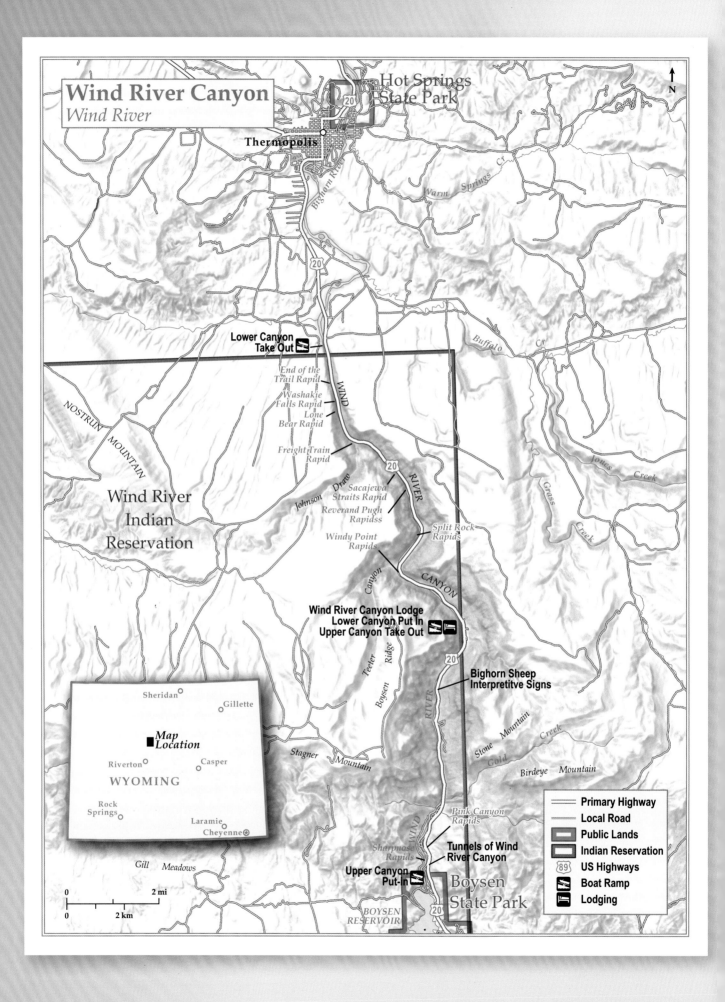

Wind River Canyon
Wind River

Hot Springs
State Park

Thermopolis

Warm   Springs   Cr.

Bighorn River

20

Lower Canyon
Take Out

Buffalo   Cr.

*End of the
Trail Rapid*

WIND

*Washakie
Falls Rapid*

*Lone
Bear Rapid*

*Freight Train
Rapid*

NOSTRUN MOUNTAIN

20

RIVER

Jones   Creek

Draw

*Sacajewa
Straits Rapid*

Johnson

*Reverand Pugh
Rapidss*

Wind River
Indian
Reservation

*Split Rock
Rapids*

Grass   Creek

*Windy Point
Rapids*

Canyon

CANYON

Wind River Canyon Lodge
Lower Canyon Put In
Upper Canyon Take Out

Teeter Ridge

Boysen Ridge

20

Bighorn Sheep
Interpretitve Signs

RIVER

Stone   Mountain

Gold   Creek

Sheridan

Gillette

**Map
Location**

Stagner   Mountain

Birdeye   Mountain

Riverton

Casper

WYOMING

Rock
Springs

Laramie
Cheyenne

*Pink Canyon
Rapids*

WIND

Gill   Meadows

*Sharpnose
Rapids*

Tunnels of Wind
River Canyon

Upper Canyon
Put-In

**Boysen
State Park**

*BOYSEN
RESERVOIR*

20

	Primary Highway
	Local Road
	Public Lands
	Indian Reservation
89	**US Highways**
	Boat Ramp
	Lodging

0   2 mi

0   2 km

N

➤ **Location:** Two miles south of Thermopolis, in west-central Wyoming, on the Wind River Indian Reservation, home of the Eastern Shoshone and Northern Arapaho tribes.

Closest commercial air: Riverton, Wyoming, 1-hour drive; Worland, Wyoming, 30-minute drive; United Airlines and Great Lakes Airline Commuter Service through Denver. Nearest cities: 6½ hours northwest of Denver, 6 hours northeast of Salt Lake City.

"The fish and other wildlife along the river, they are our relations, if they start going we are gone too . . . "
—WES MARTEL, Eastern Shoshone Tribal Council Chairman

The Shoshone and Arapaho tribes consider the Wind River Canyon a place of historic, spiritual, and cultural significance. A traditional story says when the wind is right, an eagle feather released into the breeze at the top of the canyon will carry the entire length of the canyon before it comes back to rest on the surface of the water. For these same reasons, the Wind River Canyon is closed to trespassing, hiking, rock climbing, private boating (rafting, canoeing, kayaking, or any other activity) with the exception of fishing. Fishing on the Wind River Indian Reservation is akin to fishing on private property, and treating it with a high degree of respect allows access to continue and is highly promoted and requested by Wind River Canyon Whitewater & Fly Fishing (WRCW&F) and the Shoshone and Arapaho Tribes (SAT). Floating the Wind River Canyon, per the regulations set forth by the SAT, is allowed only with the guide service of WRCW&F, a tribally owned and operated business.

This stream has been described as one of the finest wild brown trout fisheries in the West. Though stocked below the Wind River Canyon with cutthroat and rainbow as the river leaves the reservation, there is no stocking on the reservation itself. The predominant species is brown trout. This 15-mile stretch of river varies from slow, wide sections that seem to meander endlessly to fast-moving, boulder-filled pocket water, explosive rapids, long riffles, soft banks with overhanging vegetation, and deep, fast-moving runs. Each of these areas holds large, feisty wild brown trout, although there are also rainbow and cutthroat trout found throughout the river. And don't forget about the carp!

The river is a moderate-size tailwater with flows varying throughout the year between winter lows of 500 cfs, to average summer flows of 1,400 cfs. The variability depends

The Wind River offers spectacular scenery and fishing without the crowds. Terry Gunn

on water storage levels in Boysen Reservoir and the annual snowpack levels on the eastern slope of the Wind River Range and the upper reaches of the southern slope of the Absaroka Mountain Range. In a high-snowpack year, June and early July can often see 4,000–6,000 cfs!

Beginning below Boysen Reservoir, the character of the river is wide, flat, and serene with long slicks of calm. However there are sections that are anything but calm:

Darren: *Jack, do you want to put that rod away? This is a pretty good rapid!*

Jack Dennis: *No, I got an eye on it back here. I want it out so that I can have both rods ready.*

Darren Calhoun pointing out the trout that Wendy Gunn is going to stalk and catch. Terry Gunn

At the bottom of the ensuing 200-yard-long rapid and an exciting ride:

Jack Dennis: *Hey, what happened to that rod? Did you guys see it? Damn it, I had it right here . . . !*

Rivers and the rapids on them in the West are classified from Class I to VI, with the higher number equaling increased difficulty, although this system is admittedly highly subjective. The "classes" of the rapids in the Wind River Canyon vary with water flows, but there are undoubtedly several rapids in this stretch of river that are a minimum Class III and bigger at flows of 2,000 cfs and above, with technical requirements that, if not closely followed, can result in consequences less than desired by most anglers.

Though the river is best fished with a guide from a boat, wade fishing is allowed with purchase of a Wind River Reservation fishing license and recreation stamp. The license and stamp can be purchased by the day, 7-day increment, or annual/seasonal. The wading is not for the beginner, and being in good physical condition is a must. The banks are steep and rocky, there is abundant poison ivy, and this is rattlesnake

country. There are numerous stories of anglers taking nasty spills trying to reach "that spot." Fording/crossing the river, though it is within the regulations, is not recommended due to safety and trespassing issues—the Burlington Northern Santa Fe (BNSF) Railroad on the west side of the river prohibits trespassing, should you contemplate a walk along their tracks.

Darren: *Here try one of these, Mike.* (Hands him a #4 terrestrial.)

Mike Lawson: *You're kiddin' me right? I mean look at this thing* (dubious look) *. . . seriously?*

Darren: *Yep, and cast it into that super-thin water right next to that bank, then move it.*

Mike: *That water?* (Pointing) *Seems awfully thin . . . are you sure?*

Darren: *Yep.*

Mike: *OK, I guess, but I am just—Whoa! Did you see that?*

What is unique about this stream is the limited impact promoted and practiced by WRCW&F and the Shoshone and Arapaho tribes, allowing the experience for anglers to be something not easily found elsewhere, casting to large trout that are not under constant pressure. WRCW&F follows a self-imposed two guided boats per day in the 15 miles of water in the Wind River Canyon—one in the upper section of the canyon and one in the lower section.

The most frequently asked question of all rivers is "When is the best time to fish there?" And the standard answer here is: "Depends on what you want to fish." If you are a nymph fisherman, come in the spring or early summer (April to early June) or the late fall (late October or November). If it is dry-fly action you seek, then do a trip from early to mid-June through mid-September. If you are a streamer junkie, then late spring or early summer (May and June) and early to late fall, September to November.

There are several prolific hatches. Like most Western rivers, they are all dependent on weather and water temperatures. A couple of the best: Yellow Sallies, early to mid-June, lasting into early July; several different varieties of caddis beginning in early July lasting through early September. There is a cicada hatch, however it only occurs on roughly a 7-year cycle and is heavily dependent on hot, dry spring conditions as a precursor. It last happened in 2012.

Nymphing can be maddening at times due to the excessive suspended moss in the water (typically mid-June to September) but is a productive method in early spring and late fall as well as during the winter, sans moss. Standard nymphs such as the Beadhead Prince, Copper John, Hare's-ear, Rolling Rock Caddis, and San Juan Worm are all typically quite successful in a #16 or #18 with standard 9-foot tapered leaders and tippet in the 2- to 4-pound range. Double-fly nymph rigs are often a good bet with one of the previously mentioned nymph patterns and a black or brown Woolly Bugger as a second/trailer fly.

Streamers are a highly productive technique to move big fish during certain times of the year. The river is filled with crayfish, several varieties of minnows, and sculpin; the size of the fish leaves little doubt that food is plentiful. The average trout in the Wind River Canyon is a very healthy 17 to 18 inches, with 20-inch fish appearing regularly. Some of the more productive patterns are Galloup's T&A, JJ's Special, McCunes Sculpin, Dennis Kiwi Muddler, and big ugly Woolly Buggers in black, brown, and olive can also be very productive. Did I mention the carp? The carp here are worthy quarry, with many anglers regularly taking them on streamers, dry flies, and with nymph rigs. Most of these fish are in the 10-pound-plus range, and are beasts to land!

Dry-fly fishing seems to be everyone's favorite, and the dry-fly enthusiast will be impressed if she/he is here at the right time and in some cases the right year. In the years of the cicada, it is not uncommon to have days where numerous big

Wendy Gunn preparing to release a sight-caught carp. This is part of the Wind River Slam: carp, rainbow, brown, and cutthroat trout. Terry Gunn

This brown fell for a streamer crawled across the bottom, imitating one of the crayfish that inhabit the Wind. Terry Gunn

trout (20 inches+ come to have a look at your fly before they crush it! The terrestrial fishing can also be exciting, with hoppers and other large bugs. If properly presented, they often draw large trout that otherwise may not look up to the surface for food; there is nothing more exciting than watching a large brown come to the surface slowly (testing your patience the entire time) and decide to eat a big dry fly. The fish count here is not prolific, so dry-fly fishing often requires covering lots of water, good eyesight, and patience to find a fish willing to look up. Even during the major hatches, the rises are subtle and rarely happen with abandon.

➤ **Hatches:** The Wind River is not a classic "match-the-hatch" stream; therefore, most dry-fly fishing is using attractor patterns and terrestrials, such as grasshoppers, beetles, crickets, and the like. However, there are times of the year (depending on weather) when some regular hatches take place:

Early June: Tricos, Yellow Sallies, and on a somewhat irregular 6- to 7-year cycle we do see cicadas.

July: Several types of caddis in late evenings.

September and October: Depending on water levels and air temperatures, crane fly, and October Caddis.

➤ **Regulations:** Wind River Reservation Fishing License and Recreation stamp required.

Cost: Non-Wyoming resident: $25/daily Wind River Reservation Recreation stamp $5 (required yearly); $120/annual permit. Wyoming Resident: $15/daily Wind River Reservation Recreation Stamp $5 (required yearly $80/annual permit. There are several local vendors available for Wind River Reservation fishing licenses and recreation stamps. Creel limits, allowable tackle, and other regulations are subject to change annually at the discretion of the Eastern Shoshone and Northern Arapaho Tribal Joint Business Council. Therefore we recommend referring to the most current Shoshone and Arapaho Tribal fish and game regulations, which are handed out with each permit sale.

A big brown hugging the shore swings out to eat a drifted nymph. This is classic New Zealand-style sight-casting with coaching from above. Terry Gunn

➤ **Tackle:** Use a 6-weight rod with medium-fast action or flex due to wind, heavy water, size of fish, and the ability to change gear (nymphing, dry fly, streamers) as conditions dictate. Rods lighter than a 5-weight are discouraged. Floating line is standard; sink-tips and sinking lines can be productive if you're committed to fishing streamers. Leader and tippet sizes depend on flies, with 4 to 6 pounds being adequate.

Wendy Gunn hitting pocket water on the fast-moving Wind River.

DARREN CALHOUN, born and raised on the Wind River Indian Reservation, is an enrolled member of the Northern Arapaho Tribe and descendant of the Eastern Shoshone Tribe. At the age of 8, he learned to cast a fly rod from legendary outdoor filmmaker Gordon Eastman, who taught Darren that fly fishing is not about catching fish, rather "it is about fooling them." Darren established Wind River Canyon Whitewater & Fishing with his father Melvin "Pete" Calhoun, a member of the Eastern Shoshone Tribe, in 1992.

CLOSEST FLY SHOP

Wind River Canyon Whitewater & Fly Fishing
210 Hwy. 20 South, Suite #5
Thermopolis, WY 82443
307-864-9343 or 888-246-9343
cell 307-851-2456
www.windrivercanyon.com

There are other "tackle stores" in Thermopolis, however, this is the only fly shop.

BEST HOTELS
Best Western
116 E. Park St.
Thermopolis, WY 82443
888-919-9009 or 307-864-2939
http://bestwesternwyoming.com/thermopolis-hotels

Days Inn
115 E. Park St.
Thermopolis, WY 82443
800-225-3297 or 307-864-3131
www.daysinn.com/hotels/wyoming/thermopolis/days-inn-thermopolis/hotel-overview

BEST RESTAURANT
Stones Throw Restaurant at The Golf Course/Airport
143 Airport Rd.
Thermopolis, WY 82443
307-864-9494
Tuesday–Thursday 5–8:30 P.M.;
Friday and Saturday 5–9:00, closed Sunday and Monday. The best meals served in Hot Springs County, along with full bar and a great selection of beer and wine.

Safari Club at the Days Inn
115 E. Park St.
Thermopolis, WY 82443
307-864-3131
www.daysinn.com/hotels/wyoming/thermopolis
Great drinks, wide selection of good food, and an amazing display of fish and game from around the globe; photo display of numerous hunting and fishing adventures.

LODGING
Wind River Canyon Lodge
Wind River Canyon Whitewater & Fishing is in the process of building a small set of cabins that will be riverside in the Wind River Canyon, and offered to our guests

for accommodations. The projected opening date for this lodging/cabin rental is May 2014. Please check for updates: www.windrivercanyon.com, or call us at 888-246-9343.

Best Western (left)
Days Inn (left)

CLOSEST EMERGENCY MEDICAL HELP
Hot Springs County Memorial Hospital
150 E Arapahoe St.
Thermopolis, WY 82443
307-864-3121

CELL PHONE SERVICE
There is no reliable cell phone service in Wind River Canyon; in the town of Thermopolis, cell phone service from regional and national carriers (Union, Verizon, Sprint, AT&T, T-Mobile) is reliable.

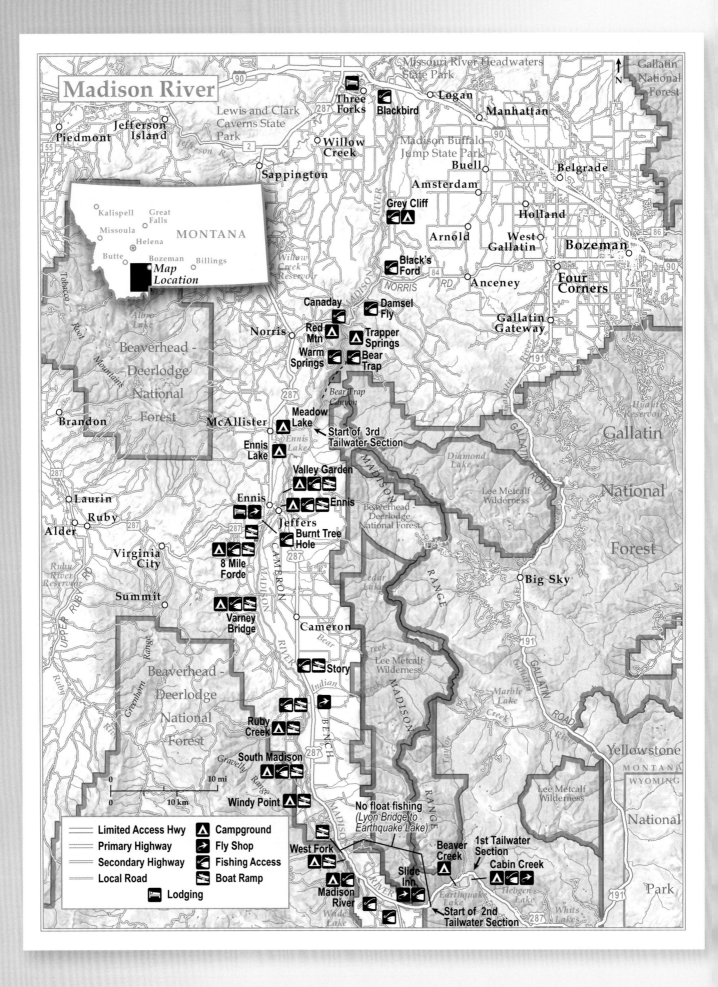

Madison River (Montana)

➤ **Location:** Southwest Montana where Idaho, Montana and Wyoming come together at the west entrance to Yellowstone National Park at the Town of West Yellowstone, Montana. It is 5 hours from Salt Lake City, 2 hours from Idaho Falls, and 3 hours from Billings, Montana.

An old friend and veteran Madison River angler told me that one cannot own a river except in one's heart. He knew the river and it was in his heart, he loved the Madison, and the same goes for me. I fish it over one hundred days a year.

Anglers try to fish it as they would their home rivers, and never get to experience the Madison's best. The three sections of the river are quite different. To succeed, a fly fisher has to be adaptable.

Here are two helpful hints:

Pick one section of the river and get to know it.

Bring a reasonable expectation. While the river holds many fish 20 inches and larger, the average is 15 inches, and a typical day for an experienced angler would mean anywhere from 10 to 20 fish between 12 and 18 inches.

The Madison River is made up of three tailwaters. The upper section begins below Hebgen Dam, 20 miles northwest of West Yellowstone, Montana. The middle tailwater begins 28 miles northwest of West Yellowstone, downstream of Earthquake Lake. The lower tailwater section starts 5 miles downstream of Ennis, below the Ennis Dam on Meadow Lake, 70 miles northwest of West Yellowstone and 55 miles southwest of Bozeman, Montana. There is commercial air service to both West Yellowstone and Bozeman airports.

➤ **Section 1: Hebgen Dam to Earthquake Lake**

The uppermost Madison River tailwater begins downstream of Hebgen Dam at the bottom end of Hebgen Lake. Anglers reach this by driving north out of West Yellowstone 8 miles on Highway 191, then turning left onto Highway 287 northwest along the shoreline of Hebgen Lake, 13 miles to the Hebgen Dam. The water here is open to the public, as most of it is U.S. Forest Service property. This tailwater was created in 1905 when the dam was built for a water-storage reservoir. Flows from the dam are stable for most of the year, the only exception being during spring runoff when the snowmelt brings the lake to full pond and surplus water is released above normal flows. Once the lake is full, water releases from the dam might be raised, but only for a short time, rarely affecting the fishing for more than a week or two in late June.

This is the shortest tailwater section of the three. After flowing 1½ miles, the tailwater ends in Earthquake Lake. The river here is open all year long. This section is characterized by its huge boulders and heavy runs, with deep, rough-and-tumble water that holds some of the largest fish in the river. Just downstream of the dam, a dirt road comes into the highway from the left. Turning onto this road, you will parallel the river for about a mile and dead end in a parking area at the lake. There are several boulders, side channels, pockets, and runs that hold rainbow and brown trout, as well as native mountain whitefish. The trout here—and on all sections of the river—are wild, not planted.

The water is clear all year for the first ½ mile until Cabin Creek enters the Madison and spills its late-June runoff (with turbid snowmelt) into the mix for a week or two until the 4th of July.

Winter fishing on the Madison above Earthquake Lake. John Juracek

From late January to mid-June, the river is packed with pre-spawning and spawning rainbows, as well as a few huge brown trout that run up from Earthquake Lake to devour the rainbows' spawn. Nymphing is usually the most consistent producer of rainbows that average 16 inches, but larger stonefly nymphs and streamer patterns can bring larger rainbows and browns, some up to 14 pounds. Be prepared for both midge and early- and late-season *Baetis* mayfly emergences that can bring trout to the surface from January to June and again from September to November.

113

The Madison River below Hebgen Dam. John Juracek

If snowmelt comes at the "normal" time, after mid-June, this section of the river offers up some of the most predictable Blue-winged Olive emergences of the early season. The fishing is best on the lower river, just above Earthquake Lake, where trout can take the #20 to #22 emerging *Baetis* duns easier than in the rough-and-tumble water upstream. In early July, big Green Drakes as well as both Golden and Giant Stoneflies hatch. While these emergences happen over a few days, it is tough to plan a trip to fish them. If you are here, it is worth checking, as they always bring big trout to the surface.

Around July 4, the river clears of any snowmelt below its junction with Cabin Creek, and evening caddis begin to hatch. From then until October, several caddis species come off and bring good rises most evenings.

Midsummer brings terrestrials like ants, beetles, bees, and grasshoppers, along with spruce moths. Fishing imitations of these insects can be epic. From July through September, expect great fishing during the heat of the day with terrestrial patterns.

Anglers are advised to always carry bear spray in this area. Grizzly as well as black bears are often seen along the river, as are cow and calf moose. Stay clear of any cow moose with a calf. Be aware of all wild animals when fishing this section of the river.

► **Section 2: Earthquake Lake to Ennis Lake**
The middle tailwater section begins where the river leaves Earthquake Lake at a natural dam created by an earthquake on August 1, 1959, and ends 44 highway miles downstream at Ennis Lake. Highway 287 runs along the river the entire length, offering several public access points in what is known as "The Madison Valley." Not only is this section known for its incredible wild trout population, but over 50 percent of the Madison is protected against harmful streamside development. Wildlife corridors for elk, pronghorns, grizzly and black bears, wolverines, moose, and other species will forever remain free of subdivisions, which could negatively impact their fragile natural habitat. Public access to the riv-

er is plentiful here. Several U.S. Forest Service and Bureau of Land Management camping and parking areas, as well as State of Montana and conservation easement river corridors provide access along the river.

The first 20 miles, from Earthquake Lake to McAtee Bridge, is open to fishing from the third Saturday in May through the end of February. The river then closes to protect spawning rainbows. The river is open to fishing year-round below McAtee Bridge, and downstream to the bridge at the town of Ennis, about 18 highway miles. From Ennis Bridge downstream about 6 miles to Ennis Lake (where angling is not permitted from boats), one can fish from the third Saturday in May through February.

The first 9 miles, from the Earthquake Lake to Lyon Bridge, is full of boulders, pockets, and pools, and contains the most wild trout and whitefish per mile of the entire river. The browns and rainbows average 15 inches. Anglers can only wade this area; float fishing is not allowed. At the lower end of this stretch, just above Lyon Bridge, the West Fork of the Madison enters the main river. During snowmelt, this tributary dumps mud into the main river, at times making it unfishable. Between June 1 and July 4, it is always best to phone ahead and check conditions.

This stretch of river is noted for its evening caddis fishing. On most warm, calm evenings during July and August, caddis emergences bring up incredible numbers of rising trout from 7 to 10 or 11 P.M. The secret to catching the biggest trout of the trip is to stay on the river late. Never leave the water until 10 P.M. or later.

Several species of mayflies emerge here, too: Blue-winged Olives, Western March Browns, Pale Morning Duns, small Western Green Drakes, Green Drakes, and Pink Ladies, all in good numbers to bring trout to the surface.

This stretch is also noted for its phenomenal winter midge fishing. During February, we experience several days when daytime temperatures reach into the 30s and 40s. On these days, when calm conditions prevail, anglers have great dry-fly fishing.

Stoneflies emerge here in good number also. Salmonflies come off in early July, along with Golden Stones; Little Yellow Stoneflies emerge in July and August.

Terrestrials provide some of the best fishing of the season on this water. Ants, beetles, bees, grasshoppers, spruce moths, and crickets are active here from late June into October. Flying ant swarms always provide dry-fly action in mid-August, and big trout can be found rising to them. Anglers drive along the Madison on this section looking for mating swarms of ants that appear like mini tornadoes. Once the funnel cloud of swarming flying ants is located, the dry-fly action is fast and furious. Insects soon fall to the surface

and a feeding frenzy begins. This bonanza does not last long, and anglers soon find they cannot "flock-shoot," spraying casts into the middle of the wolf pack of rising trout. To be successful, fly fishers must single out the big risers and accurately cast to them!

This section offers some of the finest nymph and streamer fishing for wild trout anywhere. Large sculpin patterns and beadhead caddis, mayfly, and stonefly imitations will provide fine results all season long.

From Lyon Bridge to Ennis Bridge begins the "float stretch" of the Madison. This 30-highway-mile stretch is open to fishing from boats. The first half is the Lyon Bridge to McAtee Bridge section. Many anglers refer to this section as the "30-mile riffle," as at a casual glance the river looks much the same along its length here. This water is difficult to learn without a guide; the water looks easy to fish, and anglers must cover lots of water to do well. There are long stretches here that are too shallow to provide trout-suitable cover and habitat. First-time anglers will find a guide invaluable whether they choose float or wade fishing. The guide will not only point out access points, but show the angler holding areas, seams, pockets, slicks, and other fishy spots, as well as picking the best fly patterns and describing the fishing techniques to use.

I prefer to use a drift boat for transportation, getting out of the boat to fish. However, most anglers fish from the boat, which is a different deal altogether. If you spend too much time false casting you'll lose chances at prime lies. Most successful drifting anglers say that to be successful fishing from a boat, they've learned to fish one drift with the fly while glancing downstream to pick out the next target ahead of the boat, then presenting a quick, slack-line quartering cast. They rely on their peripheral vision to spot rising fish or prime water ahead of the moving craft. Experienced drift fishers know that presenting dead-drifted dry flies and nymphs from a drift boat is very effective. Both boat and fly move along at the same speed, so it is a deadly method of drifting flies into the many boulders, pockets, seams, and runs, without telltale drag.

I find fishing dry flies from a boat usually affects fly selection, as three characteristics become paramount: visibility, floatability, and durability. Most effective will be flies that I can see, that float well, and that stand up to catching and releasing several trout. I enjoy fishing attractor patterns like Royal Wulffs and Trude Cripples, Stimulators, and PMX patterns, which fit the above criteria.

This section has the most predictable Salmonfly and Golden Stonefly hatches. From late June until July 4, anglers can expect to meet and fish these huge insects and the big trout that rise to them. No other insect creates as much excitement among anglers as the Giant Salmonfly! This stretch also has wonderful caddis, mayfly, and terrestrial fishing, so anglers are advised to be ready to also fish these important insects.

During the early season, when snowmelt and turbid water conditions are present, you can expect great angling pitching big sculpin patterns into the banks from a drift boat. I especially like the huge articulated patterns with trailing stinger hooks. Once the streamer lands, I let it sink for a few seconds, then give it a couple of short, quick strips, then pick it up and cast again. This method, on this section of the river, is responsible for taking more large trout than any other. I always look forward to a day or two of this each season.

The next 12 miles, from McAtee to Varney Bridge, is open to angling year-round. The river here lacks the big boulders and pocket water that are present upstream, but it holds large trout. There is public access and a good boat launch at the bridge, and another access a couple miles off Highway 287 downstream of McAtee Bridge, but float fishing is the best way to fish this water, since most of it runs through private property. This stretch gets great Salmonfly and Golden Stone emergences, as well as caddis and mayflies, but for the most part it is best for stonefly and terrestrial fishing, as well as attractor dry flies. Large nymphs and streamers always seem to work well here, too. Winter and early spring midge fishing is always productive just downstream of the bridge on the left side of the river, before the irrigation takeout. Often between noon and 4 P.M. you will see fish rising to emerging midges.

Local anglers in the know tell of fishing the "olive highway" during the summer. They are referring to the olive-green scum on the bottom of the river here. This line of scum extends from midriver toward the shoreline, and trout often concentrate on the edge of it.

As you drift to the end of this piece of water near Varney Bridge, you will note the river and landscape beginning to change. Huge cottonwoods line the shore, and deep runs and sweepers create large holding areas, hinting at the water lying downstream.

In the 8 river miles from Varney Bridge to Ennis Bridge, at the town of Ennis, the river remains open to fishing from drift boats or wading all year. The fish are mostly browns, and some of the largest on the river. There is limited access, as much of this stretch flows through private lands. Varney Bridge, Eight Mile Ford, and Burnt Tree are the public access points.

This water is next to impossible to learn on your own. The price of hiring a guide is reasonable to pay to learn this incredibly productive water. A guide can show you which channels offer the best fishing, as well as which channel has a dangerous dam. The water is braided, with plenty of islands and deep side channels, logjams, and sweepers to explore.

Most of the fish you will catch are rainbows, even though browns predominate. Expert anglers stalk and hunt the big browns to catch them where they hold in the shade near cover under sweepers and in deeper runs and undercuts. Rainbows can be taken in the easy-to-fish spots in the middle of riffles and where currents merge below islands. Here, too, anglers have a chance at rare Montana grayling. Look for them around Burnt Tree and Eight Mile Ford. If you are fortunate enough to see one rise, they can almost always be taken on any pattern resembling a natural insect. If they rise to your offering, you prick one, and it misses your fly, simply wait a minute and recast; the grayling will take again. Remember, they must be released immediately upon bringing them to hand. Their fragile population fluctuates widely on the Madison.

A great time to fish this stretch is in early spring, from March to May, when big rainbows run up from Ennis Lake to spawn. It is not uncommon to catch rainbows up to 25 inches on big stonefly and egg patterns.

The 6 miles of the Madison River between Ennis Bridge and Ennis Lake has several large islands, undercuts, deep runs, and pools, along with some very large trout. On the right side of the river halfway down to the lake is Valley Garden access, which is the only access on this stretch. From this point downstream, the river's flow slows and the side channels can resemble spring creeks. Every deep pool will contain huge trout, and on occasion they will attack smaller fish you have hooked.

This piece of river offers some great terrestrial fishing. Huge beetles, grasshoppers, ants, crickets, wasps, and bees can bring fish to the surface all summer and fall. The best time to fish terrestrials is in the heat of the summer from August to mid-September. All that is needed is a grasshopper, wind, and a bright, warm, sunshiny day, and you will take some fine fish from noon to 5 P.M.

Big streamer patterns can also take big trout here. Big brown and rainbow trout are always looking for juvenile whitefish, sculpin, and small trout, and streamers imitating these naturals can bring vicious takes on this piece of water.

► Section 3: Ennis Dam to Three Forks, Montana

Until a few years ago, few anglers fished this section. Most felt the river warmed up too much. In summer, anglers might see hundreds of tubers—youngsters beating the heat as they floated this stretch in inner tubes on hot, sunny days. While some anglers fished the river in winter during midge times, few tried it during summer months. During the last several years, a new flow regime has evolved to keep the river's summer temperatures at an optimal level for trout. Since then, pulse flows are released from upstream dams if water

The middle section of the Madison River as afternoon thunderstorm approaches. John Juracek

temperatures approach critical high levels, providing cooling flows to the river below, and allowing trout to flourish.

For the first 10 miles downstream of Ennis Dam, the river runs through Bear Trap Canyon in the Lee Metcalf Wilderness Area. This nasty piece of canyon water has claimed several floaters' lives, so *do not* attempt it unless you are with one of the licensed few who can operate safely on this stretch.

If canyon water is your game, you can reach the canyon from the Bear Trap Canyon Road between Norris and Black's Ford Access; the road runs along the river here. Or you can come in from the North Ennis Lake Road and head south off the Bear Trap Canyon Road at Bear Trap Bridge off Highway 84.

Early-season fishing begins in January, when midges begin emerging during the afternoon hours. This action last until Blue-winged Olive (*Baetis*) mayflies begin hatching in early April and continue into May. Another great insect on this stretch is the Mothers Day Caddis, which comes off about the same time as the holiday for which it is named. This hatch dominates the fishing here simply because of the blizzard of insects. This area's emergence is different than

others, for it is on this stretch that the caddis is reliable from year to year. It emerges when the water is clear here while other waters may be in runoff stage. On the Madison, this important hatch not only is reliable, but it also lasts from the end of April through mid-May!

Early-season streamer fishing can be great, too. A Woolhead Sculpin, #4 to #6 in natural or olive, is killing.

In fall, terrestrials like ants, beetles, bees, and grasshoppers will bring trout to the surface. Generally, anglers will do well by floating the river, however I find that when insects are active I prefer to wade and cover little water, concentrating on those areas where the current is slow and convenient enough to allow fish to rise comfortably to insect activity.

During the heat of summer, I much prefer to fish the upper river above Ennis. If you are in the area during the early or late parts of our season, give the lower section a try. To most, it seems nondescript and puzzling, with long glides and wide riffles, but a good guide will help you solve its mysteries.

Anglers will find good fishing all the way to Three Forks. And, while trout populations are low compared to the upper

Fall Baetis *fishing on the Madison, downstream of Earthquake Lake. John Juracek*

sections of the Madison, the fishing can be great—especially when the upper stretches are covered in snow.

➤ **Hatches:** With so many different types of river habitat and three lakes within the system, it is virtually impossible to list the hatches here. For a more comprehensive hatch chart, visit the website for Craig Mathews's Blue Ribbon Flies at www.blueribbonflies.com.

Blue-winged Olives: April through early June.

Pale Morning Duns: June and July.

Western Green Drakes: mid-June through July.

Tricos: mid-July through September.

Grannoms: late April through May, and July through early August.

Spotted Sedges: late May through late July.

Little Sister Sedges: June through early September.

Salmonflies: mid-June through July.

Golden Stones: July.

Yellow Sallies: July and August.

Midges: All year.

CLOSEST FLY SHOPS

Blue Ribbon Flies
305 Canyon St.
West Yellowstone, MT 59758
406-646-7642
BRF@blueribbonflies.com
www.blueribbonflies.com

Madison River Outfitters
117 N. Canyon St.
West Yellowstone, MT 59758
406-646-9644
www.madisonriveroutfitters.com

Jacklins
105 Yellowstone Ave.
West Yellowstone, MT 59758
406-646-7336
www.jacklinsflyshop.com

Arrick's
37 Canyon
West Yellowstone, MT 59758
406-646-7290
arrick@arricks.com
www.arricks.com

West Yellowstone Fly Shop
40 Madison Ave.
West Yellowstone, MT 59758
406-646-1181
flyfish@wyflyshop.com
www.wyflyshop.com

Bud Lilly's Fly Shop
39 Madison Ave.
West Yellowstone, MT 59758
406-646-7801
info@budlillys.com
www.budlillys.com

Campfire Lodge
155 Campfire Lane
West Yellowstone, MT 59758
406-646-7258
www.campfirelodgewestyellowstone.com
(Shops downstream from West Yellowstone)

Slide Inn in Cameron
150 U.S. Hwy. 287 S.
Cameron, MT 59720
406-682-4804
www.slideinn.com

Madison River Fishing Co.
109 Main St.
Ennis, MT 59729
800-227-7127
mrfc@3rivers.net
www.mrfc.com

The Tackle Shop
127 Main St.
Ennis, MT 59729
800-808-2832
info@thetackleshop.com
thetackleshop.com

Beartooth Fly-Fishing
2925 U.S. Hwy. 287
Cameron, MT 59720
406-682-7525
info@beartoothflyfishing.com
www.beartoothflyfishing.com

CLOSEST OUTFITTERS

The shops listed above also offer guide services on the Madison. In addition, you might want to try:

Montana Trout Stalkers
P.O. Box 1406
Ennis, MT 59729
406-581-5150
joe@montanatrout.com
www.montanatrout.com

CLOSEST LODGES

Bar N Quest Ranch
890 Buttermilk Creek Rd.
West Yellowstone, MT 59758
406-646-0300
www.bar-n-ranch.com

Madison Valley Ranch
307 Jeffers Rd.
Ennis, MT 59729
800-891-6158 or 406-682-7822
fishing@madisonvalleyranch.com or
mvr@3rivers.net; www.madisonvalleyranch
.com.

➤ **Fishing regulations:**

Section 1: Five trout, only one over 18 inches, daily and in possession; open year-round.

Section 2: Earthquake Lake to Lyon Bridge: no float fishing, catch-and-release, flies and artificials only.

Lyon Bridge to Varney Bridge: same as above, but float fishing allowed.

Varney Bridge to Ennis Lake: same as above, catch-and-release for rainbow trout, but anglers may keep five brown trout, only one over 18 inches, daily and in possession.

Section 3: Ennis Dam downstream: five trout daily and in possession.

➤ **Tackle:** I recommend a soft-action rod like a Winston B3x, 9-foot, 5- or 6-weight, and a RIO Gold line with a 9-foot, 3X or 4X leader to attach appropriate tippets. Patagonia Rock Grip Aluminum Bar wading boots are needed for the slippery wading conditions of the Madison River.

Author Craig Mathews. John Juracek

In 1980, CRAIG MATHEWS and his wife Jackie founded Blue Ribbon Flies in West Yellowstone, Montana. Craig has authored several important books on fly fishing, and their business has won many conservation awards for their work in and around Yellowstone and southwest Montana. Learn more at www.blueribbonflies.com.

BEST HOTELS

Section 1

Faithful Street Inn
120 Faithful St.
West Yellowstone, MT 59758
406-646-1010
www.faithfulstreetinn.com

Best Western Desert Inn
133 N. Canyon St., U.S. 20, 191 & 287
West Yellowstone, MT 59758
800-568-8520
wyellowstone.com/desertinn

Section 2

El Western
PO Box 487
Ennis, MT 59729
800-831-2773

Fan Mountain Inn
204 Main St.
Ennis, MT 59729
406-682-7835
www.fanmountaininn.com

BEST CAMPGROUND

Westfork Cabins
24 Sundance Bench Rd.
Cameron, MT 59720
406-682-4890

BEST RESTAURANTS

Section 1

Campfire Lodge
155 Campfire Lane
West Yellowstone, MT 59758
406-646-7258
www.campfirelodgewestyellowstone.com

Section 2

The Grizzly Bar and Grill
1409 U.S. Hwy 287 N.
Cameron, MT 59720
406-682-7118

Continental Divide
47 Geyser St.
Ennis, MT 59729
406-682-7600

BEST PLACES TO GET A COLD, STIFF DRINK

Driftwaters Resort
31 Sagebrush Way
Cameron, MT 59720
406-682-3088

Grizzly Bar
1 Main St.
Roscoe, MT 59071
406-328-6789

CLOSEST EMERGENCY MEDICAL HELP

West Yellowstone Clinic
11 S. Electric St.
West Yellowstone, MT 59758
406-646-9441

Madison Valley Hospital and Clinic
59729 305 E Main St.
Ennis, MT 59729
406-682-6862

CELL PHONE SERVICE
On and off depending on location; mostly inconsistent.

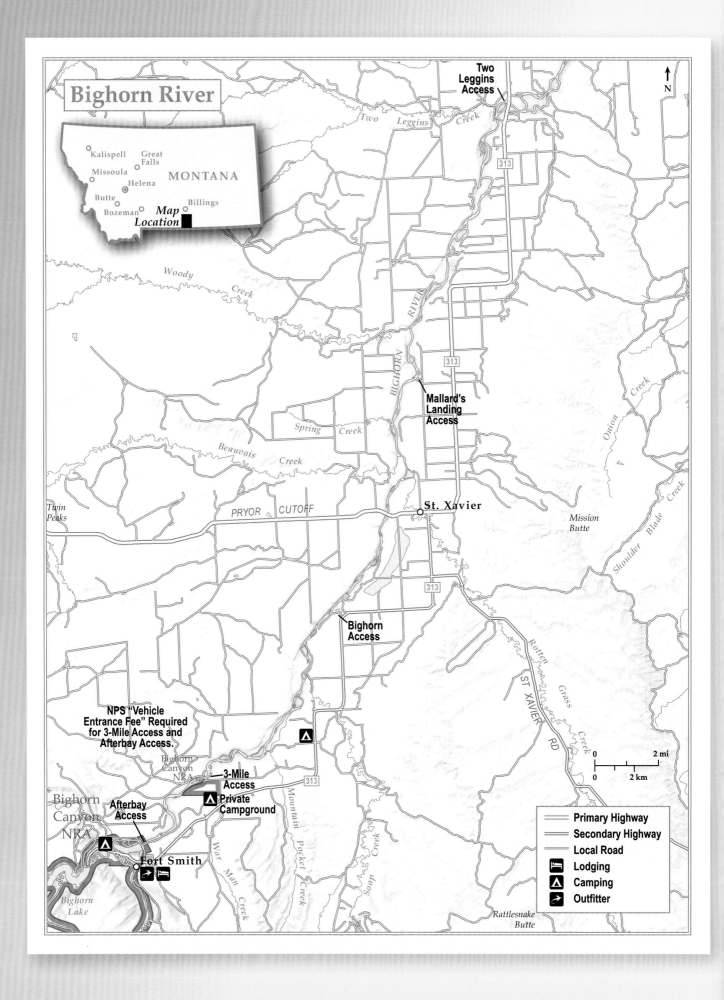

Bighorn River

MONTANA

Kalispell
Great Falls
Missoula
Helena
Butte
Bozeman
Billings
Map Location

N

Two Leggins Access

Two Leggins Creek

313

Woody Creek

BIGHORN RIVER

313

Mallard's Landing Access

Spring Creek

Beauvais Creek

Onion Creek

PRYOR CUTOFF

St. Xavier

313

Mission Butte

Twin Peaks

Shoulder Blade Creek

Bighorn Access

Rotten Grass Creek

ST XAVIER RD

NPS "Vehicle Entrance Fee" Required for 3-Mile Access and Afterbay Access.

Bighorn Canyon NRA

3-Mile Access

313

Mountain Pocket Creek

0   2 mi
0   2 km

Bighorn Canyon NRA

Afterbay Access

Private Campground

Fort Smith

War Man Creek

Soap Creek

Bighorn Lake

Rattlesnake Butte

	Primary Highway
	Secondary Highway
	Local Road
🛏	Lodging
⛺	Camping
➹	Outfitter

Bighorn River (Montana)

➤ **Location:** Montana's Bighorn flows northeastward through the Crow Indian Reservation, where 75 miles later it joins the Yellowstone River near the town of Custer, Montana. People commonly fly into Billings, Montana, or Sheridan, Wyoming (95 miles). There is also a paved airstrip in the vicinity of Afterbay Dam for those with private aircraft.

The Bighorn River is one of the most famous trout destinations in the United States. Created in 1967 by the completion of Yellowtail Dam, this former large prairie river was transformed into a trout-fishing paradise. The most productive trout fishing is found on the upper 20 miles of the river below Afterbay Dam, although fishable trout populations exist downstream of Hardin, Montana.

The Bighorn is a large river, and flows of 2,500 to 4,000 cfs are considered normal. It is very rare that the river becomes unfishable due to water conditions, and it is a popular destination when other Montana rivers are high and muddy due to spring runoff. During an average year, the Bighorn will experience higher flows in late May and June, but water clarity remains excellent and fishing productive on a variety of fly patterns.

The river's water chemistry is highly alkaline, contributing to the growth of algae and aquatic grass. Think of the Bighorn as a giant spring creek. An abundance of crustaceans, such as scuds and sow bugs, along with prolific insect hatches, create a super-fertile fish environment. Trout growth rates are impressive, and fish in the 14- to 16-inch range are common. Fish 20 inches and over are not rare. Brown trout are the dominant species, but rainbows are numerous as well. While the river's rainbows are highly prized, the sheer numbers of brown trout make this river unique. Bighorn browns are renowned for their sporting qualities. They are very strong, leap well when hooked, and tend toward golden hues in coloring. The river has excellent spawning habitat, and is managed by the State of Montana as a wild-trout fishery. There is no stocking program.

The midge hatch kicks off the dry-fly season. Midges can be found throughout the year, but the months of April and May are prime time. Anglers take fish on a variety of adult midge and emerger patterns, but cluster patterns work well when the hatch is heavy.

Late April sees the beginning of the *Baetis* mayfly hatch, and these insects continue through May and into June.

Pale Morning Duns emerge in July and August. These graceful mayflies provide outstanding surface action in late morning and early afternoon. The spinner fall can also be significant, morning or evening.

Black Caddis are the main event in late August and September. Anglers do well on pupa patterns fished deep, or on unweighted flies just under the surface.

Trico mayflies hatch in September and October. Trico duns tend to hatch early in the morning, or later in the eve-

Wintertime Mount Merritt hook-up! Hale Harris

ning. The Trico spinner fall is an impressive event, with huge pods of fish gorging themselves on these tiny, spentwing insects.

Tan caddis and fall *Baetis* round out the dry-fly season in September, October, and November. The fall *Baetis* hatch can continue into November. Some of the best dry-fly fishing can be found when the snow is flying.

The timing and intensity of all the aforementioned hatches can vary somewhat from year to year, depending on water flows and water temperature. During some years, grasshoppers provide outstanding dry-fly opportunities in July and August, with some of the biggest fish in the river looking for these large insects.

A beautiful spring day near the Red Cliffs section of the Bighorn River, 2 miles below Afterbay Dam. Hale Harris

Despite the excellent dry-fly opportunities, nymph fishing accounts for the majority of fish landed. A 9-foot leader with 4X or 5X tippet is standard. Anglers generally fish two flies on this rig, and use split-shot or tungsten putty to weight the setup. Strike indicators are recommended. Thingamabobbers, balloons, and yarn are popular. Scud and sow bug patterns are staples, as are a variety of smaller mayfly imitations. Small sizes tend to work best, as most of the insects and crustaceans in the Horn are relatively small. Usually, you'll do best fishing patterns in the #16 to #22 size range. Exceptions are the San Juan Worm, an effective pattern that imitates an aquatic worm, and various streamer patterns.

There are three fishing access sites on the upper river, with boat ramps at all of them. Afterbay Access is located immediately downstream of the Afterbay Dam. There are actually two dams on the Bighorn River. Yellowtail Dam is the large hydroelectric dam that backs up the 70-mile reservoir, Bighorn Lake. Afterbay Dam is a small dam located 1½ miles below Yellowtail Dam. Between the two dams is a small body of water called the Afterbay. The Afterbay may fluctuate dramatically during the course of the day, depending on releases from Yellowtail. However, the Afterbay serves to moderate flows on the river—anglers don't have to worry about large fluctuations on a daily basis, and fish habitat benefits as well. River fishing begins below Afterbay Dam.

Three Mile Access, also known as Lind Access, is about 3 river miles downstream of Afterbay Dam. This is an excellent wade-fishing access point with a series of channels in the vicinity. During lower flows, anglers can wade across some of these channels, all of which can provide excellent fishing. Upstream from this access, there is a nice trail along the river, and above the channel section is a nice dry-fly flat. Be advised that both Afterbay and Three Mile Access are managed by the National Park Service, and anglers are required to purchase a daily use permit.

Twelve river miles below Afterbay Dam is Bighorn Fishing Access. This state-managed access site is the most popular takeout point for area float anglers. Wade fishing is available here, although you will generally fare better at the access sites upstream.

Downriver from Bighorn Fishing Access are Mallard's Access (Mile Marker 21) and Two Leggins Access (Mile Marker 31.7). Trout populations tend to decline the farther downriver you get. This decline is due to siltation from irrigation return and feeder streams, and, to a lesser degree, from higher water temperatures during the summer. That said, fishing can be outstanding on these lower float sections, and the fishing pressure is greatly reduced. Just remember that water clarity can be an issue, especially during spring runoff or after a rainstorm. Also, powerboats can be used on the float sections below Bighorn Access, and bait fishing is allowed.

The Bighorn River Valley is rich in history. The Bozeman Trail crossed the river just 2 miles downstream of Afterbay Dam, and the site of Fort C.F. Smith is located just outside the small town of Fort Smith. The original fort's purpose was to provide protection to settlers as they traveled through territory inhabited by hostile Sioux and Cheyenne tribes. The famous Little Bighorn Battlefield, known for General Custer's demise, is located 55 miles away near Crow Agency.

Fort Smith, Montana is the epicenter of Bighorn River fly fishing, as the upper Bighorn provides the most consistent fishing. The town is 1 mile from Afterbay Dam, and there are several fly shops and lodges in the immediate area, all of which provide guide service and lodging. Other lodges are located farther down the valley; a couple of prominent lodges are near Hardin.

While most fly anglers practice catch-and-release fishing, current regulations mandate the use of artificials only (no bait allowed), and anglers can keep five trout, with only one over 18 inches.

➤ **Hatches:** All hatch dates are approximations and vary year to year depending on weather and water levels.
Midges: March 1–June 15.
Blue-winged Olives (Baetis): April 15–June 15.
Pale Morning Duns: July 15–August 15.
Grasshoppers: July 10–August 30.
Yellow Sallies: July 20–August 20.
Pale Olives (Baetis): August 1–September 30.
Black Caddis: August 5–September 2.5
Tricos: August 20–October 20.
Blue-winged Olives (Baetis): October 10–November 15.

➤ **Fishing regulations:** Open year-round. Nonmotorized vessels only on the upper 12 miles below Afterbay Dam. Artificial flies and lures on upper 12 miles. Bait fishing allowed below Bighorn Access. Bag limit: five fish, brown or rainbow, only one fish over 18 inches.

➤ **Tackle:** Use 9-foot, 5- or 6-weight rods for nymph or streamer fishing, and 9-foot 4-weights for dry-fly fishing. Reels should be large enough to hold at least 50 yards of 20-pound backing.

Breathable waders and wading shoes are recommended.

World champion Spey caster Whitney Gould. Hale Harris

HALE HARRIS grew up fishing the trout rivers of the Rocky Mountain West. He has worked as a guide in Alaska and western Montana. He currently makes his home in Fort Smith, Montana, where he is the co-owner of Bighorn Trout Shop (www.bighorntroutshop.com), one of the premier fly shops and lodges on the Bighorn River.

CLOSEST FLY SHOPS
There are three primary fly shops in Fort Smith. These shops also have lodging and guide service. There are a number of other independent outfitters and lodges without retail shops.
Bighorn Trout Shop
P.O. Box 7477
Fort Smith, MT 59035
406-666-2375

Bighorn Angler
P.O. Box 7578
Fort Smith, MT 59035
406-666-2233

Bighorn Fly & Tackle
P.O. Box 7497
Fort Smith, MT 59035
406-666-2253

CLOSEST LODGES
Forrester's Bighorn River Resort
P.O. Box 795
Fort Smith, MT 59035
406-666-9199

Kingfisher Lodge
P.O. Box 7828
Fort Smith, MT 59035
406-666-2326

CLOSEST AND BEST CAMPGROUNDS
Afterbay Campground is a public, free-camping campground managed by the National Park Service. It is located just west of Fort Smith. Campers must have a Park Service daily-use permit, or annual Park Service pass.

Cottonwood Campground is a private campground located near Three Mile Access. Full RV hookups, showers, cabins, and laundry service are available.
Cottonwood Campground
P.O. Box 7667
Fort Smith, MT 59035
406-666-2391

CLOSEST AND BEST RESTAURANT
Polly's Place
11 Main St.
Fort Smith, MT 59035
406-666-2255

BEST PLACE TO GET A COLD, STIFF DRINK
The river is located within the confines of the Crow Indian Reservation, where the sale of alcohol is prohibited. Closest bars are located in Hardin, MT.

CLOSEST EMERGENCY MEDICAL HELP
Big Horn County Memorial Hospital
17 N Miles Ave.
Hardin, MT 59034
406-665-2310

WIRELESS ACCESS
The local restaurant and fly shops have wireless access.

CELL PHONE SERVICE
None.

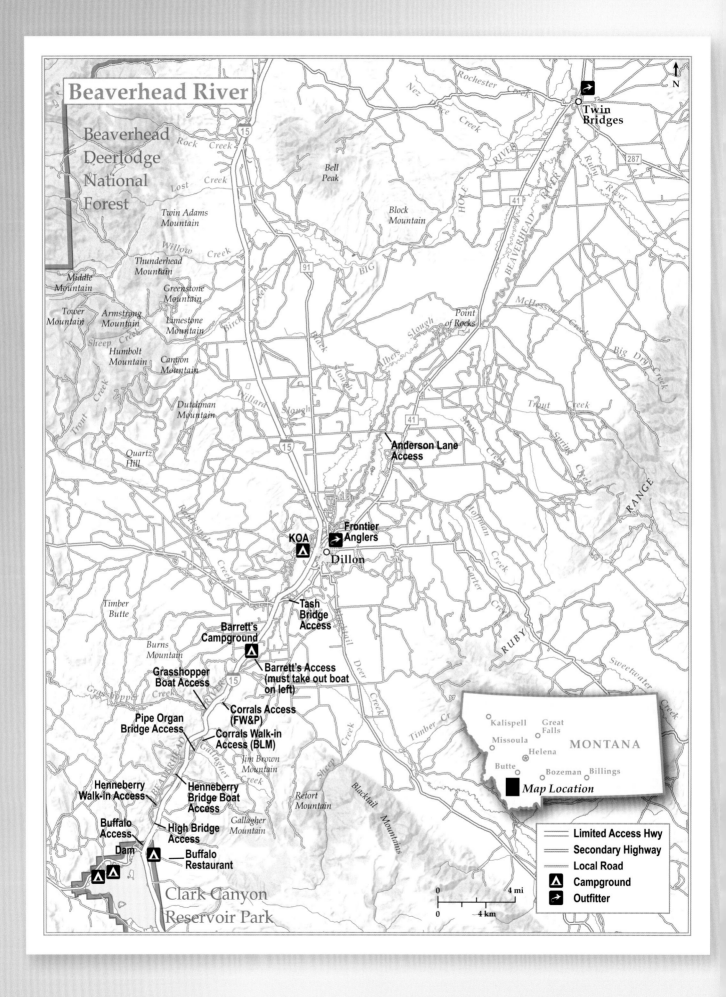

Beaverhead River

Beaverhead
Deerlodge
National
Forest

Rock Creek

Lost Creek

Twin Adams Mountain

Willow Creek

Bell Peak

Block Mountain

Thunderhead Mountain

Middle Mountain

Greenstone Mountain

Tower Mountain

Armstrong Mountain

Limestone Mountain

Humbolt Mountain

Canyon Mountain

Sheep Creek

Trout Creek

Birch Creek

Park Creek

Dutchman Mountain

Quartz Hill

Willard Slough

Hotel Creek

Albers Slough

Point of Rocks

Nez Perce Creek

Rochester Creek

Twin Bridges

BIG HOLE RIVER

BEAVERHEAD RIVER

McHessor Creek

Big Dry Creek

Trout Creek

Stone Creek

Ruby River

287

41

Anderson Lane Access

Hoffman Creek

Carter Creek

RANGE

KOA

Frontier Anglers

Dillon

Tash Bridge Access

Barrett's Campground

Grasshopper Boat Access

Barrett's Access (must take out boat on left)

Timber Butte

Burns Mountain

Grasshopper Creek

Corrals Access (FW&P)

Pipe Organ Bridge Access

Corrals Walk-in Access (BLM)

Jim Brown Mountain

Gallagher Creek

Henneberry Walk-in Access

Henneberry Bridge Boat Access

Retort Mountain

Gallagher Mountain

Blacktail Deer Creek

Sheep Creek

Timber Cr

Blacktail Mountains

RUBY

Sweetwater Creek

Buffalo Access

Dam

High Bridge Access

Buffalo Restaurant

Clark Canyon Reservoir Park

Kalispell

Great Falls

Missoula

Helena

MONTANA

Butte

Bozeman

Billings

Map Location

──	Limited Access Hwy
──	Secondary Highway
──	Local Road
⛺	Campground
→	Outfitter

0   4 mi

0   4 km

Beaverhead River *(Montana)*

➤ **Location:** An hour's drive south of Butte, 2 hours southwest of Bozeman, and 3 hours south of Missoula. Each of these Montana cities provides full accommodations, as well as daily flight services to and from most major airports, and car rentals.

The Beaverhead River is one of the finest tailwater trout fisheries in Montana, with a long and renowned history. From Lewis and Clark to the present, the Beaverhead River has been at the forefront of our Western heritage. To aid the reader, we will divide the river into sections. We will start with the top section, drift down a few miles, and keep on going.

The Beaverhead River begins its course at the base of Clark Canyon Reservoir. Joined by the highly regarded Ruby River just upstream from the town of Twin Bridges, it gains momentum before its final confluence with the famous Big Hole River, forming another legendary river, the Jefferson. This confluence lies only a few miles north of Twin Bridges. It has been said that if you were to straighten out the Beaverhead, it would reach to the other side of Montana. There is roughly 85 miles of river compared to some 50 miles of road, reflecting its twisting and winding nature.

As with all bottom-release dams, the first pool is very deep, but from this point on the river takes on its own distinct appealing character and becomes a trout haven. This is big-fish water, all the way down to High Bridge, but these large rainbows and browns have a keen interest in survival.

Access in this area is by wade fishing or floating. Wade fishing by the dam is difficult, but downstream the river shallows and even at high flows some wading can be found. There is some very deep water between Buffalo Bridge and High Bridge, but the water becomes shallow again before entering the High Bridge area. There are boat launch sites at the dam, Buffalo Bridge, and High Bridge.

The insect life in this entire section is off the charts. Most of the activity will be below the surface, but dry-fly fishing from July through October can be exceptional. The large fish,

Stalking large fish along a section of the Beaverhead. Tim Tollett

Beaverhead Rock, where Sacajawea led Lewis and Clark through Beaverhead Country. Tim Tollett

both rainbows and browns, are savvy, and fly presentation needs to be accurate and drag-free, which provides a fair challenge. Pale Morning Duns, Blue-winged Olives, Little Yellow Sallies, crane flies, and caddisflies make up the bulk of the insect population, but small forage fish, snails, sow bugs, scuds, and everything else that lives in the area constantly add to an already rich diet.

From High Bridge downstream to Pipe Organ Bridge is classic Beaverhead River fishing. Enticing riffles, winding bends, and deep runs blend together, offering a unique and distinctive fishery. The river runs through a varied environment with lots of bank and streambed structure. Trying to wet a fly can be challenging to say the least. During midsummer, the river flows bank-full. Trout population is around 3,700 fish per mile, one of the highest concentrations anywhere. There are big browns and rainbows throughout this section. You can lose a lot of flies trying to catch these trout, but every penny spent on flies usually comes back in big rewards.

"It's like we're standing on a streambed of moving insects," a friend said years ago while wading below Henneberry Bridge. As with most of the Beaverhead's journey, prolific hatches of PMDs, BWOs, caddisflies, crane flies, and Yellow Sallies keep these fish well fed. Nymphing is most productive, but tossing a well-presented dry fly will prove valuable at times. A box of streamers should also be handy. If you ask our local fishery biologist about the health and overall productivity of the Beaverhead River, you will find much of his research based in this area. The proportion of brown trout to rainbows is roughly 70/30 percent, although down toward Pipe Organ the population of rainbows lessens.

Access for floaters is at High Bridge, but limited wade fishing can be found here also. The Henneberry Access Site is strictly for waders. Other access sites are at Henneberry Bridge and Pipe Organ Bridge, both offering wading and float access. There is also another fishing access site across Henneberry Bridge.

Pipe Organ to the Grasshopper area, 4 or 5 miles, the river is rich in quality trout habitat and, with a healthy population of 2- to 4-year-old wild trout, and the catch rate increases. Hatches are basically the same, but in the last 10 years or so we are seeing more large insects such as Green Drakes and Golden Stones.

From Grasshopper to Barrett's Diversion Dam marks the last section of what is referred to as the upper river. The wading access is limited here, but the Corrals, located on the frontage road, will give anglers a place to exercise some trout. The Grasshopper and Barrett's access sites both provide float and limited wade fishing.

Insect life remains the same for this area, with abundant caddis. Although the rainbow population diminishes, good-size browns are plentiful and offer quality fishing.

From Barrett's downstream, the river becomes more re-strictive and access is an issue. You can float from Barrett's down to Tash Bridge, but there are low bridges that, during high flows, can become hazardous. At Tash Bridge, you will find float access with some wading available. The next take-out is at Cornell Park just down the road from KOA. This float is called Tash to Trash. The river runs much smaller down here, so boat size should be considered.

Bug life is similar, but differs in that, come August, most aquatic insect hatches will slow and terrestrials become more important. When I started fishing the Beaverhead, this was my favorite area to fish—and still is, especially for lunch breaks. It is loaded with nice trout, mostly browns with the occasional good rainbow.

From the bridge at Cornel Park downstream, access is ex-tremely limited. The area around the park does provide good wading, but then the river flows through a section that is tight and hardly worth the effort. Selway Bridge to Anderson Lane marks what I would consider the last of the best-quality water to fish and should be floated, as the river flows through private land. There are fish below Anderson Lane, but the count drops significantly to around 300 fish per mile, and access is at bridges only. There are some very large trout here. They have to be to survive, but water quality and catch rates are low. The floats between the bridges should only be con-sidered during high flows, as you'll need a sleeping bag oth-erwise.

➤ **Bugs for the Beaverhead River:** Zebra Midge in olive, black, and brown, #18 and #20; Pheasant-tail Nymph, #14- to #18; PT Cruiser in olive, orange, and yellow, #14 to #18; Troth's Elk-hair Caddis, #10 to #16; Yuk Bug in black and olive, #4 to #8; Zonker in pearl, copper, and olive, #2 to 8; T-Bur Stone in #4. T-T Tupps, #14 and #16; Sparkle Spider in light and dark

A large brown taken on one of Tim's famous Sparkle Spider dry flies. Tim Tollett

olive, #16 to #18. Smidget in chartreuse, olive, and gray, #16 and #18; Partridge and Peacock, #12 to #16; MVP in olive, black, and gray, #16 and #18; Brown Bear Brown, #6 to #14; Tim's Crayman, #6 to 10. Ray Charles in orange, pink, gray, and white, #16 and 18.

➤ **Flow rates:** Winter flows vary from 50 to 200 cfs. During peak water releases, June through the first part of August, flows may reach 800 to 900 cfs. Wade fishing becomes much easier below 600 cfs.

➤ **Hatches:** Beaverhead hatches kick into gear in March with prolific hatches of Blue-winged Olives and midges. Blue-wingeds will continue until late April/first part of May, with midges present the entire season.

PMDs (Pale Morning Duns) start around June 20, and some years will provide great fishing as late as the end of Au-gust.

Little Yellow Sallies begin their summer emergence around June 15 and will continue into the first part of September.

Caddis hatches start with the famous Mothers Day Cad-dis hatch toward the end of April/first part of May, taper off a bit, and then explode from late June until late September with the large October Caddis.

Crane flies can be found throughout the season, but are heaviest from the end of July through mid-September.

Tricos start in mid-August and last until mid-September.

A piggish rainbow. Fish like this really put on a show and most are never landed. Tim Tollett

➤ **Fishing regulations:** The Beaverhead is open all year from Pipe Organ Bridge to its confluence with the Big Hole River. The section from Clark Canyon Dam to Pipe Organ Bridge is open from the third Saturday in May through November 30.

Daily and possession limit is five trout, one rainbow, and one over 18 inches.

High Bridge Fishing Access Site to Henneberry FAS is closed to float fishing by nonresidents and float outfitting each Saturday from the third Saturday in May through Labor Day. The section from Henneberry Bridge FAS to Pipe Organ Bridge is closed to float fishing by nonresidents and float outfitting on each Sunday from the third Saturday in May through Labor Day. From Tash Bridge (Highway 91 South) to Selway Bridge, the river is closed to float outfitting from the third Saturday in May through Labor Day.

➤ **Please Note:** Wading anglers are not bound by these regulations.

Although motors up to 9.9 horsepower are allowed, the Beaverhead is much too small for motors, and the serenity would be ruined.

➤ **Tackle:** Nine-foot rods for 4- to 6-weight lines are generally preferred. Most anglers use floating lines. Personally, I favor 10-foot rods for 3- and 4-weight lines. They are more

useful when dealing with tricky Beaverhead currents. Sinking lines can prove valuable at times. A quality fly reel with a strong drag system that will hold at least 30 to 50 yards of backing is a must. Beaverhead trout will abuse your tackle.

Nine-foot leaders tapered from 0X down to 5X are standard, depending on fly choice, but longer leaders offer an advantage when drift is a concern. Using two flies, whether streamers, dry flies, nymphs, or any combination thereof, is standard procedure. There are a number of different methods to attach two flies, but most combinations are tied "inline"— tie the second fly off the bend of the first hook. The second fly should be attached to a 12- to 22-inch tippet section, depending on fly choice—shorter for nymphs, longer for a dry fly/ nymph combo or streamer rig. Most nymph anglers prefer to place split-shot between the two flies, but some attach it at the end of the leader with two short (6- or 8-inch) drop tippets arranged 8 inches or so up from the shot. Always, as with any dropper setup, don't tie the flies too close together or they'll tangle. When using the inline method, tie either a blood or surgeon's knot to keep split-shot from sliding. When placing split-shot at the bottom, put an overhand knot below the shot.

During the cooler months, breathable chest waders are recommended. Layer up as needed for cool morning and evenings. Summer is wet-wading time. The Beaverhead is not very slippery, and most of the time wading boots with

A beautiful, healthy Beaverhead brown trout that fell victim to a size #18 Get-R-Dun. Tim Tollett

TIM TOLLETT grew up in a fly-fishing family; his dad showed him the ropes at a young age. He started tying flies commercially in 1964, and began his guiding career in 1977 working for Al Troth. In 1980, he and his wife Teresa opened Frontier Anglers, one of the West's largest fly-fishing shops.

rubber soles will suffice. A wading staff can be a nice addition.

Montana weather changes fast, so be prepared. It can turn cold during any month. Rainjackets and a few add-ons can make or break a day on the water.

CLOSEST FLY SHOPS

Tim Tollett's Frontier Anglers
680 No. Montana St.
Dillon, MT 59725
406-683-5276
frontieranglers@gmail.com
www.frontieranglers.com

Backcountry Anglers
426 South Atlantic St.
Dillon, MT 59725
406-683-3462
backcountry@backcountryangler.com
www.backcountryangler.com

Four Rivers Fishing Company
201 North Main St.
Twin Bridges, MT 59754
406-684-5651
4R@4RiversMontana.com
www.4riversmontana.com

Stonefly Inn
409 North Main St.
Twin Bridges, MT 59754
406-684-5648
info@thestoneflyinn.com
www.thestoneflyinn.com

CLOSEST LODGES

Expedition Lodge
1120 Eliason Lane
Dillon, MT 59725
406-925-1684
justin@tightlinemontana.com
www.tightlinemontana.com

Ruby Springs Lodge
2487 Montana 287
Sheridan, MT 59749
406-842-5250
info@rubyspringslodge.com
www.rubyspringslodge.com

CLOSEST AND BEST HOTEL

The Guest House Inn
580 Sinclair St. (Exit 63)
Dillon, MT 59725
406-683-3636
dillon.mt@guesthouseintl.com
www.guesthouseintl.com

CLOSEST AND BEST CAMPGROUND

KOA
735 West Park Street
Dillon, MT 59725
406-683-2749
koa.com/campgrounds/dillon

CLOSEST RESTAURANT

Buffalo Lodge
155 Lake Front Road
(Just off of Exit 44 on I-15,
across from Clark Canyon Dam)
406-683-5535

BEST RESTAURANT

Lion's Den
725 North Montana St.
Dillon, MT
406-683-2051

BEST PLACES TO GET A COLD, STIFF DRINK

Buffalo Lodge (above)

Mac's Last Cast/Blacktail Station
265 Montana St.
Dillon, MT
406-683-6611

CLOSEST EMERGENCY MEDICAL HELP

Barrett Hospital
600 Montana Hwy. 91 South
Dillon, MT 59725
406-683-3000

CELL PHONE SERVICE
Good throughout the area.

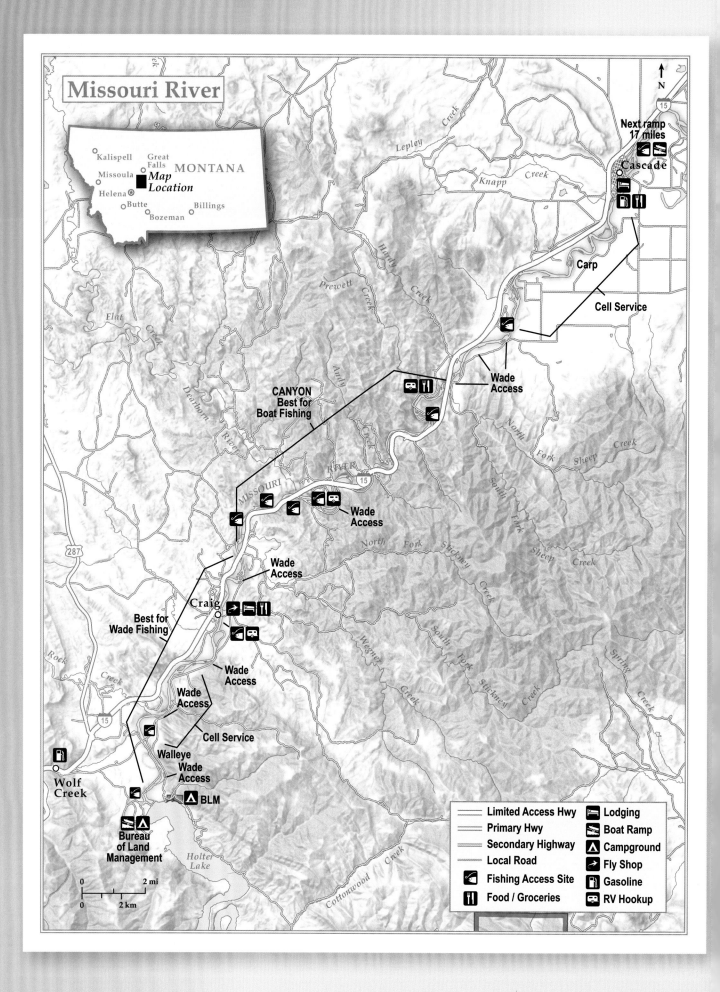

Missouri River

MONTANA

Kalispell
Great Falls
Missoula
Map Location
Helena
Butte
Billings
Bozeman

N

Next ramp 17 miles

Cascade

Carp

Cell Service

Wade Access

CANYON
Best for Boat Fishing

Wade Access

Wade Access

Wade Access

Craig

Best for Wade Fishing

Wade Access

Wade Access

Cell Service

Walleye Wade Access

Wolf Creek

BLM

Bureau of Land Management

Holter Lake

| 0 | | 2 mi |
| 0 | | 2 km |

▬▬▬	Limited Access Hwy		🛏	Lodging
▬▬▬	Primary Hwy		🚤	Boat Ramp
▬▬▬	Secondary Highway		⛺	Campground
▬▬▬	Local Road		➤	Fly Shop
◼	Fishing Access Site		⛽	Gasoline
🍴	Food / Groceries		🚐	RV Hookup

Missouri River *(Central Montana)*

➤ **Locations:** The upper Missouri River and Holter Dam are 45 miles south of Great Falls and 45 miles north of Helena—both have daily commercial flights. Missoula and Bozeman are 2½ hours away, and Calgary, Alberta and Spokane, Washington approximately 6 hours away.

The longest river in North America, the Missouri begins at Three Forks, Montana, at the confluence of the Madison, Gallatin, and Jefferson Rivers. Most of the Missouri holds little interest to fly anglers, but the 35-mile, crystal-clear tailwater between Holter Dam and Cascade offers some of the best trout fishing in the West. Known for its massive hatches and phenomenal dry-fly fishing, this giant river also offers some of the most user-friendly wade and float fishing to be found in the state.

The Missouri's waters flow reliably clear. During June runoff, when many Montana rivers are high and dirty, the Missouri is clear. This holds true even at high flows over 20,000 cfs. Off-color conditions are produced by small tributaries below Holter Dam (Little Prickly Pear Creek, Dearborn River, Stickney Creek) but typically last only a short time. Holter Dam is a hydro-generating gravity dam, and spills water from just below the top of the reservoir. Because of this, water temperatures fluctuate more dramatically than on many bottom-release Western tailwaters. This results in a wider temperature range and more diverse insect populations. Daily fluctuations are rare and small, as Holter is a run-of-the-river dam.

The village of Craig is the angling center. Lodging, fly shops, food and beverages, and the latest conditions can always be found in Craig, one of the last great rural "trout towns," with a fun social scene during the summer.

The Holter region can be divided into three sections. From Holter Dam to the mouth of the Dearborn River, the Missouri flows at a moderate pace over a small limestone gravel bottom. This is classic "spring creek" water, with islands, side channels, and almost unlimited access. It offers fantastic dry, nymph, and streamer fishing.

From the mouth of the Dearborn River to Sheep Creek, the Missouri flows through the "Canyon." Limestone cliffs surround the river, and the water is more reminiscent of a big freestone river. Faster riffles lead to large, deep pools. Riprap banks are common, and the water is more suited to attractor fishing and prospecting with nymphs and streamers. While access is still plentiful, this section is most often fished from a boat.

At Sheep Creek, the river spills out onto the Great Plains. It slows and broadens to well over 100 yards in most places. The easy, flat flow on this section offers some of the best selective dry-fly fishing anywhere. Access is somewhat limited, and floating is the rule. Strong winds coming off the Front Range can make a float on this section a gamble, and you must pay close attention to the weather forecast. The trout fishing doesn't end at Cascade, but access points become few and far between below this point.

Trout populations are very dense (4,000–6,000 per mile), both rainbow and brown trout. You may encounter the occasional brook trout, and whitefish are present. Spillover walleye from upstream reservoirs have increased to the point

Sunset at the village of Craig. Mark Raisler

that they are quite common, and fly fishers even target them in spring and fall. There is no limit on walleye, and retention is encouraged.

Trout average 16 to 18 inches, and fish from 20 to 24-plus inches are not uncommon. It can be argued that the Missouri has the largest average fish size in Montana. Tippet-snapping runs make quality reels and terminal tackle critical. These trout are known for their incredible strength and addiction to feeding on the surface.

The Missouri is famous for its tremendous hatches and unrivaled dry-fly fishing. Well-known hatches include March

Guide Ben Hardy with a fat springtime brown. Mark Raisler

Browns, *Baetis*, Pale Morning Duns, Tricos, *Pseudobaetis*, and *Callibaetis*. Caddis hatches are phenomenal all season, but peak in late June and July when they cover the water from early morning until past dark. Yellow Sallies hatch in good numbers, especially on the middle reaches of the Canyon. Midges are important all year. Giant Golden Stones and occasional Salmonflies make their appearance, but are localized. Scuds, sow bugs, and leeches are also important parts of the biomass, as are juvenile trout, whitefish, and carp.

Fishing techniques depend on stream flows. The Missouri River runs from 3,500–20,000 cfs, depending on snowpack and season. Flows between 4,000–7,000 cfs are the most common. Nymph fishing is effective at all flows; adjust your depth and weight. Dry-fly fishing is much more flow-dependent. In general, flows at or below 6,000 cfs afford the best dry-fly fishing. When flows increase to 8,000–10,000 cfs, dry-fly fishing is almost nonexistent. Streamer fishing is also best at lower flows (below 10,000 cfs). Flows between 3,500–6,000 cfs prevail for most of the season.

Dry-fly fishing attracts crowds from all over the world, and is largely technical. Bring your spring-creek tactics and you will do fine. Downstream presentations are by far the most effective when targeting rising fish, whether wading or boating. Most anglers use fast-action 9-foot, 5-weight rods. Leaders should be 10 to 15 feet long, tapered to 4X or 5X.

Many anglers use drift boats to float from pod to pod, anchoring up and across from the fish before taking turns. This is the most common technical dry-fly approach. Missouri River trout are not as tippet-shy as one might expect, but are ultrasensitive to poor presentations and noise. A stealthy approach is required, and in mid- to late summer, long casts must be perfect on the first attempt.

Even so, there are times when dry-fly fishing is easier. Springtime brings the first big hatches of the year—BWOs, March Browns, Mothers Day Caddis, and *Skwalas*—and

fishing can be phenomenal. In mid- to late summer, terrestrials are critical to your success. Hoppers are obviously important, but ant and beetle patterns probably account for more fish in the net.

Nymphing is extremely effective. "Right-angle" techniques are the most effective in the relatively slow flows. Straight leaders 4 to 12 feet long with split-shot and tandem nymph rigs are the most common. Takes can be very subtle, and a high-floating but sensitive indicator is a must. The most common nymph patterns imitate caddis, mayflies, scuds, and midges.

"Inside-out" nymphing from the boat is somewhat unique to the Missouri, and involves running the boat down the shallow "beach" side of the river, casting weighted nymph rigs toward the center. This allows you to drift at a slower pace, and move quickly to the shore to land fish. This seam is where most Missouri River trout do their subsurface feeding.

"Short-leash" nymphing has become increasingly popular. The short-leash method employs a very small indicator and a short (1- to 2-foot) unweighted nymph rig using small caddis and mayfly patterns. Essentially a "hopper-dropper" rig with no hoppers and two droppers, it can produce amazing results during the afternoon when surface activity is slim.

Most nymph anglers use a 9- to 10-foot, fast-action rod that throws a 5- or 6-weight line. Longer rods are very popular during June, when nymph rigs may be as long as 12 feet from indicator to split-shot.

Streamer fishing is very popular, and you can literally fish the entire side of the river on any float. The slower flows give the trout an extended opportunity to view your offering, and short strikes are not uncommon during late summer and early fall. The best patterns are small, flashy baitfish imitations. A floating or intermediate sink-tip line is all that is required during most of the season, though heavy tips are popular during the winter. Due to fly size and the long cast required, 6- or 7-weight rods are preferred.

Fishing generally ramps up in April, and the first big hatches of the year typically begin around May 1. Early summer often means higher flows, and nymphing is both popular and effective through June. By July 1, the river has dropped and we are in the peak of dry-fly season. Terrestrial fishing takes over in August and September, before the fall hatches return with cooler weather. Fishing remains excellent through December 1.

The Missouri is a year-round river, and while most fishing takes place from April through October, there is a fair amount of off-season traffic during the winter. Midges keep fish rising with the proper weather conditions. Streamer and nymph fishing are very effective as well. Finding fish in slower and deeper water is necessary, but easy during this time. Many Montana anglers take advantage of this quiet time of year.

➤ **Hatches:**

Baetis: April–May, October–November.

March Browns: April–May.

PMDs: June–August.

Callibaetis: June–September.

Tricos: July–September.

Brown Drakes: June–July.

Pseudocloeons: August–September.

Caddis: May–September, peak late June and July.

Yellow Sallies: July–August.

Hoppers: July–September.

Midges: October–November and February–April.

➤ **Fishing regulations:** Open year-round.

Holter Dam to Cascade Bridge: combined trout three daily and in possession, only one over 18 inches, and only one may be a brown trout. Walleye: no limit.

Floating is allowed, as are powerboats with no motor restrictions.

➤ **Tackle:**

Rods: Fast-action, 8½- or 9-foot 5- and 6-weights. Tapered leaders 10 to 15 feet, 3X to 5X.

Nymphs: Fast-action 9- to 10-foot 5- and 6-weights. Straight, 10-foot, 2X leaders, fluorocarbon tippet 3X to 5X.

Streamers: 9-foot 6- and 7-weights.

Reels: Strong, smooth drag with at least 50 yards of backing; expect long, fast runs.

JOHN ARNOLD has been guiding in the northern Rockies for over 25 years and is the co-owner of Headhunters on the Missouri River near Craig, Montana. When not working, he spends time chasing steelhead, trout, and saltwater species with his wife Julie and daughter Adair.

CLOSEST FLY SHOPS

Headhunters Fly Shop
145 Bridge St.
Craig, MT 59648 (406-235-3447)
info@headhuntersflyshop.com
www.headhuntersflyshop.com

Montana River Outfitters
515 Recreation Rd.
Wolf Creek, MT 59648 (406-235-4350)
flyshop@montana.com
www.montanariveroutfitters.com

Crosscurrents
311 Bridge St.
Craig, MT 59648 (406-235-3433)
crosscurrentsflyshop@gmail.com
www.crosscurrents.com

Prewitt Creek Fly Shop
2468 Old U.S. Hwy. 91
Cascade, MT 59421 (406-468-9244)
prewettcreekinn.com
reservations@prewettcreekinn.com

The Trout Shop
275 Bridge St.
Craig, MT 59648 (800-337-8528)
flyshop@thetroutshop.com
www.thetroutshop.com

CLOSEST OUTFITTERS AND GUIDES

John Arnold
Falls Outfitters
P.O. Box 522
Cascade, MT 59421 (406-235-3447)
www.headhuntersflyshop.com

Mark Raisler
Get the Drift Outfitters
P.O. Box 74
Wolf Creek, MT 59648 (406-235-3447)
www.headhuntersflyshop.com

CLOSEST LODGE

Missouri River Ranch
2655 Craig River Rd.
Craig, MT 59648 (406-235-4116)
www.missouririverranch.com

BEST HOTEL

Craig Lodging
145 Bridge St.
Craig, MT 59648 (406-235-3447)
info@headhuntersflyshop.com
www.craiglodging.com

BEST CAMPGROUND

Holter Lake Recreation Site
406-235-4314
www.blm.gov/mt
search for Holter Lake

BEST RESTAURANT

Izaak's Restaurant
105 Bridge St.
Craig, MT 59648 (406-235-3456)
replies@izaaks.com
www.izaaks.com

BEST PLACE TO GET A COLD, STIFF DRINK

The Craig Bar (Joe's)
50 Main St.
Craig, MT 59648 (406-235-9994)

CLOSEST EMERGENCY MEDICAL HELP

Benefis Hospital
1101 26th St. South
Great Falls, MT 59405 (406-455-5000)

CELL PHONE SERVICE

Wolf Creek to Craig, and near Cascade. Much of the river and many rental homes have no service. Headhunters in Craig is a cell phone and WiFi hotspot.

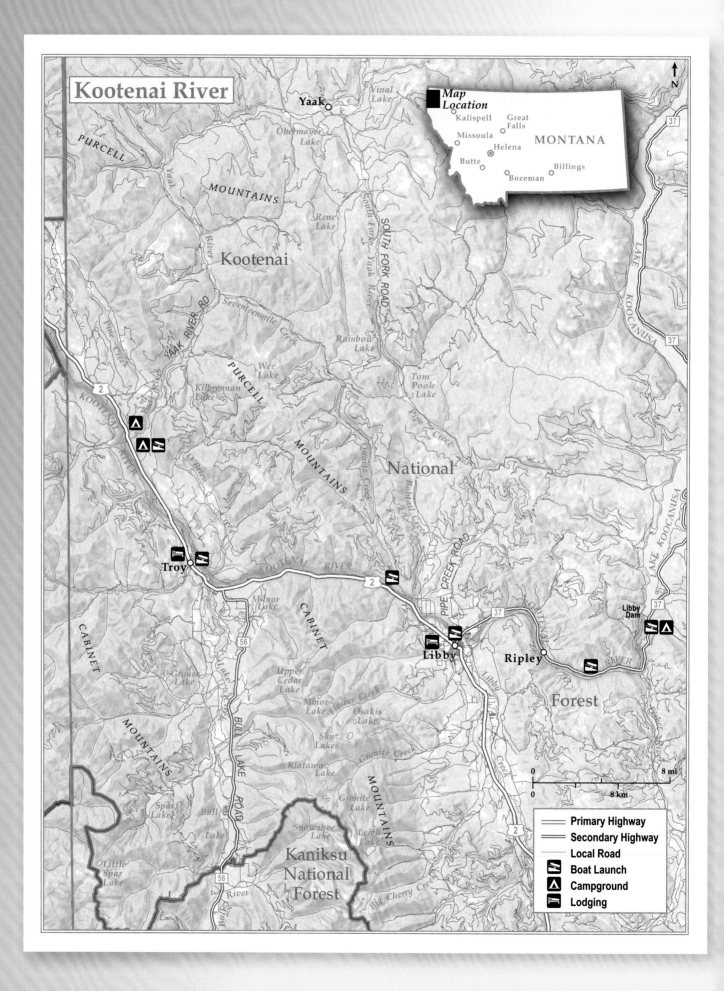

Kootenai River

MONTANA

Map Location

Kalispell
Great Falls
Missoula
Helena
Butte
Bozeman
Billings

Yaak

PURCELL

MOUNTAINS

Obermayer Lake

Vinal Lake

Rene Lake

Kootenai

Yaak River

SOUTH FORK ROAD

South Fork Yaak River

YAAK RIVER RD

Seventeenmile Creek

PURCELL

Wee Lake

Kilbrennan Lake

Rainbow Lake

Tom Poole Lake

MOUNTAINS

Pipe Creek

National

Bobtail Creek

Quartz Creek

O'Brien Creek

Pine Creek

Troy

KOOTENAI RIVER

KOOTENAI RIVER

2

CABINET

Milnor Lake

PIPE CREEK ROAD

2

Libby

37

Ripley

Libby Dam

Forest

LAKE KOOCANUSA

37

KOOTENAI RIVER

56

CABINET

MOUNTAINS

Upper Cedar Lake

Minor Lake

Flower Creek

Osakis Lake

Skyr Lakes

Granite Creek

Libby Creek

Grouse Lake

BULL LAKE ROAD

Bull Lake

Klatawa Lake

Granite Lake

MOUNTAINS

Spar Lake

Bull Lake

Snowshoe Lake

Leigh Lake

Little Spar Lake

56

Bull River

Kaniksu National Forest

Big Cherry Creek

2

0   8 mi
0   8 km

Primary Highway
Secondary Highway
Local Road
Boat Launch
Campground
Lodging

Kootenai River *(Northwest Montana)*

➤ **Location:** The Kootenai River is located in the extreme northwest corner of Montana. Three major airports serve this area—Spokane, Washington, about 3 hours away; Kalispell, Montana, about 2 hours; and Missoula, Montana, about 4 hours.

The Kootenai is Montana's largest tailwater fishery, with over half its drainage located in British Columbia. To that end, it's a major headwater tributary of the Columbia River and an arm of the Columbia hydropower system. The Libby Dam is located 18 miles north of Libby, Montana. The trout fishery begins immediately below the dam, offering approximately 40 miles of fishable water to the Idaho border. Above the Libby Dam, Lake Koocanusa Reservoir extends over 100 miles into the Canadian Rockies.

This northwest corner of Montana is not typical Big Sky Country. Instead, it's a place of dense coniferous forests, lush mountains, and river bottoms, and a place where the Pacific rainforest ecosystem crashes into the spine of the northern Rocky Mountains. The Kootenai Basin is unique, in that the river actually runs at only about 3,000 feet in elevation, making it one of the lowest riparian zones in the state. Weather and conditions throughout the winter are likely more mild than one might imagine.

The Kootenai flows through the towns of Libby and Troy, Montana. Greater Libby has a population of approximately 10,000, and Troy is far smaller, with around 2,000 full-time residents. Logging supported this area for many years and is still responsible for a portion of the economic base, although it's much diminished as an industry. You will be welcomed here with a smile; tourism dollars are greatly appreciated.

Primarily a rainbow trout fishery, the Kootenai boasts the state's only native strain, called inland-redband rainbows. Known for being strong, hard fighting, and extraordinarily acrobatic, Kootenai rainbows average 12 to 20 inches. It's not uncommon for a Kootenai rainbow to rip off 50 feet of line and jump three or four times before your skills catch up with your adrenaline. Westslope cutthroat trout are also native to the Kootenai, as well as bull trout. Bull trout are actually members of the char family, and are awesome natives, thrilling to catch, and range from 5 to 10 pounds. When float-

ing over bull trout holes, anglers are often reminded to keep hands and feet inside the drift boat.

The Kootenai is broad, wide, and big water by any standards, and most efficiently fished from a drift boat. It offers consistent, steady flows throughout the season. Pre-runoff fishing begins in March when daytime temps start to warm. While this time of year is primarily about nymphing, for a period of 4 to 6 weeks sporadic hatches of March Browns, *Baetis*, and midges are sufficient to provide some early season dry-fly action. Snowmelt and runoff starts in earnest around the first of May, and the gates of the Libby Dam are

Kootenai River rainbow catching some air. Jim Lampros

wide open. It's a vast basin, and this time of year the river is unfishable for the most part. But by mid-June the annual runoff event is largely over, discharge from Libby Dam is reduced, and the official summer season kicks off.

Consistent dry-fly fishing is the *modus operandi* of the summer season, and the Kootenai's long runs and flat pools are perfectly suited for endless drifts. With steady flows and temperatures from Libby Dam throughout the season, hatches of Pale Morning Duns and caddis are predictable and always have fish looking up. As the summer deepens, terrestrials like hoppers and ants add new opportunities for anglers and trout alike. Due to the lack of fishing pressure, attractor patterns like Royal Wulffs, Parachute Adams, Stimulators, and Tarantulas are still very effective. Swinging soft

135

Old haul bridge on the Kootenai River. Tim Linehan

hackles during hatches is an excellent Kootenai technique. If the fish aren't looking up for dries, nymphing and pulling streamers through specific runs and boulder gardens is always productive as well.

Four-, 5-, and 6-weight rods, floating lines, and 9-foot 5X leaders cover most bases from a dry-fly and nymphing point of view. Be sure to have a spool of 6X as well, especially during the fall. The Kootenai is still user-friendly in this respect. But that's not to say the average rainbows and cutthroat are pushovers. The Kootenai is flat and smooth for the most part and as the season progresses becomes absolutely gin-clear. Flies must be presented well and drag-free. But it's safe to say the resident trout here are far less sophisticated than they are on the more popular and famous tailwaters around the state. For running flies deep with sinking heads and streamers in search of truly large fish 7- and 8-weight rods are better tools. And two-handers and switch rods are also gaining in popularity and can be very effective tools for the big runs and pools of the Kootenai River.

The Kootenai is best fished from a drift boat, employing traditional float-and-wade techniques. Even at minimum flows, you cannot wade across the river. Drift boats offer access to the many midstream islands that have half-acre riffles at the heads and tails. These are prime spots only accessible by

boat. That's not to say the wading opportunities aren't worthy as well. Depending on annual snowpack, there are generally plenty of wading opportunities by about the middle of July, and access up and down the river is good.

The Kootenai may well be the biggest tailwater in Montana you've never heard of. But that's its inherent charm. Far less traveled, boasting good hatches, hard-fighting rainbows, and a friendly Northwest flavor, the Kootenai River is a solid blue-ribbon fishery.

➤ **Hatches:**
March: Blue-winged Olives, midges, Western March Browns.
April: Blue-winged Olives, midges, Western March Browns.
May: Blue-winged Olives, Western March Browns, Little Black Caddis, Grannom Caddis.
June: Little Black Caddis, Grannom Caddis, Blue-winged Olives, Pale Morning Duns.
July: Grannom Caddis, Pale Morning Duns, Green Drakes.
August: Grannom Caddis, Pale Morning Duns, Little Green Drakes, and terrestrials: hoppers, ants, and beetles.
September: Grannom Caddis, October Caddis, Little Green Drakes, Blue-winged Olives, and hoppers, ants, and beetles.
October: Blue-winged Olives, midges, Grannom Caddis, Microcaddis, October Caddis.

➤ **Fishing regulations:** The Kootenai is open to fishing throughout the entire year. Special regulations are in effect for certain stretches of the river. The Kootenai River is closed for bull trout; any bull trout caught must be immediately released.
Libby Dam to Highway 37 Bridge, near Fisher River:
Open June 1 through February 28.
Combined trout: one daily and in possession, 28-inch minimum length.
Highway 37 Bridge, near Fisher River, to Idaho border:
Open entire year.
Combined trout: four daily and in possession, includes three under 13 inches and only one over 18 inches.

➤ **Tackle:** Rods: 8½- or 9-foot with 5- or 6-weight floating line; 3- or 4-weight rod for small streams; 5- or 6-weight rod for bigger rivers. Matching reels and lines, including a sinking-tip line. Leaders and tippets: 9- to 12-foot tapered leaders, and spools of 3X, 4X, 5X, and 6X tippet material. Most versatile leader is a 9-foot 4X.

Waders and wading boots: lightweight, breathable waders with layers underneath; sticky rubber-soled wading boots with metal cleats. Long-sleeved, quick-drying fishing shirts, pants, and shorts.

Jimmy L. with his first Kootenai bull trout.
Linehan Outfitting Company

Donkey Kootenai River rainbow below Libby Dam.
Linehan Outfitting Company

TIM AND JOANNE LINEHAN own and operate Linehan Outfitting Company on the Kootenai River in northwest Montana. Since 1992, Tim has been guiding anglers on the Kootenai River and other rivers around the state. It's never been the Linehans' ambition to be one of the biggest companies in Montana—just one of the best. Visit www.fishmontana.com for more information.

CLOSEST FLY SHOPS

Kootenai Angler
13068 Hwy. 37 North
Libby, MT 59923
406-293-7578
www.montana-flyfishing.com

Kootenai River Outfitters
1604 Hwy. 2 East
Troy, MT 59935
406-295-9444
www.kroutfitters.com

CLOSEST OUTFITTERS AND GUIDES

Linehan Outfitting Company
482 Upper Ford Rd.
Troy, MT 59935
406-295-4872
www.fishmontana.com
linehan@fishmontana.com

Kootenai Angler
13068 Hwy. 37 North
Libby, MT 59923
406-293-7578
www.montana-flyfishing.com

Kootenai River Outfitters
1604 Hwy. 2 East
Troy, MT 59935
406-295-9444
www.kroutfitters.com

CLOSEST LODGES

Linehan Outfitting Company/
Kootenai River Lodge
1795 Kootenai River Rd.
Libby, MT 59923
406-295-4872
www.fishmontana.com
linehan@fishmontana.com

Linehan Outfitting Company/
Yaak Valley Log Cabins
35309 Yaak River Rd.
Troy, MT 59935
406-295-4872
www.fishmontana.com
linehan@fishmontana.com

Kootenai Angler
13068 Hwy 37 North,
Libby, MT 59923
406-293-7578
www.montana-flyfishing.com

BEST HOTEL

Sandman Motel
31901 U.S. Hwy. 2 West
Libby, MT 59923
406-293-8831
www.sandmanmotel.us

BEST CAMPGROUND

Dunn Creek/Libby Dam
U.S. Army Corps of Engineers
17877 Hwy. 37
Libby, MT 59923 (406-293-5577)
www.usace.army.mil; search for
"Libby Dam."

CLOSEST RESTAURANT

Red Dog Saloon
6788 Pipe Creek Rd.
Libby, MT 59923
406-293-8347

BEST PLACE TO GET A COLD, STIFF DRINK

Treasure Mountain Restaurant and Lounge
485 Hwy. 2 West
Libby, MT 59923 (406-293-8763)
www.libbytreasuremountain.com

CLOSEST EMERGENCY MEDICAL HELP

St. John Lutheran Hospital
350 Louisiana Ave.
Libby, MT 59923
406-293-0100

CELL PHONE SERVICE

In Libby, but spotty up and down the Kootenai River.

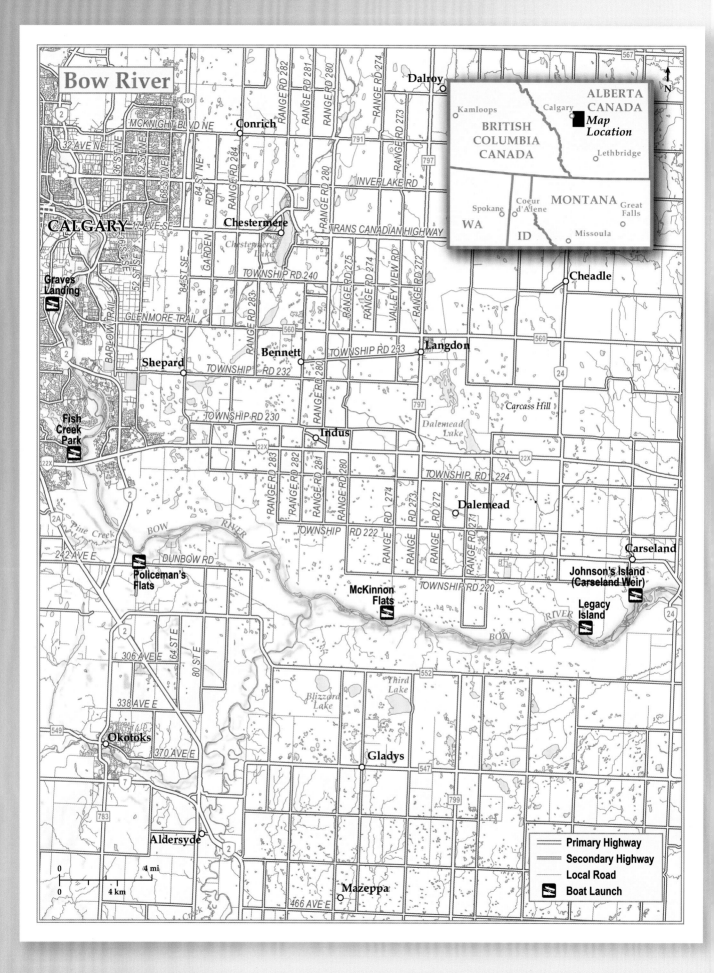

Bow River

CALGARY

Dalroy

Conrich

Chestermere

Cheadle

Graves
Landing

Shepard

Bennett

Langdon

Fish
Creek
Park

Indus

Carcass Hill

Dalemead
Lake

Chestermere
Lake

Dalemead

Carseland

Pine Creek

Policeman's
Flats

McKinnon
Flats

Johnson's Island
(Carseland Weir)

Legacy
Island

Okotoks

Gladys

Aldersyde

Mazeppa

Third
Lake

Blizzard
Lake

MCKNIGHT BLVD NE

32 AVE NE

GLENMORE TRAIL

BARLOW TRAIL

INVERLAKE RD

TRANS CANADIAN HIGHWAY

TOWNSHIP RD 240

TOWNSHIP RD 233

TOWNSHIP RD 232

TOWNSHIP RD 230

TOWNSHIP RD 224

TOWNSHIP RD 222

TOWNSHIP RD 220

DUNBOW RD

242 AVE E

306 AVE E

338 AVE E

370 AVE E

466 AVE E

BOW RIVER

Inset map

**ALBERTA
CANADA**

*Map
Location*

Kamloops

Calgary

Lethbridge

**BRITISH
COLUMBIA
CANADA**

Spokane

Coeur
d'Alene

MONTANA

Great
Falls

WA

ID

Missoula

N

Legend

— Primary Highway
— Secondary Highway
— Local Road
⊟ Boat Launch

0   4 mi

0   4 km

➤ Location: The river runs right through Calgary, Alberta. Calgary is a city of some 1.1 million people with full airline service, auto rentals, and all other accommodations for the visiting fly fisher and family.

Many anglers consider the Bow the go-to river in western Canada. Over the years, the Bow has received a great deal of recognition from Lefty Kreh and other fly-fishing celebrities, who praised its hard-fighting trout, the size of those trout, and the lack of crowds.

The Bow River begins its journey from glacier-fed Bow Lake in Banff National Park, then heads south and east, cutting through the Alberta Rockies, and then onto the Great Plains, where it meets the Oldman River and forms the South Saskatchewan River. It then continues north and east, eventually ending up in Hudson's Bay.

From a trout-fishing perspective, the stretch of river that gets the nod from anglers is the 40 miles located in and below Calgary, referred to as the Lower Bow. Above Calgary, the river is a victim of fluctuating flows from a number of hydro dams—this, coupled with cold water and low nutrients, results in low trout population and slow growth rates below the Banff town site. At the western edge of Calgary, the river enters the Bearspaw Reservoir, which stabilizes the flow and forms the tailwater. As the river winds through the city, it picks up nutrients from Calgary's sewage treatment plants. In this stretch it becomes a very healthy trout river loaded with browns and rainbows and diverse aquatic insect life that gets the trout looking up.

The Bow River fly-fishing experience is unique, in that most visiting anglers spend evenings in a Calgary hotel or motel before heading out to one of six different floats—including the City Stretch, literally downtown! Below Calgary, the river is on the prairie. The river has carved a spectacular valley teeming with wildlife, with the land adjacent to the river being primarily cattle and horse ranches and farms. These inhibit public access, therefore floating is a necessity. The Bow is a big river, flowing at an average of 3,500 cfs, so it can be a tough river to wade.

What separates the Bow River from the rest of the pack is the size of the trout that are caught and how hard they fight. With a fish population varying between 2,500 and 3,500

browns and rainbows over 10 inches—with an average of 19 inches—it's easy to see why the Bow is rated as one of the best big-fish rivers in western North America. Interestingly, despite the close proximity to Calgary, the river receives less fishing pressure than other well-known trout rivers in the area.

The Bow River is open year-round, however the main season is after runoff, which takes place from late May until the last week of June or the first week of July. Although the pre-runoff fishing can be good, the weather can be hit

Floating a Bow River side channel. Dave Brown

or miss. Post-runoff fishing can be great—trout are hungry and have not seen very many flies. Usually the Golden Stoneflies are hatching, giving anglers shots at 20-inch-plus trout on big dries. This season lasts until late July. In addition to the Golden Stoneflies, hatches of PMDs, caddis, and Tricos also get Bow River trout looking up. During nonhatch periods, successful anglers fish deep nymph rigs including hopper-droppers and streamers while searching for snouts. Despite the numbers of fish, the trout can be extremely finicky, and successful anglers must be able to employ a multitude of tactics to pull off a good day and should approach the river with an open mind. The other factor that anglers face is the strength and acrobatics of Bow River fish. These will be some of the strongest you will ever encounter. They go ballistic once hooked, which can be a challenge

. . . especially when you're fishing dries on light tippets.

Given the river's northern latitude, the days are quite long, making for some great evening fishing. During the summer months, local anglers take advantage of this. During the late season—September into early October—the river traffic slows down, though late-season fishing is some of the best of the year. Along with hatches of *Baetis*, the large October Caddis is also around. Hopper fishing remains consistent, and water boatmen are active in the eddies and near weed-lined banks with slow water. The lower flows and cooler temps encourage the river's browns to start thinking about spawning. It's an exciting time! Anglers will find themselves casting streamers on floating lines, fishing hoppers with beadhead boatman imitations, or casting to rising fish with small flies, light tippets, and long leaders—all of which are challenging and very rewarding. After the first week of October, fishing can remain excellent, but weather can be a factor.

The Bow is a very easy river to float, as there are no major obstructions in and below Calgary. Most anglers focus on the stretch of river from Calgary to about 40 miles below, which is broken up into a combination of four floats ranging from 2 to 15 miles. Although the land along the river is private, the river is home to many islands, which are public or Crown Lands, making for ideal camping. Like every trout river, the Bow has its own nuances, therefore first-time visitors should book a day with a guide before heading out on their own.

Within a few hours' drive of Calgary there are numerous other rivers worthy of a visit. Bow River tributaries such as the Highwood and Sheep offer decent fishing for bull trout, cutthroat, and rainbows. Farther south, the Oldman River and its tributaries, including the Crowsnest, offer anglers a wide array of water ranging from small alpine cutthroat creeks to slow-flowing prairie tailwaters. An angler can spend a great deal of time fishing the Bow and then other streams.

► **Hatches:**
Midges: year-round.
Baetis: April–May; September–October.
Western March Browns: May.
Caddis: May–September.
Golden Stoneflies: late June–July.
Pale Morning Duns: July–August.
Pseudos: August–early September.
Tricos: August–early September .
October Caddis: September–October.
Hoppers: late July–October.
Water boatmen: August–October.

► **Fishing regulations:** From Bearspaw Dam downstream to Western Headworks Diversion (WHD) Weir, including the Elbow River below Glenmore Reservoir: closed from April 1 to May 31, and from October 1 to November 30.

Below, Sight fishing with hopper patterns in a side channel. Inset: Beautiful Bow River brown trout. Both photos by Dave Brown.

June 1 to September 30, and December 1 to March 31: trout limit one under 35 cm; all trout over 35 cm must be released; mountain whitefish limit of five over 30 cm; maggots are the only bait allowed, and only in the river.

August 16 to September 30 from the Western Headworks Diversion (WHD) Weir downstream to the Carseland Weir (includes 500 m of the Highwood River) but excluding all waters in the Inglewood Bird Sanctuary. Open all year.

April 1 to March 31: trout limit one under 35 cm; all trout over 35 cm must be released; mountain whitefish limit five over 30 cm; bait banned.

➤ **Tackle:** Use a 9-foot 6-weight for streamers, hoppers, and nymphs; a 9-foot 5-weight or 8½- or 9-foot 4-weight for dries. Use 9- to 12-foot, 4X leaders for dries; 9-foot 2X or 3X for nymphs and streamers. Use WF floating lines for all but a 10-foot HD sink-tip for the 6-weight; standard trout reels with a minimum of 40 yards of backing. Bring breathable waders, wading boots with cleats, a rainjacket, polarized sunglasses, wet-wading gear (July–August), fleece top, Windstopper fleece jacket, sunscreen, and a hat.

DAVE BROWN, owner of Dave Brown Outfitters, began his Bow River guiding and outfitting career in 1988. Since then, he has worked as a fly shop manager, owner, fly-fishing guide, and outfitter. Dave Brown Outfitters is the first multi-river guide service in western Canada. In 2009, Dave emigrated to the United States and calls Patagonia, Arizona home. Visit www.davebrownoutfitters.com.

Evening caddis hook-up. Dave Brown

CLOSEST FLY SHOPS

Country Pleasures Fly Fishing
10816 Macleod Tr. #100
S. Calgary, Alberta, T2J 5N8
403-271-1016
info@countrypleasures.com
www.countrypleasures.com

Fishtales Fly Shop
12100 Macleod Trail SE #626
Calgary, AB T2J 7G9
403-640-1273
North American toll free: 866-640-127
sales@fishtales.ca
www.fishtalesflyshop.com

Westwinds Fly Shop
9919 Fairmount Drive S.E. #109
Calgary, Alberta, Canada T2J 0S3
403-278-6331
flyshop@telusplanet.net
www.westwindsflyshop.com

OUTFITTERS AND GUIDES

Dave Brown Outfitters
Box 884
Patagonia, AZ 85624
800-453-3991
Dave@DaveBrownOutfitters.com
www.davebrownoutfitters.com

Country Pleasures Fly Fishing (above)

Fishtales Fly Shop (above)

BEST HOTEL
The Glenmore Inn
2720 Glenmore Trail SE
Calgary, T2C 2E6, Canada
403-279-8611
www.glenmoreinn.com

BEST RESTAURANT

Caesar's Steak House
110 Willow Park Dr. SE
Calgary, AB
403-278-3930
www.caesarssteakhouse.com

CLOSEST PLACE TO GET A COLD, STIFF DRINK

Caesar's Steak House (above)

CLOSEST EMERGENCY MEDICAL HELP

Foothills Hospital
1403 29 Street NW
Calgary, Alberta, T2N 2T9
403-944-1110

CELL PHONE SERVICE
Reception varies.

THE SOUTH

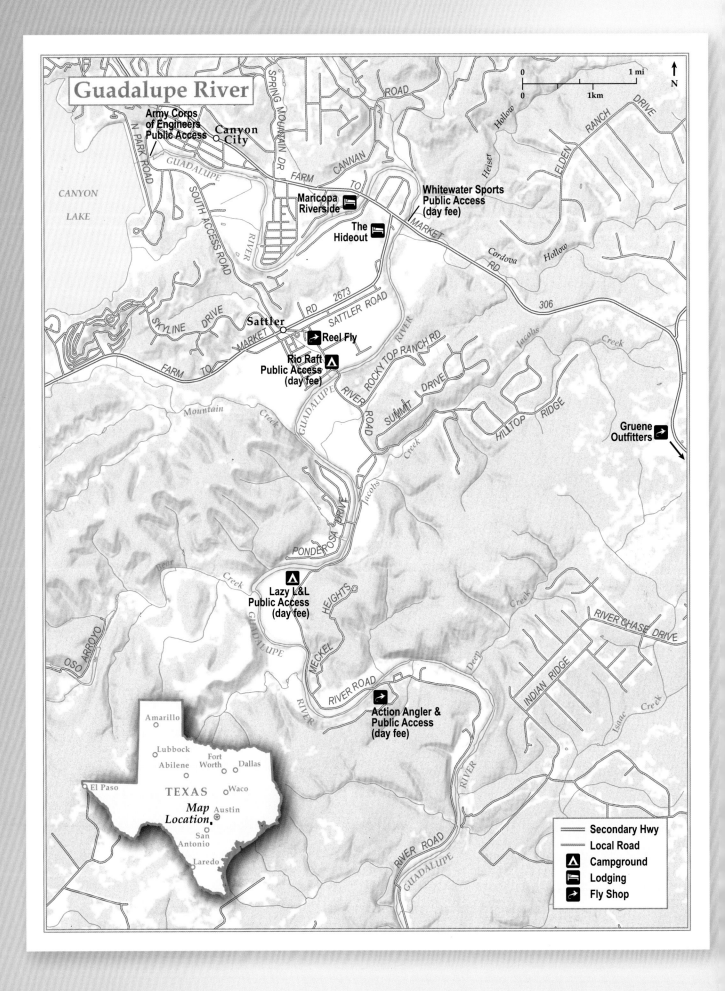

Guadalupe River

Army Corps of Engineers Public Access

Canyon City

CANYON LAKE

Maricopa Riverside

The Hideout

Whitewater Sports Public Access (day fee)

Sattler

Reel Fly

Rio Raft Public Access (day fee)

Gruene Outfitters

Lazy L&L Public Access (day fee)

Action Angler & Public Access (day fee)

N PARK ROAD

SOUTH ACCESS ROAD

GUADALUPE RIVER

SPRING MOUNTAIN DR

FARM TO MARKET CANNAN ROAD

Heiser Hollow

ELDEN RANCH DRIVE

Cordova RD

Hollow

306

SKYLINE DRIVE

FARM TO MARKET

RD 2673

SATTLER ROAD

GUADALUPE RIVER ROAD

ROCKY TOP RANCH RD

SUMMIT DRIVE

HILLTOP RIDGE

Jacobs Creek

Mountain Creek

Jacobs

PONDEROSA DRIVE

MECKEL HEIGHTS

Bear Creek

GUADALUPE RIVER

RIVER ROAD

Deep Creek

Creek

INDIAN RIDGE

RIVER CHASE DRIVE

Issac Creek

OSO ARROYO

GUADALUPE RIVER

RIVER ROAD

GUADALUPE

TEXAS

Amarillo

Lubbock

Abilene

Fort Worth

Dallas

Waco

Map Location

Austin

San Antonio

Laredo

El Paso

0 ——— 1 mi
0 ——— 1km
N

	Secondary Hwy
	Local Road
▲	Campground
🛏	Lodging
➡	Fly Shop

➤ **Location:** Central Texas, 16 miles northwest of New Braunfels, between Austin and San Antonio. During the winter months, fly fishers focus on the trophy trout zone located near the small town of Sattler. Warmwater species can be pursued the entire length of the river.

Birthed from limestone springs on the Edwards Plateau in the Texas Hill Country, the north and south forks of the Guadalupe converge in Kerr County near the town of Hunt to form the main stem of the river. There, it begins the journey to San Antonio Bay on the Gulf of Mexico, covering nearly 230 miles as it negotiates cypress-lined canyons, cliffs, and coastal plains.

The river ran generally unmolested to the Gulf until 1964, when the Army Corps of Engineers completed the construction of Canyon Dam. The dam was installed to help moderate the notorious mood swings of nature found in this region, holding back floods from tropical rains and providing water storage against droughts for municipal, industrial, and agricultural needs.

The use of the dam to protect lives and property was successful, but it created a 10-mile segment of the river too cold for native fish to thrive. The U.S. Fish and Wildlife Service determined that the river held promise as a coldwater fishery. Enter Lone Star Beer.

The owner of Lone Star Brewery at that time was an ardent trout fisherman who sponsored trout tanks at various events around the state, to increase interest in angling. Afterward, the trout were dumped into local waters for sport fishers to enjoy. Lone Star approached Texas Parks and Wildlife (TPWD) about potentially stocking the Guadalupe River with trout and eying its potential as a year-round fishery. The brewery donated 10,000 fish for the first stocking in collaboration with Texas Parks and Wildlife. This was the genesis of the southernmost sustainable trout stream in the United States.

Although a trout fishery was established, access to the river is challenging. Still, armed with a little information, anglers should have little difficulty enjoying this slice of Eden. In Texas the vast majority of property is privately held, including the banks of the Guadalupe River. With the exception of access near Canyon Dam, the public has few options to sample the fine fishing and paddling that the river pro-

vides. To best access the river, there are four primary options: free access locations provided by Texas Parks and Wildlife; purchasing a day pass from one of the local rafting venues; hiring a reputable local guide; or purchasing a membership in the Guadalupe River Trout Unlimited lease access program. Be sure to check the TPWD web page (www.tpwd .state.tx.us) for the latest information on their access points. These change from year to year depending on funding and landowner participation. Information on the GRTU lease

Hooked up on another Lone Star State rainbow. Daniel Johnson

access program may be found on their website, www.GRTU .org.

One final note about access: Once in the riverbed, you may generally wade up- or downstream at your leisure. However, if you exit the river you may be guilty of trespassing if you scale the bank above the normal waterline. The best rule of thumb to avoid confrontations with landowners is to keep your feet wet until you exit at an access site that you have permission to use.

Now that you are on the water, how can you have a successful day fly fishing the Guad?

Recommended rods range from 3- to 6-weights, depending on wind and flow. A 9-foot rod will help with line management while nymphing, and provides the ability to deliver a dry fly when conditions merit. Due to the very real possi-

Sight fishing for trout downstream from Mushroom Rock. Emily Johnson

bility of hooking a 20-inch or larger trout, a good reel with a smooth drag will give you an advantage.

A 7½- to 9-foot tapered leader from 4X to 6X with tippet to match will manage most situations. In extremely clear water, fluorocarbon tippet may provide an advantage in stealth. Split-shot is an effective tool in managing the various depths you will need. Be sure to have various weights available to accommodate a range of water depths and speeds.

Successful fly fishers on the Guadalupe utilize nymphs most of the time. Streamers and dry flies have their places here, but your go-to box should be well stocked with a good sampling of attractors and small dark nymphs in black, brown, gray, and olive. Two-nymph rigs are common, with an attractor in sizes #12 to #18 as the lead fly, trailed by a smaller nymph in sizes #16 to #22. Most fish will take the trailing or dropper fly.

Successful attractor patterns are San Juan Worms and eggs of various colors. Nymphs include standards such as Hare's-ears, Prince Nymphs, Brassies, and midge, caddis, and scud imitations. Soft-hackles can be deadly on a down-and-across drift.

If you're familiar with chasing trout in freestone streams, some sections of the Guadalupe River will be similar, with fast riffles, runs, pools, and pocket water. However, there are also slow, deep sections of the river that can be very productive once you unlock how to fish them. The key in many of these slower sections is to locate cuts or ledges, and drift your flies tight to those pieces of structure. A familiar mantra on the Guadalupe is to look for the green waters (indicating greater depth), and fish them thoroughly.

Prime trout season on the Guadalupe is generally October through April. However, the real key is not the month of the year, but water temperature. In years of good water flows of 150 cfs or greater through the summer, trout can be ethically targeted as long as anglers are conscientious about checking water temperatures. Fishing for trout when water tempera-

tures approach 68 degrees F is discouraged, as the stress from even the best-managed fight can be fatal to the fish. Water closer to the dam is colder, so moving upstream is one way to enjoy trout fishing even during the sometimes brutal Texas summer months.

The river can also provide incredible warmwater species fishing, including the State Fish of Texas, the Guadalupe bass. This bass has habits more like a trout, preferring fast water over the slow-water habitat of its well-known largemouth cousin. Poppers, divers, and streamers can all take this iconic fish. Other residents of the river include largemouth bass, smallmouth bass, sunfish, and redhorse suckers. The Guadalupe is considered (perhaps in a tongue-in-cheek way) to be a world-class redhorse sucker fishery; you will often catch them while drifting nymphs for trout. They are strong fighters and worthy of respect, even though they have a face only a mother could love.

If big fish are your thing, there are huge resident striped bass in some of the deeper pools. The state fly-rod record striper of just over 36 pounds was taken a few years ago in the trophy trout zone. Texas Parks & Wildlife removed two specimens to be used as broodstock from the same pool that produced the record fish that were in the 40-pound range in 2011.

The Guadalupe is truly a fly-fishing paradise, offering year-round opportunities for beginners and experts alike.

➤ **Hatches:** Hatches on the Guadalupe are not especially prolific, but it is worthwhile to have some caddis and mayfly patterns in your box. Check out the hatch chart for the Guadalupe tailrace is at: www.guadalupefly.com/hatch.html.

➤ **Fishing regulations:** In the 10-mile special-regulations zone, only one trout over 18 inches can be kept per day and the trout can only be retained if caught with a fly or other artificial lure. Trout caught with live or dead bait must be released immediately. We encourage catch-and-release fishing with flies or lures having barbless or debarbed hooks to reduce trout mortality.

Most of the property on both banks of the river is privately owned. Unless you have permission from the landowners, accessing the river is best done through one of the local campgrounds, which charge a small day-use fee for fishing.

Once in the river, you may wade up- or downstream as far as you wish, but if you leave the riverbed you may be guilty of trespassing. The best advice is to keep your feet in the river, and exit at the same point where you entered.

➤ **Tackle:** Use a 9-foot, 3- to 6-weight rod with floating line. A 5X leader with 5X to 7X tippet will cover most situations.

Since most of the trout angling on the Guadalupe is in wintertime, a good pair of waders and a wading staff are recommended. The riverbed is mainly limestone, so studded, rubber-soled wading boots will ensure good footing. Many areas of the river have ruts in the limestone, so a wading staff is helpful in negotiating them.

Remember:

Flows above 550 cfs are unsafe to wade.

Flows from 300–550 cfs should be undertaken only by those who have experience wading in swift-water conditions. Preferably, you would have knowledge of the riverbottom and would have waded the area previously. Much of the river will be too swift and too deep to wade safely. The potential to be swept off your feet is high!

Flows from 200–300 cfs can be undertaken by most experienced waders. There are still areas that may be too swift or deep to wade. Inexperienced waders should be aware.

Flows below 200 cfs have moderate current. A few areas may have the potential to cause a loss of footing.

Flows below 100 cfs have slow current.

Flow information can be obtained at www.grtu.org or the GBRA site at www.gbra.org/conditions/data.aspx

Author Mark Dillow. Kevin Wall

MARK DILLOW is the chapter president of the Guadalupe River Chapter of Trout Unlimited, the largest TU chapter in the nation with 5,000 members. When not chasing trout, he can be found fly fishing for warmwater species on various Texas Hill Country rivers, or pestering local fly-shop employees.

CLOSEST FLY SHOPS

Gruene Outfitters
1629 Hunter Rd.
New Braunfels, TX 78130 (830-625-4440)
www.grueneoutfitters.com

Action Angler
9751 River Rd.
New Braunfels, TX 78132 (830-708-3474)
www.actionangler.net

Living Waters Fly Fishing
309 West Main St. Suite 110
Round Rock, TX 78664 (512-828-FISH)
livingwatersflyfishing.com

Sportsman's Finest
12434 Bee Cave Rd.
Austin, TX 78738 (512-263-1888)
www.sportsmansfinest.com

Orvis
10000 Research Blvd.
Space B04B
Austin, TX 78759 (512-795-8004)
www.orvis.com

Reel Fly
1642 FM 2673 #3
Canyon Lake, TX 78133 (830-964-4823)
www.reelfly.net

CLOSEST OUTFITTERS/GUIDES

Living Waters Fly Fishing/
Chris Johnson (left)

Alvin Dedeaux Fly Fishing
3605 Counselor Dr.
Austin, TX 78749 (512-663-7945)
www.alvindedeaux.com

Livin2Fish/Clint Jackson
Austin, TX (512-576-4231)
Clint@livin2fish.com
www.livin2fish.com

CLOSEST LODGES

The Hideout on the Horseshoe
11860 FM 306
New Braunfels, TX 78133 (830-964-4540)
www.stayandfloat.com

BEST HOTEL

Courtyard New Braunfels River Village
750 IH 35 North
New Braunfels, TX 78130 (830-626-4700)
www.marriott.com
search for New Braunfels

BEST CAMPGROUND

Rio Raft & Resort
14130 River Rd.
New Braunfels, TX 78132 (830-964-3613)
rioraft@gvtc.com
rioraft.com/index.php

BEST RESTAURANT

The Gristmill
1287 Gruene Rd.
New Braunfels, TX 78130 (830-625-0684)
www.gristmillrestaurant.com

BEST PLACE TO GET A COLD,
STIFF DRINK

Gruene Hall (Texas's oldest dance hall)
1281 Gruene Rd.
New Braunfels, TX 78130 (830-606-1281)
tracie@gruenehall.com; gruenehall.com

CLOSEST EMERGENCY MEDICAL HELP

CHRISTUS Santa Rosa Hospital
600 N. Union Ave.
New Braunfels, TX 78130 (830-606-9111)

CELL PHONE SERVICE

Yes, in most areas.

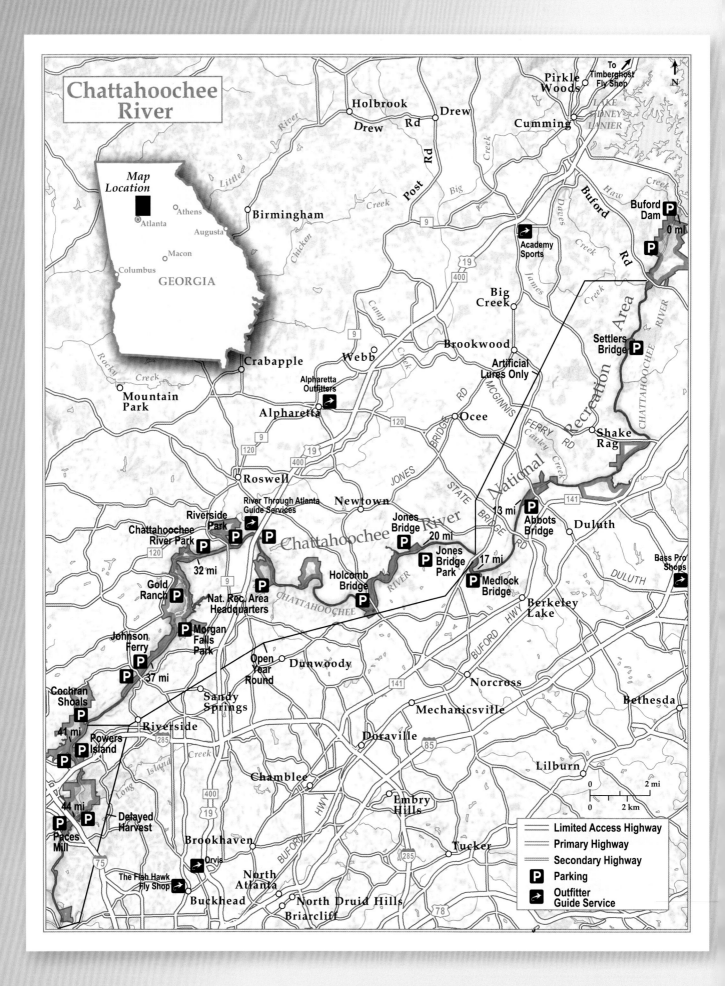

Chattahoochee River

Map Location

Athens
★ Atlanta
Augusta
Macon
Columbus
GEORGIA

Pirkle Woods
To Timberghost Fly Shop
N

Holbrook
Drew Rd
Drew
Cumming
LAKE SIDNEY LANIER

River
Little

Creek

Post Rd
9

Big Creek
James Creek
Daves Rd
Buford Rd
Haw Creek

Academy Sports

Buford Dam
0 mi

Settlers Bridge

Chicken Creek

Camp Creek

9

Big Creek

Brookwood

Artificial Lures Only

MCGINNIS RD

FERRY RD
Cauley Creek

National

Recreation Area

CHATTAHOOCHEE RIVER

Shake Rag

Crabapple

Webb

Alpharetta Outfitters

Alpharetta

Ocee

120

9
120
19
400

Roswell

River Through Atlanta Guide Services

Newtown

JONES BRIDGE RD

STATE BRIDGE RD

13 mi
141

Abbots Bridge

Duluth

Mountain Park

Rocky Creek

Riverside Park
Chattahoochee River Park

Jones Bridge
20 mi

Jones Bridge Park
17 mi

Medlock Bridge

Chattahoochee River

DULUTH

Bass Pro Shops

32 mi

Gold Ranch

Nat. Rec. Area Headquarters

Holcomb Bridge

CHATTAHOOCHEE RIVER

Berkeley Lake

Johnson Ferry

Morgan Falls Park
37 mi

Open Year Round

Dunwoody

BUFORD HWY

Norcross

Bethesda

Cochran Shoals

41 mi

Sandy Springs

Riverside

285

Long Island Creek

Chamblee

141

Mechanicsville

Doraville

85

Lilburn

Powers Island

400
19

44 mi

Delayed Harvest

Paces Mill

75

Brookhaven

Orvis

North Atlanta

The Fish Hawk Fly Shop

Buckhead

Embry Hills

285

Tucker

North Druid Hills

Briarcliff

78

0   2 mi
0   2 km

Legend

	Limited Access Highway
	Primary Highway
	Secondary Highway
P	Parking
↗	Outfitter Guide Service

Chattahoochee River (Georgia)

► **Location:** Forty miles north of the Atlanta perimeter at Buford Dam on the south end of Lake Sidney Lanier. The tailwater section of the Chattahoochee River meanders for 48 miles through the linear, 10,000-acre Chattahoochee River National Recreation Area, ending at Standing Peachtree Creek within the Atlanta city limits.

The Chattahoochee River forms the southern half of the Alabama–Georgia border, as well as a portion of the Florida border. It is a tributary of the Apalachicola River, a relatively short river formed by the confluence of the Chattahoochee and Flint Rivers and emptying from Florida into Apalachicola Bay in the Gulf of Mexico. Better known by locals as the "Hooch," it is one of the South's best-kept fly-fishing secrets and the source of the Georgia state record brown trout (just over 18 pounds) in 2006. In 2000, Georgia Department of Natural Resources biologists documented natural reproduction of brown and rainbow trout throughout a 35-mile section of the river between Buford Dam and Morgan Falls Dam. In this same stretch, DNR has embarked on a Trout Unlimited–funded growth and migration study of brown trout, indicating a healthy, self-sustaining population of wild fish. Trout Unlimited National listed the Chattahoochee as one of the top 100 trout streams in the United States. It is difficult to wrap your mind around the fact that this river is clean and cold enough to support trout this far south, not to mention having Atlanta looming just downstream.

The tailwater section gushes from the penstocks of Buford Dam with a minimum flow of 700 cfs and maximums of 10,000 cfs from a lake depth of 130 feet from 38,000-acre Lake Lanier, which sits 1,070 feet above sea level. There are some shoal areas considered Class II rapids with over 120 feet of relief on this 48-mile reach of riverbed. Anglers should lean toward caution, as dramatic fluctuations in water flows released from Buford Dam can increase some rapids to Class IV. To reach the source of the river, one must follow it 130 miles north to the Appalachians, to a small spring called Chattahoochee Gap at 3,500 feet. A combination of high elevations and water storage in this massive lake are the keys to the Hooch's success. Because of mild, long, cool winters and long, hot summers, Lake Lanier has two distinct thermal layers of stored water, causing the impoundment to stratify once a year. Typically, midsummer water temperatures at Buford Dam range from 47 to 49 degrees F; typically the warmest water at the dam in early winter ranges from 59 to 63 degrees F, just before the lake "turns over" or mixes to become uniformly cold. While the dam was originally designed to control flooding and to produce hydropower and drinking water for Atlanta, little did the engineers know this river was ideally designed for trout, with an annual average temperature of 56 degrees F!

Morgan Falls Dam is 37 river miles below Buford Dam and is where the river changes in character. Morgan Falls Dam controls water levels in a network of backwater sloughs and flats teeming with carp, bream, and bass. Watercraft are needed to access these silted waters, but the main river holds trout. One hundred miles downstream of Morgan Falls is

The Chattahoochee follows the Brevard Fault Line. River Through Atlanta Guides

a shallow impoundment called West Point Lake, where in summer striped bass take refuge in the cooler waters of Morgan Falls, and gorge on trout and crayfish. West Point also holds a newly identified endemic bass species called a shoal bass, or "shoalie," a river-adapted largemouth that acts and fights like a smallmouth. The other good news about Morgan

149

The "Hooch" is not just a trout fishery.

The Chattahoochee River. Both photos by River Through Atlanta Guides

Falls is that the striped bass cannot breach this dam, which protects 37 miles of trout water upstream from these voracious predators.

The Chattahoochee is a very wide and deep river, so drift boats or other types of watercraft are needed to access the many productive gravel bars and shoals. Inflatable float tubes and pontoons are most popular, but canoes, john boats, rafts, and open kayaks are excellent, too. Because the vast majority of land adjacent to the river is private, watercraft are essential for getting off the beaten path to fish remote, less-pressured water. The National Park Service has excellent public parks along the river totaling 10,000 linear acres of passive parklands, with some restroom facilities, boat launches and ramps, and hiking trails. Visit www.nps.gov/chat.

➤ **Hatches:** *Caddis:* Black Caddis (case builders) and Tan Sedges (free-living) begin emergence in early March, peak in mid-May, and taper down in mid-June. Fall, or October Caddis emergence begins in mid-September and is sporadic but steady through November.

Stoneflies: Large Salmonflies are found in shoal areas, but not in sufficient numbers to create a dry-fly bite; large black to brown nymph patterns are deadly from late February through May. Little Winter Stoneflies begin emergence in mid-December, peak in mid-February, and taper down in mid-March.

Mayflies: Blue-winged Olives hatch year-round, but the main emergence begins in early September, peaks in January, and tapers down in February. A sparse and sporadic Yellow Drake (burrower) hatch occurs from mid-August through October. Light Cahill emergence begins in mid-March, peaks in mid-April, and tapers down in late May.

Midges: Black, cream, gray, and olive, either blackflies or midges emerge year-round, but peak in mid-January.

Large crane fly: Larvae available year-round. Emergence begins in late July, peaks in mid-September, and tapers down in mid-November.

Crustaceans: Scuds, sow bugs, and crayfish abound year-round.

Annelids: Aquatic and terrestrial worms occur year-round.

Baitfish: Blueback herring and threadfin shad occur in the reservoir winter and summer, and are dispensed downstream dead and dying after passing through the dam turbines; dace and sculpins occur year-round.

Because of a mild climate, the Georgia Piedmont does not receive its first hard frost until late November or early December, so fishing terrestrial fly patterns through December can be successful. The terrestrial bite is mid-June through December. Ants, flying ants, Japanese and June bug beetles, yellowjackets, grasshoppers, tent and Catawba worms (caterpillars) are standards.

➤ **Fishing regulations:** There are 48 miles of designated trout water, with 15 miles of artificials-only water from the Georgia Highway 20 bridge to Medlock Bridge 141. There are 6 miles of Delayed Harvest regulations from Sope Creek to Paces Mill Park, where anglers must release all trout immediately and use only artificial lures and flies with single barbless hooks. The use of additional "dropper" flies on one line is permitted. Delayed Harvest is from November 1 to May 14.

The additional 27 miles of river is under Georgia state trout stream regulations. Visit www.gofishgeorgia.com.

➤ **Tackle:** Use 5- and 6-weight rods, and 6- or 7-weights for streamer fishing on windy days. WF floating line is ideal for most situations, but serious streamer guys will need at least an intermediate sink-tip. Rods for striped and shoal bass below Morgan Falls should be 9 to 10 feet for 7- to 10-weight lines. Recommended rods for carp fishing above Morgan Falls are 9-foot, 7- or 8-weights.

Breathable or Neoprene waders are needed, as the Hooch is quite cold. Wading shoes should be EcoTraX with cleats. A wading staff, belly boat, or float tube is invaluable, as the average stream depth is 4 feet. An inflatable life jacket or normal PFD is required, even while wading on the first 2 miles of river below the Buford and Morgan Falls Dams. Carry a cell phone in a waterproof case to check the dam release schedules periodically.

CHRIS SCALLEY (on left) grew up fishing, trapping, and hunting the Chattahoochee River and surrounding watershed. Chris started River Through Atlanta guide service in 1994 and is an Orvis-endorsed guide. Chris founded the Chattahoochee Cold Water Fishery Foundation, for which *Field & Stream* magazine recognized him with its Heroes of Conservation Award.

CLOSEST FLY SHOPS

Orvis
3275 Peachtree Rd. NE #210
Atlanta, GA 30305
404-841-0093
www.orvis.com/atlanta

The Fish Hawk
3095 Peachtree Rd. NE
Atlanta, GA 30305
404-237-3473
www.thefishhawk.com

CLOSEST OUTFITTERS

Fly Box Outfitters
840 Ernest W. Barrett Pkwy. #568
Kennesaw, GA 30144
678-594-7330
www.flyboxoutfitters.com

Alpharetta Outfitters
79 S. Main St.
Alpharetta, GA 30009
678-762-0027
www.alpharettaoutfitters.com

GUIDE SERVICES

River Through Atlanta Guide Service
710 Riverside Rd.
Roswell, GA 30075
770-650-8630
www.riverthroughatlanta.com

CLOSEST LODGE

Lake Lanier Islands Resort (upscale Legacy Lodge and Conference Center; lake house and cabin rentals)
7000 Lanier Islands Pkwy.
Buford, GA 30518
770-945-8786
reservations@lakelanierislands.com
www.lakelanierislands.com

CLOSEST AND BEST HOTEL

Hotel 400/Roswell
1500 Market Blvd.
Roswell, GA 30076
866-539-0036
(Great breakfasts and close proximity to the river.)

CLOSEST AND BEST CAMPGROUND

Shoal Creek Campgrounds
6300 Shadburn Ferry Rd.
Buford, GA 30518
678-482-0332
www.lakelanierparks.com/Shoal_Creek_Campground.html

BEST RESTAURANT

Greenwoods
1087 Green St.
Roswell, GA 30075
770-992-5383
www.greenwoodsongreenstreet.com

BEST PLACE TO GET A COLD, STIFF DRINK

Harp Irish Pub
1425 Market Blvd #1330
Roswell, GA 30076
770-645-01188
www.harpirishpub.com

CLOSEST EMERGENCY MEDICAL HELP

North Fulton Hospital
3000 Hospital Blvd.
Roswell, GA 30076
770-751-2500
www.nfultonhospital.com

CELL SERVICE
Generally available.

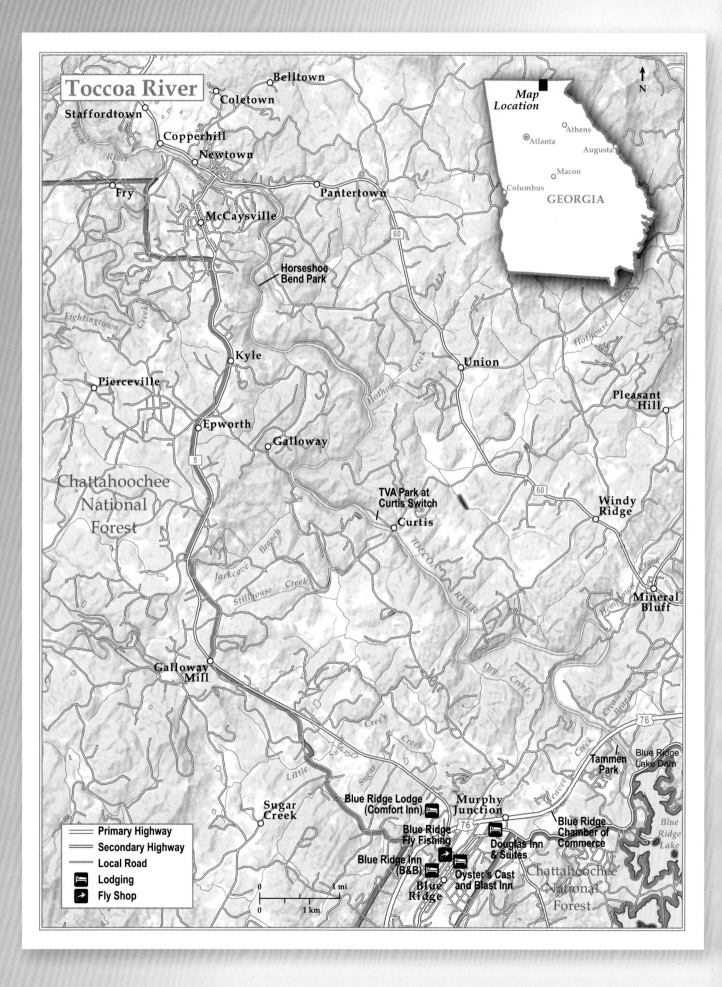

➤ **Location:** North Georgia, about 1½ hours north of Atlanta; 2 hours east of Chattanooga, and 2½ hours south of Knoxville, Tennessee.

Trout-angling opportunities on Georgia tailwater streams are scarce, but the Toccoa River near the eclectic little community of Blue Ridge has become one of the favored Southeast destinations for fly anglers. Flowing north out of Lake Blue Ridge, the Toccoa has more than 15 miles of clear, cold Appalachian water running hard up against the Tennessee and North Carolina borders. But the Georgia section is the one known for impressive trout fishing.

The Tennessee Valley Authority (TVA) sets generation schedules, but a strong working relationship among the Authority, the Georgia Department of Natural Resources, and Trout Unlimited has resulted in much more angler- and trout-friendly discharges in recent years than prevailed previously. As a result, the town of Blue Ridge is now officially recognized as the Trout Capital of Georgia.

This North Georgia river has the traits characteristic of most tailwater trout fisheries—cold water and good insect populations. The hard granite substrate of most southern Appalachian trout streams is known for great water quality, but poor aquatic insect populations due to the almost neutral pH. But on the Toccoa tailwater, TVA installed a dissolved oxygen injection system several years ago at the bottom release from Lake Blue Ridge, resulting in impressive hatches year-round. Seasonally, you'll find the ubiquitous midges, Little Black Stones, Quill Gordons, and March Browns, or tasty Blue-winged Olives, Sulphurs, Light Cahills, and terrestrials. Moving through the year, you'll encounter massive winter hatches of Black Caddis that will transition into Gray Caddis, then Olive, Tan, and October Caddis. Any month, Pheasant-tail Nymphs are consistent fish producers here, so don't discount the benthic zone.

Interestingly, when TVA generates power on the Toccoa River, you'll find little to no insect bite. However, if you have access to a raft or drift boat, the streamer fishing for very large rainbows and browns can be epic. Throwing big, meaty, articulated streamers on a 7-weight rod with a sinking line

doesn't produce large numbers of fish, but the quality of each fish can be noteworthy. When hunting with streamers, big-fish anglers have legitimate shots at trout closing in on the 24-inch mark. In 2009, DNR shocked up a 14-pound, 28.3-inch brown while conducting a stream survey. If you don't have access to a good boat that can handle high water, you don't fish the Toccoa during generation. With only one generator at the dam, the water is either on or off. Off is when you wade or float. On is floating only, and requires an experienced oarsman to safely navigate a couple of old, abandoned bridges along the way.

Public access to the river presents the angler with a paradox. On the one hand, there are only four places on the entire tailwater where an angler can legally access the river without permission from private landowners. On the other hand,

Mark Whitney on the Toccoa River in summer, early morning fog. Jimmy Harris

anglers able to float the river have little competition once they leave the vicinity of these public access points. Normal flows on the Toccoa when there is no generation are 120–150 cfs. There are no rapids, but there are several ancient Native American fish traps throughout this section of the river that you may have to drag your boat over. A canoe, kayak, or personal pontoon boat is ideal for floating and fishing the long stretches of river between launch areas. Low-profile drift boats and skiffs are excellent craft for two or three anglers. A typical approach is to fish from the boat when

Unicoi Outfitters Guide Rex Gudgel on Toccoa River. Jimmy Harris

Winter sunrise on the Toccoa River. Jimmy Harris

floating the deep water between shoals, and getting out to wade-fish the shoals.

➤ **Tackle:** Rod selection here is like what you'd want on most other trout streams: an 8½- or 9-foot 5-weight with a floating line, but 3-, 4-, and 6-weights are fun for different applications. Pods of fish rising to #20 BWOs are pretty darned entertaining on a 3- or 4-weight, and lobbing split-shot, an indicator, and two nymphs with a 6-weight is a blast when there's no surface action. Packing more than one rod can give you the versatility to adapt as conditions change.

The trout population in the Toccoa River runs about 9:1 rainbows to browns. Understanding how to read the water and the tactics needed for each species is important. It's even more so on certain reaches of this river, depending upon the geologic features of the riverbottom. Gravel bottoms harbor mostly rainbows, while deeper, low-gradient stretches with sandy bottoms are prime brown trout habitat. Cracking the

code to the river is always part of the fun, but it requires time. If time is at a premium, there are some good outfitters offering both wade and float trips on the Toccoa River tailwater. There's nothing like the experience of a professional guide to shorten your learning curve.

➤ **Hatches:** As with other tailwaters, noted hatch times are generally for peaks; hatches often occur to a somewhat lesser degree a few weeks earlier and later. For a more complete hatch chart with suggested imitations, visit www.unicoioutfitters.com/toccoa-river-tailwater-hatch-chart.shtml.
Midges: October through January.
Black Stoneflies: November through February.
Blue-winged Olives: March through April; October through December.
Olive Caddis: April through May.
Light Cahills: June through September.
Tan Caddis: June through September.
Yellow Drakes: July through September.
Terrestrials: July through September.

➤ **Fishing regulations:** Trout season is year-round, with a daily creel limit of eight fish per angler with no size limitation. TVA's predicted generation schedule is available online at www.tva.gov/lakes or by calling 1-800-238-2264 and pressing 4, then 23, then # to hear a recording of the anticipated schedule for the next day.

A map of the river with approximate river distances and the time it takes rising water to reach specific landmarks is available online at www.unicoioutfitters.com.

Unicoi Outfitters guide Jake Darling with a
Toccoa River rainbow. Jimmy Harris

Author Jimmy Harris. Jeff Dumiak

JIMMY HARRIS is one of the owners of Unicoi
Outfitters, an Orvis-Endorsed Outfitter and retail
fly shop 90 miles northeast of Atlanta, Georgia near
the southern Appalachian town of Helen. Jimmy
purchased a 50 percent interest in Unicoi Outfitters
in 1998 after wading Georgia trout streams over the
previous 25 years and guiding on them for 4 years.
His fly-fishing passions run the gamut from small,
rhododendron-covered wild trout streams to the
cold tailwaters of the Southeast.

CLOSEST FLY SHOPS

Unicoi Outfitters
7280 S. Main St.
Helen, GA 30545
706-878-3083
flyfish@unicoioutfitters.com
www.unicoioutfitters.com

Blue Ridge Fly Fishing
490 E. Main St.
Blue Ridge, GA 30513
706-258-4080
www.blueridgeflyfishing.com

Oyster Fine Bamboo Fly Rods
494 E. Main St.
Blue Ridge, GA 30513
706-374-4239
shannen@oysterbamboo.com
www.oysterbamboo.com

CLOSEST LODGING

A variety of riverside rental cabins with
accommodations for from 2 to 4 people up
to 10 or 12, as well as local motels, can be
reached through the Fannin County
Chamber of Commerce, 706-632-5680;
www.blueridgemountains.com.

BEST CAMPGROUND

There are no camping facilities directly on
the Toccoa tailwater. However, Fannin
County is home to 106,000 acres of the
Chattahoochee National Forest with
over 500 developed campsites scattered
throughout.

BEST RESTAURANTS

Downtown Blue Ridge is a food lover's
delight, with cuisine to satisfy any appetite.
Harvest on Main is our personal favorite:
576 E. Main St., 706-946-6164;
www.harvestonmain.com

BEST PLACES TO GET A COLD,
STIFF DRINK

Visit Harvest on Main for after-dinner
wine and cocktails, or take a short walk to
The Blue Ridge Brewery, 187 Depot St.;
706-632-6611; www.blueridgebrewery.com

CLOSEST EMERGENCY MEDICAL HELP

Fannin Regional Hospital
2855 Old Hwy. 5 North
Blue Ridge, GA 30513
706-632-3711
www.fanninregionalhospital.com

CELL PHONE SERVICE

Cell phone service is available along most
of the Toccoa River tailwater. The primary
service providers are AT&T and Verizon.

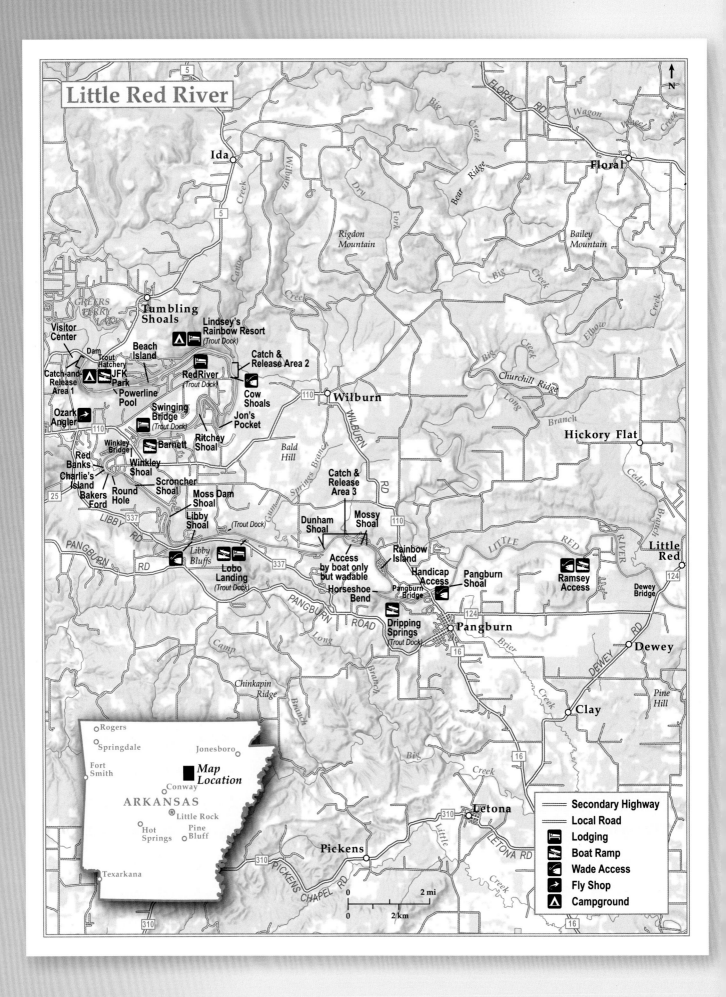

Little Red River

Ida

Floral

FLORAL RD.

Wagon Creek

Big Creek

Bear Ridge

Rigdon Mountain

Dry Fork

Bailey Mountain

Canoe Creek

Big Creek

Churchill Ridge

Tumbling Shoals

Visitor Center

Lindsey's Rainbow Resort
(Trout Dock)

Beach Island

Catch & Release Area 2

Dam

Trout Hatchery

RedRiver
(Trout Dock)

Catch-and Release Area 1

JFK Park

Powerline Pool

Cow Shoals

Wilburn

Long Branch

Hickory Flat

Ozark Angler

Swinging Bridge
(Trout Dock)

Jon's Pocket

Barnett

Ritchey Shoal

Bald Hill

Cedar Branch

Red Banks

Winkley Bridge

Winkley Shoal

Scroncher Shoal

Catch & Release Area 3

Charlie's Island

Bakers Ford

Round Hole

Moss Dam Shoal

Dunham Shoal

Mossy Shoal

LITTLE RED RIVER

Little Red

Libby Shoal

(Trout Dock)

Rainbow Island

Ramsey Access

Dewey Bridge

LIBBY RD.

Libby Bluffs

Access by boat only but wadable

Handicap Access

Pangburn Shoal

Pangburn Bridge

Dewey

PANGBURN RD.

Lobo Landing
(Trout Dock)

Horseshoe Bend

Dripping Springs
(Trout Dock)

Pangburn

DEWEY RD.

Pine Hill

Camp Creek

Long Branch

Brier Creek

Clay

Chinkapin Ridge

Branch

Big Creek

Letona

LETONA RD.

ARKANSAS

Rogers

Springdale

Jonesboro

Map Location

Fort Smith

Conway

Little Rock

Hot Springs

Pine Bluff

Little Creek

Texarkana

Pickens

PICKENS CHAPEL RD.

	Secondary Highway
	Local Road
	Lodging
	Boat Ramp
	Wade Access
	Fly Shop
	Campground

0   2 mi

0   2 km

N

Little Red River *(Central Arkansas)*

➤ **Location:** Central Arkansas, 65 miles north of Little Rock. Major cities are Memphis, 3 hours east; Tulsa, 4 hours west; Dallas, 5 hours southwest; and St. Louis, 6 hours north. Little Rock is served by all the major airlines. All types of accommodations, including motels, resorts, and even private rentals on or near the river, are available in the Greers Ferry Lake, Little Red River, and Heber Springs area.

Nestled in the foothills of the Ozarks is a little-known gem of a tailwater fishery. The Little Red River's 35 miles provide anglers of all skill levels several classic types of water in which to catch—and release—trophy rainbow and brown trout. Greers Ferry Lake and the Little Red River are not far from several large cities, but the area is generally unknown to most of the angling world.

Trout fishing in the Little Red is made possible by the Greers Ferry Dam, constructed by the Army Corps of Engineers in the early 1960s. The dam holds some 40,000 acres and controls the floodwaters of the Little Red drainage. The other primary function of the dam is to generate hydroelectric power through its two turbines, which can generate up to 100 megawatts. This coldwater release allows the growth of trophy trout, even a 40-pound, 4-ounce world-record brown trout caught in May 1992.

The Corps of Engineers maintains a fish hatchery below the dam for rearing rainbow and brook trout. The presence of brown trout, on the other hand, is the result of some local fly-fishing clubs, which, with the blessing of the Corps and the Arkansas Game and Fish Commission, stocked the river with browns. In 1975, club members floated the river in canoes and planted fertilized, Bitterroot-strain brown trout eggs—contained in Whitlock-Vibert boxes—in the gravel-covered shoals. The following year, they came back with a supplemental stocking of 5,000 fingerlings. This was the last time the river was stocked with brown trout. Sixteen years later, the world record was landed in the upper part of the river.

The Little Red River features excellent access points, even though it flows through private land for most of its course. The access below the dam is also a Corps of Engineers full-service campground, with facilities including a fishing area reserved exclusively for handicapped people and children. There are nine points with both walk-in access and boat launch ramps. Several offer walking access both up- and downstream for 1,000 yards, with riffles, pools, downed timber, and eddies. The entire river is available and fishable once an angler has entered by public access.

Fishing on the Little Red River varies from point to point. The tailwater below the dam has more fishing pressure because of the campground, but the fishing access is one of the better spots on the river. With the coldest water near the dam, midge hatches predominate, most often #18 through #26 in

Tranquil morning fly fishing the Little Red.

black, gray, cream, and olive. Populations of scuds and sow bugs provide an ample and ever-present food source when nothing is hatching. The uppermost part of the dam area offers the best opportunity to catch brook trout. They thrive in the very coldest water—and away from the browns. In the fall, brookies are sometimes seen spawning in the gravel.

The middle of the river contains the largest populations of brown trout. The 3 miles below Cow Shoals contain enormous weed beds, which provide the food sources for rapid growth, plus give the juvenile trout cover to hide from the cannibalistic adults. The aquatic insect life in this section includes mayflies and caddisflies along with the sow bugs. Mayfly hatches are frequent in the spring and fall, along with good hatches of caddis during late spring and summer.

Perfect brown trout.

The Little Red River. Kevin Krai

Of the access points, the Swinging Bridge area provides the wading angler the greatest variety of water and insect populations. Water types include riffles, pools (some very deep), runs, and eddies. This area also affords easy access by automobile, and therefore gets high fishing pressure during the prime months. The Swinging Bridge area also provides the most interesting fishing because of the diversity of water. Some days you will have access to riffles and pools, and on other days the only spots might be deep, slow pools. This forces you to pause and think, which makes fly fishing more challenging and fun. Mayfly and caddis hatches here are very good from early spring through summer, along with late-summer terrestrials and dragonflies during hot weather.

Libby Shoals access is easy to find along the road, but does not seem to get as much pressure as other areas. The path from the parking area to the river has a set of concrete stairs leading right down to the water, providing nice, level wading—possibly the easiest on the river. The water riffles over good, clean gravel, into deep runs with some big, deep rocks. Upstream from the riffle is a large, very deep, slow pool—a great place for a float tube, kick boat, or kayak. This gives you good access up through a long, structure-covered channel running at least a mile upstream. Intermittent hatches of caddis and mayflies, along with the river's constant staple, the sow bugs, are good through the channel and down through the shoal, ending at the public boat ramp. On summer afternoons, the short float down to the boat ramp can yield some very large fish off the weed beds and all the downed timber along the shore. Bigger brown trout like the solitude of timber with quick access to deep water. Dragonfly and damsel nymphs stripped toward the surface during the heat of the summer can draw some aggressive strikes.

The Pangburn Bridge access is some 23 miles downstream of the dam, again easy to find, and with good but limited wading. Up from the walk-in are large, slow, deep pools filled with weed beds that provide good fishing on deep nymph rigs. The gravel shoal is quite shallow and runs off into deeper water. The early spring has some good hatches of March Brown mayflies, with caddis coming later in the spring, plus strong late-summer and early fall Blue-winged Olives. One thing to watch for on the lower river is rising water due to releases from the dam. During the summer, releases may be timed such that the water never really goes down enough to allow safe wading. The autumn water is much more stable because typically the lake has been lower throughout the summer, given the high demand for power. Through September and October the weather is much cooler, lessening the demand for power, yielding lower water and better wading.

The last area that suits the wading angler is Ramsey Access. It has a classic riffle with large runs, slicks, eddies, and some pockets emptying into a deep pool. The fast water here is good for nymphing with indicator rigs, with some good dry-fly opportunities during hatches. Hatches consist of March Browns in spring, some caddis in early summer, good dragonfly and damsel action in August, and the fall BWOs. During the summer, fish are always on the lookout for crayfish, minnows, and other forage. The influx from several creeks and the hot, humid Arkansas summers tend to warm the water slightly. This little change in water temperature can sometimes trigger bigger fish into chasing some large flies. Fishing pressure is not as great here as on the upper parts of the river. Ramsey can be unwadable at times during the summer because of water releases. The last three months of the year are the best time to fish down in the lower parts of the river.

➤ **Hatches:**

March Brown mayflies: spring.

Caddis: late April through May.

Sulphur duns: small populations in midsummer.

Dragonflies and damsels: during the heat of summer.

Fall BWOs: good populations in late August through September.

Midges: populations good year-round.

➤ **Fishing regulations:** Visit www.agfc.com for maps, requirements, techniques, and rules.

➤ **Tackle:** Use 3-, 4-, and 5-weight rods with floating lines for most fishing situations. Streamer anglers find 7- and 8-weight rods with heavy sink-tip or streamer lines perform well during high-water periods. Use knotless leaders tapered to 5X or 6X. Wear breathable waders with Vibram rubber soles.

Standard fly patterns including midge larvae; midge pupae in black, olive, and red; Pheasant-tails; Gold-ribbed Hare's Ears; Woolly Buggers in black and olive, sow bugs in several different colors such as gray, tan, brown, and black; caddis pupae; caddis larvae; and a selection of soft-hackles will cover most subsurface conditions. Elk-hair Caddis, Adams, March Browns, BWOs, Griffith's Gnats, and Parachute Adams are good to have during hatches. Seasonal flies such as hoppers, ants, crayfish patterns, Zonkers, and dragonfly nymphs are good during nonhatch periods. Nymphs should be #14 to #20, and dry flies from #14 to #22, with midges a little smaller. Streamers should be #1/0 to #8, depending on the pattern.

They may be tiny, but our larger trout can sure find 'em. Kevin Krai

After a 20-year career as an aircraft mechanic and pilot, TOM HAWTHORNE opened The Ozark Angler. In 1990, he started guiding full time, with summers spent guiding for Bud Lilly's Trout Shop in West Yellowstone, Montana. In 1995 he opened his second store in Heber Springs, Arkansas, near the Little Red River.

CLOSEST FLY SHOPS
The Ozark Angler
659 Wilburn Rd.
Heber Springs, AR 72543
501-362-3597
www.ozarkangler.com

CLOSEST OUTFITTERS/GUIDES
The Ozark Angler (above)

Jamie Rouse Fly Fishing Adventures
501-691 2252
www.arkansasflyfishingguides.com
Jamie@Jamierouse.net

Little Red Fly Fishing Guide Service
501-365-3330
www.littleredflyfishingtrips.com
greg.seaton@littleredflyfishingtrips.com

CLOSEST LODGES
Lobo Landing Resort
3525 Libby Rd., Hwy. 337
Heber Springs, AR 72543
501-362-8502

BEST HOTEL
Red Apple Inn
1000 Club Rd.
Heber Springs, AR 72543
800-733-2775

BEST CAMPGROUND
The Army Corps of Engineers operates many around the lake and river. Closest to the river are the JFK and Dam Site parks. Visit www.recreation.gov; search "Little Red River" for more information and online reservations.

BEST RESTAURANT
Chuck's Steak House
35 Swinging Bridge Dr.
Heber Springs, AR 72543
501-362-2100

BEST PLACE TO GET A COLD, STIFF DRINK
None; Heber Springs is in a dry county.

CLOSEST EMERGENCY MEDICAL HELP
Baptist Health Medical Center
1800 Bypass Rd.
Heber Springs, AR 72543
501-887-3000

CELL PHONE SERVICE
Good on the river.

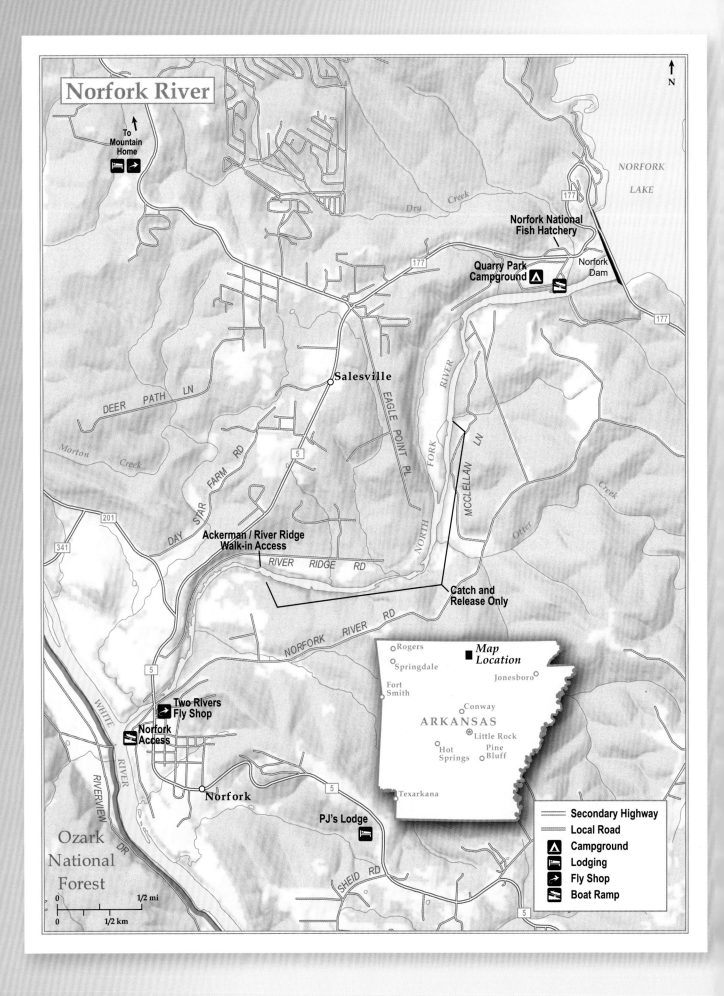

Norfork River

To Mountain Home

NORFORK LAKE

177

Dry Creek

Norfork National Fish Hatchery

Quarry Park Campground

Norfork Dam

177

177

RIVER

DEER PATH LN

Salesville

EAGLE POINT PL

NORTH FORK

MCCLELLAN LN

Otter Creek

Morton Creek

5

DAY STAR FARM RD

201

341

Ackerman / River Ridge Walk-in Access

RIVER RIDGE RD

Catch and Release Only

NORFORK RIVER RD

5

WHITE RIVER

Two Rivers Fly Shop

Norfork Access

RIVERVIEW DR

5

Norfork

PJ's Lodge

SHEID RD

5

Ozark National Forest

0   1/2 mi

0   1/2 km

Rogers
Springdale
Fort Smith
Jonesboro
Conway
ARKANSAS
Little Rock
Hot Springs
Pine Bluff
Texarkana

■ Map Location

	Secondary Highway
	Local Road
▲	Campground
	Lodging
	Fly Shop
	Boat Ramp

➤ **Location:** North-central Arkansas, about a 3-hour drive from Little Rock, a 2¼-hour drive from Fayetteville, Arkansas, or Springfield, Missouri, and 4 hours from Memphis, Tennessee. All four cities have full-service airports.

The 4.8-mile section of the North Fork of the White River is known as the Norfork River. It originates in southern Missouri and flows south through the Ozark Plateau into Arkansas, where Norfork Dam creates a year-round tailwater fishery for rainbow, brown, cutthroat, and brook trout. Beautiful wooded Ozark foothills and limestone bluffs line the banks of this short jewel of a tailwater down to its confluence with the White River.

Like the White, the Norfork was a warmwater fishery until the 1944 completion of Norfork Dam changed the ecosystem in favor of trout. Rainbows were subsequently stocked and grew phenomenally fast in such a nutrient-rich environment. Norfork National Fish Hatchery was opened just below the dam in 1957 to stock the river, along with other White River system tailwaters. Trout between 5 and 10 pounds soon became common. In 1988, the Norfork gained worldwide fame when a 38-pound, 9-ounce world-record brown was caught one summer evening.

Most trout in the Norfork average 10 to 14 inches. Larger fish, especially browns up to and well over 20 inches, are caught regularly. Abundant scuds, sow bugs, midges, sculpin, and crayfish grow trout to trophy proportions quickly. Every year somebody catches a true hog around the 10-pound or 30-inch mark, usually a brown. The Norfork is one of the few places east of the Rockies where cutthroat are stocked and caught regularly. The Snake River fine-spotted cutthroat planted in the Norfork average 10 to 14 inches, but can easily grow to over 20.

Norfork Dam is a hydroelectric dam, and water releases can vary greatly on an hourly basis depending on several factors. Generation usually occurs during peak power demand, so weekdays and periods of hot or cold weather typically bring higher flows. Expect significant generation on hot summer afternoons and cold winter mornings. Low water is more common during mild weather and on weekends. Lake levels and seasonal rains also affect releases. Spring floods can prompt generation and/or floodgate releases to lower the lake. Water temperature averages around 58 degrees year-round, and the clarity varies from gin-clear in summer to slightly stained in fall and winter, due to turnover in Lake Norfork.

At zero generation—or "dead low" as locals call it—the river trickles along at less than 50 cfs. Riffles, gravel runs, deep slow pools, and lots of interesting limestone bedrock features down the length of the river all hold lots of fish. Drift fishing from a john boat or drift boat is by far the most productive way to fish high water, and it's best to hire an experienced guide the first time out. The Norfork has lots of fast water with barely submerged bedrock structure, and running it blind can be dangerous. The two generators at Norfork Dam have a total release of 7,200 cfs when both units are online at maximum capacity, but the river can vary in flow by any amount, up to that level. The Norfork is capable of rising over 6 feet in an hour, so both wade and boat fly fishers should be aware at all times. Pick a particular rock or

Floating down the Norfork in low water. Steve Dally

landmark on the bank to monitor water levels, and always have an escape route in mind.

Nymphing is the predominant way to catch fish. Zebra-style midges, sow bugs, scuds, soft-hackles, and various beadheads all work well under an indicator, both with and

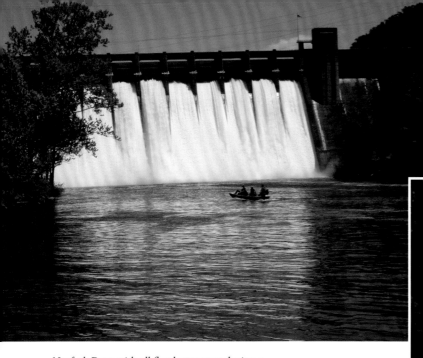

Norfork Dam with all floodgates open during a
heavy spring flood release. Ben Levin

*Below. Summertime is hopper time
with Ben Levin. Steve Dally*

without a split-shot. High-vis flies like San Juan Worms and eggs, along with streamers stripped off the banks, are productive in high water. Swinging or stripping small Woolly Buggers will always catch fish on any water level.

There are some great hatches and dry-fly opportunities at certain times of the year and under specific conditions. Spring kicks off with a great caddis hatch starting in late March that continues through early May. Size #14 or #16 caddis—including Elk-hair and Parachute-style patterns in olive, tan, and light green—work great, along with green-bodied soft-hackles and pupa patterns.

Redbuds and dogwoods in full bloom along the riverbanks, wild turkeys strutting and gobbling in the bottoms, and mild weather make spring a beautiful time to fish and enjoy one of the best hatches of the year. Then Sulphurs start coming off in May and can last sporadically into July. Sulphur Compara-duns and yellow parachute-style patterns in #14 to #16 work great, while Pheasant-tails with and without beads are deadly under an indicator. Midges and crane flies hatch year-round. Small Parachute Adams and Griffith's Gnats are always good to have for risers at any time of year. Hopper fishing can be excellent, too, especially during high summer flows while drift fishing. The best days for all hatches on the Norfork tend to be warm, low-water days.

Quarry Park below the dam has public wade access, boat ramps, tent/RV camping, and bathrooms. Dry Run Creek, a natural stream enhanced by effluent water from the hatchery, runs nearby and is a phenomenal fishery exclusively for children under 16 and licensed handicapped adults. The number of large trout in this small creek has to be seen to be believed.

The Ackerman/River Ridge Walk-In Access off Highway 5 is very popular with wade fishers and offers a nice variety of water during no generation. Norfork Access at the confluence with the White is the last public fishing access/boat ramp.

➤ **Hatches:** When you fish the Norfork and other nearby rivers, you are definitely in caddis country. While there can be prolific mayfly hatches, caddis imitations are your go-to, bread-and-butter flies.
Tan Caddis and Green Caddis: March through April.
Spotted Caddis: April.
Various Microcaddis: April through October.
Sulphur mayflies: May and June.
Blue-winged Olives: November through February.
Midges: All year.
Crane flies: March through October.
Scuds and sow bugs: All year.
Hoppers and terrestrials: June through October.

➤ **Fishing regulations:** Catch-and-release only (where marked by signs) and barbless hooks between Long Hole and Ackerman/River Ridge Walk-In access. Anglers are allowed to keep fish from the rest of the river. Refer to AGFC regulations for limits. No drag chains from boats.

Phone 870-431-5311 for a recorded message on current generation.

Go to www.swl-wc.usace.army.mil and search "Norfork" for a tabular water release chart displaying actual cfs up to one hour behind real time.

Typical rainbow from Norfork's catch-and-release section. Sow bugs, scuds, and crayfish give fish in the tailwater rich colors year-round. Ben Levin

➤ **Tackle:** A 5-weight rod, floating line, 5X or 6X fluorocarbon tippets, and small indicators will cover low water. For high water, use a 6-weight with floating line, long 3X to 5X leaders, a larger indicator like a Thingamabobber, two flies, and just enough split-shot to fish the bottom. Streamer fishing is with 7- or 8-weights, sink-tip lines, 10- to 15-pound tippet, and larger articulated flies.

BEN LEVIN was born and raised in Arkansas and grew up catching trout and smallmouth bass in the White River system since age five. He has been guiding professionally for more than 15 years, and has guided in Idaho and Alaska as well as in his native Arkansas. Ben has a B.A. in English from the University of Arkansas. He guides full time for trout for Dally's Ozark Fly Fisher on the White and Norfork tailwaters, as well as for smallmouth bass across the Ozarks. Ben lives on Crooked Creek, near the Norfork, where he guides, fishes, writes, takes pictures, and hunts critters—all with his chocolate Lab, Soco.

CLOSEST FLY SHOPS

Dally's Ozark Flyfisher
1200 West Main #7
Cotter, AR 72626
870-435-6166
steve@theozarkflyfisher.com
www.theozarkflyfisher.com

Two Rivers Fly Shop
13718 Hwy. 5 South
Norfork, AR 72658
870-499-3060
tworiversflyshop@gmail.com

CLOSEST OUTFITTERS

Dally's Ozark Flyfisher (above)

Two Rivers Fly Shop (above)

CLOSEST LODGING

River Ridge Inn
57 River Ridge Rd.
Norfork, AR 72658
870-499-7775
jimsmith@riverridgeinn.com

Norfork River Resort
13386 Arkansas 5
Norfork, AR 72658
870-499-5757
resorts@centurytel.net

Whispering Woods Cabins
4245 Hwy 177 South
Jordan, AR; 72519
870-499-5531
whwoods@centurytel.net

BEST HOTEL

River Rock Inn and Hotel
1350 Hwy 62 W
Mountain Home, AR 72653
870-425-5101

BEST CAMPGROUND

Quarry Park at Norfork Dam
870-499-7216

BEST RESTAURANTS

PJ's Restaurant and Lodge
384 Lodge Lane
Norfork, AR 72658
870-499-7500
www.pjslodge.com

Norfork Café
14198 Arkansas 5
Norfork, AR 72658
870-499-7400

BEER, LIQUOR, AND GROCERIES

The Woodsman
59 Fisherman St.
Norfork, AR 72658
870-499-7454

CLOSEST EMERGENCY MEDICAL HELP

Baxter Regional Medical Center
624 Hospital Dr.
Mountain Home, AR 72653
870-508-1000

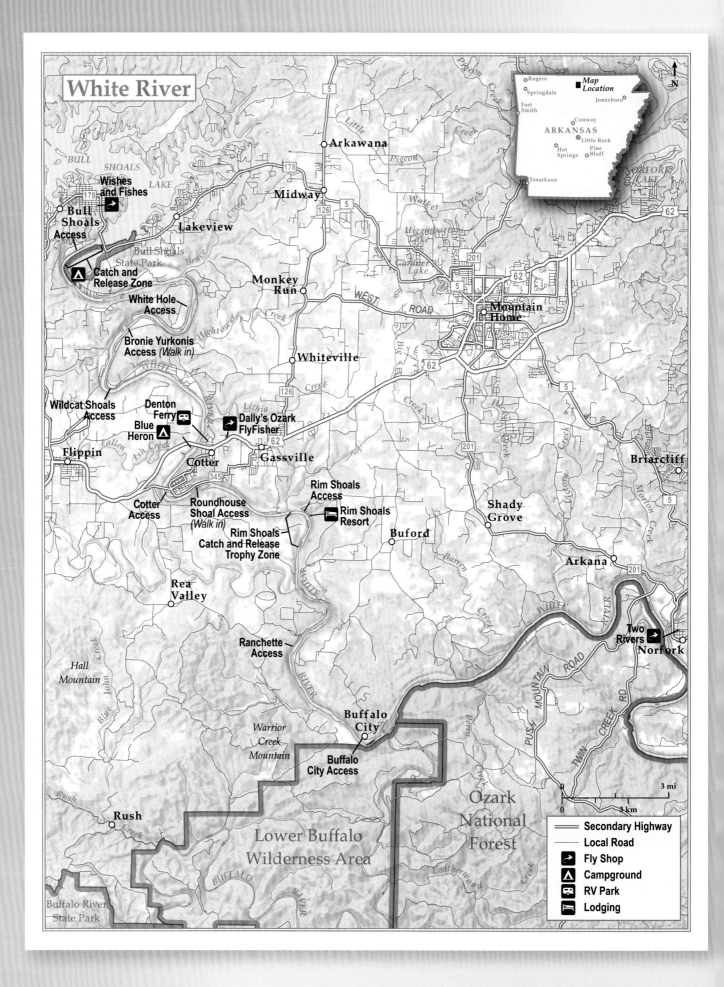

White River

Arkawana

Midway

Arkansas
- Rogers
- Springdale
- Fort Smith
- Conway
- Little Rock
- Hot Springs
- Pine Bluff
- Jonesboro
- Texarkana

■ Map Location

NORFORK LAKE

BULL SHOALS LAKE

Wishes and Fishes

Bull Shoals Access

Lakeview

Catch and Release Zone

White Hole Access

Bronie Yurkonis Access *(Walk in)*

Monkey Run

Mountain Home

Whiteville

Wildcat Shoals Access

Denton Ferry

Blue Heron

Dally's Ozark FlyFisher

Flippin

Cotter

Gassville

Briarcliff

Cotter Access

Roundhouse Shoal Access *(Walk in)*

Rim Shoals Access

Rim Shoals Resort

Shady Grove

Rim Shoals Catch and Release Trophy Zone

Buford

Arkana

Rea Valley

Ranchette Access

Hall Mountain

Warrior Creek Mountain

Buffalo City

Two Rivers

Norfork

Buffalo City Access

Ozark National Forest

Rush

Lower Buffalo Wilderness Area

Buffalo River State Park

| 0 | 3 mi |
| 0 | 3 km |

=== Secondary Highway
— Local Road
▶ Fly Shop
△ Campground
RV Park
Lodging

➤ **Location:** North-central Arkansas, close to the Arkansas–Missouri border. Cotter, Arkansas is 2¼ hours from Springfield, Missouri; 2½ hours from Fayetteville; 3 hours from Little Rock; and 4 hours from Memphis, Tennessee, all with full-service airports. Branson, Missouri offers limited flights, and is 90 minutes from Cotter.

The White River tailwater below Bull Shoals Dam is the finest tailwater in the Lower 48 to hunt for trophy browns—or if you are looking for plenty of action. Big brown trout (24 to 30 inches) get all the attention, but the White River fishery is more layered and nuanced—dedicated nymph and midge fishers will be right at home. Wet-fly and Euro nymph fishers can find their water, while streamer addicts and dry-fly aficionados can find outstanding brown trout fishing.

The White offers something for every fly fisher. She bolsters the confidence of novices through plenty of bent-rod positive reinforcement via the bounty of rainbows from Norfork Federal Fish Hatchery. Experts challenge themselves hunting the river's trophy brown trout or figuring out the abundant midge hatches. But the White is harder to know intimately. The power station releases can fluctuate from 50–24,000 cfs—occasionally within a single day—but variations of up to 10,000 cfs are more common. So seeking advice from guides and shops makes good sense, both for safety and to maximize your fishing experience. And local know-how is essential for trophy hunters. Trout feeding behavior, holding lies, and the best methods to catch them change with the flows.

The 32-mile stretch below Bull Shoals Dam (down to Buffalo City) has the highest trout density—and the most public accesses and fishing pressure—but fly-fishing activity becomes scarce below the confluence with the Norfork Tailwater.

The two catch-and-release, barbless-hooks-only trophy zones (the first immediately below Bull Shoals Dam, and the second 20 miles downstream at Rim Shoals) draw fly fishers like a magnet. Bull Shoals does hold some of the best rainbow trout in the river, but in reality, neither zone is large enough to offer significantly better fishing than other sections.

Wade fishers traditionally enjoy the "zero-generation," 50-cfs flows, when the broad expanses of the White can be crossed and the long, slow, flat glides and the steeper riffles—known locally as "shoals"—can be remarkably productive.

As flows increase, wade fishing is possible only near the banks, and fishing from a watercraft becomes more productive. At lower flows, personal watercraft such as pontoon boats, kayaks, and canoes can help you move between the

Drift boats are joining traditional White River john boats as the preferred craft. Steve Dally

wadable shoals and islands. And anglers can successfully fish the White up to its wide-open, 24,000-cfs flows both from traditional 20-foot motorized White River john boats and from Western-style drift boats, which are growing in popularity here.

Both styles of boats allow anglers to fish longer and cover more water than they could by wading. However, the key to getting the best from the White River is to remain flexible in one's approach, adapting locations and tactics according to the ever-changing flows and conditions.

The White has long been known as a wet-fly fisher's dream, with flies either drifted or fished subsurface more actively. Wet flies imitate multiple food sources, including midges, scuds, sow bugs, and (periodically) caddis and mayflies. Beadhead midges, eggs, Woolly Buggers, and worm imitations are essential patterns year-round.

Look for local patterns such as Davy Wotton's Whitetail Midges and Knowles's Ruby Midge. Both are must-haves, and Wotton's Sow Bug patterns are essential.

Gabe Levin's 32-inch White River brown trout caught on a Conrad Sculpin, with brother and guide Ben Levin. Steve Dally

The White River glides under the historic Rainbow Bridge at Cotter, Arkansas. Steve Dally

In March, around the Sowbug Roundup fly-tying festival, the spring caddis hatches of *Hydropsyche* and *Rhyacophila* begin, prompting some of the best dry-fly fishing of the year at lower flows. The spring caddis hatch can rival the famous Mothers Day Caddis hatch out West, with big browns up to 26 inches dining on the surface, as long as the spring flows aren't too volatile.

Trout can sometimes still be found rising in eddies, in current lines along the bank, and in tucked-away backwaters at surprisingly high flows. But generally, switching to nymphing or wet-fly techniques will be more productive. Prince Nymphs, Graphic Caddis, Wotton's Transparent SLF Pupae, and Dally's Tailwater Soft Hackles in Caddis Green are must-haves. On top, Elk-hair Caddis, E/C Caddis, and Spotlight Caddis are all good. The caddis hatch runs into early May, working its way upstream to Bull Shoals.

By June, the Sulphurs (usually #16 or #18) will begin a more geographically haphazard hatch, which is nonetheless spectacular at its peak. Midsize browns will take both dries (Parachutes or Compara-duns) and nymphs (Pheasant-tails and Copper Johns) with alacrity, resulting in catches out of proportion to their relative population in the river.

By July, experienced hands are looking for some power-generation flows to bring out larger terrestrials along the banks for quality brown trout. Slapping down a hopper in the current along a grassy bank can bring slashing takes or surprisingly delicate sips from trophy browns. While they're not common, 30-inch browns are a possibility. In 2010, our guide team put clients onto two such fish on terrestrials. Terrestrial action can continue into October with mild fall weather and the right water flows, and is truly one of the White's most spectacular events.

Fall brings the brown trout spawn, and the White River tradition of targeting spawning fish. This is still legal (as of this writing) but increasingly controversial, and is fading in popularity as concern grows for protecting the spawning browns.

Post-spawn, with water temperatures in the 50s, the brown trout feed aggressively on larger food items: minnows, sculpin, and stocked trout, particularly in the stronger current of higher flows. January and February, which bring higher water releases, are the prime months, but streamer tactics can work year-round at the right flows, generally 5,000 cfs and higher.

Generally, streamer anglers are divided into two camps. Some people fish conventional and Western patterns (anything from Buggers and coneheads up to 5-inch articulated flies such as Dungeons, Zoo Cougars, and the like) and catch good numbers of smaller browns and rainbows. The White River/Michigan camp prefers bigger-profile baitfish patterns such as Schmidt's Double Deceivers to imitate juvenile trout. This excludes the bycatch, but markedly increases your chances of landing a 24-inch or larger cannibal brown. You get to choose between regular action or hunting a trophy.

You'll also occasionally stumble across a smallmouth or largemouth bass when fishing streamers on the White in winter. If that holds some appeal, look to the White River tributaries. Crooked Creek and the Buffalo River are small, beautiful creeks holding smallmouths up to 19 inches.

➤ **Hatches:**

Streamer fishing for trophy browns is best from December through to the end of February.

Caddis hatches start in March and are good through April.

Sulphurs are best in June and early July.

Terrestrials start in May, but the best action fires with the hoppers in August and September.

The renowned shad kill—when threadfin (known locally as "yellowtail") and gizzard shad in Bull Shoals Lake get sucked through the dam's power-generating turbines, and big browns in the White gorge themselves on the dead and maimed baitfish—is a more temperamental "hatch," but February is best.

➤ **Fishing regulations:** The White River is open to all types of tackle, apart from two catch-and-release trophy zones: the first immediately below Bull Shoals Dam, and the second 24 miles downstream at Rim Shoals. In both, all trout species must be released and barbless (or crimped) hooks used. Multiple-fly rigs are now permitted in the trophy zones. The Bull Shoals trophy zone is closed from November 1 to January 31. For more details, check the full regulations at agfc.com, or pick up an AGFC trout regulations guide from local fly shops.

➤ **Tackle:** A 9-foot, 5-weight rod with a floating line is an easy all-around selection for your first White River trip and covers most of your needs. A 9-foot 6-weight is probably a better bet for hopper fishing with large foam hoppers up to #4. For streamer fishing, use a fast-action 6- to 8-weight rod and a shooting head sink-tip with a 6- or 7-inches-per-second sink rate.

Australia-born STEVE DALLY has been guiding on the White River system since 2004 and from Cotter since 2006. He is a partner and manager of Dally's Ozark Fly Fisher fly shop and guide service in Cotter. A former journalist, he has traveled extensively across the U.S., writing largely for Australia and New Zealand publications. He is the gear columnist for Australia and New Zealand's premier fly-fishing publication, *FlyLife*.

CLOSEST FLY SHOPS/OUTFITTERS

Dally's Ozark Fly Fisher
1200 West Main #7
Cotter, AR 72626
870 435 6166
www.theozarkflyfisher.com
info@theozarkflyfisher.com

Two Rivers Fly Shop
13718 Hwy. 5 S.
Norfork, AR 76258
870 499-3060
tworiversflyshop@gmail.com

Wishes & Fishes Fly Shop
627 Central Blvd.
Bull Shoals, AR 72619-0751
870 445-3848
flyfisharkansas.com/flyshop

HOTELS AND LODGES

The White River Inn (5-star lodge)
924 County Road 174
CotterAR 72626
870 430-2233
www.thewhiteriverinn.com

Rim Shoals Resort
(river cabins, bunkhouse, dock, and river taxi)
153 Rim Shoals Camp
Mountain Home, AR 72653
870 435-6144
rimshoals.com

White River Trout Lodge
(riverfront accommodations)
752 County Rd. 703
Cotter, AR 72626
(877-848-7688)
www.whiteriverlodge.com

BEST CAMPGROUND

Bull Shoals–White River State Park
(riverfront campground)
870 445-3629
www.arkansasstateparks.com/BullShoals-WhiteRiver.

Blue Heron Campground & Resort
150 Blue Heron Dr., P.O. Box 1253
Flippin, AR 72634
870 453-4678
www.blueheroncampground.com
blueheron@ozarkmountains.com

BEST RESTAURANTS

KT's Smokehouse BBQ
(lunch and dinner)
406 E. Main St.
Gassville, AR 72635
870 435-5080

178 Club Restaurant
2109 Central Blvd.
Bull Shoals, AR 72619
870 445-4949
www.178club.com

CELL PHONE SERVICE

Service is patchy on the White River due to the surrounding hills and valleys. Regular service in the towns.

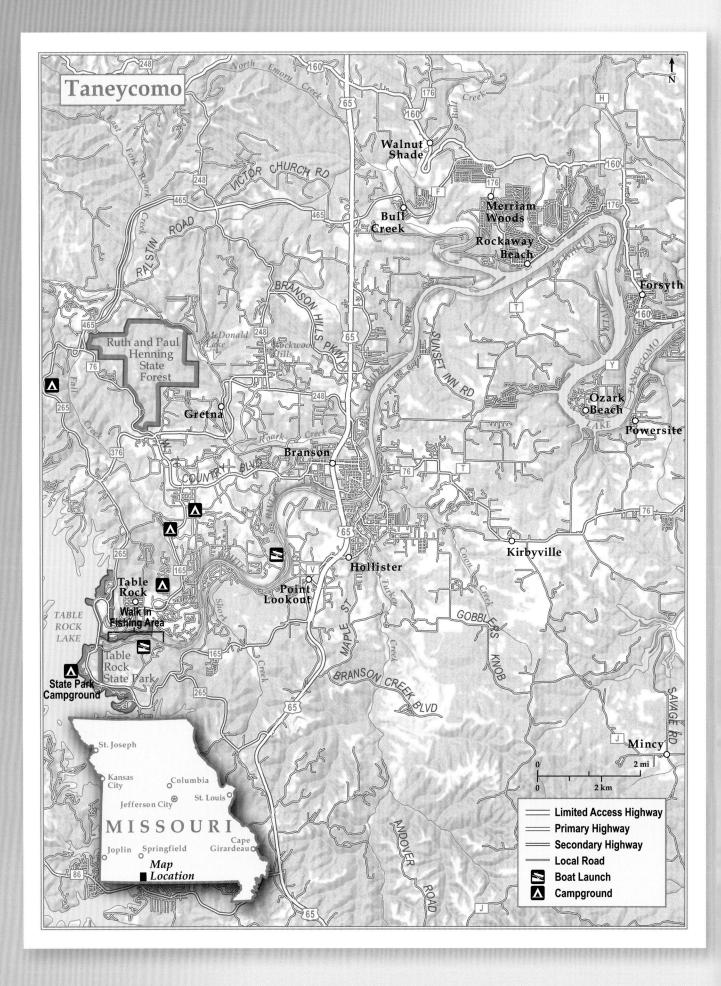

Taneycomo

Walnut Shade

Bull Creek

Merriam Woods

Rockaway Beach

Forsyth

Ruth and Paul Henning State Forest

McDonald Lake

Rockwood Hills

Gretna

Branson

Ozark Beach

Powersite

WHITE RIVER

LAKE TANEYCOMO

Kirbyville

Hollister

Point Lookout

Table Rock

Walk in Fishing Area

Table Rock State Park

TABLE ROCK LAKE

State Park Campground

VICTOR CHURCH RD

RALSTIN ROAD

BRANSON HILLS PKWY

SUNSET INN RD

COUNTRY BLVD

MAPLE ST

BRANSON CREEK BLVD

GOBBLERS KNOB

Coon Creek

Turkey Creek

ANDOVER ROAD

SAVAGE RD

Mincy

East Fork Roark Creek

North Emory Creek

Bull Creek

Roark Creek

Fall Creek

Short Creek

MISSOURI

St. Joseph

Kansas City

Columbia

Jefferson City

St. Louis

Joplin   Springfield

Cape Girardeau

Map Location

0   2 mi
0   2 km

	Limited Access Highway
	Primary Highway
	Secondary Highway
	Local Road
	Boat Launch
	Campground

N

➤ **Location:** The lake is near Branson, Missouri, in the southern part of the state. It is a 3½-hour drive from either Kansas City or St. Louis. There are commercial flights directly into Branson, or Springfield, about a 45-minute drive.

Lake Taneycomo is a 22-mile impounded section of the White River formed in 1913 by the construction of Powersite Dam at the lower end. In 1958, Table Rock Dam was completed at the upper end. Table Rock Dam's primary functions are flood control and power generation. It is one dam in a grid of more than 20 others, which provide electricity to several states. This makes the generation schedule for releasing water interesting, to say the least. The side effect from this dam was the creation of a coldwater lake and ideal conditions to support trout. Water temperature stays around 48 degrees, with year-round access and fishing.

Spring fishing seems to provide the greatest numbers of fish caught in a day, but fall is the best time to catch larger fish when they are moving up for the spawn.

The best accesses and best conditions for wade fishers are located in the upper portion of the lake just below the dam. This section probably has the highest concentrations of trout on any given day. The land just below and on either side of the dam belongs to the Missouri Department of Conservation (MDC). In this area MDC operates a hatchery to raise trout for local stocking and for relocation to other fisheries in Missouri and a few neighboring states. There are paved parking areas, walking trails, and stairs for easy access to some of the wading areas. On March 1, 1997, in an effort to improve the quality of fish in Taneycomo, MDC designated this area from 750 feet below the dam down to the mouth of Fall Creek as a Special Management Area, with regulations specific to this portion of the lake. All rainbow trout between 12 and 20 inches must be immediately released unharmed, and only flies and artificial lures can be used. On the remainder of the 22-mile lake, there is no length limit, except on browns—20 inches—and no bait or lure restrictions.

We often joke that fishing Taneycomo is like fishing 365 different rivers in one year. The generation flows can be ex-

treme. Our normal tailwater level with no generation will be somewhere around 701.6 feet above sea level. Table Rock Dam has four generators, each of which can flow approximately 3,500 cfs and raise the level about 3 feet. Therefore, the lake can go from almost no flow to 14,000 cfs, and the level from 701.6 feet to 713.6 feet. Fortunately, this is not an everyday occurrence. However, during peak power demand in the summer, or in case of a need for flood control, we can see these extremes. In the upper portion of Taneycomo, a horn system is in place to warn people that a water release is about to occur. Prior to release, a horn is sounded for each generator to be opened. *Always* heed these warnings and get to a safe location. Oftentimes, if only one or two generators are opened up, anglers can still find locations in this upper area to safely wade and continue fishing.

River Run Outfitters guide Gina Leitle preparing to release a fish. River Run Outfitters

Rainbow trout were first stocked into Lake Taneycomo in 1958. One interesting aspect about the Taneycomo rainbows is that somewhere in their makeup is the McCloud strain, from the McCloud River in California. Officials first introduced McCloud-strain rainbows into Missouri's Crane Creek in the late 1880s, and McCloud rainbows were part of

04/23/2012

Wading area close to the dam and in the area of the hatchery. Note the rock bank, which is pretty typical of the bottom structure of this lake/river. River Run Outfitters

River Run Outfitters guide Jim Lund with pretty rainbow. River Run Outfitters

early attempts to develop the best strain of trout for Taney-como. Brown trout were not introduced until 1980, and have done very well. Over the past 14 years, at least three browns over 20 pounds have been caught.

Unfortunately, brown fishing is not at its prime. Major flooding in 2011 impacted the brown trout population. The MDC is has increased stocking to get back the brown trout fishery Taneycomo anglers once enjoyed. On the other hand, the floods did not seem to negatively affect the rainbow trout. Taneycomo has lots of nice rainbows to be caught, with an average size of 14 to 15 inches, and fish over 20 inches are always a possibility. Whether due to the influence of McCloud-strain rainbows or other factors, Taneycomo rainbows spawn twice yearly: in the fall from September into November, and then again generally starting in February, but sometimes as early as January.

Taneycomo is much like many other tailwater fisheries in that our primary food sources for the trout are crustaceans—scuds and sow bugs—and midges. We also have good populations of sculpin and various other small fish, as well as worms and leeches. Especially in the upper section of the lake, mayflies and caddis are very limited, and stoneflies nearly nonexistent.

The best dry-fly fishing probably occurs in the fall, when we do well fishing imitations of various terrestrials such as beetles, hoppers, and ants. However, on any given day when a nice midge hatch is occurring and we have low-water conditions with fish rising, you can catch a lot of fish on a #18 Adams or Mosquito, or by stripping a soft-hackle fly.

When all power generators are going, a boat is a must. There are some places near the hatchery where one can fish around the outlets from the rearing ponds, which flow into the lake. Most of the water here is gin-clear, so 6X tippet is indicated for nymph-style fishing. Sometimes in the fall, the water is even clearer, and the dissolved oxygen may be low. During these times a 7X tippet may be your only ticket.

Not only do we have excellent trout fishing, but we are in the middle of a great family-oriented area. Branson is noted for its theme parks, water parks, warmwater activities, live entertainment, and lots of shopping.

➤ **Hatches:** Although we see an occasional mayfly or caddis in the spring, our consistent hatches are midges in a wide variety of sizes and colors. We can have midge hatches 365 days a year. The other main food sources in Taneycomo are crustaceans: scuds and sow bugs. Small fish, especially sculpin, are also available.

➤ **Fishing regulations:** Open year-round, 365 days a year, 24 hours a day. No restrictions on boat size or motors.

Statewide regulations and limits of four trout daily and eight in possession apply, except that only one brown trout may be included in the daily limit, and it must be at least 20 inches. Rainbow trout from 12 to 20 inches must be released unharmed immediately after being caught in Lake Taneycomo from the closed zone 760 feet below Table Rock Dam to the mouth of Fall Creek. There is no length limit on rainbow trout downstream from the mouth of Fall Creek. Only flies and artificial lures may be used on Lake Taneycomo above the mouth of Fall Creek.

Unscented soft plastic baits, and natural and scented baits (including natural fish foods, dough bait, putty- or paste-type bait, and any substance designed to attract fish by taste or smell and any fly, lure, or bait containing or used with such substances) are specifically prohibited above the mouth of Fall Creek.

While you're on Lake Taneycomo, all trout must be kept with the head, tail, and skin intact. A trout permit is required to possess trout anywhere on the lake and is required of all anglers above the Highway 65 bridge.

➤ **Tackle:** Use 8½- or 9-foot, 4- to 7-weight rods; 4-weights for soft-hackles and dries. Use 7½- to 9-foot leaders tapered to 5X or 6X. For midging, nymphing, and fishing scuds and sow bugs, a 9-foot, 5-weight rod with 5X or 6X tippet is ideal. There are times, especially in the fall, when 7X tippet is necessary due to the clarity of the water. Consider fluorocarbon tippet material. With the fluctuating water levels, sink-tip fly lines with varying sink rates can be the method of choice, and 6- or 7-weight rods can handle these better. Use 3X or 4X tippet when pulling streamers.

Water temperatures in Taneycomo can range from 48 to 52 degrees. Layer accordingly. Much of the wading area is fairly shallow, so waist-high or full waders will work. Missouri implemented a no-felt-soles policy in 2012, so only rubber-soled wading boots are allowed.

CAROLYN PARKER and her husband Stan started River Run Outfitters fly shop and guide service in Branson, Missouri in 1999. Carolyn is a full-time instructor and guide, running a Western-style drift boat on the Taneycomo portion of the White River.

CLOSEST FLY SHOPS

River Run Outfitters
2626 State Hwy. 165
Branson, MO 65616
417-332-0460
shop@riverrunoutfitters.com
www.riverrunoutfitters.com

Anglers & Archery Outfitters
138 Eden Way
Branson, MO 65616
417-335-4655
www.anglersandarchery.com

Bass Pro Shops
1 Bass Pro Dr.
Branson, MO 65616
417-243-5200
www.basspro.com

Chartered Waters Trout Shop
1326 Acacia Club Rd.
Hollister, MO 65617
417-334-1005
customerservice@charteredwaters.com
www.charteredwaters.com

CLOSEST OUTFITTERS/GUIDES

Anglers & Archery Outfitters (above)
Chartered Waters Trout Shop (above)
River Run Outfitters (above)

CLOSEST LODGES AND MOTELS

Lodge at the Falls
3245 Falls Parkway
Branson, MO 65616
417-336-3255

Fall Creek Inn and Suites
995 Hwy. 165
Branson, MO 65616
417-648-1683
www.fallcreekinn.com

BEST HOTEL

Chateau on the Lake
415 N. State Hwy. 265
Branson, MO 65616
417-334-1161
www.chateauonthelake.com

BEST CAMPGROUND

Table Rock State Park
5272 State Hwy. 165
Branson, MO 65616
417-334-4704

CLOSEST RESTAURANT

Danna's Bar-B-Q & Burger Shop
963 State Hwy. 165
Branson, MO 65616
417-337-5527
www.dannasbbq.com

BEST RESTAURANT

Candlestick Inn Restaurant
127 Taney
Branson, MO 65616
417-334-3633
www.candlestickinn.com

BEST PLACE TO GET A COLD, STIFF DRINK

Kickin Aces Saloon
120 Montgomery
Branson, MO 65616
417-335-2620
www.kickinacessaloon.com

CLOSEST EMERGENCY MEDICAL HELP

Cox Medical Center
Branson Landing Blvd. & Skaggs Rd.
Branson, MO 65616
417-335-7000

CELL PHONE SERVICE

Available almost everywhere on Lake Taneycomo.

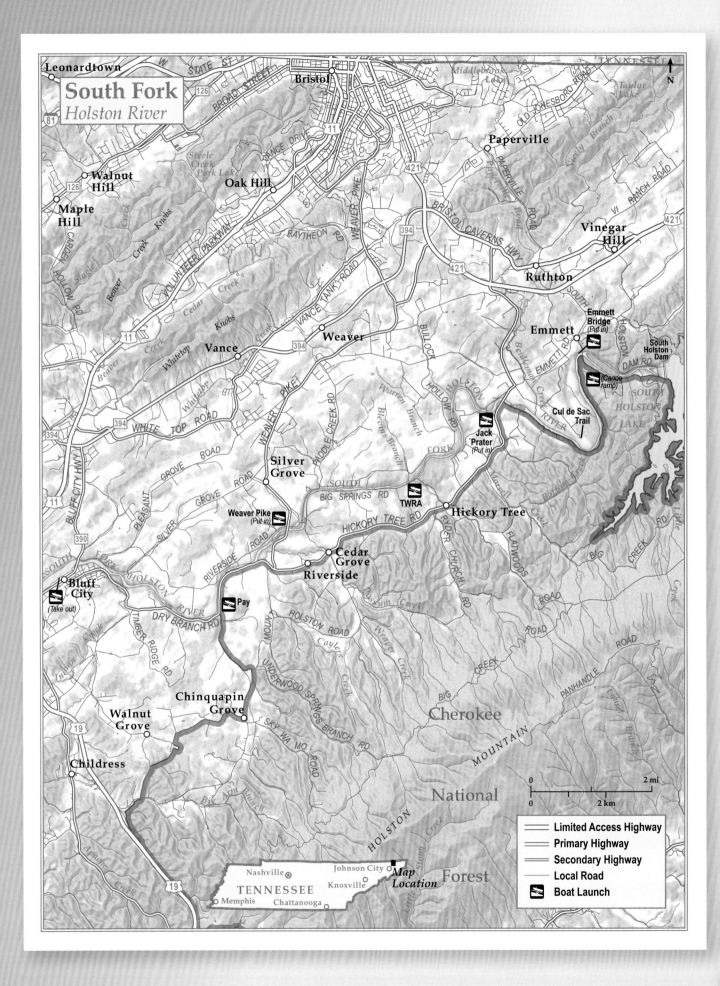

South Holston River *(Tennessee–Virginia)*

➤ **Location:** The South Holston River (aka SoHo tailwater) is in upper east Tennessee near Bristol, Tennessee/Virginia. The water that flows into the South Holston Lake actually comes from Virginia. Central to several states in the region, it is within minutes of east Tennessee, southwest Virginia, and western North Carolina.

The South Holston Dam was completed in 1950, creating South Holston Lake, which covers approximately 7,580 acres and is 13½ miles long, with 160 miles of shoreline. Stocking of the lake with brown and rainbow trout began in 1954. Each year we see 90,000 to 100,000 rainbows introduced into the waters to supplement their population. Browns have not been stocked in these incredible waters since 2003. To date, the largest brown caught was 43 inches, with an approximate weight of 33 pounds. The best news is that it was caught *and* released!

A 2006 survey showed 37 percent of all fishing on the SoHo is fly fishing. The river is a tremendous economic resource for the surrounding area. Nearby Bristol Motor Speedway hosts two of NASCAR's biggest races annually, and many race fans come early during race weeks to experience the SoHo's great fishing. You have your choice of floating or wading. As on all tailwaters, you need to be aware of the release schedule from the dam. Go online at tva.com to get the projected water flow.

If you would like to bring your own drift boat, you will find several river access points, though I strongly suggest hiring a local guide. It is the guides' job to know the best places to find fish. It's important to remember that you will be unable to float the SoHo on low water—the limestone bottom will hang you up and hold you, and will do a terrible number on your boat bottom. There is plenty of access to wade also, if that is your choice.

The river will give an angler just about every type of water you would ever want. You can fish slow, flat water that will let you spot fish and do some sight fishing. You can locate some riffles in all sections of the river. If you're interested in deep-water nymphing, the middle and lower sections are where you want to be. Dry-dropper rigs, indicator rigs, high-sticking, and free nymphing can all bring results for a patient, observant angler.

Among all the rivers listed in this book, the South Holston has a truly unique personality and is one of the most technical rivers you will ever fish. It's just like being in a relationship: As soon as you think you have someone figured out, you find out you had it all wrong to begin with. Similarly, the SoHo can be cruel, but if you take your time and listen, you will be greatly rewarded. To fish one of the best and most beautiful trout streams in the U.S., come visit the South Holston.

South Holston float with Kent Klewein from the "Gink & Gasoline" blog and David Grossman from the "Southern Culture on the Fly" blog. Steve Seinberg

➤ **Hatches:** The SoHo is known not only for its beautiful browns, but for the Sulphur mayfly hatch from mid- to late April until the first part of October. The Sulphur hatch here can put you in dry-fly heaven if you come at the right time and look for rising fish.

But the Sulphurs are not the only show in town. The South Holston is also excellent for anglers who enjoy fishing streamers, nymphs, or terrestrials such as hoppers and beetles. In the summer when the water is low, fishing a Japanese beetle can be productive in the early mornings. As the day progresses, you may want to add a dropper to the beetle to increase the excitement. Zebra Midges in various colors and sizes can produce great results.

The farther upriver you go, the smaller the insects become. Be prepared to fish flies from #14 all the way down to #26 to #30. You read that right, #30! (You may want to bring along some good 7X and even 8X tippet for those little flies.) But except for the really small stuff, 5X to 6X will work great.

Wading low water with Josh Garris. Steve Seinberg

Beautiful South Holston brown. Steve Seinberg

SoHo brown. Steve Seinberg

➤ **Fishing regulations:** The Tennessee Wildlife Resources Agency (TWRA) has set aside two prime brown-trout spawning areas on the SoHo to protect spawning brown trout. These areas are closed to all fishing from November 1 through January.

In addition, TWRA has implemented a slot limit—16 to 22 inches—to allow the SoHo to produce outstanding trophy-size fish. This allows anglers to harvest one fish 22 inches or larger. All fish within the 16- to 22-inch "slot"—also called the protected length range (PLR)—must be returned to the water immediately. For up-to-date information and regulations, visit the Tennessee Wildlife Resources Agency website at www.tn.gov/twra.

➤ **Tackle:** Bring 9-foot, 4- to 6-weight rods. You'll want floating lines for fishing dries and nymphs, and sink-tips for streamers. Leaders should be 9 to 15 feet and normally tapered to 4X to 6X. To go smaller, add finer tippet, down to 8X if necessary.

Wear breathable waders with Vibram or "sticky rubber" soles. You may want studs for more stability, because parts of the SoHo's riverbottom are very slick. A wading staff is also a very good idea.

The weir dam below South
Holston Dam. Mike Adams

I grew up in Alabama, fishing farm ponds for bass and bluegills.
When in the Army, I was stationed in Alaska and caught my
first trout on a fly. I was hooked. I have been blessed to have
lived near some of the best trout fishing in the U.S. I have been
living in East Tennessee for the last 16 years, guiding the South
Holston, Watauga, and Caney Fork Rivers. I have been tying
commercially for 22 years and also build rods. I have been
married for 45 years and have 3 children and 7 grandchildren.

Life has been good.
—MIKE ADAMS

CLOSEST FLY SHOPS

Mahoney's
830 Sunset Dr.
Johnson City, TN 37604
800-835-5152
www.mahoneysports.com

South Holston River Fly Shop
608 Emmett Rd.
Bristol, TN 37620
423-878-2822
ForeverFlyFishing@yahoo.com
southholstonriverflyshop.com

EFO
102 Willmary Rd.
Johnson City, TN 37604
423-928-2007
efo@easternflyoutfitters.com
easternflyoutfitters.com

Mountain Sports Ltd.
1021 Commonwealth Ave.
Bristol, VA 24201
276-466-8988
mountainsportsltd.com

CLOSEST OUTFITTERS/GUIDES

Mike Adams Fly Fishing Outfitters
2914 Watauga Rd. #304
Johnson City TN 37601
423-741-4789
www.adamsflyfishing.com

Watauga River Lodge
643 Smalling Rd.
Watauga, TN 37694
828-208-3428
booking@wataugariverlodge.com
www.wataugariverlodge.com

South Holston River Lodge
1509 Bullock Hollow Rd.
Bristol, TN 37620
877-767-7875
reservations@SouthHolstonRiverLodge.com
www.southholstonriverlodge.com

CLOSEST LODGES

South Holston River Lodge (above)

Sleep Inn Suites
2020 Franklin Terrace Ct.
Johnson City, TN 37604
423-915-0081
www.sleepinn.com

BEST CAMPGROUND

Lake View RV Park
4550 Highway 11 E.
Bristol, TN 37618
866-800-0777
camping@lakeviewrvpark.com
www.lakeviewrvpark.com

BEST RESTAURANT

Prices Store
Hwy. 44
Bluff City, TN
423-538-3337

Peerless Restaurant
2531 N. Roan St.
Johnson City, TN 37601
423-282-2351

CLOSEST PLACE TO GET A COLD, STIFF DRINK

Jack City Grill/Restaurant
1805 N. Roan St. #A1
Johnson City, TN 37601

Cootie Brown's
2715 N. Roan St.
Johnson City, TN 37601

CLOSEST EMERGENCY MEDICAL HELP

Bristol Regional Hospital
1 Medical Park Blvd.
Bristol, TN 37620
423-844-1121

Piney Flats Urgent Care
6070 Hwy. 11 E.
Piney Flats, TN 37686
423-538-5202

CELL PHONE SERVICE
Yes. Pretty much unlimited.

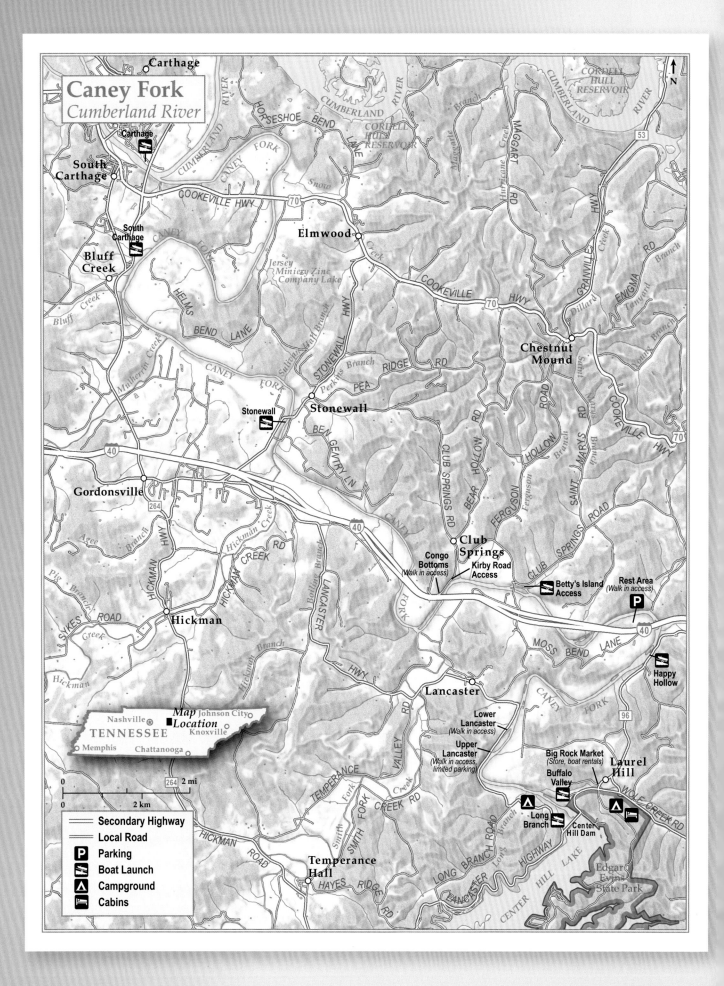

Caney Fork
Cumberland River

Carthage

Carthage

South Carthage

South Carthage

Bluff Creek

Elmwood

Chestnut Mound

Stonewall

Stonewall

Gordonsville

Club Springs

Congo Bottoms
(Walk in access)

Kirby Road Access

Betty's Island Access

Rest Area
(Walk in access)

Hickman

Lancaster

Happy Hollow

Lower Lancaster
(Walk in access)

Upper Lancaster
(Walk in access, limited parking)

Big Rock Market
(Store, boat rentals)

Laurel Hill

Buffalo Valley

Long Branch

Center Hill Dam

Edgar Evins State Park

Temperance Hall

TENNESSEE
Map Location
Nashville
Memphis
Chattanooga
Johnson City
Knoxville

0   2 mi
0   2 km

— Secondary Highway
= Local Road
🅿 Parking
🛥 Boat Launch
⛺ Campground
🛏 Cabins

CORDELL HULL RESERVOIR

CUMBERLAND RIVER

CORDELL HULL RESERVOIR

HORSESHOE BEND

CUMBERLAND LAKE

COOKEVILLE HWY 70

COOKEVILLE HWY 70

40

264

96

53

Center Hill Lake

Edgar Evins State Park

WOLF CREEK RD

Caney Fork River *(Central Tennessee)*

➤ **Location:** The Caney Fork River is in Middle Tennessee, approximately 1 hour east of Nashville and 2 hours west of Knoxville on I-40.

The Caney Fork River is a typical Southern hydroelectric tailwater, situated below the Center Hill Dam, which is operated by the Army Corps of Engineers. Daily releases of cold, trout-sustaining water from Center Hill Dam meander 26 miles through the gentle Tennessee hills. The river crosses under I-40 five times before joining the Cumberland River near the town of Carthage, Tennessee.

At first glance, the river is not your classic trout stream environment. The gentle riffles, runs, and deep pools of the Caney Fork lack structure and cover, making it a tricky river to read, and locate trout. The river also lacks the prolific mayfly hatches found in the tailwaters of eastern Tennessee. Crustaceans and midges dominate the food base. Do not let the lack of classic hatches fool you—anglers are pleasantly surprised by the numbers of quality rainbows, browns, and brook trout found throughout the river. Recent water quality improvements and trophy trout regulations continue to improve both sizes and numbers of fish.

A few important things to know about the river: The Caney Fork is a year-round fishery; it runs at approximately 250 cfs when the Corps is not generating power or releasing water through a sluice or floodgate. Water releases can reach volumes upward of 15,000 cfs. Wadable water levels are found during times of no water releases, 300 cfs and lower. The river is also very fishable during higher water with a drift boat, canoe, or other motorboat. Most anglers prefer a water level below 5,000 cfs, as the river can be a dangerous float at higher water levels. Make sure you check the water release schedule for the day—water levels can go from the top of your wading boots to over your head in a matter of minutes! Release schedules are always subject to change, so be sure to check in the morning before departure. Water release schedules are online at www.tva.gov/river/lakeinfo/index.htm.

The upper 8 miles of the river (from the dam to Betty's Island) supports the majority of fish, anglers, recreational paddlers, and guides. This section of the river can be extremely crowded due in summer due to easy access, proximity to a campground, the high numbers of fish per mile, and the recent proliferation of canoe and kayak liveries. The upper 8 miles also has the two shortest floats on the river. From May through September, fishing on weekdays offers a far better experience than on weekends. The middle and lower river has less traffic, but there is very little legal access other than by boat or canoe.

On the Caney Fork, always have plenty of midge, blackfly, scud, and sow bug patterns in your fly box. These are the big four trout foods here, top to bottom, year-round. Sow bugs are my go-to patterns when the fish are tight-lipped, in winter, spring, summer, or fall.

April usually kicks off the season on the Caney, with caddis hatches in the middle and lower sections and scuds, sow bugs, and midges dominating the upper section. Fishing in

David Buxbaum setting the hook.

the spring is usually fast and furious. After long periods of high water, the fish are fat, strong, and usually less selective.

June to October is midge and blackfly time. Long leaders and fine tippets rule the day during the summer. The river is usually very wadable and fishes like a big spring creek this time of year. If sight casting to feeding fish in thin, clear water is what you like, you will love the river in summer. The fish can be very size- and color-selective. They will not move

Left. Summer fog on the Caney Fork.
Above. Caney Fork brown.

far for the fly. Fish will even move away from bright-colored strike indicators in thin water. Summer months in Tennessee can also bring some great terrestrial fishing. Grasshoppers, beetles, and ants can always be found struggling in the surface film. October usually brings caddis back into the middle and lower sections.

From November through the end of March usually requires a boat, because this is our rainy season. It is not uncommon to have no wadable water for months on end. This winter fishing calls for streamers and big sink-tips—8- or 9-weight rods with 200- to 450-grain sinking tips are the norm. The winter months on the Caney Fork are the big-fish time of year.

When the stars align correctly, we have just the right amount of precipitation so the river doesn't blow out, and air temperatures stay cold enough to start killing shad in Center Hill Lake above the dam . . . then, get ready! Dead and dying shad get sucked through the generators in massive numbers and create a feeding frenzy downriver. The shad "hatch" on the Caney is something every angler should experience at least once in a lifetime. Big trout, stripers, walleye, skipjack, and buffalo all get in on the buffet. Nothing beats a floating shad pattern getting crushed by a 10-pound trout or a 30-pound striper! This is our reward after months of 15-foot leaders, 8X tippets, and #26 flies.

➤ **Hatches and fly selection:**
Midges: All year.
Blackflies: All year.
Scuds: All year.
Sow bugs: All year.
Caddis: April into early July; September into early November.
Crane flies: Late June into early September.
Terrestrials: Late May into early September.
Sculpin, darters, and minnows: All year.

Midges: Larva colors include black, gray, dark olive, olive, and red. Pupa colors are black, dark olive, olive, and gray.

Adult colors: black, gray, dark olive, olive, and cream.
Sizes: #18–#28
Larva: Disco Midge, Kaufmann's Marabou Midge Larva, Biot Midge w/ and w/o beadhead.
Pupa: Palomino Midge, JT's Buxom, RS2.
Adult: Griffith's Gnat, Parachute Adams.

Scuds: Scud colors: Gray, gray olive, tan, pinkish orange.

Patterns: Your patterns should be tied two ways—on curved scud hooks and on standard straight hooks. Most scud patterns are tied too thick! Caney Fork scuds are thin and strong swimmers, #14–#22.

Sow bugs: Sow bug colors should include olive, tan, gray, dark gray, and black.

Patterns: JT's Sow Bug, Umpqua's Sow Bug, Cress Bug, #14–22. Most store-purchased sow bug patterns are poorly tied. Your patterns need to be flat, and the shells darker than the undersides.

Caddis: Caddis larva colors are bright caddis green, creamy caddis green, olive, and tan.

Pupa colors are caddis green, creamy caddis green, and brown.

Adult colors include creamy olive, creamy caddis green, and tan.

Patterns: Larva patterns (#14–#18) can be simple like a Serendipity or Lafontaine's Deep Pupa, Lafontaine's sparkle pupa, Nori's Caddis Pupa, and Soft Hackle Pupa.

Adult pattern: Elk-hair Caddis #14–#16, olive and tan.

Big Mayfly (Willowfly):
Patterns: I fish only the adult, since this is a nighttime hatch. The dun is usually cream-colored with chocolate brown on the sides, #2–#6. Any Hex or Eastern Green Drake

pattern will work here. The fish will not be selective and will explode on the fly. I like to tie a glow-in-the-dark post on a big parachute pattern.

Crane fly: Patterns: Light Cahill or Eastern Sulphur (#16) will do most of the time for the adult. Brown Bomber soft hackles and rust colored will also produce well.

Terrestrials: Patterns: Heavy on beetle patterns. Japanese beetle patterns are very strong producers. Black and big brown patterns also work well. QT Nymphs and Renegades work well to represent drowned beetles.

Ants in sizes #16–#22 can sometime tempt selective fish; black and rusty orange with cream-colored hackle.

Cricket patterns work better than hopper patterns in sizes #10–#14 black and browns.

Threadfin Shad: Patterns: Gray and white Clouser Minnows, Whitlock's Deep Shad, white Woolly Buggers, and white Zonkers, #6–#8.

Sculpin, Darters, Minnows: Patterns: Olive, black, brown, blue/green Woolly Buggers, #2–#16; olive/white, brown/white, brown/yellow, dace Clouser Minnows, #2–#16; Muddler Minnows, #2–#14.

Snails: Patterns: Size #14–#16 Borger pattern or Renegade.

➤ **Regulations:** Special trout regulations apply from Center Hill Dam downstream to the Cumberland River, including tributaries. Total daily creel of all trout in combination is five fish (rainbow, brook, and brown). Rainbows: 14- to 20-inch slot, only one fish over 20 inches. Brook trout: 14- to 20-inch slot, only one over 20-inches. Brown trout: 1 per day, 24-inch minimum length. Anglers must purchase a Tennessee fishing license and a trout stamp. www.twra.gov.

➤ **Tackle:** Low-water rods and reels: 9-foot, 4- or 5-weight with floating line; leaders 9 to 15 feet and fluorocarbon tippet, 4X to 8X. High-water rods: 9-foot, 6- to 9-weight with floating line and 30-foot Type 6 sink-tips up to 350 grains.

JIM MAURIES is the owner/operator of Fly South, a full-service fly shop in Nashville, Tennessee. Jim was born and raised in Colorado, and it was there his fly-fishing addiction took root. Jim started tying flies professionally during his college years to support his fishing habit. That was the steppingstone into working for a fly shop, which in turn led to guiding and instructing fly tiers and fly fishers. Jim has guided and taught fly fishers in Tennessee for more than 20 years. Jim pioneered fly fishing for many different species in the Middle Tennessee area, but trout remain his first love.

CLOSEST FLY SHOPS
Fly South
115 19th Ave. South
Nashville, TN 37203
615-341-0420 or 615-341-0421
flysouth@bellsouth.net
Cumberland Transit
2807 West End Ave.
Nashville, TN 37203
615-321-4069
info@cumberlandtransit.co
Game Fair, Ltd.
5703 Old Harding Pike
Nashville, TN 37205
615-353-0602
sales@gamefairltd.com
Big Rock Market (limited fly tackle)
1193 Wolf Creek Rd.
Silver Point, TN 38582
931-858-0967

CLOSEST OUTFITTER
Fly South (left)

BEST HOTELS
Stay in Nashville (only one hour away). Hotels, music, and dining.

CLOSEST LODGE
No lodges on the Caney, but cabin rentals can be found at Big Rock Market and Edgar Evans State Park.

CLOSEST CAMPGROUND
Long Branch Campground
478 Lancaster Rd.
Lancaster, TN 38569
(615) 548-8002

CLOSEST/BEST RESTAURANT
The Galley at Edgar Evins Marina
2100 Edgar Evins Park Rd.
Silver Point, TN 38582
931-858-2424
April-October

BEST PLACE TO GET A COLD, STIFF DRINK
BYOB or beer at Big Rock Market

CELL PHONE SERVICE
Fair to good, depending on location.

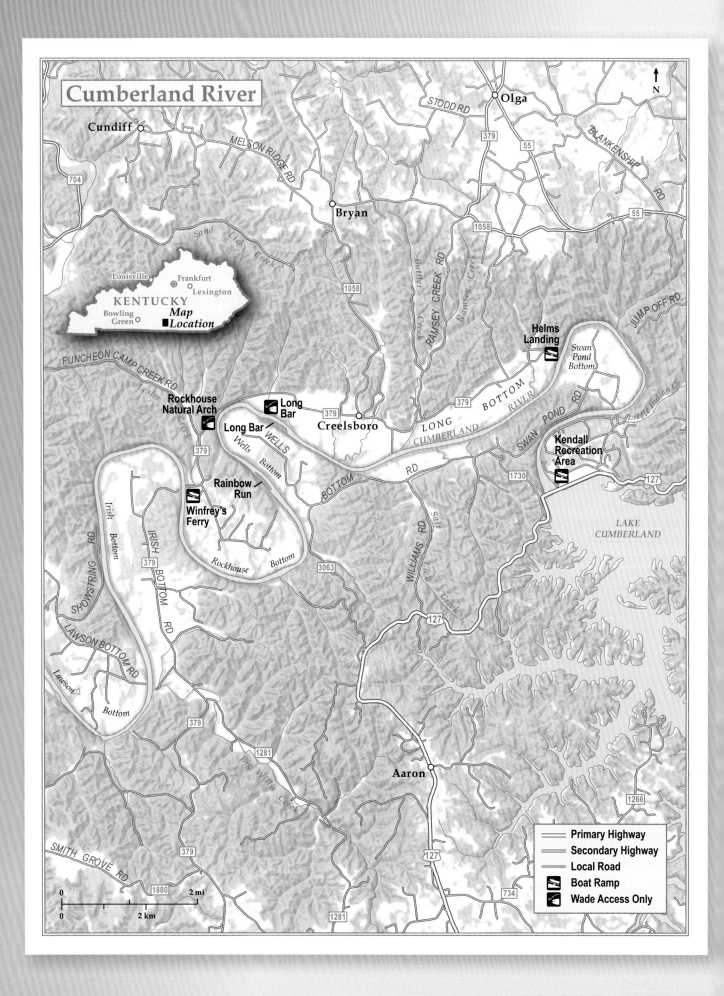

Cumberland River

Olga

Cundiff

STODD RD

379

55

BLANKENSHIP RD

MELSON RIDGE RD

704

Bryan

1058

55

Sand Lick Creek

Butler Creek

RAMSEY CREEK RD

Ramsey Creek

KENTUCKY
Louisville
Frankfort
Lexington
Map Location
Bowling Green

JUMP OFF RD

Helms Landing

Swan Pond Bottom

PUNCHEON CAMP CREEK RD

Lester Creek

Rockhouse Natural Arch

Long Bar

379

Creelsboro

379

LONG BOTTOM

CUMBERLAND RIVER

SWAN POND RD

Little Indian Cr

Kendall Recreation Area

127

Long Bar

WELLS

Wells Bottom

BOTTOM RD

1730

Rainbow Run

379

Winfrey's Ferry

LAKE CUMBERLAND

Irish Bottom

SHOWSTRING RD

IRISH BOTTOM RD

Rockhouse Bottom

3063

WILLIAMS RD

Salt Creek

LAWSON BOTTOM RD

Lawson Bottom

379

127

1281

Big Wills Creek

Aaron

1266

SMITH GROVE RD

1880

379

2 mi

127

2 km

1281

734

Cumberland River *(Kentucky–Tennessee)*

➤ **Location:** A little over 2 hours from Lexington and Louisville, and a handful of miles south of Jamestown, Kentucky, U.S. 127 passes directly across the top of Wolf Creek Dam, with Lake Cumberland on one side and the Cumberland River on the other. Although the lower stretches of river meander through Cumberland and Monroe Counties before passing into Tennessee, the majority of the access points are located in Russell County along KY 379 on the north side of the river, and KY 3063 on the south side.

The Cumberland River starts as a small mountain stream in the hills of eastern Kentucky and grows quickly as the lack of arable land funnels rainwater into the Cumberland Basin until a relatively large river emerges in the central part of the state. Flash flooding along this river became such a problem that in the 1940s that the U.S. Army Corps of Engineers built Wolf Creek Dam to create Lake Cumberland as a flood control project. It turned out to be the largest manmade lake east of the Mississippi River. Lake Cumberland is roughly 50,000 acres in area and deeper than 200 feet in some places. The Corps unintentionally killed many of the native warmwater species that once lived in the waters downstream of the dam. As a "fix" to this problem, a sizable fish hatchery was built at the base of Wolf Creek Dam to stock rainbow and brown trout into the newly created tailwater, as well as in many other streams throughout the region.

The Kentucky Department of Fish and Wildlife Resources annually stocks about 240,000 trout in the Cumberland River: about 150,000 rainbows, 50,000 browns, and 40,000 brook trout. While there is no documented trout reproduction in the river, anglers can find fish from 9 to 30-plus inches. The current state-record brown, brook, and rainbow were all caught in this tailwater: the brown was just over 21 pounds, the rainbow was 14 pounds, and the record for the newly introduced brook trout is currently being broken almost monthly.

The Cumberland is an amazing striped bass fishery as well. Twenty-pound stripers are common, and 40-pound fish are not as rare as you might think. Fish over 50 pounds are seen and caught every year, although most larger stripers are not taken on the fly.

There are also good numbers of white bass, carp, walleye, and other warmwater species that make their way up the river from time to time, and anglers have the potential to catch a wide variety of fish depending on the section of river fished.

The Cumberland is usually calm and flat and can be very difficult to read to those unfamiliar with this type of water. Double nymph fishing is the most common and successful method. However, constant adjustments are crucial, and moving the indicator a couple of inches up or down the leader can often make the difference between a strike and just another drift. Bring your polarized glasses and watch the water carefully—you'll need to study the seams and pay close attention to your drifts to have consistent success.

Beefy brown

Even though the fishing can be challenging at times, fly selection is not. Standard, tried-and-true patterns work well. Prince Nymphs, Zebra Midges, and a couple of Griffith's Gnats will cover most of the bases. During spring, there is limited dry-fly fishing, primarily with caddis and midge imitations. Typically, the most prolific hatch of the year is the Mothers Day Caddis, which can be massive or almost nonexistent. Summer is mostly spent fishing midges under indicators, but as we get into August, trout will readily rise to a grasshopper, beetle, or cicada, so put some foam in your

Limestone palisade along the river.

box if you plan to fish during the dog days.

Fall is the time for piscatorial love, and although there is no recorded reproduction in the river, fish still put on their best spawning colors and hang around the gravel bars in hopes of finding a mate. Small streamers fished during rising water can be deadly this time of year. In the winter, pack larger streamers and tiny midge patterns. Fish the midges in low water and strip big, meaty baitfish imitations in the deep stuff on a hefty sinking line.

Night fishing is not recommended at any time. The river often becomes blanketed in fog after dark, and both wading and boating become extremely dangerous, regardless of water levels.

To pursue the stripers, you will need 8- to 10-weight rods and some giant streamers. Focus your efforts below the town of Burkesville—there is good access at Traces of the Cumberland (a private facility offering river access and boat rentals) and at a public ramp located right in town. Periods of low generation are the best times to target these fish on a fly.

Starting just below the Wolf Creek Dam, the river carves its way through private property and limestone cliffs, providing only a handful of public access points. Trout fishers using boats will usually launch at three of the six public boat ramps: Kendall Recreation Area (directly below the dam), Helm's Landing, or Winfrey's Ferry. All the boat ramps are situated where you can float from one ramp to the next in one day's fishing, if you limit your wade time. Except when the river is at its lowest levels, john boats and jet sleds can put in at any ramp and motor upstream or down. As on any tailwater this size, it is extremely important to remember that constant water level fluctuations can make for dangerous conditions, regardless of what watercraft you are using.

For canoes or kayaks, a common float is from Rock House

Natural Bridge to Winfrey's Ferry. This 5-mile stretch passes through some of the most productive trout water in the river and allows you to take out about a mile down the road (KY 379) from where you put in; it is an easy walk back to your vehicle. With two cars, there are more options, but anglers are still limited to the handful of public access points.

When water levels are low enough to wade, anglers can find good access and parking at the boat ramp access points mentioned above, as well as the state-managed Long Bar Fishing Access Area and Rainbow Run Fishing Access Area, and directly below the dam. The river is wide everywhere, and there is always a relatively deep channel, so wading anglers should keep in mind that even during periods of low or no power generation, there are only a couple of spots where a person can wade completely across the river.

Current state of the river

In 2007, the Corps began a major repair project on Wolf Creek Dam. During construction, the river, the aquatic life, and the fishing all suffered immensely. However, the river is currently recovering in an amazing fashion. Water quality, clarity, and flows are all beginning to benefit anglers. Aquatic invertebrates and other insect life are again teeming in the river. A significant portion of the larger fish in the river perished during the dam repair process, but the Kentucky Department of Fish and Wildlife Resources is stocking a number of fish in the 16- to 20-inch range to help balance the sizes in the river. They are also beginning to stock triploid rainbows, a strain that does not have an interest in breeding (only in feeding), which should help rapidly boost sizes.

The Department is also creating a meandering creek that will leave the back of the hatchery and run through wooded farmland until it empties into the river about 2 miles downstream. This will provide an excellent place to fish should water levels in the tailwater be too high to wade, or too forceful to boat safely.

➤ **Hatches:**

Midges #18–#22: Year-round.

Caddis #14–#18: May–June.

Sulphurs #16–#18: May–June.

Blue-winged Olives #16–#20: June–August.

Grasshoppers, beetles, and flying ants (various sizes): August– September.

➤ **Fishing regulations:** Open year-round.

Rock House Natural Bridge

Gorgeous 'bow

A trout permit is required in addition to your fishing license, whether you plan to keep fish or not. Possession limit is five fish per angler per day. No rainbow or brown trout between 15 and 20 inches may be kept. Each angler is allowed one fish per day over 20 inches. One brown trout per day may be kept, and it must be over 20 inches. Brook trout must be at least 15 inches to keep.

➤ **Tackle:** Use 9- or 10-foot, 4- or 5-weight rods with floating lines for dries and nymphs, and 6- or 7-weight rods and sinking lines for streamers. Carry tapered mono leaders with fluorocarbon tippets down to 5X or 6X. A beaded nymph fished under an indicator is the most productive technique. Breathable waders with rubber-soled wading boots are recommended year-round.

GENE SLUSHER is the owner of The Lexington Angler, a full-service fly shop in Lexington, Kentucky. Gene is a graduate of Centre College and received his J.D. and his Master of Studies in Environmental Law from Vermont Law School. When he is not fishing, Gene enjoys gardening, sipping bourbon, and piddling around with bird dogs.

CLOSEST FLY SHOP
The Lexington Angler
119 Clay Ave.
Lexington, KY 40502
859-389-6552
www.lexingtonangler.com

CLOSEST OUTFITTERS/GUIDES
Cumberland Drifters Guide Service
859-983-2907
www.cumberlanddrifters.com

CLOSEST LODGES
Lure Lodge
Lake Cumberland State Resort Park
5465 State Park Rd.
Jamestown, KY 42629
270-343-3111
parks.ky.gov

BEST HOTEL
Lure Lodge,
Lake Cumberland State Resort Park *(left)*

BEST CAMPGROUND
Kendall Recreation Area and Campground
(directly below Wolf Creek Dam)
80 Kendall Rd.
Jamestown, KY
270-343-4660
877-444-6777
www.recreation.gov

BEST RESTAURANT
Lake Cumberland State Resort Park
parks.ky.gov

BEST PLACE TO GET A COLD, STIFF DRINK
Somerset, Kentucky (a 45-minute drive). The Cumberland River tailwater is located in a dry area, where alcohol sales are prohibited.

CLOSEST EMERGENCY MEDICAL HELP
Russell County Hospital
153 Dowell Rd.
Russell Springs, KY 42642
270-866-4141

CELL PHONE SERVICE
Yes.

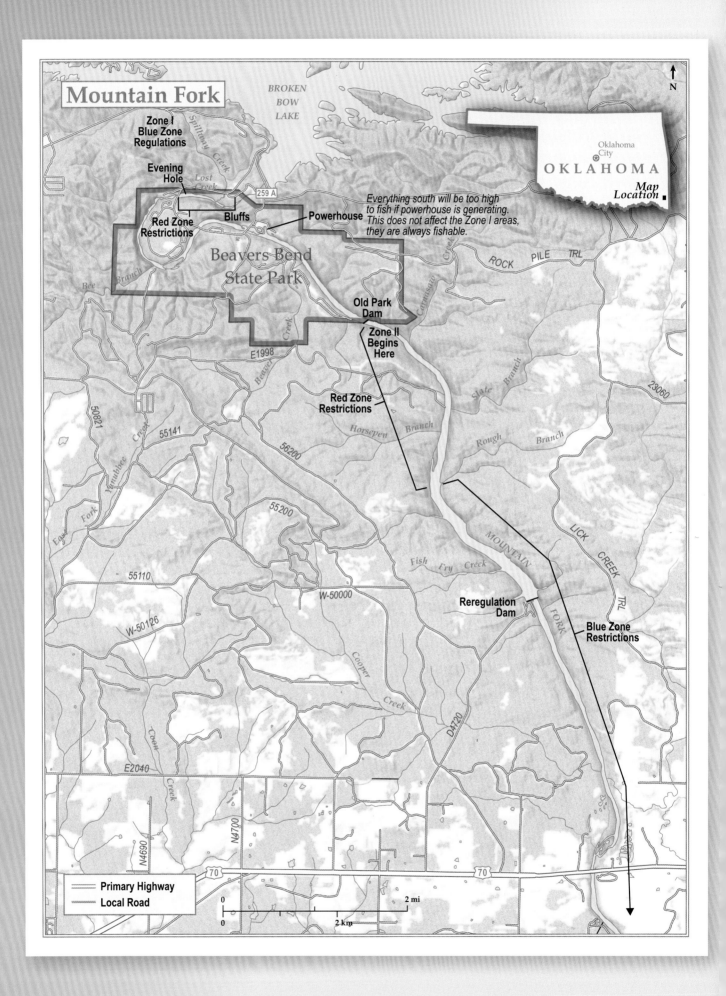

Mountain Fork

Zone I
Blue Zone
Regulations

Evening
Hole

Red Zone
Restrictions

Bluffs

Powerhouse

*Everything south will be too high
to fish if powerhouse is generating.
This does not affect the Zone I areas,
they are always fishable.*

Beavers Bend
State Park

BROKEN
BOW
LAKE

N

Oklahoma
City

OKLAHOMA

Map
Location

ROCK PILE TRL

Old Park
Dam

Zone II
Begins
Here

Red Zone
Restrictions

Slate Branch

Rough Branch

23060

55141

56200

55200

55110

W-50000

Fish Fry Creek

MOUNTAIN

LICK CREEK TRL

W-50126

Reregulation
Dam

Blue Zone
Restrictions

FORK

Cooper Creek

D4720

E2040

N4700

N4600

70

70

Primary Highway
Local Road

0   2 mi

0   2 km

E1998

50821

Yanubbee Creek

Eagle Fork

Beaver Creek

Bee Branch

Spillway Creek

Lost Creek

259 A

Carnasaw Creek

Horsepen Branch

Mountain Fork River *(Southeast Oklahoma)*

➤ **Location:** Eight miles north of Broken Bow in southeast Oklahoma and near Beavers Bend State Park. About a 3-hour drive from Dallas/Fort Worth, Shreveport, Tulsa, and Oklahoma City.

When you think fly fishing, you probably imagine Wyoming, Colorado, Alaska, or Montana. But Oklahoma? Not hardly. But then, it's unlikely you've ever heard of the Mountain Fork River in the foothills of the Kiamichi Mountains in the Sooner State. The Mountain Fork was dammed in the early 1970s, forming 22-mile long, 14,000-acre Broken Bow Lake. The 170-foot-deep lake serves for flood control and hydropower generation.

This is historic Native American country. The town of Hochatown—subsequently inundated by Broken Bow Lake—was settled by the Choctaw in the 1830s. It is one of the largest lakes within the State of Oklahoma, and a popular destination for locals and visitors from neighboring Texas.

The dam, which backs up to Beavers Bend State Park, does not discharge high volumes of water from the hydropower plant through the park. Instead, a spillway was constructed approximately ½ mile to the west side of the dam, where water is released via a gate valve and flows about 4 miles before converging with the powerhouse discharge. Thus, the park is not affected by high water flows during periods of generation.

The 12-mile trout fishery is divided into three zones. Although each zone is approximately 4 miles long, they are quite different.

➤ **Zone I**

Water is released at the spillway, and the flow is generally 80+ cubic feet per second. There is a 100+ foot drop in elevation in the first mile before it runs into the river channel and levels out. In the last 10 years, a great deal of work has been done to enhance this section. The Oklahoma Department of Wildlife Conservation installed more than a dozen small log dams, creating conservation pools, which have proved to be excellent habitat for trout. Rainbow trout started reproducing in the stream almost immediately.

Although nymphing is popular, there is some dry-fly fishing with patterns imitating caddis, March Browns, and BWOs.

A mile below the spillway, the flow is divided. The diversion was added to create an additional ¼ mile of trout water

for the fishery known as Lost Creek. The diversion is also the beginning of the special-regulations section.

A quarter mile from the diversion, the two branches converge above the Evening Hole, a ½-mile stretch that is notably the best sight-fishing area in the park. The flow is much slower, and the river has widened to 50 to 60 feet. Mayflies here include Light Cahills, Sulphurs, BWOs, March Browns, and tan and black caddis, as well as midges. Terrestrials include ants and grasshoppers. Crayfish and minnows are also significant parts of the food base. The Evening Hole Bridge marks the end of the Evening Hole and the special-regulations stretch.

The next 2-mile section of river slows considerably, and the water is typically deeper. There are two bridges located along the river that have stop logs installed at their bases from March through mid-November. These are used to raise the water level for canoeing, swimming, and other activities.

The Bluffs (Red Zone).

The logs are removed during the winter months, lowering levels and creating more wadable fishing areas. This stretch is known for its *Hexagenia* hatch during July and August.

Just below the second bridge, the powerhouse discharge enters the river. Wading is prohibited below the powerhouse to the Old Park Dam, but is allowed just above the release channel. There is limited room to wade, but it can be productive with streamers that represent the threadfin shad that come through the turbines during releases.

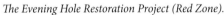
The Evening Hole Restoration Project (Red Zone).

A really good brown trout.

Rainbow release.

➤ Zone II

A half mile downstream of the powerhouse discharge is the Old Park Dam. It forms the park boundary and the beginning of Zone II. Although Zone II is approximately 4 miles long, the Re-Regulation Dam backs water up to within 1½ miles of the Old Park Dam, limiting access to only the upper stretch. Zone II is sometimes referred to as "grad school," with slow, clear, shallow water making wading and casting challenging. This is a special-regulations area, allowing trout to grow large. While trout populations are not high, fish over 20 inches are not uncommon and it's more about quality than quantity. With the exception of *Hexagenia*, you will find the same insects here that you find in the park. Streamers that represent shad are also popular. Much of the stream bottom is exposed bedrock that can be extremely slick. Sticky rubber–soled boots, studs, and wading staffs are all recommended.

Use caution when wading to the far side. High water from power-generating discharges rises rapidly and is not wadable, so always have an exit strategy.

➤ Zone III

Beginning at the Re-Regulation Dam, Zone III is fishable the entire 4-mile stretch to the Highway 70 bridge. There are two access points along the river: a state campground on the west side of the Re-Regulation Dam and a primitive campground on the east bank, halfway to the Highway 70 bridge.

Zone III has by far the best habitat and food base of the entire fishery. Its limitations come from water temperature problems that occur each summer. This has not prevented anglers from catching some big trout. The 17-pound, 4-ounce state record brown trout was caught at the base of the Re-Regulation Dam. Good hatches of BWOs, Caddis, March Browns, Light Cahills, and Sulphurs occur. Also there are large populations of sow bugs and crayfish, as well as various minnows.

➤ Hatches:

December–February: BWOs, #18–#20.

January–February: midges, #22–#24; Light Cahills, #18–#22;

The lower end of Spillway Creek (Blue Zone).

February–April: March Browns, #12–#14; caddis #14–#16;

April–August: streamers, shad patterns #6–#8; crayfish #6–#10; Sulphurs and Light Cahills. Late afternoon: *Hexagenia* #10.

Fall: midges and Light Cahills.

➤ **Fishing Regulations:** Open year-round.

Blue Zone: Six rainbow trout any size; one brown trout 20+ inches; bait fishing, fly fishing, and spin fishing are legal.

Red Zone: One rainbow trout 20+ inches; one brown trout 20+ inches; no bait or attractants, no barbed hooks allowed.

➤ **Tackle:** Use a 4- or 5-weight, 8½- or 9-foot rod and 4- or 5-weight reels and weight-forward floating lines to match; 7½- to 9-foot tapered leaders.

JESSE KING fell in love with fly fishing over a half century ago. He started instructing full time in 1996. Catching trout on the first presentation is his goal, and this comes from a great cast. Jesse and his wife Linda built Three Rivers Fly Shop and have owned and operated the business since 1997.

CLOSEST FLY SHOPS
Three Rivers Fly Shop
17 Oak Leaf Lane
Broken Bow, OK 74728
580-494-6115
3rivers@pine-net.com
threeriversflyshop.com

CLOSEST OUTFITTERS/GUIDES
Jesse King
Three Rivers Fly Shop *(above)*

CLOSEST LODGES
About 600 cabins are available, from rustic to luxurious. Recommendations at www.threeriversflyshop.com
Lakeview Lodge
9 miles north on Hwy. 259 North
Broken Bow, OK 74728
580-494-6300

BEST HOTEL
Hochatown Country Lodge
6 miles north on Hwy. 259
Broken Bow, OK 74728
580-494-6300
www.hochatownlodge.com

BEST CAMPGROUND
Beavers Bend State Park
11 miles north on Hwy. 259
Broken Bow, OK 74728
580-494-6115
www.beaversbend.com

BEST RESTAURANT
Abendigo's Grill and Patio
259 N. Stephens Gap Rd.,
Hochatown, OK 74728
580-494-7222
www.abendigos.com

BEST PLACE TO GET A COLD, STIFF DRINK
Grateful Head Pizza Oven and Taproom
10271 N. Hwy. 259
Hochatown, OK 74728
580-494-6030
www.gratefulhead.com

CLOSEST EMERGENCY MEDICAL HELP
EMS/Ambulance of Broken Bow
1003 N. Park Dr.
Broken Bow, OK 74728
580-584-2800

McCurtain Memorial Hospital
1301 E Lincoln Rd.
Idabel, OK 74745
580-286-7623
adm@mmhok.com; www.mmhok.com

CELL PHONE SERVICE
AT&T and Verizon.

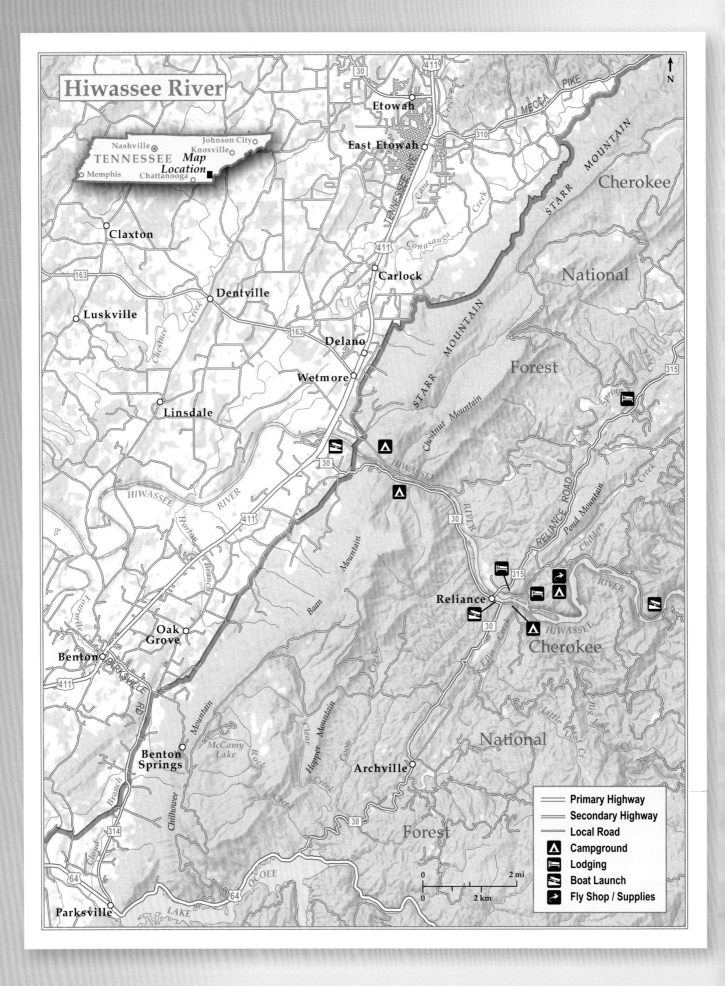

Hiwassee River

Etowah

East Etowah

Cherokee

National

Claxton

Carlock

Forest

Dentville

Luskville

Delano

Wetmore

Linsdale

Reliance

Cherokee

Oak Grove

Benton

National

Benton Springs

Archville

Forest

Parksville

	Primary Highway
	Secondary Highway
	Local Road
▲	Campground
⊟	Lodging
⇄	Boat Launch
↗	Fly Shop / Supplies

0   2 mi

0   2 km

TENNESSEE
Nashville
Knoxville
Johnson City
Memphis
Chattanooga
Map Location

Hiwassee River *(Southeast Tennessee)*

➤ **Location:** The Hiwassee runs through the southeast corner of Tennessee next to Georgia and North Carolina, with Reliance, Tennessee, being the fly-fishing hub. The nearest town on some maps will be Cleveland, Tennessee. The river is 45 minutes from Chattanooga and about 2 hours from Atlanta and Nashville.

This tailwater trout fishery begins at the north side of Unicoi Gap in Towns County, Georgia and drains 750,000 acres of the Chattahoochee National Forest before flowing into Lake Chatuge. Once the river leaves Georgia, it flows north into Hiwassee Lake in North Carolina. From this point, it flows east into Tennessee. In Reliance, below Appalachia Powerhouse, the Hiwassee River emerges as a high-mountain tailwater fishery. The icy cold water is not released from generators below the dam, but rather is piped from the base of the dam for 12 miles through the mountains through two huge tubes. This is where the 18-mile stretch locals call the "Big Hi" begins. Here, the waterway is classified as a state scenic river. It runs through the Cherokee National Forest, with virtually no development through the corridor. This wild and natural fly-fishing experience is easily accessible from many major cities in the southeast U.S.

The fishery is predominantly rainbow and brown trout, with a few native warmwater species. The river is stocked with trout throughout the year, with good holdover. There is a minimum harvest allowed during spring and summer, with catch-and-release from October through February. There is also some natural reproduction in the mountain feeder streams. Some remote gravel bars of the upper river may contain fall brown trout spawning areas.

The river can be divided into three distinct sections, each with its own character and demeanor. The three sections fish differently as the seasons progress and the hatches and flow of the river change. The upper stretch begins at the powerhouse and goes to Reliance. This is the most popular float section, about 6 miles. This is true whitewater driftboat fly fishing at its best. The river is 300 yards wide at several locations, with sections of Class I and II whitewater. Some areas of interest

are Colonels Island, Fox's Cabin, Towee Falls, Big Bend, and the Stairstep Rapids. The river flows through a gorge only accessible by foot or boat before tumbling over the Class III Devils Shoals and coming back into contact with civilization at Reliance. The upper stretch can be waded on low or medium water flows, but really comes into its own on full generation, when you must fish from a drift boat. Most of the shoal areas are steep, with only one line for the drift boats.

There is no room for error here! Navigation requires a skilled driftboat captain who is familiar with the lines and experienced in whitewater rowing. The middle section begins

Boats at the train trestle.

at the train trestle boat launch in Reliance and runs down to Highway 411. This stretch is also about 6 miles long. Here, the river starts to make its transition from a high-gradient mountain river to a calmer and more typical TVA tailwater. Just below the river bridge, the river flows through Webb's Fields and some of the best gravel shoals on the river. This spot is known for the Hendrickson mayflies and caddis that pop from the riffles. Drifting this section will bring you to the Brownie Hole, Power Line Shoals, and Gee Creek Fish Traps. The third section, from Highway 411 to the mouth of

Beautiful spot on the Hiwassee Devils Shoals.

the Ocoee River, is the longest float stretch, about 8 miles. Here, the river has left the mountains to the east and flows through fields and fertile farmland on its way to the Tennessee River. The water ambles here, and is typical of pastoral east Tennessee tailwaters, with long, slick glides interrupted by bubbling shoals and fish traps. This section is best fished in early spring and is known for early caddis hatches.

The Hiwassee River is most noted for its wonderful dry-fly fishing. Even though it is huge by comparison, the river's personality and character are those of a mountain freestone river. The river holds an enormously diverse insect population. The whitewater shoal areas keep the cold water highly oxygenated and provide the perfect habitat for mayflies, caddis, and stoneflies. Shallow areas combined with such a diversity of bugs means that hatches and subsequent dry-fly fishing can happen any day. Early in the year it is not uncommon to find small Winter Stones, baby Blue-wingeds (or *Pseudocloeons*), and midges making up the topwater fare. Very early spring brings out the Hendrickson mayflies for the first real hatch of the year. This can be one of the most prolific and blanketing hatches. When it starts, it happens daily for several weeks. The Hendrickson hatch fades right into the Sulphurs in April. The Sulphurs will typically last into June and be joined by various caddisflies in the spring months. The signature hatch of the Hiwassee River is the

Isonychia bicolor. The Big Slate Drakes begin in June and some will still be found in September. The *Isonychias* are not a blanket hatch here, but sporadic daily for the entire summer season. Hiwassee River trout will eat a dry *Isonychia* pattern on almost any day during the summer. For fall, there's the October Caddis hatch. Nymph and streamer fishing is also excellent as there is a substantial baitfish, sculpin, and crayfish population. The river experiences a winter shad hatch that brings the big browns to the upper river for some very exciting streamer action during our mild winters.

➤ **Hatches:** *Early Brown Stones:* early April into June.
Hendricksons: mid-April through May.
Blue-winged Olives: April through June and early September through November.
Grannoms: April and then again in August.
Brown Caddis: April into December with prime months May through September.
Isonychia: April through August or early September.
Tricos: May through August.
Midges: During cooler weather both early and late in the year.
Others: The Hiwassee can be a veritable smorgasbord of insect life. Be on the lookout for Sulphurs, White Mayflies, Winter Stoneflies, and assorted caddis almost any day.

190

Sliding down the steps.

Hiwassee brown trout.

➤ **Fishing Regulations:** PFDs are required while floating or boating; no alcohol of any kind is allowed on the water. Creel limits from the Powerhouse to Reliance from March 1 to September 30 are six trout, only two of which can be browns and must be over 14 inches. From October 1 to February 28 is catch-and-release only.

➤ **Tackle:** Use a 9-foot 4- to 7-weight rod. A 9-foot 5- or 6-weight will cover most situations from small dries to heavy streamer or nymph rigs. I recommend 9-foot tapered to 6X to 2X. Have polarized sunglasses and a cap or hat. Pack a light rainjacket, as pop-up thundershowers are always a possibility. In the summer, wear lightweight breathable clothing and bring sunscreen.

DANE LAW is a product of the University of Georgia, Athens. He began guiding in Iliamna, Alaska in 1987. He started Southeastern Anglers in 1999. Dane is considered an authority on the coldwater tailraces of the Southeast, and his specialties include smoked chicken and cicada fishing. More info on the whole crew can be found at www.southeasternanglers.com.

CLOSEST FLY SHOPS
Reliance Fly and Tackle
588 Childers Creek Rd.
Reliance, TN 37369
423-338-7771
www.relianceflyshop.com

CLOSEST OUTFITTERS/GUIDES
Southeastern Anglers
Dane Law
149 McCormick Rd. SW
Cartersville, GA 30120
770-655-9210
danelaw@southeasternanglers.com
www.southeasternanglers.com

BEST HOTEL
Red Roof Inn
600 N. Tennessee Ave.
Etowah, TN 37331
423-781-7459

BEST CAMPGROUND
Reliance Fly and Tackle
588 Childers Creek Rd.
Reliance, TN 37369
423-338-7771
www.relianceflyshop.com

BEST RESTAURANT
Reliance Fly and Tackle (above)

BEST PLACE TO GET A COLD, STIFF DRINK
Reliance Fly and Tackle (left)

CLOSEST EMERGENCY MEDICAL HELP
Woods Memorial Hospital
886 Hwy 411 North
Etowah, TN 37331 (30 minutes away)
423-263-3600

CELL PHONE SERVICE
None.

191

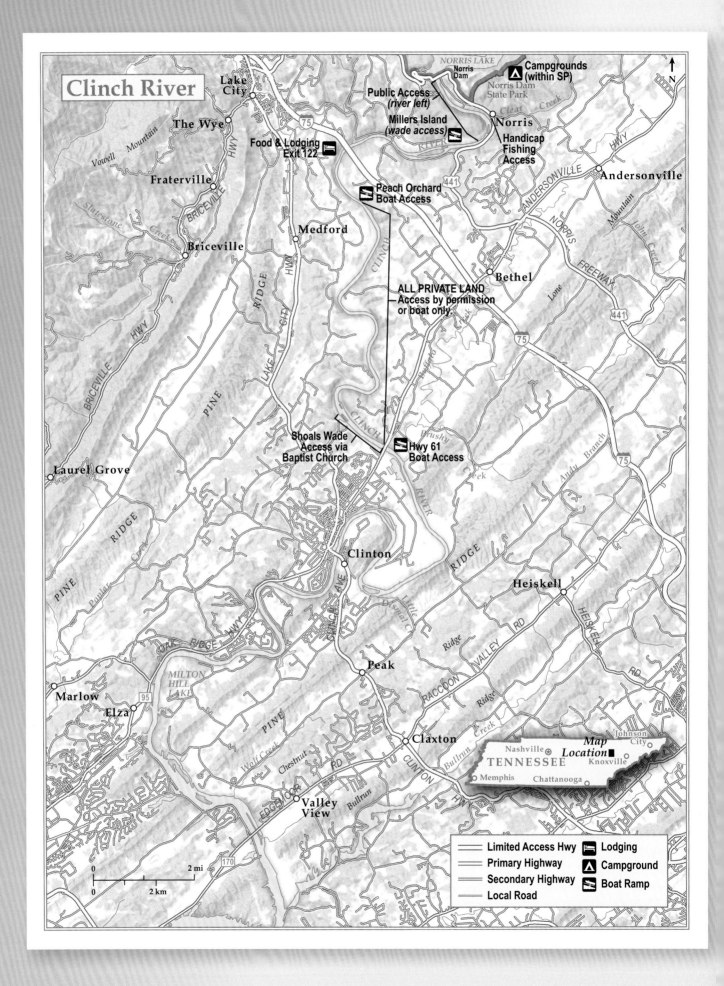

Clinch River

Lake City

The Wye

Fraterville

Briceville

Medford

Vowell Mountain

Statestone Creek

BRICEVILLE

BRICEVILLE HWY

PINE RIDGE

LAKE CITY HWY

PINE RIDGE

Poplar Creek

Laurel Grove

Marlow

Elza

95

MILTON HILL LAKE

OAK RIDGE HWY

EDGEMOOR RD

Wolf Creek

Chestnut

BULL RUN RD

Valley View

170

Bullrun

Food & Lodging
Exit 122

75

Peach Orchard
Boat Access

NORRIS LAKE

Norris Dam

Campgrounds
(within SP)

Norris Dam
State Park

Public Access
(river left)

Millers Island
(wade access)

Norris

Handicap
Fishing
Access

Clear Creek

CLINCH RIVER

441

ANDERSONVILLE HWY

Andersonville

NORRIS FREEWAY

Mountain

John Creek

Bethel

Lone Creek

441

75

ALL PRIVATE LAND
— Access by permission
or boat only.

CLINCH RIVER

Shoals Wade
Access via
Baptist Church

Hwy 61
Boat Access

Brushy

CLINCH RIVER

Little Creek

RIDGE

Dismal Creek

Andy Branch

75

Clinton

MELTON HILL LAKE

Little Creek

Heiskell

HEISKELL RD

VALLEY RD

Raccoon Ridge

Peak

RACCOON VALLEY RD

CLINTON HWY

PINE RIDGE

Claxton

Bullrun Creek

Johnson City

Map
Location

Nashville

TENNESSEE

Knoxville

Memphis

Chattanooga

Legend

Limited Access Hwy	Lodging
Primary Highway	Campground
Secondary Highway	Boat Ramp
Local Road	

0   2 mi

0   2 km

➤ **Location:** Eastern Tennessee, about a 30-minute drive north of Knoxville on I-75. Use exit 122 (Clinton–Norris–Highway 61). Most major airlines serve Knoxville's Magee/Tyson airport.

The Clinch tailwater begins below Norris hydroelectric dam. Built by the Tennessee Valley Authority (TVA) and completed in 1933, Norris was the first dam constructed in the vast TVA water-management system. The portions of the river above Norris Lake support warmwater species including smallmouth bass, crappies, white bass, and many species of rough fish. However, after the dam was completed, the section below it became too cold to support most of these, leading the TVA and Tennessee Wildlife Resources Agency (TWRA) to stock trout. The first inhabitants were McCloud River rainbows, with later stockings of browns, and more recently brook trout. The water temperature proved to be ideal, but water being drawn from the bottom of the dam contained very little dissolved oxygen, therefore limiting the insect base primarily to midges. This did not create a desirable habitat for coldwater species in the lower reaches of the river. The TVA responded by constructing a weir dam 1 mile below the main dam to improve dissolved oxygen levels and moderate the drop in the water during times of no generation. Invertebrate production flourished, giving rise to the rich food base the Clinch now enjoys.

The Clinch below Norris flows through 13 miles of rolling hills, fields, and farmland before being impounded by Melton Hill Lake. The upper reaches are owned by the TVA and offer easy access to waders down to the Miller's Island boat ramp. This is a public ramp maintained by TVA, and offers both boat access and wading opportunities. From this point on, the river is bordered by private land. TWRA maintains a boat ramp about 2 miles below Miller's Island, in an area known as Peach Orchard. There is no other public access for the next 9 miles, and entry to the river must be gained either by floating or by permission from a landowner.

Arguably one of the richest and most productive tailwaters in the Southeast, the Clinch maintains a year-round temperature of about 52 degrees. Because of the extreme depth of Norris Lake, water flowing from the dam warms very little as it proceeds downstream. Because of this, rainbows and browns can be released as fingerlings and can be expected to reach growth rates of 1 to 2 inches a month, depending on time of year. This creates a proliferation of stream-reared fish almost indistinguishable from wild populations, and sets the stage for opportunities at true trophy-size individuals. The Tennessee state record brown was pulled from the Clinch, and weighed a whopping 28 pounds, 9 ounces.

Because TVA operates on the peak power principle, water levels can fluctuate as much as 6 feet or more during a single day, so it is imperative to know planned releases before heading off to the river. Obtain these either by calling the TVA phone line (800-238-2264) or accessing the website

Foggy morning float below the dam. Steve Seinberg

(www.tva.com). During times of no generation, the Clinch resembles a very large spring creek, with limestone ledges interspersed with small riffles and slow, deep, clear pools. Stealth and precise presentations are often required, and 6X or even 7X fluorocarbon tippets on 9- to 12-foot leaders, are in order. Small, dark midge patterns, beadhead nymphs, and scud patterns #18 to #22 rigged between 2 and 4 feet below yarn indicators work year-round and comprise the bulk of the flies used on the Clinch. May and June bring the mayfly

Early fall morning on the Clinch. Steve Seinberg

A big Clinch River brown. Mike Bone

hatches and a good selection of Sulphur Compara-duns, #16 and #18, will go far in ensuring success on cruising, selective trout.

When Norris Dam generates power, the water is too deep and swift for wading, and fishing can only be done safely from a boat. During generation, deep nymph rigs and streamers become the preferred methods for the Clinch's resident fish.

➤ **Hatches:** There really aren't great hatches on the Clinch. Sulphur mayflies (generally #16 and #18) hatch from late April until mid-June. There is also a Small Black Caddis (#18 to #20) hatch from mid-June through late August, usually late in the evening. Midges (#20 to #28) are available year-round, and range from yellow to dark gray.

➤ **Fishing Regulations:** No tackle restrictions. There is a slot limit whereby all fish between 14 and 20 inches must be released. The possession limit is 7 fish below 14 inches; anglers may also possess one fish over 20 inches, not to exceed 7 fish total. The Clinch is open year-around to fishing, as are almost all Tennessee tailwaters.

➤ **Tackle:** Tackle selection often depends on water generation, but a 9-foot, 5- or 6-weight rod with floating line is considered standard. The Clinch is big water with very few overhanging trees or obstructions, and the longer rod lengths help when mending over the many conflicting currents. Shorter rods and lighter lines can be used on calm days, but high winds are common, especially in the spring. Streamer

fishing is typically done from a boat when Norris Dam is generating, and requires 6- to 8-weight rods rigged with fast sink-tip lines. Full-sinking lines are generally not required.

Fish in the Clinch can be notoriously selective and spooky, especially at lower flows, so a good selection of 9- to 12-foot leaders along with 5X to 7X fluorocarbon tippets is required. Streamer fishers using sinking lines in higher flows can get away with 10- to 12-pound-test fluorocarbon leaders. Fish are much less spooky at higher water levels, and the larger tippets are often required for keeping big browns away from downed trees and midriver ledges.

Good fly selections should include beadhead nymphs and dark midge pupa patterns, #16 to 22. Mayfly hatches generally occur from late April to mid-June, so a good selection of Sulphur Compara-duns, emerger patterns, and Parachutes in size #16 to #18 ranging from bright yellow to muddy orange should be included.

Wading anglers often use small, dark Woolly Buggers and streamer patterns in #8 to #12, but as water flow increases, so should the size of the streamers. White, tan, and light olive flies in #4 to #8 are most commonly used when streamer fishing from a drift boat.

A sweeping front-seat view of the Clinch River. Steve Seinberg

A healthy rainbow caught on a #18 red Zebra Midge. Steve Seinberg

MIKE BONE began his guiding career in the Great Smoky Mountains National Park. In 1993, he switched to float-fishing trips on the larger tailwater rivers of East Tennessee. He has been the owner-operator of Clinch River Outfitters based on the Clinch River near Knoxville for the past 20 years and pioneered many of the methods and floats being used today.

CLOSEST FLY SHOPS

Three Rivers Angler
5113 Kingston Pike
Knoxville, TN 37919
865-200-5271
877-563-6424
www.3riversangler.com

Little River Outfitters
106 Town Square Dr.
Townsend, TN 37882
877-448-3474
www.littleriveroutfitters.com

CLOSEST OUTFITTERS

Mike Bone/Clinch River Outfitters
P.O. Box 185
Andersonville, TN 37705
865-494-0972; 865-567-7138
www.theriverjournal.com

CLOSEST AND BEST HOTEL

Clinch River House
526 New Clear Branch Rd.
Lake City, TN 37769
865-426-2715
www.clinchriverhouse.com

CLOSEST AND BEST RESTAURANT

Harrison's Grill and Bar
110 Hillvale Rd.
Clinton, TN 37716
865-463-6368
www.harrisonsgrill.com

BEST PLACE TO GET A COLD, STIFF DRINK

Harrison's Grill and Bar
110 Hillvale Rd.
Clinton, TN 37716
865-463-6368
www.harrisonsgrill.com

CLOSEST EMERGENCY MEDICAL HELP

Methodist Medical Center of Oak Ridge
990 Oak Ridge Turnpike
Oak Ridge, TN 37830
865-835-1000
www.mmcoakridge.com

CELL PHONE SERVICE
On most areas of the river.

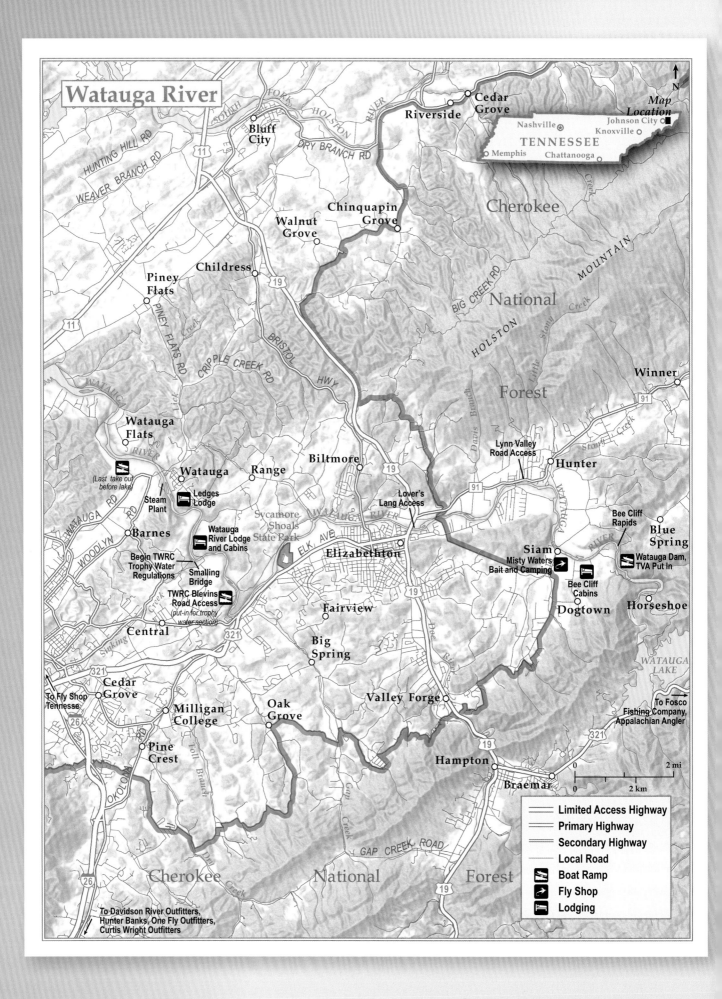

Watauga River

Hunting Hill Rd
Weaver Branch Rd

Bluff City

11

South Fork
Holston River
Dry Branch Rd

Riverside
Cedar Grove

Cherokee

Chinquapin Grove

Walnut Grove

Childress

19

Piney Flats

11

Piney Flats Rd

Cripple Creek Rd

Bristol Hwy

Big Creek Rd

National

Holston

Stony Creek

Mountain

Forest

Winner

91

Watauga Flats

Watauga River

Watauga

Range

Biltmore

19

Davis Branch

Little Stony

Lynn Valley Road Access

Hunter

(Last take out before lake)

Steam Plant

Ledges Lodge

Watauga Rd

Woodlyn Rd

Barnes

Watauga River Lodge and Cabins

Sycamore Shoals State Park

Elk Ave

Watauga River

Lover's Lang Access

91

Siam
Misty Waters Bait and Camping

Bee Cliff Rapids

Blue Spring

Watauga Dam, TVA Put In

Begin TWRC Trophy Water Regulations

Smalling Bridge

Elizabethton

Bee Cliff Cabins

Horseshoe

TWRC Blevins Road Access
(put-in for trophy water section)

Fairview

19

Dogtown

Central

321

Big Spring

Watauga River

Watauga Lake

Cedar Grove

To Fly Shop Tennessee

26

Milligan College

321

Oak Grove

Sinking Creek

Valley Forge

Doe River

321

To Fosco Fishing Company, Appalachian Angler

Pine Crest

Okolona

Toll Branch

Hampton

19

Braemar

Gap Creek

Gap Creek Road

Dry Creek

Cherokee

National

Forest

19

To Davidson River Outfitters, Hunter Banks, One Fly Outfitters, Curtis Wright Outfitters

Map Location

Nashville
Knoxville
Johnson City

TENNESSEE

Memphis   **Chattanooga**

N

Scale
0 — 2 mi
0 — 2 km

Legend
═══	Limited Access Highway
═══	Primary Highway
═══	Secondary Highway
───	Local Road
🚤	Boat Ramp
➡	Fly Shop
🛏	Lodging

➤ **Location:** The tailwater section of the Watauga River is located in northeast Tennessee, about 1 hour from Asheville, NC; 2 hours from Knoxville, 3½ hours from Charlotte, NC, and 6 hours from Washington D.C. You can fly commercially to the Watauga via Asheville or Tri Cities, Tennessee.

The Watauga River begins its 60-mile journey high in the Blue Ridge Mountains on the northwest face of Grandfather Mountain. The Watauga flows northwest through the community of Valle Crucis in Watauga County before crossing the Tennessee state line, where it forms Watauga Lake. After leaving Watauga Dam, the river is immediately impounded again by Wilbur Dam, which provides the flow for 20.6 miles of tailwater fishery before emptying into Boone Reservoir.

Both Watauga and Wilbur Dams are regulated by the Tennessee Valley Authority (TVA). Wilbur is a deepwater-release dam. As a result, the Watauga in the summer averages 51 to 54 degrees Fahrenheit. The TVA maintains a guaranteed minimum summer flow schedule for recreational use. The Watauga covers a large drainage basin, and heavy summer storms can cause the Doe River (which enters the main river near the town of Elizabethton) to flash and pump mud into the river. Depending on the size of the rainstorm, the river may be fishable in 12 to 24 hours, or it may take as long as 48 hours. Water flows are driven by power demand, rainfall, and the whims of the TVA. So anglers must always be vigilant for changing water levels. Even though generations are scheduled, they are sometimes modified. Fall drawdowns of Wilbur and Watauga Reservoirs create the largest and longest generations of the year.

The river is noted for its long, flat pools that meander through farmland and past large rock bluffs. Wade anglers will find access on the Watauga difficult. Wading access can be found around the Tennessee Wildlife Resource Agency (TWRA) access areas and around Wilbur Dam itself. However, most of the river is open to bait fishing, and you will have to contend with local worm dunkers in common areas. Wade anglers staying at The Ledges Lodge and Watauga River Lodge may gain access to the river in those areas. However, there is no high-water-mark regulation in Tennessee, and landowners own the riverbed, so wading outside designated areas is not an option.

For boating anglers, floating the Watauga also offers some challenges. Floating from Wilbur Dam to the TWRA access off Blevins Road is best when the TVA is generating power from Wilbur Dam. The upper section can be accessed by boat launches at Wilbur Dam, Lyn Valley Bridge, and Lovers Lane under the Highway 37 bridge. While floating from Wilbur Dam to the TWRA at Blevins Road is possible even without power generation, it's easier when the water is higher. Boaters starting at Wilbur Dam should be advised that Bee Cliff Rapids is a Class II rapid when the dam is in full generation. Conditions are ideal for floating the upper reach-

Floating under Smalling Bridge on a foggy summer day. Kevin Howell

es of the Watauga when the TVA is generating only one unit, if you can be on the water then.

The section from Blevins Road Access to Boone Lake can be floated at any water level, and most anglers prefer to float this section when there is no generation. This section also includes the only trophy section on the river. The trophy section allows harvesting only two fish over 14 inches, and bait fishing is not allowed. It takes approximately 4 hours for generating water to Reach Blevins Road from the time it is released. This is the most popular stretch of the river for fishing, and most anglers float from the TWRA access at Blevins Road to the TWRA Access at Wagner Road (the Old Steam Plant). A few guides and anglers will float past the Wagner Access and take out at a small, unnamed access off Riverview Drive. Once anglers float past the takeout at Riverview Drive, they must have permission from landowners to take out, or they must float into Boone Lake and row the flat water for several miles to reach a boat ramp.

The Ledges in fall. Steve Seinberg

Releasing another nice Watauga rainbow. Steve Seinberg

The Watauga is a quintessential tailwater, where small dry flies and midge nymphs seem to dominate the fishing techniques. The river has good aquatic life, which is supported not only by the coldwater releases, but also some trace amounts of limestone in the area. Anglers will find good hatches of Blue-winged Olives, Sulphurs, and most other small mayflies found in a tailwater, along with a lot of caddis and midges. Dry-fly fishing is best when there is no water generation. You'll often encounter pods of rising fish sipping dry flies so small you may need an electron microscope to identify them! But anglers willing to fish a #18 to #20 dry with an unweighted #20 soft-hackle or RS2 beneath it will hook up fairly regularly. However, most folks fish a double nymph or midge rig 3 to 7 feet beneath a strike indicator.

When there is no power generation, anglers are forced to fish 9- to 12-foot leaders with 5X to 7X tippet. When TVA is generating, the river turns a milky color and larger tippets, 3X to 5X, won't spook the trout. The heavier flow washes larger food items around, including worms. Larger nymphs, #12 to #16, and streamers are the preferred patterns during power generation.

In the fall and winter during power generation, egg patterns are preferred. Also, overhanging limbs on the river-banks offer some great, and often overlooked, terrestrial fishing in the summer.

➤ **Hatches:**
November–March: BWOs, #18–#24; midges #20–#24.
March: Small Black Caddis, #20–#24; last of the BWOs, #20–#24.
April: caddis, #10–#12.
May: Tan Caddis, #12–#16; Sulphurs, #16–#20.
June–October: Sulphurs, #16–#20, finished by July; crane flies, #16–#20; midges #18–#24; terrestrials, #10–#18.

➤ **Fishing Regulations:** Any combination of trout species: Daily limit, seven; no minimum length.

Exceptions: Only two trout in a creel may be lake trout. Brook trout must be 6 inches minimum.

Quality Trout Fishing Area (Smallings Bridge downstream to CSX railroad bridges): 14-inch minimum length,

Morning on the Caddis Flats. Steve Seinberg
Right. Author Kevin Howell with a large golden dorado

creel limit 2 trout. Use or possession of bait is prohibited. Trout less than 14 inches may not be in possession.

➤ **Tackle:** Use 9-foot, 4- or 5-weight rods with floating weight-forward lines. Leaders should be 9 to 12 feet, tapered to 6X. Waders are highly recommended due to cold water.

KEVIN HOWELL owns Davidson River Outfitters in Pisgah Forest, NC and is a partner in Andes Drifters in Argentina. He has been a Fly Fishing Masters Champion and a Signature Fly Designer for Umpqua. Kevin has been a guide in North Carolina and Tennessee for 25 years. In addition to guiding, he has written countless articles and been featured on numerous television shows.

CLOSEST FLY SHOPS

Davidson River Outfitters
95 Pisgah Highway
Pisgah Forest, NC 28768
davidsonflyfishing.com
888-861-0111

Curtis Wright Outfitters
5 All Souls Crescent
Asheville, NC 28803
curtiswrightoutfitters.com
828-274-3471

Fly Shop of Tennessee
102 Willmary Rd.
Johnson City, TN 37601
423-928-2007
flyshopoftn.com

Foscoe Fishing Company
8857 North Carolina 105
Boone, NC 28607
Foscoefishing.com
828-963-6556

Hunter Banks
29 Montford Ave.
Asheville, NC 28801
Hunterbanks.com
828-252-3005

Mahoney's
830 Sunset Dr.
Johnson City, TN 37604
800-835-5152
mahoneysports.com

One Fly Outfitters
112 Cherry St.
Black Mountain, NC 28711
Oneflyoutfitters.com
828-669-6939

CLOSEST OUTFITTERS

Davidson River Outfitters (left)

Hunter Banks (left)

Watauga River Lodge & Outfitter
643 Smalling Rd.
Watauga, TN 37694
828-208-3428
wataugariverlodge.com

CLOSEST LODGES

Watauga River Lodge & Outfitter (above)

Bee Cliff Cabins
141 Steel Bridge Rd.
Elizabethton, TN 37643
423-542-6033
beecliffcabins.com

Watauga River Cabins
720 Smalling Rd.
Johnson City, TN 37601
800-334-6720
wataugarivercabins.com

BEST HOTEL

Holiday Inn Express
2 Orr Court
Johnson City, TN 37615
423-328-0500

BEST CAMPGROUND

Misty Waters Bait and Camping
246 Wilbur Dam Rd.
Elizabethton, TN 37643
423-543-1702

CLOSEST EMERGENCY MEDICAL HELP

First Assistant Urgent Care
314 Rogosin Dr.
Elizabethton, TN
423-542-8929

CELL PHONE SERVICE
While there are a few dead spots, most of the river has cell phone reception, especially with Verizon Wireless.

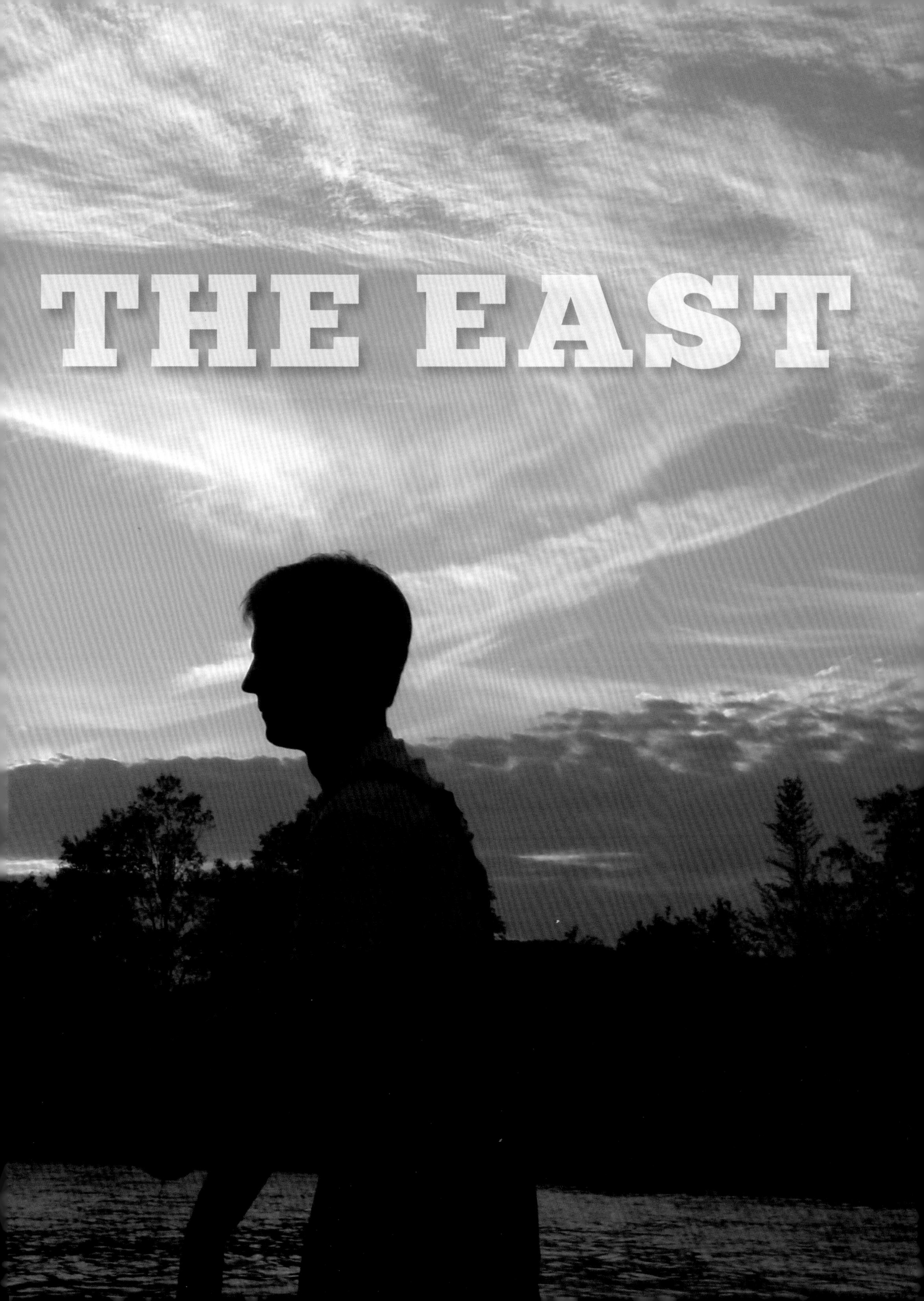
THE EAST

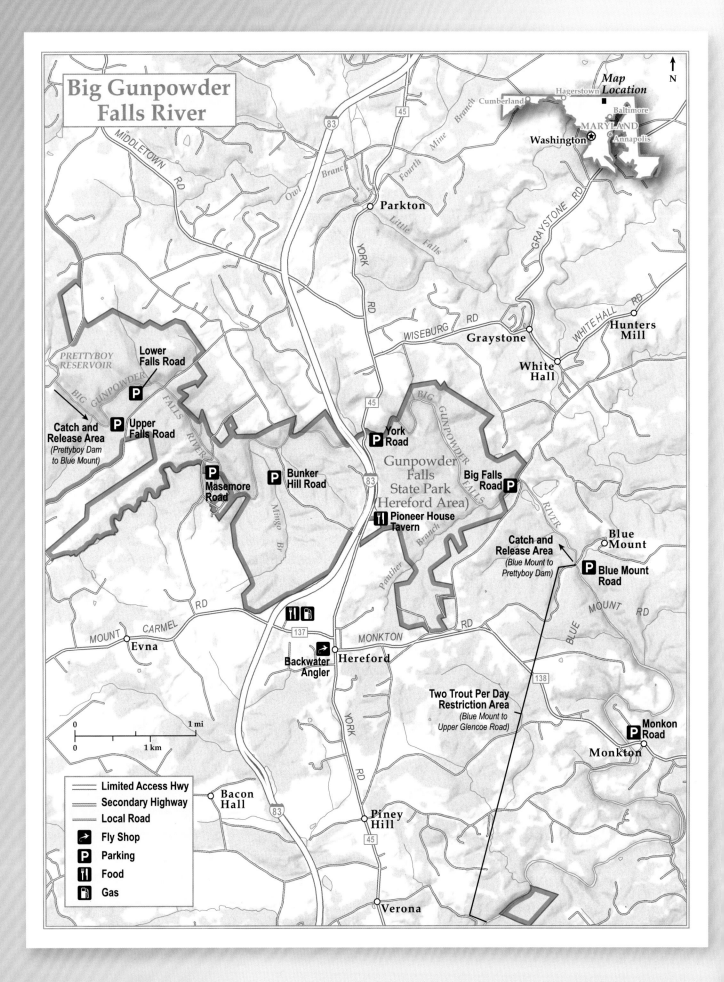

Big Gunpowder Falls River

Map Location

MARYLAND

Hagerstown
Cumberland
Baltimore
Annapolis
Washington

N

MIDDLETOWN RD

83
45

Owl Branch
Mine Branch
Fourth Branch

Parkton

YORK RD

Little Falls

GRAYSTONE RD

WISEBURG RD

Graystone

WHITE HALL RD

Hunters Mill

White Hall

PRETTYBOY RESERVOIR

Lower Falls Road

BIG GUNPOWDER FALLS RIVER

Upper Falls Road

Catch and Release Area
(Prettyboy Dam to Blue Mount)

Masemore Road

Bunker Hill Road

Mingo Br

York Road

83
45

BIG GUNPOWDER FALLS

Big Falls Road

Gunpowder Falls State Park (Hereford Area)

Pioneer House Tavern

Panther Branch

Blue Mount

Catch and Release Area
(Blue Mount to Prettyboy Dam)

Blue Mount Road

BLUE MOUNT RD

RIVER

MOUNT CARMEL RD

Evna

137

MONKTON RD

Hereford

Backwater Angler

YORK RD

138

Two Trout Per Day Restriction Area
(Blue Mount to Upper Glencoe Road)

Monkon Road

Monkton

Bacon Hall

83

Piney Hill

45

Verona

Legend

Limited Access Hwy
Secondary Highway
Local Road

Fly Shop
P Parking
Food
Gas

0   1 mi

0   1 km

➤ **Location:** The Big Gunpowder Falls River is located in upper Baltimore County, Maryland, about 20 miles north of Baltimore. It is about a 30-minute drive from Baltimore and about 90 minutes from Washington D.C.

The river flows 20-plus miles from its headwaters in northern Baltimore County before entering the Chesapeake Bay. The 7.2-mile stretch of river downstream of Prettyboy Reservoir is recognized for some of the finest tailwater trout fishing in the country.

The Gunpowder, as most call it, is the primary water supply for the City of Baltimore. The city is responsible for controlling water flows in the river. A noble effort in the early 1980s on the part of a local Trout Unlimited chapter resulted in a minimum water flow agreement with the city, and the Gunpowder tailwater fishery as we now know it was born. Brown trout fingerlings raised from stock from surrounding creeks were placed in the Gunpowder. The trout were now guaranteed enough cold water through the warm summer months to survive and reproduce naturally. The 1¼-mile stretch of river immediately downstream of Prettyboy Reservoir was designated Special Regulation Trout Water by the state. Regulations demand catch-and-release fishing only, with artificial lures and flies.

Brown trout began to thrive in the regulated area of the stream, and annual surveys showed exceptional trout numbers and successful reproduction. Fisheries managers were prompted to expand the regulated area. Today we have 7.2 miles of water managed solely as catch-and-release fishing for stream-bred trout. Recent surveys have shown wild brown densities of more than 4,000 trout per mile in some areas.

The Gunpowder is a tailwater with many faces. There are six road crossings within the regulated catch-and-release portions of the river. River access and marked parking lots are available at each road crossing. The uppermost portion of the stream below Prettyboy Reservoir and above Falls Road, boasts some of the highest trout numbers in the river. This 1¼-mile section of stream also features some of the most fabulous landscapes anglers will encounter on the stream. Long stretches of riffles and runs just below the dam give way to a narrow river valley full of pocket water and deep boulder pools.

Anglers can fish this stretch of stream year-round. Spring brings some of the best fishing as Sulphur mayflies and cad-

dis begin to hatch in mid-May. The Sulphur hatch is popular among anglers fishing dry flies, and is one of the most consistent hatches on the stream. A Sulphur dun on a dead-drift has fooled many a big brown. Many anglers can be on the stream well after dusk on June evenings, hoping to catch the Sulphur spinner fall. Caddis hatches are also consistent

Gunpowder mist. Jeff Lewatowski

through spring and early summer. Anglers targeting the riffles will find good success with a well-presented olive-bodied caddis. The pocket water stretches on this portion of stream are great for high-stick nymphing, and this technique will consistently fool some of the biggest trout.

Trout fishing is allowed year-round on catch-and-release sections of the Gunpowder. More than 90 percent of the

The wooded backdrop of the Big Gunpowder River. Theaux LeGardeur

A nice Gunpowder brown trout. Jeff Lewatowski

trout are browns. All the browns are wild, and average 8 to 12 inches. The browns are vividly colored gold and beautifully spotted. There are few more stunning sights than a November-caught Gunpowder brown sporting its spawning colors. They are energetic fighters and love to jump when hooked. Though big browns are wary and difficult, determined anglers take brown trout over 20 inches on a fairly regular basis. Native brook trout are also in the river and in many of the tributary creeks. A strain of Kamloops River rainbow trout was stocked in recent years as fingerlings, with the hope of developing some natural reproduction. The stocking was on the upper portion of the catch-and-release area, and anglers will still encounter rainbow trout there on occasion. Much of the Gunpowder below the catch-and-release area is managed as put-and-take trout water, and is stocked by the state in spring and fall.

The central portions of the catch-and-release water extend from Masemore Road downstream to York Road. The river changes face through this area as it widens, and flows soften. Riffles and runs dominate and provide great dry-fly opportunities. Anglers probe the riffles on April afternoons with Hendrickson and Quill Gordon mayflies. The long, slow glides within this section of stream are favorite spots for anglers fishing midges to rising trout. On summer mornings trout can be seen through early morning mist gobbling up Trico mayflies on these slower glides. A variety of techniques work well on the Gunpowder. Successful anglers alter their techniques with the seasons.

The lower portion of the catch-and-release area includes the 2-mile section of stream between York Road and Big Falls

Road, designated as State Wildlands. This section meanders slowly through beautiful deciduous forest. The river is full of deadfalls and logjams. Many of the banks are overgrown, and deep, slow-moving pools are present in many areas. Anglers fishing this stretch can typically avoid the crowds and find some solitude. Many cast heavily weighted streamers to the banks or root piles. Dark-colored Zonkers or sculpin patterns will often move some beastly browns. Many of the 20-plus-inch fish caught each year fall for big streamers. Terrestrial fishing is also great through this portion of the stream through the warmer months. Ants, beetles, and hopper patterns fished along undercut and brushy banks will fool some good fish. Those hoping to cure cabin fever in February and March may encounter Winter Stoneflies dancing across the stream. Sunny days bring the best stonefly hatches, usually Little Black or Brown Stones. Trout will rise eagerly to a heavily hackled stonefly pattern skated across the stream during a winter hatch.

Steal away to the Gunpowder for the day while on business or just passing through Baltimore or D.C., and find yourself a world away on one of our nation's best tailwaters.

➤ **Hatches:** December through March: Little Black and Little Brown Stoneflies, blackflies, variety of midges.

April into May: Hendrickson mayflies, Quill Gordons, Blue-winged Olives, caddis, midges.

Mid-May through July: Sulphur and Blue-winged Olive mayflies, caddis, midges.

July through October: Trico and Blue-winged Olive mayflies, caddis, terrestrials, midges.

Early spring and fish on! Jeff Lewatowski

Sulphur imitations. Jeff Lewatowski

➤ **Fishing Regulations:** Gunpowder River Special Regulation Trout Management Area—catch-and-release, artificial lures and flies only. Maryland Non-Tidal Fishing License and Trout Stamp needed.

Typically wade-fishing access. Kayak and canoe access is available, but useful only at periods of high flow.

➤ **Tackle:** Use 8½- or 9-foot 4- and 5-weight fly rods with floating lines and 9- to 12-foot leaders. Use 10- to 12-foot leaders tapered to 5X or smaller when fishing dries. Chest waders are recommended. Felt soles are illegal; wear the newer sticky rubber–type soles with metal cleats.

JEFF LEWATOWSKI has been a professional fisherman and guide for more than 20 years. He has guided and fished waters from Alaska to the offshore Atlantic Ocean. He presently operates his own fly-fishing guide service in Maryland on the Big Gunpowder Falls River, Chesapeake Bay, and the Atlantic Coast. Learn more at www.fishlews.com.

CLOSEST FLY SHOPS
Backwater Angler
16938 York Rd.
Monkton, MD 21111
410-357-9557
info@backwaterangler.com
www.backwaterangler.com

CLOSEST OUTFITTERS/GUIDES
Lew's Fly Angler
Jeff Lewatowski
3433 Old Level Rd.
Havre de Grace, MD 21078
410-808-5105
jlewatowski@gmail.com
www.fishlews.com

Backwater Angler (left)

CLOSEST AND BEST HOTEL
Hunt Valley Marriott
221 International Circle
Hunt Valley, MD 21030
800-447-4136

BEST RESTAURANT
Pioneer House Restaurant
17717 York Rd.
Parkton, MD 21120
410-357-4231
pioneerpubandrestaurant.com

CLOSEST EMERGENCY MEDICAL HELP
GBMC
6701 N. Charles St.
Towson, MD 21204
443-849-2000

CELL PHONE SERVICE
Most cell phones will have service on the stream.

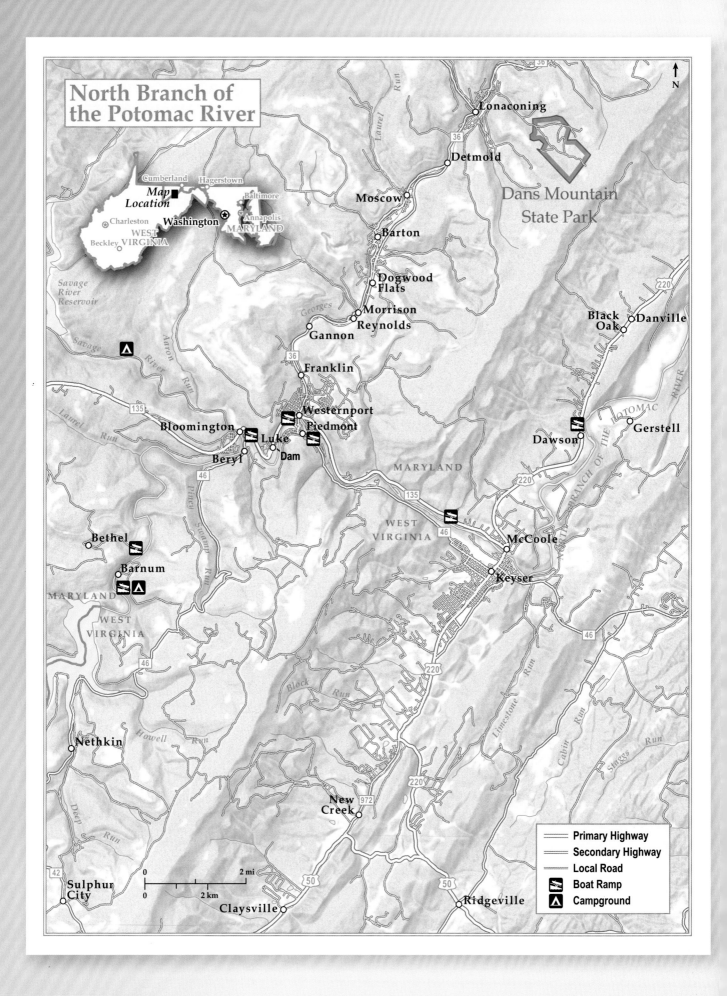

North Branch of
the Potomac River

➤ **Location:** The North Branch is in western Maryland, forming the border between West Virginia and Maryland. It is 2½ hours from Pittsburgh, and 3 hours from the Baltimore/Washington, D.C./Northern Virginia metropolitan area. Hagerstown, Maryland Regional Airport is 2 hours away; Morgantown, West Virginia Regional Airport is 1½ hours away.

The North Branch of Potomac tailwater section begins below Jennings Randolph Lake and holds trout for 19 miles. Jennings Randolph Lake was completed in 1982 for flood control and water-quality improvements. The North Branch (or NB) was a dead river due to acid mine drainage for more than 100 years, but with the advent of the dam, plus five lime dosers upstream of the lake, the pH has increased enough to sustain trout. The first rainbow and brown trout stockings began in the late 1980s. While there is some natural reproduction in the river, the Maryland Department of Natural Resources and the West Virginia Division of Natural Resources stock fingerlings in the catch-and-release areas, and keeper-size fish in the put-and-take areas.

Water temps in the early spring hover in the mid-40s to 50 degrees and rarely rise above 65. Wade anglers should look for flows below 350 cfs, and be careful; this is a slick-bottomed river that runs fast and deep with the very clear water. The State of Maryland has banned the use of felt-soled wading boots in all streams. Float fishers want water flows from 200–600 cfs. Inflatables are the way to go, due to the very rocky nature of the river. All the guides use rafts on the upper 7 miles. There are four weekend whitewater releases in the spring, starting in mid-April and running every other weekend through May. Flows during these releases are 1,000 cfs when they ramp up early on Saturday, with the flows continuing through Sunday afternoon. The dates of these releases are set in early January and posted on the Army Corps website. The rest of the time, flows are dictated by the lake level and the amount of rain and snow received in the area. Flows are very predictable through the summer and into the winter.

The mile-long catch-and-release area just below the dam is walk-and-wade, accessed through West Virginia from Barnum Road, then walking upstream of the parking lot along the old railroad bed, which is open only to foot traffic and bicycles. This is artificial lures only, and anglers must have no

Wading the Potomac and changing flies. Harold R. Harsh

bait of any kind in their possession. The two wires crossing the river at the upper and lower ends of this section are clear indicators of the boundaries. There are three large pools in this section, with pocket water between them.

Below this catch-and-release section is the 1¼-mile put-and-take area. It is stocked through the summer with keeper-size fish (9 to 15 inches) by both Maryland and West Virginia. Access is along River Road, which runs the entire length. The first boating access is at the big parking lot in Barnum. There are no tackle restrictions in the put-and-take area, except that anglers are allowed no more than two rods; you may keep five fish, with no size restrictions. The put-and-take section ends at Blue Hole, a big, pondlike pool

Wading the upper North Branch. Harold R. Harsh

The many pools break into classic pocket water and smooth runs. The gradient picks up below Blue Hole, and the river drops about 1,000 feet in the 6 miles. At fishable flows, the river is rated a Class I whitewater, but there are a few places where you could get into trouble in a smaller boat. If you plan to float it yourself, check the river from land or hire a guide the first time you visit.

Because of the absence of vehicle traffic below Blue Hole, this section gets fished the least, except for guided float fishing, and the farther downstream you go the less likely you are to see other anglers. The states of West Virginia and Maryland own the land on both sides of the river, so there are no houses or other structures until you reach the town of Bloomington, Maryland, toward the end of the 6 miles.

Because the river had been dead for 100+ years and the dam is fairly new, the insect population has been slow to come back. In the past 20 years that I have been working here, it has improved annually. Little Black Stoneflies and midges are the main hatches in the winter and early spring. Caddis hatch once the water starts to warm through the fall. While there are hatches of mayflies, BWOs early and late, March Browns from May through July, and Sulphurs in mid-June, the hatches are often sparse and sporadic. The *Isonychia* hatch in late June through July has been the exception. Large hatches of this mayfly in early afternoon, and spinner falls toward dark have most of the fish in the river looking up! Large Golden Stoneflies hatch throughout the summer, usually after dark. Ants, hoppers, and beetles round out the summer fishing, with most of the guides throwing hopper-dropper rigs through the summer and into the early fall.

From the public ramp in Bloomington downstream to the Westernport wastewater treatment plant is put-and-take. This is a walk-and-wade area from the takeout to the small dam at the paper mill. The next boat access is in the town of Westernport, Maryland and Piedmont, West Virginia, about ¼ mile downstream from the paper mill. This begins the next 5-mile section of the river. While there are some walk-and-

downstream of where the road is gated. The next boat access is at the head of this pool, and motorized traffic ends in the parking lot. Only foot and bicycle traffic is allowed from the gate across the railroad bed, downstream to Bloomington, Maryland. This is also the beginning of the lower catch-and-release area—artificials only, no bait in possession. This section is a wild trout management area. No keeper-size fish are stocked, only fingerling browns and cutthroats. From Blue Hole to the next takeout in Bloomington is 6 miles, and is some of the best run-riffle-pool water you could hope to fish.

Red spots! A North Branch brown. Harold R. Harsh

West Virginia golden trout. Harold R. Harsh

wade opportunities, this section is mainly fished by floating. This is an urban float through the town of Westernport, downstream to the boat ramp in McCoole, Maryland. Maryland Route 135 runs along the left bank of the river, and you float over the effluent pipes from the treatment plant. From the treatment plant, the regulations are zero creel limit, which means any angling practices are allowed (including bait), but no fish can be kept. While the water from the plant is nontoxic, is does add color to the river from this point downstream. It also adds nutrients to the water, making it more fertile. The fish below here grow faster than in the upper sections, and the warmer water coming out of the plant keeps them more active and feeding in the cold winter months.

While water temps on the upper river drop into the low to mid-40s in winter, the temps from here down stay in the upper 40s to mid-50s in the same period. In the summer, the cold water from the Savage River tailwater enters the NB to help keep it cooler, but the effluent heats the water, and if flow drops, it can warm the water to lethal temps.

Since the water is more fertile, there are more insects here, but because of the water clarity very rarely do you see fish rise. Most of the fishing is with double nymph rigs or streamers. Crayfish and hellgrammite patterns along with flash flies seem to work the best. Big stonefly nymphs along with black Woolly Buggers with a Pheasant-tail dropper work well under a strike indicator.

From the next boat access at McCoole, the river clears as the particulates drop to the bottom. This 5-mile section ends at the Gary Yoder Memorial Park and boat ramp. While still an urban float, the river does get away from the road and into farmland after a couple of miles. The water here is warmer, but still cold enough to sustain trout as long as the flows stay

up, but the water is warming up enough that we start catching smallmouth bass. While you may see more fish rising because of water clarity, we still do most of our fishing with nymphs and streamers.

➤ **Hatches:** *Midges (cream or gray):* January through March; October through December.
Black Stoneflies: December through February.
Quill Gordons: April, possibly into early May.
Hendricksons: April, possibly into early May.
Blue-winged Olives: April; August through September.
Tan Caddis: March through May; September and October.
March Browns: April through September.
Hoppers: July through mid-September.
Crickets: July through early October.
Others: Olive Caddis, Sulphurs, Light Cahills, Dun Variants, and Red Quills hatch at various times during the year.

➤ **Fishing Regulations:** Open year-round. Catch-and-release 1 mile from below upper wire to lower wire.
Put-and-take 1.4 miles from wire to end of Blue Hole.
Catch-and-release 5 miles from end of Blue Hole to Bloomington, Maryland.
Put-and-take 2 miles from Bloomington to the wastewater treatment plant.
Zero creel limit 9 miles from wastewater plant to Gary Yoder Memorial Park.

➤ **Tackle:** Use a 9-foot, 4- to 6-weight rod with a floating line and a 7½-foot, 3X to 5X leader. For streamers, use a 9-foot, 7-weight rod with a sink-tip with a 4- to 6-foot 1X or 2X leader.

Fall on the upper catch-and-release section. Harold R. Harsh

210

Rick Moran with a rainbow from the upper tailwater float. Harold R. Harsh

HAROLD HARSH is a lifelong resident of western Maryland, and his Spring Creek Outfitters was the first fly shop and guide service on the North Branch of the Potomac. Except for his time serving his country in the Marine Corps, he has lived and fished in Garrett County, where he guides more than 150 days a year.

CLOSEST FLY SHOPS

Spring Creek Outfitters
86 Big Frog Lane
Oakland, MD 21550
301-387-6587
harold@springcreekoutfitter.com
www.springcreekoutfitter.com

CLOSEST OUTFITTERS/GUIDES

Spring Creek Outfitters (above)
Sang Run Outfitters
10852 Oakland Sang Run Rd.
McHenry, MD 21541
301-387-6726
outfitters@hughes.net
www.sangrunoutfitters.com

North Branch Angler
6135 Oakland Sang Run Rd.
Oakland, MD 21550
301-387-5314
kenpavol@pennswoods.net

P.J. Daley
Oakland, MD 21550
703-999-8504
savageriverangler@gmail.com

CLOSEST LODGES

Savage River Lodge
1600 Mt. Aetna Rd.
Frostburg, MD 21532
301-689-3200
info@savageriverlodge.com
www.savageriverlodge.com

BEST HOTEL

Keyser Inn
51 Josie Dr. (off Route 220 South)
Keyser, WV 26726
304-788-0913
www.keyserinn.com

BEST CAMPGROUND

Cabins on the North Branch, Barnum, WV. Contact Mineral County Parks and Recreation
150 Armstrong St.
Keyser, WV 26726
304-788-5732
parks@mineralcountywv.com
www.mineralcountywv.com

BEST RESTAURANT

Pine Lodge Steakhouse
1520 Deep Creek Dr.
McHenry, MD 21541
301-387-6500
www.pinelodgesteakhouse.com.

BEST PLACE TO GET A COLD, STIFF DRINK

UNO'S Bar and Grill
19746 Garrett Hwy.
Oakland, MD 21550
301-387-4866
www.deepcreekuno.com

CLOSEST EMERGENCY MEDICAL HELP

Garrett Memorial Hospital
251 N. 4th St.
Oakland, MD 21550-1375
301-533-4000
www.gcmh.com

CELL PHONE SERVICE

Spotty at best.

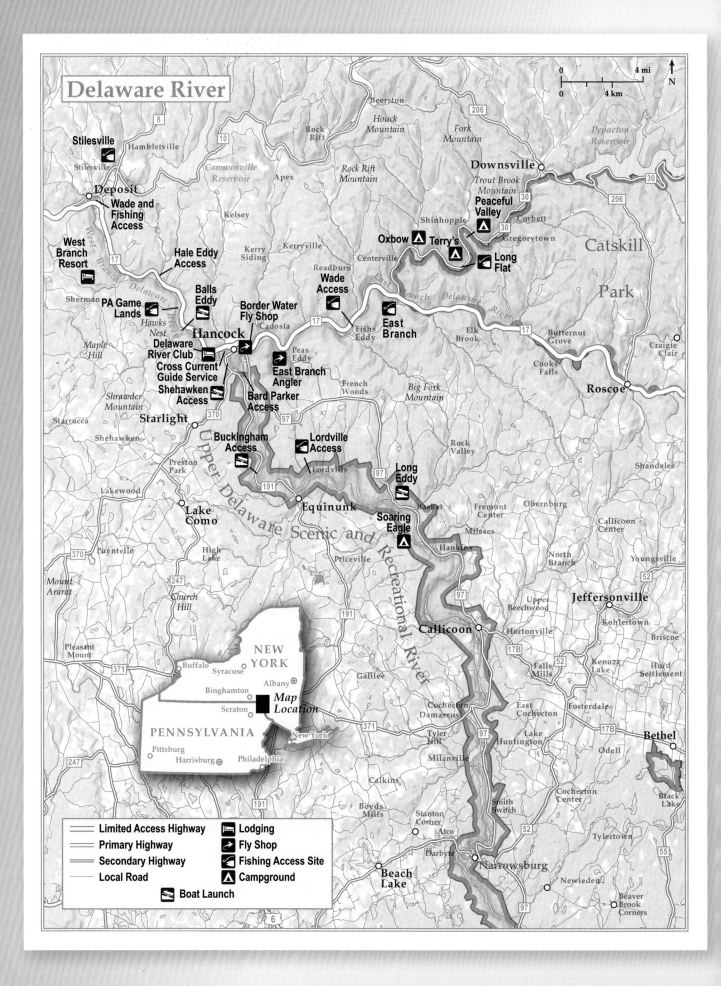

Delaware River

Stilesville

Hambletville

Deposit

Wade and Fishing Access

West Branch Resort

Hale Eddy Access

PA Game Lands

Balls Eddy

Hancock

Delaware River Club

Cross Current Guide Service

Shehawken Access

Bard Parker Access

Border Water Fly Shop

East Branch Angler

Buckingham Access

Lordville Access

Starlight

Lake Como

Equinunk

Long Eddy

Soaring Eagle

Wade Access

East Branch

Oxbow

Terry's

Long Flat

Peaceful Valley

Downsville

Catskill Park

Roscoe

Callicoon

Jeffersonville

Bethel

Narrowsburg

Beach Lake

Map inset:

NEW YORK

Albany

Binghamton

Syracuse

Buffalo

Scraton

New York

PENNSYLVANIA

Pittsburg

Harrisburg

Philadelphia

Map Location

Legend

Limited Access Highway	Lodging
Primary Highway	Fly Shop
Secondary Highway	Fishing Access Site
Local Road	Campground
Boat Launch	

0   4 mi
0   4 km
N

6

Upper Delaware River *(New York–Pennsylvania)*

➤ **Location:** The Upper Delaware System is located in the Catskill Mountains—the history-rich birthplace of American fly fishing—approximately 150 miles from New York City, on the border of New York and Pennsylvania. Flights are available to Binghamton, New York and will leave you about a 45-minute drive. In less than a half day's drive, you can reach the river from the metropolitan areas of Boston and Baltimore; Philadelphia is even closer, about a 3-hour drive.

The system is made up of three rivers: the West Branch, East Branch, and main stem of the Delaware. The West Branch and East Branch join at the village of Hancock, New York, to form the main stem. Both create tailwaters from New York City drinking water reservoir dams, which provide cold, pristine water. The Delaware reservoir water doesn't require any filtration.

The East Branch is about 27 miles long and an excellent trout fishery for wild rainbow and brown trout from the season opener on April 1 through mid-June. The changing character of this waterway allows it to be treated as two separate rivers. From mid-June into September, the lower stretch of the river—from the junction of the Beaverkill, downriver—gets too warm until mid-September. Then, the river is once again cool enough for trout until season's end on November 30. This is big water with spring flows that are often too high to wade. Public access is very limited, making floating the best option.

The East Branch upriver of the Beaverkill has ample cold water to fish all season. The section upriver from Shinhopple, New York closes on October 15 to protect spawning brown trout. You'll find ample public access along New York 30. These parking/access areas are well marked by the New York Department of Environmental Conservation (DEC). Think "spring creek" on this stretch, and you'll have the opportunity to spot and stalk a few trophy browns. Far-and-fine is the norm here, unless the water is highly stained from a rainstorm; then it gets easier . . . but never easy.

The West Branch is a much shorter river, running about 17 miles from the dam to its junction with the East Branch. Its shorter length, and its use—to provide minimum flow levels to the main stem of the Delaware—give the river more coldwater releases. Barring a drought year, it's fishable for its entire length. Access is good and available near the Town of Deposit, New York, and through the Pennsylvania

Game Lands #299 off Penn-York Road. The more consistent flows give the West Branch the highest fish populations of the whole system. It's also the most popular with anglers. By some standards, when the water is at a good wading height, the river can get crowded, but not so crowded that everyone can't have a good experience by playing nice in the sandbox and by practicing common courtesy.

The main stem can be the most challenging to fish, partly due to its larger size and partly due to access. In the spring, the main river has excellent fishing for about 25 miles. As the season progresses, the coldwater length of the river shrinks. During the summer, the river will stay cold for about 5 miles

The height of spring. Joe Demalderis

downriver from the junction of the East and West Branches. In a very warm, low-water year, this can shrink to 3 miles or less.

When looking at the rivers for the first time, you'll quickly recognize the riffle-run-pool structure of your typical Eastern freestone, with one exception: the riffles, runs, and pools are much longer. The main stem has some pools that are a mile long, some riffles almost as long, and runs that fall somewhere in between. If you give the river permission to intimidate you, it will. Instead, focus on what's in reach and set yourself up to have an enjoyable, though challenging, day.

Fly selection is easy. Early season and high water are for streamer fishing, as the trout are focused on alewives, which

Above. Ah, the East Branch! Joe Demalderis
Inset. On his way home. Jimmy Fee

are predominantly white in color. The spring has more adult baitfish in the river, since the young of the year haven't been born yet, while the late summer and fall have more juvenile baitfish swimming around.

Keep this in mind in selecting streamer sizes. Add into the mix of protein the large numbers of American shad smolts descending the East Branch and main stem in late summer and fall. Adults that made the 300-mile journey from the ocean spawned the shad in late spring. Think white. Zonkers and their hybrids are good go-to patterns. Yellows and browns are good fall colors when the browns get their pre-spawn aggressive behavior going. These colors mimic young brown trout, and big browns are cannibalistic. Use that to your advantage. And never hesitate to go formal, with basic black.

Nymphs and wets work well during nonhatch periods. The trout will be in the usual holding places such as seams, logs, rocks, cuts, and the like. The big, broad riffles are ideal for swinging wets, and the hard tug of the average 15- to 16-inch trout boosts your adrenaline. Match your wets to the fly du jour—for example, a Partridge and Yellow is good when Sulphurs are hatching.

All nymphing techniques are productive on the river; just match your technique to the water. High-sticking, indicator style, or any of the European persuasions, regardless of the nationality, all work under the right circumstances. Again, match your fly to what's been hatching and keep in mind that there are always stonefly nymphs and midge pupae in the river.

Dry-fly fishing is the attraction of the Delaware system. Every major hatch in the East occurs. Hatches typically start in mid-April and last through October. Hendicksons, March Browns, Green Drakes, Brown Drakes, Sulphurs, and sever-al caddis hatches all occur in great numbers in the spring. Early-season hatches occur during the civilized midday to evening hours. As the season progresses, the most productive times change to early and late in the day, often to well after dark. The exception is on the upper sections of the West and East Branch, where midday to evening summer Sulphur hatches are prolific and attract a good bit of attention from both fish and fishers.

Dry-fly selection should focus on flush-in-the-film patterns in the style of parachutes, Compara-duns, and emergers. Soft wing materials such as CDC tend to give the selective trout a more realistic profile. Snowshoe emergers also provide a good profile, and their extra durability can save time in the sometimes short frenzy of a pod of fish feeding heavily, especially during *Isonychia* hatches in the main stem riffles.

Terrestrials such as flying ants, beetles, and spruce moths are numerous enough to grab a trout's attention, especially flying ants in the late summer.

➤ **Hatches:** You'll find Brown Stoneflies from late March to early May in sizes 12/14; with Blue-winged Olives at roughly the same time in sizes 18/20. From early April to mid-May the water comes alive with Little Black Caddis in sizes 18–20. Look for both Blue Quills and Mahogany Duns from the second week in April to the second week in May. You can pretty much set your watch by the regularity of those hatches. Quill Gordons, Hendricksons, and Sulphurs in sizes 12/4 follow – mid-April to mid- or late June. The Grannom Caddis, Sulphurs, and Pale Evening Duns won't be far behind or will occur shoulder-to-shoulder with earlier hatches. For a more comprehensive hatch chart visit www.crosscurrent guideservice.com/hatches.html.

➤ **Fishing Regulations:** The sections of the West Branch and main stem that border New York State and Pennsylvania stay open year-round. The West Branch—entirely in NY—and the East Branch from the dam down to Shinhopple are open April 1 to October 15. The rest of the East Branch is open April 1 to November 30.

The vast majority of anglers practice catch-and-release. The West Branch in the town of Deposit has a catch-and-release section that extends from the Route 17 overpass downriver for 2 miles. The rest of the West Branch has a 2-fish, 12-inch-minimum limit from April 1 through October 15; then it's all catch-and-release.

The East Branch has a 2-fish, 12-inch limit from April 1 to October 15; October 16 to November 30 it's catch-and-release.

The season on the main stem of the Delaware begins the first Saturday after April 11 and extends to October 15. There is a one-fish-per-day limit for fish exceeding 14 inches; it's all catch-and-release at other times of year. The Upper Delaware is a wild trout fishery, and catch-and-release fishing is something that cannot be emphasized enough.

➤ **Tackle:** If you bring one rod to the Delaware, make it a medium-fast to fast-action, 9-foot 5-weight. Four- and 6-weights are fine and also make excellent secondary rods for nymphing and streamers, or in the case of 4-weights, dry flies. The average wild trout in the river is 15 to 16 inches, with plenty of smaller fish to keep it fun, and plenty of bigger fish in the 20- to 23-inch range to keep it exciting. There are even some 2-foot-plus jumbos lurking around to make it heart-stopping at times.

JOE DEMALDERIS guides fly fishers, and hosts and books trips to some of the world's great fly-fishing destinations. His primary water is the Upper Delaware River system, which he's been fishing since the mid-1970s and has guided since 1993. In 2010, Joe was named the Orvis-Endorsed Fly-Fishing Guide of the Year.

CLOSEST FLY SHOPS

Border Water Fly Shop
159 East Front St.
Hancock, NY 13783 (607-637-4296)
www.borderwateroutfitters.com

West Branch Resort
150 Faulkener Rd.
Hancock, NY 13783 (607-467-5525)
www.westbranchresort.com

CLOSEST OUTFITTERS/GUIDES

Cross Current Guide Service & Outfitters
PO Box 721
159 East Front St.
Hancock, NY 13783 (914-475-6779)
www.crosscurrentguideservice.com
www.flyfishthedelaware.com

East Branch Outfitters
1471 Peas Eddy Rd.
Hancock, NY 13783 (607-637-5451)
www.eastbranchoutfitters.com

CLOSEST LODGES

West Branch Resort
150 Faulkener Rd
Hancock, NY 13783 (607-467-5525)
www.westbranchresort.com

BEST HOTEL

Hancock House Hotel
137 E. Front St.
Hancock, NY 13783 (607-637-7100)
www.newhancockhouse.com

Smith's Colonial Motel
23085 New York 97
Hancock, NY 13783 (607-637-2989)
www.smithscolonialmotel.com

Delaware River Club
1228 Winterdale Rd.
Starlight, PA 18461 (570-635-5800)
www.thedelawareriverclub.com

BEST CAMPGROUND

Oxbow Campsites
3026 Rt. 30
East Branch, NY 13756 (607-363-7141)
www.oxbowcampsites.com

BEST RESTAURANT

Bluestone Grill Restaurant
62 W. Main St.
Hancock, NY 13783 (607-637-2600)
www.bluestonegrill.com

Circle E Diner
369 E Front St.
Hancock, NY (607-637-9905)

CLOSEST PLACE TO GET A COLD, STIFF DRINK

Lydia's Crosstown Tavern
6031 Hancock Hwy.
Starlight, PA 18461 (570-635-5926)

CLOSEST EMERGENCY MEDICAL HELP

Barnes-Kasson Hospital
2872 Turnpike St.
Susquehanna, PA 18847 (570-853-3135)

CELL PHONE SERVICE

Some limitations on the East Branch between the dam and Route 17 and on the main stem more than 5 miles from Hancock.

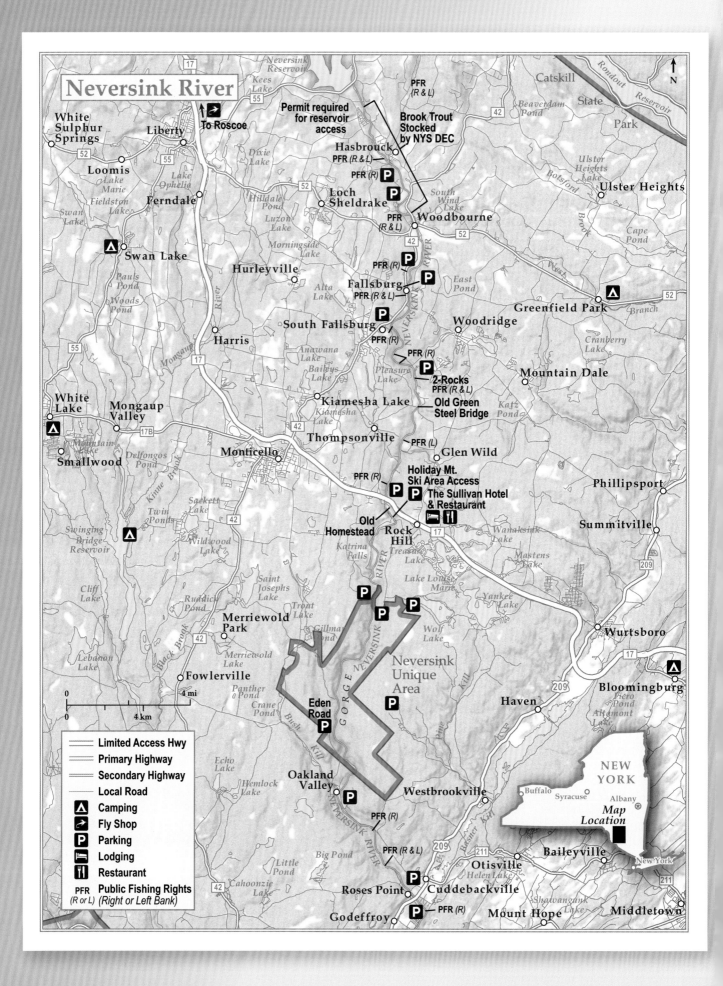

Neversink River

White Sulphur Springs

Liberty

To Roscoe

Loomis

Ferndale

Kees Lake

Neversink Reservoir

Dixie Lake

Permit required for reservoir access

Brook Trout Stocked by NYS DEC

PFR (R & L)

Hasbrouck

PFR (R & L)

PFR (R)

Loch Sheldrake

PFR (R & L)

Woodbourne

Catskill

State

Park

Beaverdam Pond

Rondout Reservoir

N

Ulster Heights Lake

Botsford

Ulster Heights

Lake Marie

Swan Lake

Fieldston Lake

Lake Ophelia

Hilldale Pond

Luzon Lake

Morningside Lake

Hurleyville

Alta Lake

Fallsburg

PFR (R & L)

South Wind Lake

East Pond

Cape Pond

West Brook

Greenfield Park

Pauls Pond

Woods Pond

South Fallsburg

PFR (R)

Woodridge

Cranberry Lake

Mountain Dale

Harris

Anawana Lake

Baileys Lake

Pleasure Lake

PFR (R)

2-Rocks

PFR (R & L)

Old Green Steel Bridge

Katz Pond

Kiamesha Lake

Kiamesha Lake

Thompsonville

PFR (L)

Glen Wild

Phillipsport

White Lake

Mongaup Valley

Mountain Lake

Smallwood

Delfongos Pond

Monticello

Holiday Mt. Ski Area Access

The Sullivan Hotel & Restaurant

PFR (R)

Old Homestead

Rock Hill

Treasure Lake

Wanaksink Lake

Summitville

Swinging Bridge Reservoir

Kinne Brook

Sackett Lake

Twin Ponds

Wildwood Lake

Katrina Falls

Lake Louise Marie

Lake

Yankee Lake

Mastens Lake

Wurtsboro

Cliff Lake

Ruddick Pond

Saint Josephs Lake

Trout Lake

Gillman Pond

Wolf Lake

Neversink Unique Area

Lebanon Lake

Merriewold Park

Merriewold Lake

Bloomingburg

Fiero Pond

Fowlerville

Panther Pond

Crane Pond

Eden Road

GORGE NEVERSINK RIVER

Haven

209

Altamont Lake

0   4 mi
0   4 km

Echo Lake

Oakland Valley

Hemlock Lake

NEVERSINK RIVER

Westbrookville

PFR (R)

PFR (R & L)

Otisville

Helen Lake

Baileyville

NEW YORK

Buffalo   Syracuse

Albany

Map Location

Little Pond

Big Pond

Cahoonzie Lake

Roses Point

Cuddebackville

Shawangunk Kill

Mount Hope

Middletown

Godeffroy

PFR (R)

New York

Legend

— Limited Access Hwy
— Primary Highway
— Secondary Highway
— Local Road
▲ Camping
➤ Fly Shop
P Parking
🛏 Lodging
🍴 Restaurant
PFR (R or L) Public Fishing Rights (Right or Left Bank)

➤ **Location:** New York's Catskill Mountains, approximately 1½ hours north and northwest of New York City. The Catskills do not have the high peaks of the Western United States, but contain seven major rivers, allowing fly fishers in the Northeast lots of opportunity. These rivers offer some of the best trout waters in the U.S., none better than the Neversink.

The Neversink begins atop Slide Mountain and flows to Port Jervis. It starts with two branches, the East and the West, which converge in Claryville, above the Neversink Dam. Except for the extreme upper reaches of both branches—as well as a small parcel of land owned by the Frost Valley YMCA—all land from Slide Mountain to the Neversink Dam is under private ownership and has been since the 1800s. Theodore Gordon's former home water is under the dam, which was completed in 1950. The dam ensures that the Neversink River has consistent water flows with temperatures ranging from 40 to 60 degrees all season. An agreement between the City and the State of New York requires that water temperatures remain at 75 degrees or lower at the town of Bridgeville.

We divide the river from the dam to the Neversink River Recreational Area (the Gorge) into three distinct areas: the upper area immediately below the dam to Fallsburg; from Fallsburg to the Gorge; and the Gorge itself.

The upper reaches below the dam is a classic tailwater fishery, with grass beds, long, flat pools, and a gravel bottom making for easy wading. The area requires careful stalking and long, fine leaders. These waters hold only wild brookies and browns. This area has the best fishing all season due to consistently cold water. If you decide to fish the area near Hasbrook, look for the oft-reported ghost of a small man, weighing only about 90 pounds, fishing a long cane rod. That's Theodore Gordon, and some claim to have seen him on this stretch of the river. The river varies in width from a small stream just below the dam to about 60 feet when it reaches Woodbourne. Access is off Hasbrook Road outside the small town of Woodbourne.

The middle section from Woodbourne to the Gorge is transitional water going from a tailwater fishery to a freestone-style stream. This section is stocked with browns, as well as holding a good population of wild browns. Route 42, between Woodbourne and Fallsburg, has public access areas that are well marked. Use Exit 100 off Route 17, then Route 52 East to Route 42. Try the area by the gravel company, the one with the big, red barn, and go either up- or downstream. Or, try the pool opposite the phone company (another DEC public fishing area) and use your skill in the slow-moving, crystal-clear water. Nice fish can be found under the far bank,

Confluence of East and West Branches of the Neversink River, and beginning of main stream, near Claryville. Daniel Case

but be careful—the large pool is deeper than you think. You might try fishing by the green bridge in Woodbridge.

The last section is the Neversink River Recreational Area (the Gorge), which was purchased from a private landowner by the State of New York about 15 years ago. This purchase created a fly-fishing paradise. Bring your camera to capture the stunning panorama. The Gorge holds only wild browns with some wild brookies, and regulations dictate no-kill and artificial lures only. We recommend barbless hooks. Fish average about 14 inches. This is a freestone-type of stream, with

"Hiram's Hole" in Neversink Gorge. Art Salomon

Left. A perfect brookie.

Above. Remaining abutment from aqueduct carrying Delaware and Hudson Canal over Neversink River near Cuddebackville. Daniel Case

and limited fishing pressure. We highly recommend this area to experience fly fishing the way it used to be. Lack of development ensures you an experience available nowhere else in the Catskills. Bring a wading staff at high-water times, and always wear waders with "sticky rubber"-type soles and metal studs everywhere on the Neversink.

After heavy rains, the Neversink clears quickly, even while other Catskill streams remain muddy or off-color. Temperatures, even in the heat of summer, remain relatively cool, especially in the upper reaches. Except during early-season stocking times, the Neversink receives less fishing pressure than most other Catskill streams.

➤ **Hatches:** Sulphurs come off from mid-May through September. Count on small Blue-winged Olives on the water throughout the season.

Early-season favorites are Blue-winged Olives, Blue Quills, and Caddis in #18 and #20. Hendricksons and Quill Gordons in #12 and #14 are abundant from mid-April through mid-May. March Browns, Grey Foxes, and Light Cahills #10 to #14 are fished from mid-May through mid-June. Look for the *Potamanthus* in #8 and #10 anytime after mid-June in the slower sections of the river.

Summer is terrestrial time. Fish grasshoppers and crickets in #10 to #14 along the banks. From early July through the first frost, look for Tricos #22 to #26. Starting in June and again in September, look for *Isonychias* in #10 to #14. The

pockets, riffles, and deep pools. Fishing starts improving in early to mid-May as water temperatures rise. The Gorge has the largest population of stoneflies of any river in the Catskills. It has excellent water quality, with large populations of caddis and mayflies. Attractor patterns such as Royal Wulffs and Ausable Wulffs are always good choices. The Gorge is located off Katrina Falls Road in Rock Hill, Exit 111 off Route 17. After parking at the end of the road, it's about a 30-minute walk down to the river along a small trail. Wearing regular hiking shoes will make your trip out of the Gorge much easier. Don't forget to sign in at the metal box at the top of the trail so DEC personnel know who's in the area. This area is widely regarded as one of the most stunningly beautiful places to fish, with its natural, untouched terrain heaviest concentrations of *Isonychias* are in the Gorge and other fast-running water. When in doubt, fish a DS Emerger #14 to #18, which is effective all season.

➤ **Fishing Regulations:** www.dec.ny.gov or 866-426-3778; license year is October to September 30. Fishing season is April 1 to October 15.

➤ **Tackle:** A 9-foot, 5-weight will be the rod of choice. Waders are a must in early season, while waist-highs are fine for late in the season.

➤ **Flies:** Early season: Hendrickson #12–#14, Quill Gordon #12–#14, stoneflies #10–#14.

Midseason: Grey Fox #12–#14, March Brown #10–#12, Blue-winged Olive #16–#24.

Summer: terrestrials such as ants, beetles, and grasshoppers.

Fall: streamers, midges #20–#24, Olives #18–#24, and *Isonychia* imitations #10–#14.

DENNIS SKARKA was born in rural eastern Long Island. Being a rebel even at age 12, he traded in his Schwinn bike for a fly rod. His love of history and fly fishing brought him to the Catskills after his service in Vietnam. In 1998, he opened Catskill Flies in Roscoe and continues to guide and develop innovative fly patterns for his customers.

CLOSEST FLY SHOPS

Catskill Flies
6 Stewart Ave.
Roscoe, NY 12776
845-434-4473
www.catskillflies.com

Beaverkill Angler
52 Stewart Ave.
Roscoe, NY 12776
607-498-5194
www.beaverkillangler.com

Baxter House River Outfitters
2012 Old Route 17
Roscoe, NY 12776
607-290-4022
www.baxterhouse.net
bhoutfitters@aol.com

Dette Trout Flies
68 Cottage St.
Roscoe, NY 12776
607-498-4991
www.detteflies.com
flyshop@catskillflies.com

CLOSEST OUTFITTERS
Catskill Flies (above)

Beaverkill Angler (left)
Baxter House River Outfitters (left)

CLOSEST AND BEST LODGING

Reynolds House
1394 Old Route 17
Roscoe, NY 12776
607-498-4422
www.reynoldshouseinn.com

Downsville Motel
6964 River Rd.
Downsville, NY 13755
607-363-7575
www.downsvillemotel.com

Baxter House River Outfitters
2012 Old Route 17
Roscoe, NY 12776
607-290-4022
www.baxterhouse.net
bhoutfitters@aol.com

BEST RESTAURANTS

Riverside Café
16624 County Hwy 17
Roscoe, NY 12776
607-498-5305
www.riversidecafeandlodge.com

Roscoe Diner
1908 Old Route 17,
Roscoe, NY 12776
607-498-4405
www.theroscoediner.com

Raimondo's Restaurant & Pizzeria
62 Stewart Ave.
Roscoe, NY 12776
607-498-4702

Rockland House
159 Rockland Rd.
Roscoe, NY 12776
607-498-4240
www.rocklandhouse.com

CLOSEST EMERGENCY MEDICAL HELP

Catskill Regional Medical Center
68 Harris Bushville Rd.
Harris, NY 12742
845-794-3300

CELL PHONE SERVICE
Hit and miss—it's OK by the reservoir, nonexistent in the canyon.

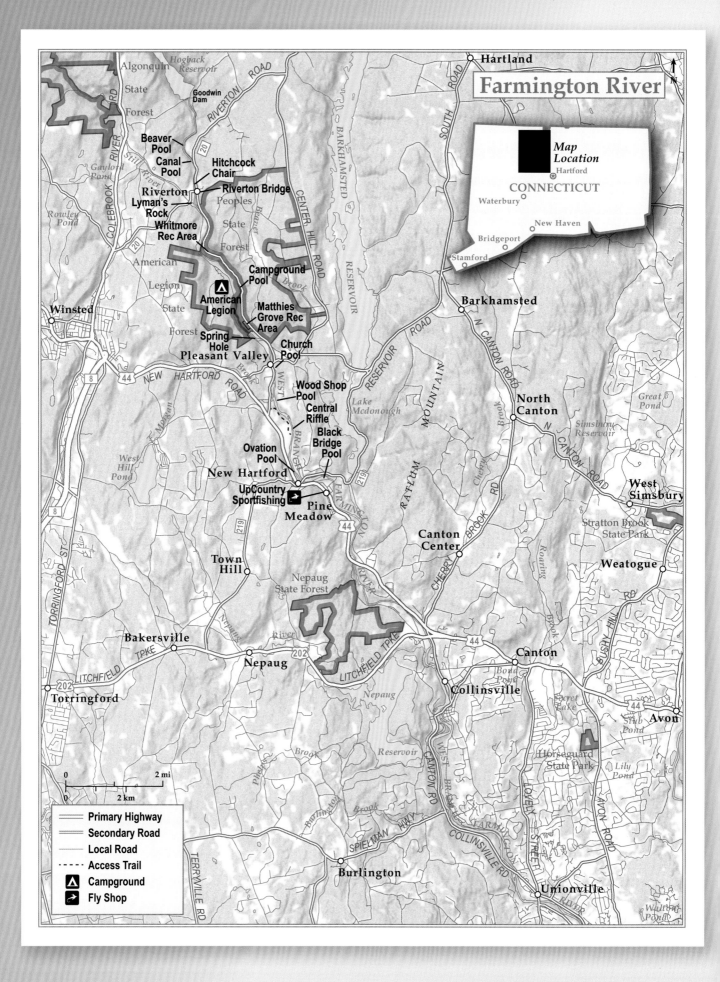

Farmington River *(Northwest Connecticut)*

➤ **Location:** Northwest Connecticut, about a 2-hour car ride from Boston; about 3 hours from New York City. Bradley International Airport is 40 minutes away in nearby Windsor, Connecticut.

The Farmington River tailwater flows from Hogback Reservoir, providing about 30 miles of fishable trout stream. Anglers from all over New England, New York, and New Jersey come to the river during the summer months to take advantage of the cold waters that teem with an abundance of rainbow, brook, and brown trout. The trout are a mix of wild and stocked with a 12-inch average size, though it is not uncommon to land trout in the 20- to 28-inch range. The popularity of the river comes from its fantastic management practices. A full 6 miles of year-round catch-and-release and an additional 15 miles of seasonal catch-and-release area ensures good fishing all year.

The banks of the Farmington River were once home to the Tunxis tribe of Native Americans, who farmed its fertile meadows and caught Atlantic salmon as they ran upriver to spawn. By the mid-1800s, both the Native Americans and the salmon were gone, with the dams of the Industrial Revolution blocking salmon passage. Today, all that is left of the Atlantic salmon are the small parr stocked as part of a restoration program. Floods in the 1930s and 1950s erased most of the factories built along The Farmington and facilitated the building of the dams and reservoirs, which now protect the valley and provide cold water for the trout.

The upper portions of the Farmington River flow through a combination of state forest lands and widely spaced homes. It is protected by its National Wild and Scenic designation, which keeps development from its banks and ensures good, consistent flows from the dam for recreation. The source of the tailwater, the Goodwin Dam, does generate power; however, the dam's main purpose is flood control, and you'll see mostly steady flows during a day of fishing. The Farmington is largely a gentle wading river, with some canoe traffic during the summer months. Drift boats are seen occasionally during the higher flows of the early spring and fall, but are absent during the summer.

There is nearly unlimited access to the river, with quiet roads following all of its length and easy pull-offs to park along its sides.

The Farmington River is a medium-size freestone river with typical flows in the 200- to 600-cfs range. The fishing season on the Farmington never closes, and the river rarely ices up, so even on the coldest days of January you will see at least a few anglers. Early March to early April sometimes brings high flows as the melting snow raises water levels. In a typical year, flows moderate by mid-April, and several months of great hatches begin. By August, the river is at its

Fall on the Farmington. Ken DeFusco

lowest point of the year, and ultralight fly rods and tiny dry flies are the norm.

The Farmington boasts year-round hatches of mayflies and caddis. The traditional kickoff comes in late April with the Hendricksons, followed by March Browns, Grey Foxes, Tan and Green Caddis, as well as the much-beloved Sulphur Duns. Blue-winged Olives of various sizes hatch all year, as do the unique Winter/Summer Caddis (*Dolophilodes distinctus*). The Winter/Summer Caddis emerges on the surface as a pupa, and swims to the nearest shore or rock before trans-

Upper Farmington River. Mark Swenson

Inset. Farmington mayfly. Todd Kuhrt

forming into a small, dark brown, mottled adult. The odd behavior of the pupa creates a challenge, as often a trout will eat an imitation only if it is twitched or skated before reaching the trout's downstream lie.

The largest brown trout in the Farmington River are primarily carnivores and night feeders. Often anglers fishing to rising trout near dark will hear the water's surface explode, as the large fish target the smaller trout and Atlantic salmon parr. As a result, the Farmington has a small legion of dedicated anglers who venture out after sundown with headlamps, 6-inch streamers, and mouse patterns, often with spectacular results.

All methods of fly fishing work on the Farmington. While the largest numbers of anglers come to fish dry flies—with lots of success—a well-swung wet fly can often coax surface-wary trout into striking. Those employing nymphs on the riverbottom during the day are rewarded with larger trout, which avoid showing themselves during the sunlit hours. Both spring and fall, streamers bring numbers of trout to the net, and on summer evenings, giant streamers find the true trophy-size brown trout. The best anglers come prepared for all situations and rarely go away fishless.

➤ **Hatches:** An excellent source of current hatch information (including suggested sizes of imitations) may be found at the Nutmeg Trout Unlimited website, www.nutmegtrout.org.

Winter Caddis: March and April; July through September.
Black Caddis: March through June, with the heaviest concentrations in April and May.
Cinnamon/Spotted Tan Caddis: May through September; heaviest in June and July.
Blue-winged Olives: March through June, heaviest in April and June; later September and October,
Little Mahogany Duns: April through June, with most prolific hatch April and May; September.
Midges: All year.
Terrestrials: April through October.

➤ **Fishing Regulations:** Open year-round; 6 miles of catch-and-release, 15 miles of seasonal catch-and-release from September 1 to the third Saturday in April. There is a two-trout limit, 12-inch minimum length, from the third Saturday in April to August 31. Barbless hooks only.

➤ **Tackle:** Bring a 9-foot, 5-weight rod with a floating line and a spare spool with a sink-tip. A 3- or 4-weight rod is adequate for dry flies during the summer. The fish in the Farmington see a lot of anglers, so you need light tippet in the 6X to 8X range for dry-fly fishing; 4X or 5X for nymphs; and 1X to 3X for streamers. Chest waders are necessary, as almost all access requires wading in various depths from calf-deep to mid-torso.

Fall on the Farmington. Ken DeFusco

GRADY ALLEN owns UpCountry Sportfishing, located on the banks of the Farmington River. He is the vice president of the Farmington River Anglers Association and has spent his life promoting the conservation of Connecticut's fishing resources.

CLOSEST FLY SHOPS

UpCountry Sportfishing
352 Main St.
New Hartford, CT 06067
860-379-1952
upcountrysports@gmail.com
www.farmingtonriver.com

CLOSEST OUTFITTERS/GUIDES

Bruce Marino
B-Mar Flies and Guide Service
46 Fern Hollow Dr.
Granby, CT 06035
860-653-8288
www.bmarflies.com

Fred Jeans
The Selective Angler
P.O. Box 750
New Hartford, CT 06057
860-693-6642
www.selectiveangler.com

Mark Swenson Guide Services
203-632-0206
marcus2@charter.net

Antoine Bissieux (Orvis-endorsed)
860-759-4464
www.bissieux.com

BEST HOTEL

Riverton Inn
436 E. River Rd.
Riverton CT
860-379-8678
innkeeper@rivertoninn.com

BEST CAMPGROUND

Austin F. Hawes State Campground
Barkhamsted, CT 06063
877-668-2267
(located in the Pleasant Valley section of Barkhamsted on the river)

BEST RESTAURANT

Blue Sky Foods
431 Main St.
New Hartford, CT 06057
860-379-0000;
www.blueskyfoods-ct.com

BEST PLACE TO GET A COLD, STIFF DRINK

Chatterley's
2 Bridge St.
New Hartford, CT 06057
860-379-2428
www.chatterleysct.com

CLOSEST EMERGENCY MEDICAL HELP

Hartford Medical Group Walk-In Clinic
339 W. Main St. (Route 44)
Avon, CT 06001
860-696-2150

CELL PHONE SERVICE

Yes, but weak in some areas.

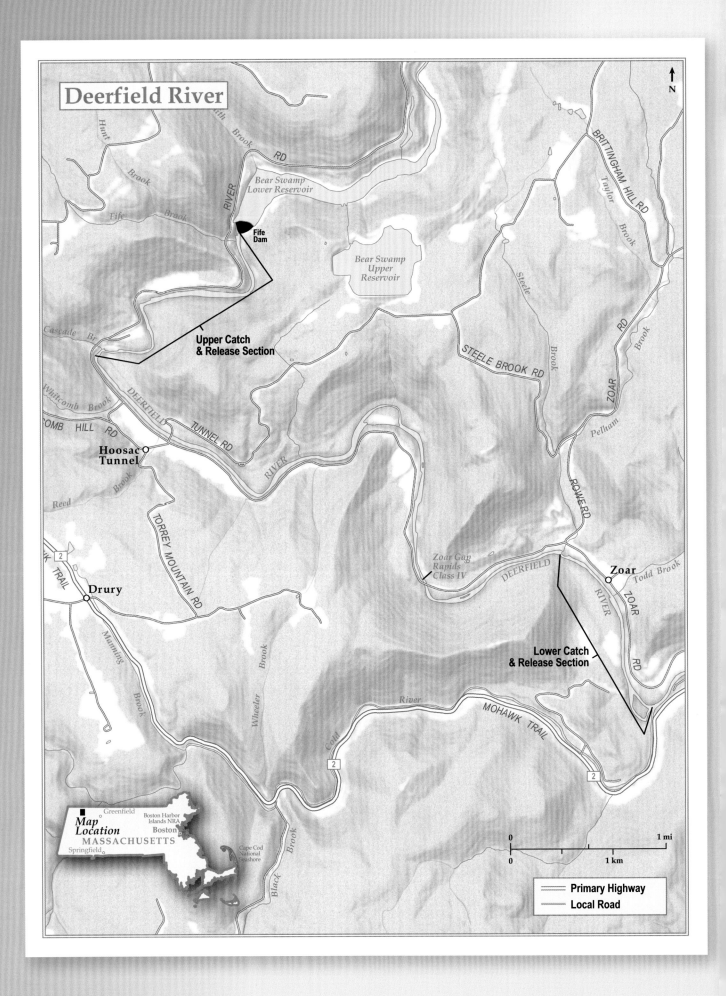

Deerfield River

N

Hunt Brook

Brook

Fife Brook

RIVER

Brook RD

Bear Swamp
Lower Reservoir

Fife
Dam

Bear Swamp
Upper
Reservoir

BRITTINGHAM HILL RD

Taylor Brook

Steele Brook

ZOAR RD

Pelham Brook

STEELE BROOK RD

Cascade Br

Upper Catch
& Release Section

Whitcomb Brook

DEERFIELD

COMB HILL RD

Hoosac
Tunnel

TUNNEL RD

RIVER

Brook

Reed

TRAIL

2

Drury

TORREY MOUNTAIN RD

Manning Brook

Wheeler Brook

Zoar Gap
Rapids
Class IV

ROWE RD

DEERFIELD

Zoar

Todd Brook

ZOAR RD

RIVER

Lower Catch
& Release Section

River

Cold Brook

2

MOHAWK TRAIL

2

Black Brook

Greenfield

Boston Harbor
Islands NRA
Boston

Map
Location
MASSACHUSETTS

Springfield

Cape Cod
National
Seashore

	0		1 mi
	0	1 km	

— Primary Highway
— Local Road

➤ **Location:** Northwest Massachusetts, about a 2-hour ride from Boston; about 3 hours from Hartford, Connecticut and Manchester, New Hampshire. Full-service airports are available in all three cities.

I'm a fly shop owner from Maine, but I'm writing about a river in Massachusetts. Why? Because the Deerfield River is one of the finest trout fisheries in the Northeast. Because I caught my first trout on a hatch-matched dry fly there. I also caught my first fish on a nymph rig there. I even rowed my first drift boat there.

The Deerfield River below Fife Brook Dam is a true success story. It is the all-too-rare river that fishes better today than it did 20 or even 10 years ago. This success is due to progressive fisheries management and the decommissioning of the Yankee Atomic Plant, which previously warmed the river by up to 15 degrees.

To call the Deerfield a "working river" is an understatement. Few rivers have been dammed up, rerouted, dewatered, and otherwise manipulated more than the Deerfield. Complete with every type of dam imaginable, a mountaintop reservoir and pumping system, a 150-foot-wide overflow pipe that acts as a circular top-flow dam in high water, and miles of manmade sluices, the Deerfield is veritable museum of hydro-engineering.

The Deerfield is in a rugged valley surrounded by steep, wooded hills. The sun comes late to the river and leaves early. Annual rainfall is above average for the region. The valley is lightly developed with only a small number of modest homes. Bankside development is almost nonexistent.

Much of the Deerfield can be accessed from Zoar Road, which parallels the river from Route 2 to Fife Brook Dam. Some of the better sections require a bit of a walk or climb. The entire length is floatable, with the exception of Zoar Gap, which is a challenging Class III+ drop, best attempted by experienced boaters only.

The Deerfield is a medium-size freestone river with flows in the 125–1,000 cfs range. Flows are controlled by Fife Brook Dam and are of the feast-or-famine variety. Minimum flow is 125 cfs. High flows are in the 1,000 cfs range. Flows in between are rare. The good news is that the flow regime does not seem to affect the fish. As for the anglers, they seem to have worked things out, with the waders fishing the low flows and the boaters fishing the high flows.

Between Fife Brook Dam and Route 2 there are more than 8 miles of river. The river flows uninterrupted through gentle riffles, deep runs, slow pools, boulder fields, and the occasional rapid. In addition to anglers, kayakers, whitewater canoeists, and commercial rafts filled with thrill seekers all take advantage of this wonderful resource.

Deerfield brown in a picturesque setting. Harrison Anglers

The Deerfield River can be waded during low flows. It is tough to wade during high water. Fishing from a boat—raft—is the best way to fish during high water. Using a boat of any type in low water—even a canoe or kayak—results in more dragging than fishing, and is not recommended.

The Deerfield River is open to fishing year-round. While prime time may be April through November, you can fish the river all winter long if you pick your days. In fact, I have had some very productive days in the dead of winter when many other New England rivers are closed to fishing, not fishable, or not fishing well.

The Deerfield River is primarily a rainbow and brown trout fishery. The ratio of rainbows to browns varies from year to year, but usually favors the former. There is a mix of

Deerfield River

Below. Angler John Vacca with a rainbow from below Fife Brook Dam. Bob Mallard

stocked and wild fish. The ratio of stocked versus wild fish also changes from year to year. It also varies by species, with more wild browns than rainbows. Rainbows average 10 to 14 inches, with fish up to 18 inches caught. Browns average slightly larger and grow to rather impressive sizes, with fish up 24 inches.

➤ **Hatches:** While not necessarily strong, the hatches on the Deerfield are predictable. Midges hatch year-round—especially near the dam. Mayfly hatches start in April and run intermittently through June. Caddis start later and go longer. Stoneflies can hatch pretty much anytime. During the summer months, fish feed on terrestrials: ants, hoppers, beetles, and crickets.

While fish are taken in many different ways on the Deerfield, it is primarily a nymphing river. On overcast days, fish will take streamers, but even then you will not catch as many fish as you would if you were nymphing. Trout will feed on the surface during a hatch. Fish will also take dry attractors in the summer. But, like fishing streamers on a bright day, fishing attractors is not usually a fly fisher's best option.

➤ **Fishing Regulations:** Open year-round.

From Fife Brook Dam to Hoosac Tunnel (a 4.7-mile engineering marvel that took the lives of almost 200 workers) is the first of two catch-and-release sections. This 1.6-mile stretch of water may be the best on the river. The second

catch-and-release section runs from Pelham Brook to just above the campground at Route 2. This section is roughly 3.5 miles long.

➤ **Tackle:** A 9-foot, 5-weight rod with a floating line is your best bet for the Deerfield River most of the time. If you want to fish streamers, a 9-foot, 6-weight with a fast-sinking line is your best option. Dry-fly fishing is best done with a 9-foot 4-weight, as you may need 6X tippet to fish midge patterns effectively. While rods longer than 9 feet can work, especially for nymphing, shorter rods are not practical. Strike indicators should be large enough to float two flies and added

Angler David Peress and Guide Tom Harrison with upper Deerfield brown.

BOB MALLARD has fly fished for 35 years and owns Kennebec River Outfitters in Madison, Maine. His writing has appeared in local, regional, and national fly-fishing publications. Look for Bob's upcoming book *50 Best Places to Fly Fish the Northeast*.

weight. Flies should include Woolly Buggers, sculpin patterns, mayfly and stonefly nymphs, all stages of caddis in a variety of sizes and colors, worms, and eggs.

CLOSEST FLY SHOPS

The Lower Forty
134 Madison St.
Worcester, MA 01610
508-752-4004
www.thelowerforty.com
lowerforty@verizon.net

Concord Outfitters
84 Commonwealth Ave.
West Concord, MA 01742
978-318-0330
www.concordoutfitters.com

CLOSEST GUIDES/OUTFITTERS

Harrison Anglers
P.O. Box 2012
Buckland, MA 01338
413-626-4738
www.harrisonanglers.com
tom@harrisonangelrs.com

LODGING

Warfield House Inn Bed & Breakfast
200 Warfield Rd
Charlemont, MA
888-339-8439
www.warfieldhouseinn.com
info@warfieldhouseinn.com

Oxbow Resort Motel
1741 Mohawk Trail
East Charlemont, MA
413-625-6011
www.oxbowresortmotel.com
info@oxbowresortmotel.com

Giovanni's Red Rose Motel
1701 Mohawk Trail
Charlemont, MA; 413-625-2666
www.redrosemotel.com

CAMPGROUND

Mohawk Park Campground
Riverside Tent & RV Sites, Route 2
(just west of Zoar Road)
Charlemont, MA
413-339-4470

FOOD

Otters Restaurant
(breakfast, lunch, and dinner)
1745 Mohawk Trail
East Charlemont, MA
413-625-6011
www.oxbowresortmotel.com
info@oxbowresortmotel.com

West End Pub (lunch and dinner)
16 State St.
Shelburne Falls, MA
413-625-6216
www.westendpubinfo.com

Gypsy Apple (gourmet dining)
65 Bridge St.
Shelburne Falls, MA
413-625-6345

Mohawk Park Pub & Restaurant
(lunch and dinner)
Route 2
Charlemont, MA
413-339-4470

CLOSEST PLACE TO GET A COLD, STIFF DRINK

West End Pub
16 State St.
Shelburne Falls, MA 01370
413-625-6216
www.westendpubinfo.com

CLOSEST EMERGENCY MEDICAL HELP

Cooley Dickinson Hospital
30 Locust St. (Route 9)
Northampton, MA 01061-5001
413-582-2000

CELL PHONE SERVICE
Intermittent.

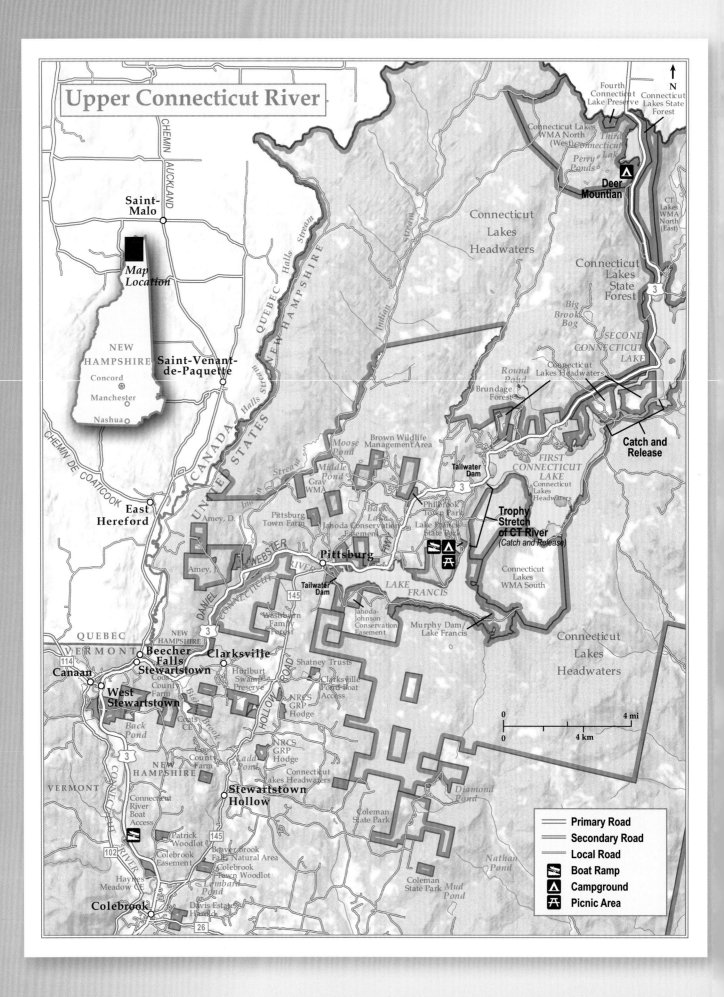

Upper Connecticut River

Saint-Malo

Map Location

NEW HAMPSHIRE

Concord

Manchester

Nashua

Saint-Venant-de-Paquette

East Hereford

CHEMIN AUCKLAND

CHEMIN DE COATICOOK

QUEBEC

CANADA

UNITED STATES

NEW HAMPSHIRE

Halls Stream

Indian Stream

Indian Stream

Halls Stream

Stream

Fourth Connecticut Lake Preserve

Connecticut Lakes State Forest

Connecticut Lakes WMA North (West)

Third Connecticut Lake

Perry Ponds

Deer Mountian

CT Lakes WMA North (East)

Connecticut Lakes Headwaters

Connecticut Lakes State Forest

Big Brook Bog

SECOND CONNECTICUT LAKE

Round Pond

Connecticut Lakes Headwaters

Brundage Forest

Catch and Release

FIRST CONNECTICUT LAKE

Connecticut Lakes Headwaters

Moose Pond

Brown Wildlife Management Area

Middle Pond

Gray WMA

Tailwater Dam

Philbrook Tower Park

Trophy Stretch of CT River *(Catch and Release)*

Pittsburg Town Farm

Amey, D.

Amey, J.

Pittsburg Town Farm

Jahoda Conservation Easement

Back Lake

Lake Francis State Park

Pittsburg

WEBSTER ROAD

DANIEL WEBSTER

CONNECTICUT RIVER

Tailwater Dam

LAKE FRANCIS

Connecticut Lakes WMA South

Connecticut Lakes Headwaters

Washburn Family Forest

Jahoda-Johnson Conservation Easement

Murphy Dam / Lake Francis

QUEBEC

VERMONT

NEW HAMPSHIRE

Beecher Falls
Stewartstown

Clarksville

Canaan

West Stewartstown

Coos County Farm

Bishop Brook

Hurlburt Swamp Preserve

HOLLOW ROAD

Shatney Trusts

Clarksville Pond Boat Access

NRCS GRP Hodge

Coats CE

Back Pond

County Farm

Ladd Pond

NRCS GRP Hodge

Connecticut Lakes Headwaters

Diamond Pond

VERMONT

NEW HAMPSHIRE

Stewartstown Hollow

Coleman State Park

Connecticut River Boat Access

Patrick Woodlot

Colebrook Easement

Beaver Brook Falls Natural Area

Colebrook Town Woodlot

Lombard Pond

Haynes Meadow CE

Davis Estate Hardch

Colebrook

Coleman State Park

Nathan Pond

Mud Pond

N

	Primary Road
	Secondary Road
	Local Road
	Boat Ramp
	Campground
	Picnic Area

0		4 mi
0		4 km

Upper Connecticut River *(Northern New Hampshire)*

➤ **Location:** Northern New Hampshire is a 4½-hour drive from Boston or Portland, Maine, and 3½ hours from Manchester, NH, the closest airport.

The headwaters of the Connecticut River rise at the U.S./Canadian border at the northern tip of New Hampshire in the town of Pittsburg. The river flows through a chain of mountain lakes—the Connecticut Lakes—before beginning its journey to Long Island Sound. Tailwater dams keep river water cold all summer below First Connecticut Lake and Lake Francis.

The Upper Connecticut has three distinctly different stretches. From below Second Lake, the river is small, with 60 cfs the common flow. This section is home to brook trout and wild landlocked salmon. Slightly stained with tannins, this freestone stretch features a cascading waterfall ("Falls in the River") along with riffles, pools, and a wonderful pond area where Dry Brook enters. Small brook trout and small salmon are in the river year-round, but in the spring (early May), large landlocks come into the mouth of the river from First Lake to feed on spring-spawning baitfish. In the fall, lake salmon return to the river to spawn, providing another chance to catch salmon 15 to 20 inches. From the dam to the bridge on Magalloway Road, regulations are fly-fishing-only, catch-and-release. From the bridge to Green's Point on First Lake, fly-fishing-only, two salmon per day, 15 inches minimum; for trout, 5 fish or 5 pounds; and for lake trout, 2 fish 18 inches or greater.

Below First Lake is the much-written-about Trophy Stretch. Here, flows are normally 150–300 cfs, with cold water flowing all summer. Dams on the Connecticut Lakes are managed for recreation. Power generation on the Connecticut occurs much farther south, a real plus for anglers. Riffles, runs, and pools are easily waded. Conservation easements along the river provide access along this forested section. Favorite pools include Doc's, Bridge, The Skating Rink, Judge's, and Jury Box. In this nearly 2-mile stretch, you'll find brook, rainbow, and brown trout, along with landlocked salmon and the occasional lake trout. Trout and salmon are in the river year-round, with the larger salmon entering in the spring, and

during the fall spawning run. Fly-fishing-only regulations apply from the dam nearly to Lake Francis, with a two-fish limit; trout above 12 inches and salmon above 15 inches.

Below Lake Francis, the last in the chain, water temps seldom exceed 50 degrees even in the heat of summer. This keeps water cold enough for trout for more than 30 miles downstream. Normal water flows are 300–500 cfs. There is no fly-fishing designation to the water in this stretch, catch limits are 5 fish or 5 pounds for trout, and two salmon above 15 inches. In this section, you'll find browns, brookies, and rainbows. Access is easy below the dam and along U.S. 3 in Pittsburg. The river becomes the New Hampshire–Vermont state line below Pittsburg, and access points become less frequent. Below the bridge in West Stewartstown/Canaan, Vermont is

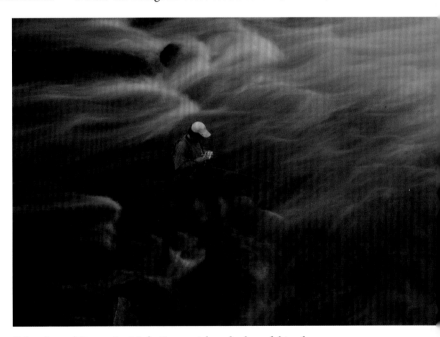

Below Second Connecticut Lake Dam, catch-and-release fishing for brook trout and landlocked salmon. Lopstick Outfitters

a fishing access for wading or launching. Kayaks, canoes, and drift boats become the preferred method for fishing, as the river has become larger with the influx from Indian, Halls, and Leach Stream tributaries. Large brown trout haunt these waters and can be found in the deeper pools.

Hatches begin in early May, during the salmon run. Overcast afternoons with temps above 50 often see Blue-winged Olive hatches. In early June, the caddis hatch begins. The Connecticut is a caddis river. Caddis are so prevalent that a properly presented imitation will bring fish to the surface even without a hatch. Other notable hatches are summer stones. In early July, look for Little Yellow Sallies, while the large Black Stones dominate the evenings in late July and August. Lower stretches of the river see more mayflies—Blue-winged Olives, Sulphurs, and *Callibaetis*—as well as terrestrials in late summer. During the last two weeks of August, an incredible hatch of Cinnamon Flying Ants occurs in the Colebrook, New Hampshire, area.

While the Upper Connecticut River is the main fishing attraction of the area, it is worthy to note the many other fishing opportunities, all within a 15-mile radius of Pittsburg and the Connecticut Lakes. The Upper Connecticut has tributary streams that hold brook trout. There are seven fly-fishing-only wilderness ponds accessed by well-maintained logging roads. The Connecticut Lakes are home to lake trout and landlocked salmon, while Back Lake has good trout and smallmouth bass fishing. From early May to October 15 (the season's close) there are always fishing opportunities no matter the weather.

➤ **Hatches:** *Caddis:* Late May–October.
BWOs: May–October.
Little Yellow Stones: July.
Sulphurs: mid-June to the end of June.
Stones: August–early September.
Light Cahills: mid-June to the end of June.
Cinnamon Ants: mid-August.
Hendricksons: mid-May to the end of May.
Midges and Griffith's Gnats: May.

➤ **Fishing Regulations:** Pittsburg Dam at Second Connecticut Lake to upstream side of logging bridge on Magalloway Road: Eastern brook trout and landlocked salmon January 1 through October 15, fly fishing only, catch-and-release.

From Magalloway Road Bridge to inlet at Green Point on First Connecticut Lake: Eastern brook trout and landlocked salmon January 1 through October 15, fly fishing only. Daily limit for brook trout is two fish.

First Connecticut Lake dam to the signs on Lake Francis: Eastern brook trout, rainbow trout, brown trout, and land-

Nice brown caught with a Bugger on the Upper Connecticut River near Colebrook. Lopstick Outfitters

Average brookie caught in the "Trophy Stretch" of the Upper Connecticut River, Pittsburg. Lopstick Outfitters

First Connecticut Lake Dam is the start of the "Trophy Stretch" of the Upper Connecticut River in Pittsburg. Lopstick Outfitters

locked salmon January 1 through October 15; fly fishing only. Daily limit for brook trout is two fish, minimum length 12 inches.

From below Murphy Dam in Pittsburg: brook trout, brown trout, rainbow trout, and their hybrids, January 1 to October 15, 5 fish or 5 pounds daily limit, whichever is reached first; no length limit.

➤ **Tackle:** A 9-foot, 5-weight rod with a floating line is a great all-around outfit for the area. Full- sinking and sink-tip lines are good in the spring for streamer fishing or pond fishing, but always carry a floating line: You can always make a floating line sink, but can never make a sinking line float. Bring both 7½-foot leaders for nymphing and 9-foot leaders for dries. For fishing in the upper sections, a softer, lighter rod such as a 3- or 4-weight can be fun for small dries and emergers, but on the lower sections where longer, accurate casts are important, a fast, 9-foot rod is preferred.

Author Lisa Savard with son Corey on the Yellowstone River in Montana.

LISA SAVARD is a licensed New Hampshire fly-fishing and upland hunting guide. Lisa has fished the Upper Connecticut and its tributaries for more than 40 years. Together with her husband, Tim, they owned Lopstick Lodge and Cabins and Lopstick Outfitters, an Orvis-Endorsed Fly Fishing Outfitter, for more than 20 years. Recently starting a new life chapter, Lisa and Tim have resettled near Missoula, Montana.

CLOSEST FLY SHOPS

Lopstick Outfitters
First Connecticut Lake
45 Stewart Young Rd.
Pittsburg, NH 03592
800-538-6659
www.Lopstick.com

North Country Fly Shop
9 Mountain Ash Dr.
Pittsburg, NH 03592
603-538-1151

Ducret's
133 Main St.
Colebrook, NH 03576
603-237-4900

CLOSEST OUTFITTERS

Lopstick Outfitters (above)

Tall Timber
Beach Rd.
Pittsburg, NH 03592
603-538-6651
www.talltimber.com

Osprey Adventures
Columbia, NH 03576
603-922-3800
www.ospreyfishingadventures.com

CLOSEST LODGING

Cabins at Lopstick
First Connecticut Lake
45 Stewart Young Rd.
Pittsburg, NH 03592
800-538-6659
www.CabinsatLopstick.com

Tall Timber Lodge
Beach Rd.
Pittsburg, NH 03592
603-538-6651
www.talltimber.com

CLOSEST CAMPGROUNDS

Lake Francis State Campground
River Rd.
Pittsburg, NH 03592
603-538-6965
www.nhstateparks.org

RESTAURANTS

Rainbow Grille & Tavern
Beach Rd.
Pittsburg, NH 03592
603-538-9556
www.rainbowgrille.com

Buck Rub Pizza Pub
Main St.
Pittsburg, NH 03592
603-538-6935
www.buckrubpub.com

Dube's Pit Stop Breakfast and Lunch
Main St.
Pittsburg, NH 03592
603-538-9944

CLOSEST EMERGENCY MEDICAL HELP

Upper Connecticut Valley Hospital
181 Corliss Lane
Colebrook, NH 03576
603-237-4971

45th Parallel EMS
46 Ramsey Rd.
Colebrook, NH 03576
603-237-5593

CELL PHONE SERVICE
Limited cell phone service in Pittsburg. Best cell service is south of Stewartstown and in Colebrook.

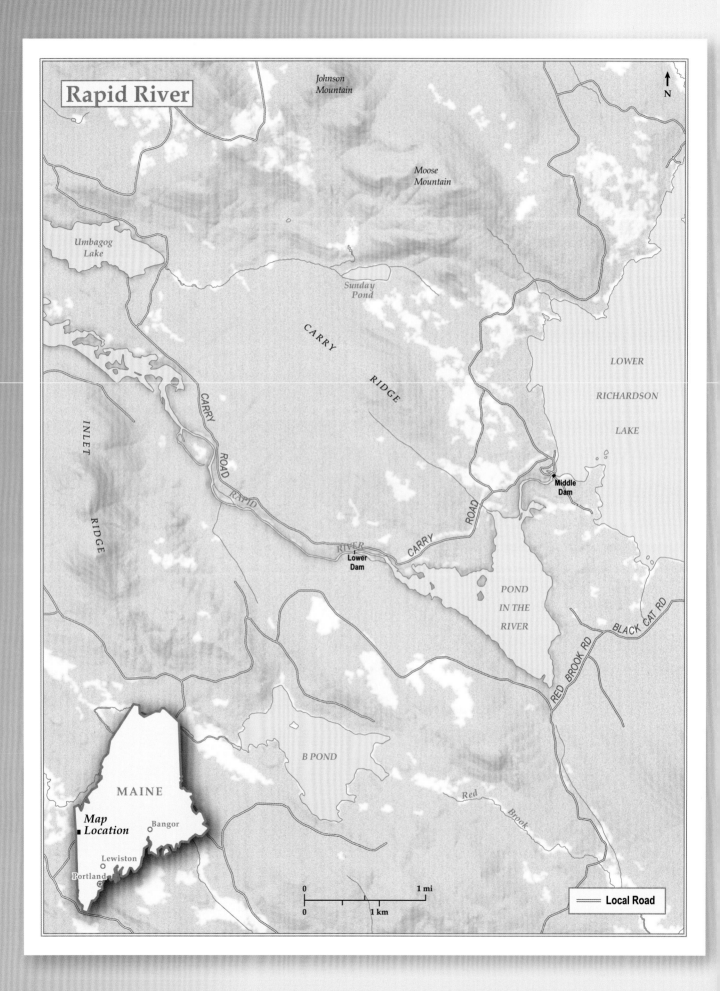

Rapid River

Johnson
Mountain

Moose
Mountain

Umbagog
Lake

Sunday
Pond

CARRY

RIDGE

LOWER

RICHARDSON

LAKE

INLET

CARRY

ROAD

RIDGE

RAPID

RIVER

CARRY

ROAD

Middle
Dam

Lower
Dam

POND

IN THE

RIVER

BLACK CAT RD

RED BROOK RD

B POND

Red

Brook

MAINE

Map
Location

Bangor

Lewiston

Portland

0   1 mi

0   1 km

Local Road

➤ **Location:** Western Maine, about a 4-hour ride from Boston; and about 3 hours from both Portland and Bangor, Maine, and Manchester, New Hampshire. Full-service airports are available in all four cities.

The Rapid River is the finest native Eastern brook trout river in the United States. Anglers would need to travel to Canada to find a better one. There are also landlocked (Atlantic) salmon in the Rapid; the salmon are introduced. The trout and salmon in the Rapid are now naturally reproducing—none are stocked.

The Rapid River is rich in angling history. Carrie Stevens developed her renowned Grey Ghost streamer just a few miles from the Rapid at Upper Dam, located between Mooselookmeguntic and Richardson Lakes. The latter is the headwaters of the Rapid. Louise Dickinson Rich wrote her book *We Took to the Woods* while staying at a cabin on the banks of the Rapid. For decades, the now defunct Lower Dam on the Rapid was synonymous with fly fishing in Maine.

The Rapid River is located in a large, working forest. It is surrounded by conservation easements prohibiting logging or development within 165 feet of the water. There is minimal development, with just a handful of small, rustic cabins. There is no power except at Middle Dam—the beginning of the river. Access is via a network of dirt roads. It is restricted by locked gates and requires a walk of roughly 30 minutes—unless you hire a guide or are staying at one of the sporting camps. The closest paved road is roughly 5 miles away.

The Rapid River is a medium-size freestone river with flows in the 300–800 cfs range. Fishing season starts early, by Northern New England standards. While many Maine rivers are running high due to snowmelt, the Rapid is usually fishable by the April 1 opener. By mid-May, fishing is in full swing. After a midsummer drop-off due to warm water, fishing picks up again in late August and keeps getting better until the season closes at the end of September.

Between Middle Dam and Lake Umbagog there are more than 3 miles of moving water. Less than a mile down from

Middle Dam, the river is interrupted by the aptly named Pond in the River. Below this 500-acre pond, the river flows unbroken to Lake Umbagog. Above and below the pond, the Rapid lives up to its name by dropping more than 800 feet in elevation before terminating at the lake.

Brook trout in the 12- to 16-inch range are common. There are a surprising number of brook trout in the 18- to 20-inch range. Fish over 20 inches are always possible. The landlocked salmon run smaller than the brook trout. Fish above 18 inches are rare, but possible. The average salmon is 12 to 14 inches. The Rapid is a true trophy fishery. Many anglers catch the "fish-of-a-lifetime" here.

Water flows are quite predictable. While you may see a bump while you are there, these are rarely more than a mi-

Lower Dam on the Rapid. Richard V. Procopio

nor inconvenience and never life-threatening. Water is usually low for the first month of the season, followed by a brief bubble coinciding with ice-out on the lakes above. By late spring, flows are low and usually stay there until the end of the season.

The Rapid is a wading river. Boating is best left to the whitewater enthusiasts. The one exception is Pond in the River where the only way to fish it is with a small boat. Anglers do, however, see small prams and canoes used to gain

The Rapid River. Richard V. Procopio

*Inset. Guide client with Rapid brook trout.
Pond in the River Guide Service*

access to hard-to-reach spots such as First and Second Current. A canoe can also be used to get from Pond in the River to Lower Dam.

While fish are taken in many different ways on the Rapid, it is primarily a nymphing river. Early in the season, fish will take streamers. After that, streamer fishing is rarely your best bet, at least in regard to numbers. Trout and salmon will surface feed when a hatch is on. They will also take the occasional attractor. But like midseason streamer fishing, attractors are generally not your best choice.

➤ **Hatches:** The trout and salmon in the Rapid River feed on minnows, insects, crayfish, and eggs. The predominant minnows are smelt, dace, and sculpin. Insects include hellgrammites, stoneflies, mayflies, caddis, and midges. Aquatic worms are also present. In early May, large brook trout feed heavily on sucker eggs. While I have never witnessed it, the brook trout are large enough to eat the occasional mouse, as do their peers in Canada.

While rarely what you would call epic, the hatches on the Rapid are fairly consistent. The first hatches of the year are in mid-May and consist of Quill Gordons and Hendricksons. Small BWOs hatch on and off all season. Stoneflies of varying sizes and colors hatch throughout the season. The largest stoneflies are the late spring–midsummer Goldens, best imitated with a #8 pattern. Caddis hatch most evenings starting in late May and ending mid-September.

➤ **Fishing Regulations:** The Rapid River is that all-too-rare fishery where the powers that be do almost everything right. Managed under fly-fishing-only, catch-and-release, and barbless-hooks-only restrictions, the brook trout are the most protected fish in Maine. The nonnative landlocked salmon are less protected, with a 3-fish, 12-inch minimum. Regulations on the pond are the same as the river, with one exception—there is a brief midsummer closure to protect fish seeking refuge from the warm river water.

➤ **Tackle:** Use a 9-foot, 5-weight rod and floating line. For streamers, you'll want a 9-foot 6-weight with a sink-tip. While longer rods can work, shorter rods are not practical. I recommend fluorocarbon leaders and tippet. Strike indi-

Late spring brook trout. Pond in the River Guide Service

cators should be large enough to float two flies and added weight. Flies should include smelt and sculpin streamer patterns; mayfly and stonefly nymphs; all stages of caddis in a variety of sizes and colors; and small, cheese-colored eggs in the spring.

BOB MALLARD has fly fished for 35 years, and owns Kennebec River Outfitters in Madison, Maine. His writing has appeared in local, regional, and national fly-fishing publications. Look for Bob's upcoming book *50 Best Places to Fly Fish the Northeast* due out late 2013 or early 2014.

CLOSEST FLY SHOPS
Rangeley Region Sport Shop
2529 Main St.
Rangeley, ME
207-864-5615
www.rangeleysportshop.com
rivertoridge@aol.com

Kennebec River Outfitters
469 Lakewood Rd.
Madison, ME
207-474-2500
www.kennebecriveroutfitters.com
info@kennebecriveroutfitters.com

Sun Valley Sports
129 Sunday River Rd.
Bethel, ME
207-824-7533
www.sunvalleysports.com

CLOSEST OUTFITTERS/GUIDES
Pond in the River Guide Service
207-864-9140
www.rangeleyflyfishing.com
info@rangeleyflyfishing.com

CLOSEST LODGES
Lakewood Camps (rustic cabins)
Middle Dam, ME
207-243-2959
www.lakewoodcamps.com

Forest Lodge (rustic cabins)
Lower Dam, ME
207-650-3890
www.rapidriverflyfishing.com

Pond in the River Guide Service
(apartment and house rentals)
Downtown Rangeley and Wilson Mills
207-864-9140
www.rangeleyflyfishing.com
info@rangeleyflyfishing.com

BEST CAMPGROUND
Cupsuptic Campground
(tent and camper/trailer sites)
Route 16
Oquossoc, ME
207-864-5249
www.cupsupticcampground.com
info@cupsupticcampground.com

BEST RESTAURANT
Loon Lodge
16 Pickford Rd.
Rangeley, ME
207-864-5666
www.loonlodgeme.com
info@loonlodgeme.com

Moosely Bagels
(breakfast, lunch, and food/coffee to go)
2588 Main St.
Rangeley, ME
207-864-5955

CLOSEST PLACE TO GET A COLD, STIFF DRINK
Parkside & Main
(lunch and dinner, full bar)
2520 Main St.
Rangeley, ME
207-864-3774

CLOSEST EMERGENCY MEDICAL HELP
Rangeley Health Center
Rangeley Health and Wellness
Rangeley, ME 04970 – 1 hour away
207-864-4397
Monday-Wednesday-Thursday-
Friday: 8 AM-4:30 PM, Tuesday 9 AM-6 PM

Franklin Memorial Hospital
111 Franklin Health Commons
Farmington, ME 04938 – 90 minutes away
207-778-6031

CELL PHONE SERVICE
Not reliable.

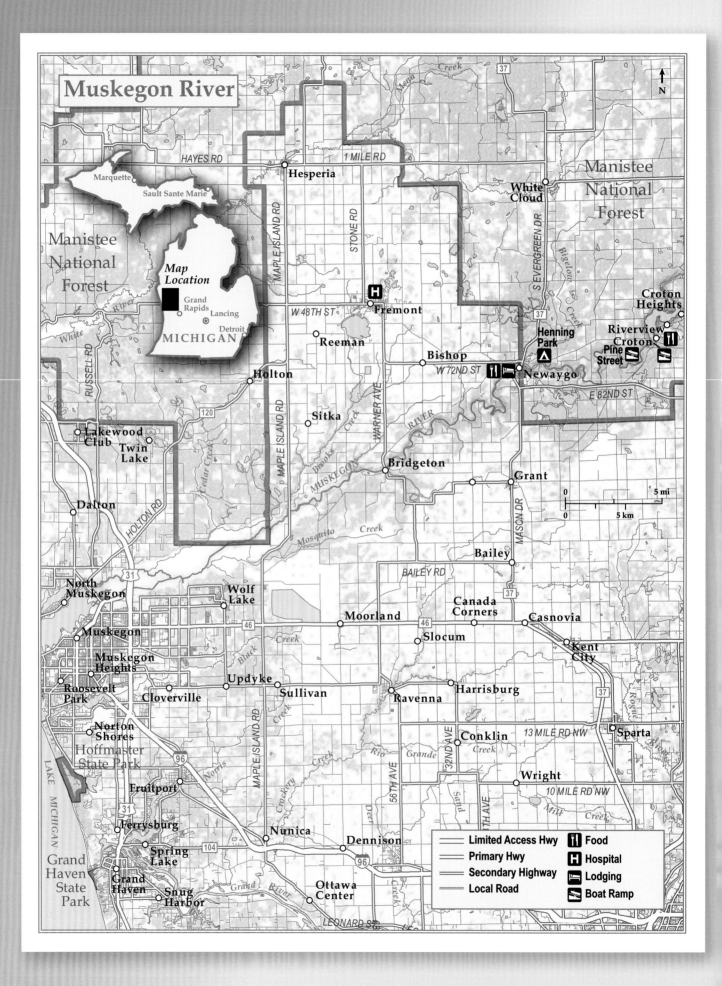

Muskegon River

Manistee National Forest

Marquette

Sault Sante Marie

Manistee National Forest

Map Location

Grand Rapids   Lancing

MICHIGAN   Detroit

HAYES RD   1 MILE RD

Hesperia

White Cloud

Manistee National Forest

RUSSELL RD

MAPLE ISLAND RD

STONE RD

S EVERGREEN DR

Bigelow Creek

Croton Heights

W 48TH ST   Fremont

Riverview Croton

Reeman   Henning Park   Pine Street

Bishop   Newaygo

W 72ND ST   E 82ND ST

Holton   WARNER AVE   RIVER

120

Sitka

MAPLE ISLAND RD   Brooks Creek   MUSKEGON

Lakewood Club   Twin Lake   Bridgeton   Grant

MASON DR   0   5 mi

0   5 km

Dalton   Mosquito Creek

HOLTON RD   Bailey

BAILEY RD

North Muskegon   Wolf Lake   37

31   Moorland   Canada Corners   Casnovia

46   Slocum   Kent City

Muskegon   Black Creek

Muskegon Heights   Updyke   Sullivan   Ravenna   Harrisburg   37

Roosevelt Park   Cloverville

Norton Shores   Conklin   13 MILE RD NW   Sparta

Hoffmaster State Park   96   Rio Grande   32ND AVE   Creek   Rogue River

LAKE MICHIGAN   Norris Creek   Wright   10 MILE RD NW

Fruitport   Crockery Creek   56TH AVE   Mill Creek

Ferrysburg   Nunica   Dennison   Said

Grand Haven State Park   Spring Lake   104   96

Grand Haven   Snug Harbor   Grand River   Ottawa Center

LEONARD ST

Limited Access Hwy	Food
Primary Hwy	Hospital
Secondary Highway	Lodging
Local Road	Boat Ramp

N

➤ **Location:** The Muskegon is located in west-central Michigan, in the state's Lower Peninsula. The river is about an hour north of Grand Rapids, and approximately a 4-hour drive from Chicago or 6 hours from Cleveland.

The Muskegon is one of the Midwest's great fishing rivers. It is a long river, flowing for 228 miles from its source in northeast Michigan to its mouth. The river is peppered with dams, with the most famous tailwater stretch below Croton Dam in Newaygo, Michigan. Below that dam, it flows for 46 miles. The river system has a long logging history, and remnants from its past can be seen in the tailwater stretches of the river. The river contains a high percentage of gravel and rock as its substrate, and this makes it excellent habitat for many species of fish and their forage.

This tailwater stretch of the river is truly a special place. The fishing is seasonal, with great trout fishing in the spring months, followed by excellent warmwater fishing for smallmouth bass during the summer. The grand finale comes in the fall, when fresh migratory steelhead and king salmon enter from Lake Michigan. The King salmon spawn and die by November, however, the steelhead remain in the river until spring. A significant run of steelhead arrives in November, with fresh fish trickling in through the winter months, meeting up with another heavy run of fish in March and April. The several species available, coupled with the fact that it generally runs clear, makes this a year-round fishery that always has great potential.

The river is renowned for its trout fishing in the spring and early summer. Starting in March and April, chunky trout are caught behind the spawning steelhead. Late-winter stoneflies also provide some good fishing. As the days get longer and we progress into May, the real fun begins. Streamer and wet-fly fishing is the first to pick up, as brown and rainbow trout gorge on salmon and steelhead fry. By mid-May, caddis are hatching. This is followed by the first emergences of Sulphur mayflies. The hatch everyone waits for on the Muskegon is the Gray Drake, which has a fantastic but unpredictable spinner fall. Below the riffles and gravel areas, anglers will find plump 13- to 15-inch trout with the occasional big fish of 20 inches or

more. The Gray Drakes are followed by wonderful *Isonychia* emergences and spinner falls. The *Isos* make for good dry-fly fishing. These bugs also make for some excellent wet-fly fishing with emergent dun patterns. As summer closes in, Blue-winged Olive hatches peak, typically around July 4.

The Muskegon gets warm during the summer months, and many anglers switch their focus away from resident trout to smallmouth bass. The Muskegon, and many of the surrounding fisheries, are excellent for hard-fighting bronzebacks. During July and August, you can expect the very best fishing for smallies on crayfish patterns fished and twitched below a small float. Stripping colorful suspending streamers is another exciting way to fish. However, the most visual form of fishing is with poppers. As you head below the town of Newaygo, you will find more and more of this excellent

Fly fishing the Muskegon on a fall morning. Kevin Feenstra

surface fishing. Typically, the lower and clearer the water is, the more smallmouth you will catch, as they rely heavily on sight to feed. Furthermore, as the summer progresses, the number of smallmouths in the river increases as fish move out of the river mouth and into the river system.

While fishing the lower reaches of the Muskegon for smallmouth, we often see the first migratory fish of the season. King salmon begin to ascend from Lake Michigan on the cooler nights in September, and salmon fishing peaks in mid-

Panorama of a fall morning. Kevin Feenstra

October. The river is quite a spectacle at that time of the year with the brilliant changing colors in the surrounding deciduous trees and thousands of salmon on their spawning run.

The Chinook (king) salmon are only a precursor to the great fish that soon arrive on their heels. By mid-October, a fish with a square tail shows up, feeding behind the spawning kings. The first steelhead to appear are caught on egg flies and nymphs, as dead leaves and weeds can make swinging flies challenging in the early weeks. By the end of October, however, conditions are prime for swinging streamer patterns. These brilliant chrome fish average 5 to 8 pounds, but may grow much larger. Traditional Western patterns do work on our steelhead, however, flies with a lot of flash shaped like native minnows and sculpin are more productive. Such patterns produce jarring, memorable strikes on a regular basis.

The Muskegon is one of the few places where anglers can fish for steelhead for over 100 days on end, from mid-October until May, with a good chance at catching fish at any time. As winter comes, swung flies can still be used effectively while fished through tailouts and slow pools. However, because the water temperatures are very cold and large numbers of fish are available, many fly anglers opt for nymph-fishing techniques during the winter months. Winter fishing is very rewarding, but be advised that it can be cold. The Muskegon is over 100 feet wide in most places, and the biting winter wind is hard to avoid. Though it is not for everyone, there is something very special about catching a steelhead on a bitter-cold Michigan winter day. You may fish for hours without a bite, fighting with ice in your guides, while enduring cold hands and feet. And then, suddenly, it happens—a large chrome fish pulling line out of your hands as the ice falls off the rod.

During these coldest weather periods, the trout are a bonus fishery. There are great local anglers who wait all year to catch trout in the winter. They use tiny midge patterns, Pheasant-tails, and Brassies under indicators to catch numerous trout. This is a very nice diversion in the dead of winter, and is accessible to the wading angler.

The Muskegon offers trout, smallmouth bass, steelhead, and salmon as its main species. But there is much more available for the angler willing to explore. Seasonally, you can catch large northern pike, largemouth bass, walleyes, channel catfish, and many other resident species. Lake-run brown trout are great migratory gamefish that are common, but largely ignored. Lake-run browns arrive in September and are available through the winter months. They will take a variety of stripped baitfish presentations.

Some parts of the river are developed, with cottages around its banks. Large tracts of the river remain undeveloped in every stretch, and it is a beautiful place throughout. It is common to see white-tailed deer, bald eagles, ospreys, herons, mink, otters, and other wildlife around this magnificent river. If you love to fly fish and appreciate natural beauty, chances are that you will find something appealing in this gorgeous and unique river system.

➤ **Hatches:** January–February: winter midge hatches, early winter stoneflies, #18–#20.

February–April: Early Brown Stones, #14–#18.

May: tan caddis, #18.

Late May to mid-June: Sulphurs, #16–#18; Gray Drakes, #10–#14.

June: *Isonychias*, #10–#14; Light Cahills, #16; Cinnamon Caddis, #18; Green Caddis, #18–#20.

July–September: Blue-winged Olives, #18–#22; various caddis, #18–#20.

Kevin's boat on a typical October morning. Kevin Feenstra

September: increasing tan caddis, #18; terrestrials such as ants, #16–#22.

October–November: tan caddis, #18, occasional; BWOs, #18–#20.

December: Midges.

➤ **Fishing Regulations:** Open year-round below Croton. Because regulations change periodically, consult the current Michigan fishing guide for creel limits. There are no restrictions on motors; flat-bottomed boats and drift boats can both be used effectively. It is common to see jet sleds on the river. There are trailer spotting services available from Croton Dam to Newaygo.

➤ **Tackle:** Rods: Use 9-foot 5- or 6-weights for trout and smallmouth bass. Use 9- or 10-foot, 8- or 9-weights for steelhead and salmon.

Two-handed rods are also excellent tools for steelhead, and the river is one of the premier Midwest rivers for Spey fishing, with 12½- to 14-foot, fast-action rods in the 8- to 9-weight category ideal.

Reels: For trout and smallmouth bass, any reel that holds a 5- or 6-weight line will be adequate. A disk drag can be helpful, as you may encounter a steelhead while trout fishing in the spring and fall. When steelhead or salmon fishing, use a large reel with a disk drag. If you are going to fish in the winter, select a reel with less porting, as it will be less likely to freeze up.

Lines: Much of the trout and smallmouth bass fishing is with weight-forward floating lines, though it is always useful to have a 200-grain sink-tip for the occasional streamer fishing for resident fish. The steelhead fishing can be very specialized—for swinging flies, an intermediate Skagit line with T14 or equivalent for tips is very good. Floating lines with tips also are adequate, but for coldwater work, it is important to get the fly deep and keep it there.

Leaders: Use long leaders for dry-fly fishing for trout. Nymphing with good-size indicators is also deadly. Trout can be caught on indicators anytime the river is clear throughout the year. The most common tippet size for trout is 5X to 6X. Whether for trout or steelhead, the leaders for sink-tip lines are short, typically 3 to 4 feet, with 10- to 14-pound tippet.

Wading gear: There is good wading access in various places. Consult with a local fly or tackle shop to make sure conditions are OK. Most of the wading is done between Croton Dam and Newaygo. Breathable waders are fine from April to November; however, during the cold winter months, boot-foot waders are highly recommended and can make the weather bearable. Capilene-style underwear is also important.

Great streamer-caught brown trout. Kevin Feenstra

The Muskegon is many things, including a great smallmouth stream. Kevin Feenstra

Facing. Quiet summer evening on the Muskegon. Kevin Feenstra

Kevin Feenstra with a nice chrome hen caught on the swung fly. Photo by Jane Feenstra

KEVIN FEENSTRA has fished the streams of western Michigan since he was very young. In his early twenties, he began guiding as an alternative to graduate school. Now 15 years later, he has never looked back. Kevin's passion is swinging flies for Midwestern steelhead, but he loves to fly fish for any predator that swims. He now resides in Newaygo, Michigan, guiding 180–200 days each year on the Muskegon River system.

CLOSEST FLY SHOPS
Great Lakes Flyfishing Company
8460 Algoma Ave. Ste. E.
Rockford, MI 49341
616-866-6060
www.troutmoor.net
glffc@troutmoor.net

Hex Shop
1144 East Paris Ave. #2
Grand Rapids, MI 49546
616-977-3655
www.thehexshop.com
info@thehexshop.com

Nomad Anglers
1600 East Beltline Ave. NE
Grand Rapids, MI 49525
616-805-4393
brian@nomadanglers.com
www.nomadanglers.com

CLOSEST OUTFITTERS/GUIDES
Feenstra Guide Service
PO Box 640
Newaygo, MI 49337
231-652-3528
www.feenstraguideservice.com
info@feenstraguideservice.com

Hulst Outfitters
5131 W 72nd
Fremont, MI 49412
231-598-2443
www.michiganriverguide.com
nathan@michiganriverguide.com

River Quest Charters
2109 E. Garber Rd.
Newaygo, MI 49337
616-293-0501
www.riverquestcharters.com
fishon@riverquestcharters.com

CLOSEST LODGES
Gray Drake Lodge
7522 S. Gray Drake Bluff
Newaygo, MI 49337
231-652 2868
www.graydrake.com

Muskegon River Lodge
2109 E Garber Rd.
Newaygo, MI 49337
616-293-0501;
info@muskegonriverlodge.com
www.muskegonriverlodge.com

BEST HOTEL
Cronk's Oakridge Hotel
9135 Mason Dr.
Newaygo, MI 49337
231-652-1288
www.cronks-oakridge.com

BEST CAMPGROUND
Henning Park (a Newaygo County park)
500 Croton Rd.
Newaygo, MI 49337
231-652 1202

BEST RESTAURANT
Hit the Road Joe
7291 Elm Ave.
Newaygo, MI 49337
231-652-6020
www.hittheroadjoe.moonfruit.com

BEST PLACE TO GET A COLD, STIFF DRINK
Northern Trails Bar/Grill
7242 East 88th St.
Newaygo, MI 49337
231-937-7604

CLOSEST EMERGENCY MEDICAL HELP
Gerber Memorial Hospital
212 S. Sullivan Ave.
Fremont, MI 49412
231-924-3300

CELL PHONE SERVICE
Cell phone service is available on the river especially near the town of Newaygo. Coverage improves every year and it is likely that you will be able to stay in touch regardless of what stretch you are fishing. As you work your way downriver past Newaygo and down toward Muskegon, there are areas that have very limited coverage.

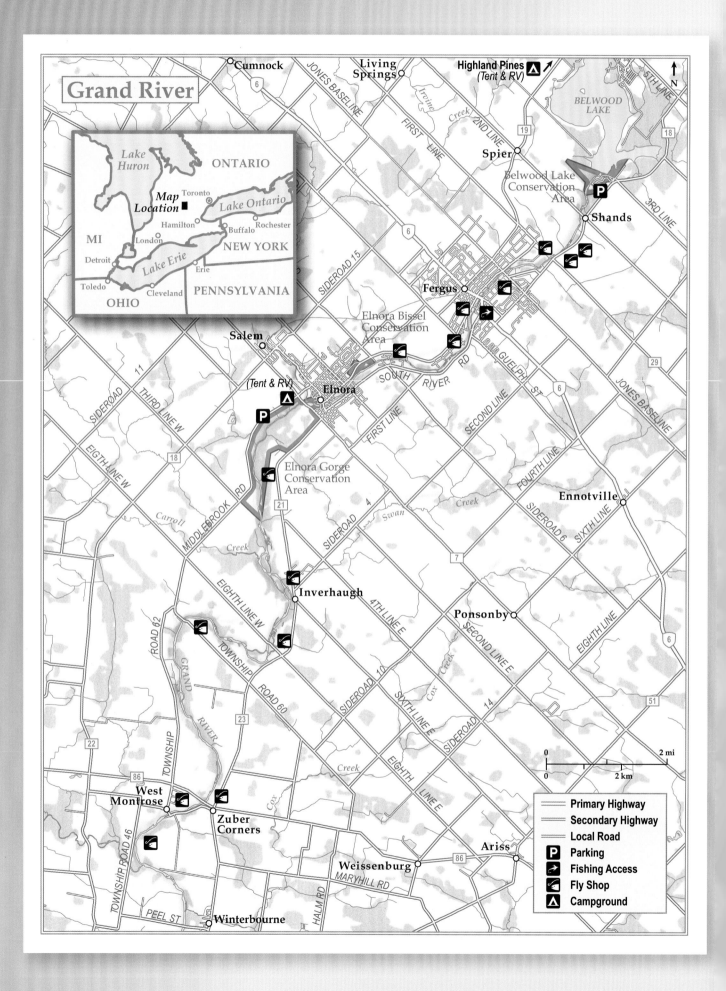

Grand River

Map Location

Lake Huron · ONTARIO · Toronto · Lake Ontario · Hamilton · Rochester · London · Buffalo · NEW YORK · MI · Lake Erie · Detroit · Erie · OHIO · Toledo · Cleveland · PENNSYLVANIA

Cumnock

Living Springs

Highland Pines *(Tent & RV)*

N

BELWOOD LAKE

5TH LINE

Spier

Belwood Lake Conservation Area

Shands

Fergus

Elnora Bissel Conservation Area

Salem

(Tent & RV)

Elnora

SOUTH RIVER

GUELPH ST

Elnora Gorge Conservation Area

Ennotville

Inverhaugh

Ponsonby

West Montrose

Zuber Corners

Weissenburg

Ariss

Winterbourne

Legend

— Primary Highway
— Secondary Highway
— Local Road
P Parking
→ Fishing Access
Fly Shop
⛺ Campground

Scale: 0 — 2 mi / 0 — 2 km

Grand River (Southwest Ontario, Canada)

➤ **Location:** The Grand River is in southwest Ontario, Canada, about 2 hours from Buffalo, 3 from Detroit, and an hour from Toronto's Pearson International airport. From its source, it flows south through Grand Valley, Fergus, Elora, Waterloo, Kitchener, Cambridge, Paris, Brantford, Caledonia, and Cayuga before emptying into the north shore of Lake Erie south of Dunnville, at Port Maitland.

Wading through the clear waters towards a pod of rising fish, surrounded by limestone bluffs, cedar trees, and clouds of mayflies, who'd have known that only a couple of decades ago this river was barren of trout? Government, community, and volunteers have made improvements to transform it into the most popular brown trout fishery in eastern Canada.

The Upper Grand tailwater has a solid brown trout fishery, and the amenities to make it a favourite destination for trout addicts. The Grand flows through the quaint villages of Fergus and Elora, towns that provide the services anglers look for that greatly add to the fishing experience. The downtowns are dominated by old limestone buildings holding friendly pubs, numerous B&Bs, fine dining, and local specialty shops. Despite its proximity to the major population centres of Toronto, Hamilton, Kitchener/Waterloo, London, Detroit, and Buffalo, the river is rarely crowded.

Constant flows provided by the Grand River Dam—commonly called the Shand Dam—allow insect populations to flourish. The cold, nutrient-rich water feeds an abundance of aquatic insects that grow fat trout. Big fish feed heavily on the surface during the day throughout the season. From May through September, there is usually some sort of hatch that brings fish to the surface every day.

This fishery was created when the Ministry of Natural Resources initiated a stocking program in 1988. The stocking continues, and is supplemented by some natural reproduction. The growth rates rival many other trophy rivers. Grand River browns are solid, strong fish.

The Grand River tailwater varies in character throughout this 28km (15 miles) of trout water, easily reached via more than 20 access points. The river's flow is usually between 4 and 7 cms (120–210 cfs). Much of the river has special regulations, where single barbless hooks are required; anglers must release all trout. This keeps the larger fish in the system to reward the skilled or lucky angler.

In general, the Grand Tailwater can be divided into three sections, each with its own unique character:

The upper reach between the Shand Dam and the town of Fergus is bedrock-controlled and heavily influenced by the dam. The Shand is a flow-augmentation and flood-control structure, not a pulsing hydropower dam. Access is easy, and big fish in the 16- to 24-inch range are common due to the consistent water conditions and wealth of food, largely caddis and midges. The upper river's limestone shelves are home to an incredible number of caddis. Bring your favorite emerger and pupa patterns, as big fish target transitional bugs. This is an area of the river that gets constant fishing pressure, so expect to see big fish working, but it may take a very good presentation to fool them.

The middle reach is characterised by limestone outcrops and cedar thickets that frame classic runs and pools. This

The Tooth of Time is the start of the Gorge. It's "treacherous hard" to get at runs and deep pools. Ken Collins

reach extends from the Town of Fergus down to the Low Level Bridge below the Elora Gorge. It is amazing that you can fish right in town and feel like you are miles away from civilization. The middle reach is where the hatches are more diverse and the crowds a bit thinner than the upper section hotspots. This is where many experienced Grand anglers stalk fish feasting on the glamour mayfly hatches.

The Elora Gorge is a highlight of a Grand River trip. Limestone cliffs up to 90 feet high frame the river and provide a perfect backdrop. However, once summer arrives, the Gorge is dominated by rubber rafts and inner tubes; fish early or

Cascade Falls in the gorge is a lovely scenic run. Ken Collins

A perfect example of what a brown trout should look like.

late. In June, the gorge features a variety of hatches including a solid *Isonychia* hatch just before the tubing season heats up.

The lower tailwater is wider, with long riffles and shallow pools. It is less influenced by the dam and has a lower density of fish, but there are some good ones. The lower river is an ideal place to hunt trout feeding on Hendricksons, Grey Foxes, Cahills, *Isonychias*, Brown Drakes, stoneflies, and caddis.

The fishing season on the Grand Tailwater runs from the fourth Saturday in April until September 30. The character of the river and the fishing changes with the seasons. From the opener to about mid-May, the best fishing is largely subsurface. The water is cold and clear, and bold streamers and well-placed nymphs account for the majority of hook-ups. But, be prepared with a few BWO emerger and dun patterns just in case.

As the water warms in mid-May, the first flushes of mayflies occur. The Hendrickson hatch in the lower and mid-reaches is the river's glory hatch; strong hatches are met with good numbers of anglers. We prefer to stay away from the crowds and begin targeting surface-feeding fish in early June, when there are overlapping hatches of Grey Fox, Light Cahill, BWO, crane fly, and caddisflies. The dry-fly action lasts throughout the day at this time of year, and the entire river fishes well through the month of June and the first couple of weeks of July.

July is our favourite. Caddis, crane flies, Cahills, and *Isonychia* are in high gear and we can usually find rising fish in solitude. The latter half of July sees the bugs getting smaller and the fishing a more technical, but by that time of year your skills are usually honed to take advantage of these opportunities.

Late July through mid-September is not the top time on the tailwater. Tiny flies, warming waters, and frequent algae blooms from the lake can make for challenging fishing. Anglers should be ready at dawn and dusk with #18 to #26 flies that imitate Tricos, caddis, midges, and BWOs. Have some flying ant imitations ready. Flying ant "hatches" are not predictable, but if they happen, you don't want to be caught without a #16 or #18 ant imitation.

Late September sees fish turning on the feedbag for fall. As the water cools, the fish become more active, and streamers and nymphs begin to account for more fish than dries. Tuck a few small caddis and *Isonychia* in your box just in case, but a bold streamer should be your first choice. Second would be nymphing fast water with small nymphs or crayfish. Many late-season outings see fish nailing streamers or nymphs with gusto. These days get you through winter dreaming of next season on the Grand River tailwater.

➤ **Hatches:** www.grandrivertroutfitters.com/river/hatch/grandriver.html is the best way to match up our slightly different timing for all the normal hatches of eastern North America.

Hatches in months listed are not carved in concrete. There will generally be light to moderate hatches in the month prior and month following the major months listed.

Hendrickson: Late May through early June.

Blue-winged Olive: (not a major hatch) early May; late July through mid-September.

Light Cahill: late June to early July. Occasional to early August.

Hexagenia: Sporadic late August to late September.

Tan Caddis: late May through June; late July through mid-August; and mid- to late September

Various Black, Spotted, and Microcaddis: June through September.

➤ **Fishing Regulations:** Over 90 percent of the river is under special regulations. *No bait* is allowed, and all trout must be released. Single, barbless hooks only. For complete info please visit www.mnr.gov.on.ca.

➤ **Tackle:** This river boasts some of the most incredible dry-fly action you will ever encounter, and 3- and 4-weight rods match the conditions perfectly. However, our fish here are big, and eat big, so bring a 5- or 6-weight to toss large streamers.

Coauthor Ken Collins

Coauthor Steve May, left

KEN COLLINS is the owner of Grand River Trout-fitters. He is also the head guide and instructor. Since the start of the 1988 GRT rehabilitation program, Ken has been involved including stream rehab, tree planting, stocking, and much more. He is the founding president of the organization Friends of the Grand River (www.friendsofthegrandriver .com), which has been taking care of this world-class fly-fishing river.

STEVE MAY has also been involved in every stage of the development of this river, with countless volunteer hours, but more importantly as a professional government employee. His employment over the years with two of the key government partners, the Ministry of Natural Resources (MNR) and the Grand River Conservation Authority (GRCA), has rewarded this fishery and its participants with key improvements and studies. He is also a professional fly tier, guide, and fly-fishing instructor for GRT.

CLOSEST FLY SHOPS

Grand River Troutfitters Ltd.
536 Anderson St.
Fergus, ON N1M 1Z7
519-787-4359
www.grandrivertroutfitters.com

Grindstone Angling
Lwr 24 Mill N.
Waterdown, ON L0R 2H0
905-689-0880
www.grindstoneangling.com

The First Cast HLS Fly Fishing Shop
380 Eramosa Rd.
Guelph, ON N1E 6R2
519-766-4665
www.thefirstcast.ca/index.html

Natural Sports
1572 Victoria St. N.
Kitchener, ON N2B 3E5
519-749-1620
www.thefishingstore.ca

Wilson's Fly Shop
199 Queen Street East
Toronto, ON M5A 1S2
416-869-3474
www.canadasflyfishingoutfitter.com

CLOSEST LODGES

We do not have any lodges in the area, but there are B&Bs and small hotels. The town of Guelph, 20 minutes away, has every big-chain hotel imaginable.

Breadalbane Inn (built in 1860 as a traditional Scottish/English pub)
487 St. Andres St. W.
Fergus, ON
519-843-4770
www.breadalbaneinn.com

BEST HOTEL

Village Inn
66 Wellington Rd. 7
Elora, ON N0B 1S0
888-733-3567
info@villageinnelora.com
www.villageinnelora.com

BEST CAMPGROUND

Elora Gorge Campground
7400 Wellington Rd. 21
Elora, ON N0B 1S0
519-846-9742
www.grandriver.ca

Highland Pines Campground
8523 Wellington Rd. 19
Belwood, Ontario
877-211-7044 and 519-843-2537
www.highlandpines.com

BEST RESTAURANT

Van Galis (Scottish)
180 St. Andrew St. E
Fergus, ON
519-787-2900
info@vangalis.ca

Breadalbane Inn (left)
Brew House on the Grand
170 St David St. S
Centre Wellington, ON
519-843-8871
www.brewhouseonthegrand.ca

BEST PLACES TO GET A COLD, STIFF DRINK

Brew House on the Grand (above)

Goofie Newfie Bar & Grill
105 Queen St. W
Centre Wellington, ON N1M 1T7
519-843-4483
goofienewfie.ca

CELL PHONE SERVICE

All major companies have good reception in this area.

MORE INFORMATION

Friends of the Grand River,
www.friendsofthegrandriver.com
Fergus Elora Chamber of Commerce,
www.elorafergus.ca

Ontario Tourism,
www.ontariotravel.net

Drift boat on the Missouri River. Mark Raisler

Philanthropy

We at Stonefly Press feel that it's important to view ourselves as a small part of a greater system of balance. We give back to that which nourishes us because it feels natural and right.

Stonefly Press will be donating a portion of our annual profits to conservation groups active in environmental stewardship. We encourage all our readers to learn more about them here, and encourage you to go a step further and get involved.

American Rivers
(americanrivers.org)

Bonefish & Tarpon Trust
(bonefishtarpontrust.org)

California Trout
(caltrout.org)

Coastal Conservation Association
(joincca.org)

Friends of the White River
(friendsofwhiteriver.org)

Riverkeeper
(riverkeeper.org)

Trout Unlimited
(tu.org)

Western Rivers Conservancy
(westernrivers.org)

A typical Missouri River hatch during July. Mark Raisler

Index

Winter midge fishing on the Middle Provo. Steve Schmidt